PLAYWRIGHTS
AT WORK

THE PARIS REVIEW

PLAYWRIGHTS
AT WORK

Edited by George Plimpton

THE MODERN LIBRARY

NEW YORK

2000 Modern Library Paperback Original

Copyright © 2000 by The Paris Review
Introduction copyright © 2000 by John Lahr

LIBRARY OF CONGRESS CATALOGING-IN-PUBLICATION DATA
Playwrights at work: Paris review/edited by George Plimpton
p.   cm.
ISBN 0-679-64021-5
1. Dramatists, American—20th century—Interviews.
2. American drama—20th century—History and criticism—
Theory, etc. 3. Playwriting. I. Plimpton, George. II. Paris review.
PS350.P58   2000
812'.5409—dc21   99-44064

Modern Library website address: www.modernlibrary.com

Printed in the United States of America

2 4 6 8 9 7 5 3 1

ACKNOWLEDGMENTS

The editor thanks the interviewers and the following staff members of *The Paris Review* for their help in preparing this volume: James Linville, Sean Rocha, and especially James Lavino.

CONTENTS

INTRODUCTION

by John Lahr

We need stories; but, as the twenty-first century begins, most of the stories we're told on television and in film are corporate creations, calculated to pick the pockets of the public. The theater's charm and its power is that it is the last bastion of the individual voice, where the secrets of the psyche and the sins of the society can be explored in community with others. "I regard the theater as the greatest of all art forms, the most immediate way in which a human being can share with another the sense of what it is to be a human being," Thornton Wilder tells *The Paris Review* in this volume. He goes on: "This supremacy of the theater derives from the fact that it is always 'now' on the stage." Ours is an age of perpetual distraction, a virtual reality which Wilder didn't live to see; "the now" is what a large part of the video-addicted public will pay anything to avoid. Entertainment has become atomized; inevitably, the cross-fertilization that is implied in the word *civilization* (whose root is the Latin for *city*) has been eroded by the new technology. The public has become habituated to its solitude; it has also grown increasingly uncomfortable in large groups. The onslaught of technological escape, which tickles the society to death, has weakened the appetite for active play. When all is provided, nothing need be sought. In the republic the result is a palpable psychic mutation—a passive, credulous, restless mass at once overexcited and underinformed. At its best, theater is an antidote to the whiff of barbarity in the millennial air. "My feeling is that people in a group, en masse, watching something, react differently, and perhaps more profoundly, than they do when they're alone in their living rooms," Arthur Miller says here. In the dark, facing the stage, surrounded by others, the paying customer can let himself go; he is emboldened. The theatrical encounter allows a member of the public to think against received opinions. He can submerge himself in the extraordinary, admit his darkest, most infantile wishes, feel the pulse of the contemporary, hear the sludge of street talk turned into poetry. This enterprise can be joyous and dangerous; when the theater's game is good and tense, it is both. "We live in *what is,* but we find a thousand ways not to face it," Thornton Wilder says. "Great theater strengthens our faculty to face it." The playwright has to call the story out of himself; the audience has to call the energy out of the actors. This responsibility has its excitements and its disappointments. Whether you talk, eat, make out, or leave a film, the performances remain the same; the movie happens without a public. The play needs an audience. So the paying customer enters the theater on his mettle; he has a certain unstated but real emotional responsibility to the group. He has to rouse himself from his inveterate entropy and to be alert. "The theater made everybody in the audience behave better, as if they were all in on the same secret," John Guare says in these *Paris Review* interviews, recalling the empowering magic of his childhood theatergoing. "I found it amazing that what was up on that stage could make these people who didn't know each other laugh, respond, gasp in exactly the same way at the same time."

A playwright is an altogether different literary species from a novelist, who marshals words merely onto the page. "What *is* so different about the stage is that you're just *there,* stuck—there are your characters stuck on the stage, you've got to live with them and deal with them," Harold Pinter says. The novelist never sees the reader walk out of his book. He is not writing in space and time; he doesn't have to coax a character he's created to speak the words as written. Consequently, a playwright is a raffish hybrid, a kind of cross between a recluse, a roughneck, and a con man. He lives both in his head and in the world. To ensure the life of his work, he has to be both a charmer and a killer. "You must keep people happy backstage because that affects what's onstage," John Guare says, describing what he privately refers to as "Diva Watch." "During a run, the playwright feels like the mayor of a small town filled with noble creatures who have to get out there and make it brand-new every night. When a production works, it's unlike any other joy in the world."

And when it fails, no failure is so public, so humiliating, and so instant. "Mr. William Randolph Hearst caused a little excitement by getting up in the middle of the first act and leaving with his party of ten," Lillian Hellman says, recalling the floperoo *Days to Come.* "I vomited in the back aisle. I did. I had to go home and change my clothes. I was drunk." The playwright learns quickly to develop a thick carcass, or at least to fake one. To succeed, the play has to surmount all sorts of obstacles—hurdles of money, casting, directing, rewriting—before it reaches the public. Because of this ferocious struggle, playwrights are a nervy, bumptious, competitive, often outrageous lot. As the reader will discover in these pages, they are also good, high-spirited company. For instance, speaking of *The Sisters Rosensweig* and aspects of herself in one of her characters, Wendy Wasserstein includes "the ability to get involved with a bisexual." She adds: "Hey—when's the mixer!" Eugène Ionesco describes the first night of *The Bald Soprano,* when members from the dadaist Collège de 'Pataphysique, to which he was a satrap, turned up at his opening wearing its highest decoration, *La Gidouille,* "which was a large turd to be pinned on your lapel.... The audience was shocked at the sight of so many big turds, and thought they were members of a secret cult." Sam Shepard recalls his contentious, alcoholic father going to see one of his plays for the first time, a New Mexico production of *Buried Child,* which was loosely based on the father's family. "In the second act he stood up and started to carry on with the actors, and then yelled, 'What a bunch of shit this is!' " Shepard explains. "The ushers tried to throw him out. He resisted, and in the end they allowed him to stay because he was the father of the playwright."

In a sense playwrights are masters of their own ceremonies—rituals whose style of provocation the public in time learns to follow and to enjoy. In *The Bald Soprano* and *The Lesson* Ionesco mounted a theatrical attack on bourgeois assumptions about psychology and language. "We achieved it above all by the dislocation of language," he tells *The Paris Review.* "Beckett destroys by language with silence. I do it with too much language, with characters talking at random, and by inventing words." The sense of unlearning—of making new paths in the public imagination—is part of theater's job description. "To have a play draw you in with humor and then make you crazy and send you out mixed up!" John Guare says, speaking of playwrights who influenced his ambition for mischief. "When I got to Feydeau, to Strindberg, Pinter, Joe Orton, and the 'dis-ease' they created, I was home." It is Samuel Beckett who has taken theater to the outer limits of uncertainty—a revelation which occurred when Beckett returned to Dublin after World War II and found his mother almost unrecognizable from Parkinson's disease. In Lawrence Sheinberg's account of his meetings with Beckett, the playwright describes his intellectual volte-face. "The whole attempt at knowledge, it seemed to me, had come to nothing," Beckett tells him. "It was all haywire. What I had to do was investigate not-knowing, not-perceiving, the whole world of incompleteness."

Although the playwrights assembled here talk about the physical circumstances of playwriting, about the history of their plays and their influences, about their lives, none of them can quite answer the question every interviewer wants to know: how does the play happen? There is no truthful way to answer such a question. "A play just seems to materialize; like an apparition it gets clearer and clearer and clearer," Tennessee Williams says. About his masterpiece *A Streetcar Named Desire,* he continues: "I simply had the vision of a woman in her late youth. She was sitting in a chair all alone by a window with the moonlight streaming in on her desolate face, and she'd been stood up by the man she planned to marry." A play is a piece of happy synchronicity where the writer's ideas, his collaborators, and his luck cohere into a narrative which is a kind of gossamer mystery. "Good plays are a mystery," Neil Simon says here. "You don't know what it is that the playwright did right." He adds: "If the miracle happens, you come out at the very place you *wanted* to."

A play is for every playwright a journey into the unknown, a trip for which each has his own idiosyncratic method and mission. For instance, Tennessee Williams, who spent eight hours a day for thirty years at his craft, says he writes plays as a kind of "*emotional* autobiography" in which his characters are correlatives who chronicle the shifting spiritual battle in his own very divided nature. Harold Pinter, by contrast, works entirely out of his unconscious. "I don't know what kind of characters my plays will have until they ... well, until they *are.* Until they indicate to me what they are." He adds: "I don't conceptualize in any way. Once I've got the clues I follow them—that's my job, really, to follow the clues." Many of the writers here bear witness to being taken over by the voices and almost channeling the voices who inhabit them. "There were so many voices that I didn't know where to start," Sam Shepard says, of beginning to write his off-off-Broadway plays. "It was splendid, really; I felt kind of like a weird stenographer." Even for a Broadway playwright like Neil Simon, the experience is the same. "I've *always* felt like a middleman, like the typist," he says. And Eugène Ionesco, true to his surrealist first principles, dictates his plays to his secretary. "I let characters and symbols emerge from me, as if I were dreaming," he tells *The Paris Review*. "I always use what remains of my dreams of the night before. Dreams are reality at its most profound, and what you invent is truth because invention, by its nature, can't be a lie." He adds: "Writers who try to prove something are unattractive to me, because there is nothing to prove and everything to imagine. So I let words and images emerge from within."

Playwrights always work against time. Their plays give shape to the moment; in turn, the moment defines them. The sense of the clock ticking is part of the unstated poignancy of both their art and their lives. Tennessee Williams, for instance, builds the sense of time's passing and the waning of creative energy into his drama. "I don't ask for your pity, but just for your understand——not even that—no," Chance Wayne says in the last line of *Sweet Bird of Youth*. "Just for your recognition of me in you, and the enemy, time, in us all." But whereas Williams's life and his art seem to flee from the prospect of an ending, Samuel Beckett's work embraces it. "It's a paradox, but with old age, the more the possibilities diminish, the better chance you have," Beckett says here. "With diminished concentration, loss of memory, obscured intelligence—what you, for example, might call 'brain damage'—the more chance there is for saying something closest to what one really is." He adds: "How is it that a man who is completely blind, completely deaf, must see and hear? It's this impossible paradox which interests me. The unseeable, the unbearable, the inexpressible." All the playwrights included here, each in his or her own way, are trying to trap what is invisible to the community and to give it shape. "If anything new and exciting is going on today, it is the attempt to let Being into art," Beckett says. He adds: "Being is constantly putting form in danger." The different shapes of the plays mirror the different shapes of the souls whose Being speaks down to us uniquely on through the eras—a powerful, beautiful, necessary spiritual connection with our moment and with our times gone by.

PLAYWRIGHTS
AT WORK

THORNTON WILDER

Courtesy of Yale Collection of American Literature,
Beinecke Rare Book and Manuscript Library

Thornton Niven Wilder was born in Madison, Wisconsin, on April 17, 1897. As a child he attended public and private schools in America and in China, where his father was a United States consul in Hong Kong. Wilder studied for two years at Oberlin College, then transferred to Yale University, graduating in 1920. He spent a year studying architecture in Rome; it was there he first became fascinated by the effects of the passage of time on individuals and societies—a preoccupation that would later surface in works such as *The Skin of Our Teeth* (1942). Returning to America, Wilder worked as a teacher at the Lawrenceville School and received a master's degree in French from Princeton University.

Wilder wrote his first drama, *The Trumpet Shall Sound*, while at Yale, but it was not produced until 1926. By then he had completed a novel,

The Cabala. His literary reputation was established with the publication of *The Bridge of San Luis Rey* (1927), his immensely popular second novel, which won him a Pulitzer Prize.

During the 1930s Wilder was a lecturer in comparative literature at the University of Chicago. In dramas such as *The Long Christmas Dinner* (1931), he began using unusual structures and techniques to explore traditional morality. *Our Town* (1938), his best-known and most frequently performed work, takes place on a bare stage and has a narrator who guides the audience through the action. It earned Wilder another Pulitzer—this time for drama.

Having served as a corporal in the U.S. Coast Artillery Corps in 1918, Wilder was commissioned by the Army Air Intelligence during the Second World War in 1942, advancing to the rank of lieutenant colonel and earning the Legion of Merit and a Bronze Star. During the war years *The Skin of Our Teeth* was produced in New Haven and New York.

In his later years Wilder was awarded the Presidential Medal of Freedom and received honorary degrees from ten colleges and universities, including Oberlin, Yale, and the University of Zurich. His late novel *The Eighth Day* (1967), considered by many his finest prose work, earned the National Book Award. Wilder died in 1975.

———

A national newsmagazine not very long ago in its weekly cover story limned Thornton Wilder as an amiable, eccentric, itinerant schoolmaster who wrote occasional novels and plays which won prizes and enjoyed enormous but somewhat unaccountable success.

Wilder himself has said: "I'm almost sixty and look it. I'm the kind of man whom timid old ladies stop on the street to ask about the nearest subway station: news vendors in university towns call me 'professor,' and hotel clerks, 'doctor.' "

Many of those who have viewed him in the classroom, on the speaker's rostrum, on shipboard, or at gatherings have been reminded of Theodore Roosevelt, who was at the top of his form when Wilder was an adolescent and whom Wilder resembles in his driving energy, his enthusiasms, and his unbounded gregariousness.

It is unlikely that more than a few of his countless friends have seen Wilder in repose. Only then do you realize that he wears a mask. The mask is no figure of speech. It is his eyeglasses.

As do most glasses, they partially conceal his eyes. The glasses also distort his eyes so that they appear larger: friendly, benevolent, alive with curiosity and in-

Bk Two chapter 1. begins on
page 44 ends p.47 ③⑥

Book TWO : chapter Two

~~Book~~ ~~TWO~~ ~~: - PAMPHILUS~~

Under the burden of perplexities and self-reproach Pamphilus decided to ~~~~ seek some light on his problem by reviving an old custom. This custom ~~~~ in frequent use among Greeks of the great age, but ~~~~ had fallen off at the time of the events of this story. Athletes still observed it several days before a race; brides ~~~~ it on the eve of their wedding, and devout soldiers about to set out upon an expedition ~~~~ (old ladies who hoped to recover some lost trinket) It ~~~~ consisted of abstaining from speech and from food from one sunrise to the next and of either passing the night in the temple enclosure or arriving there before the dawn that closed the watch. There was not thought to be any particular magic in the practice; ~~~~ : it cleared the mind of fumes, removed it from the commerce of the day, and prepared it perhaps for a significant dream. The Watcher guarded his fast and his silence, but the Greek mind did not approve of heightening the experience by any further self-denial. The Watcher moved about the home as usual; he exercised in the palaestra; if some uninformed person spoke to him, he drew his finger across his lips and the situation was understood. ~~~~

It was indeed little short of odd for a full grown man, in the even current of private life to revive this custom, but the Islanders were still sufficiently religious to respect the habits that had expressed the spiritual life of their glorious grandfathers, and now made no comment.

A manuscript page from The Woman of Andros. Reprinted by permission of the Yale University Library.

terest. Deliberately or not, he rarely removes his glasses in the presence of others. When he does remove them, unmasks himself so to speak, the sight of his eyes is a shock.

Unobscured, the eyes—cold, light blue—reveal an intense severity and an almost forbidding intelligence. They do not call out a cheerful "Kinder! Kinder!"; rather, they specify: "I am listening to what you are saying. Be serious. Be precise."

Seeing Wilder unmasked is a sobering and tonic experience. For his eyes dissipate the atmosphere of indiscriminate amiability and humbug that collects around celebrated and gifted men; the eyes remind you that you are confronted by one of the toughest and most complicated minds in contemporary America. They are the eyes of a man whose novels have enjoyed the attention and aroused the sensibilities, for thirty years now, of the whole gamut of the reading public in America and Europe. (In Germany he is generally addressed as Verehrter Dichter.*) His plays have so appreciably affected American theater tradition that few serious dramatists have ignored the fact of their existence.*

Why the mask? Ultimately, that must remain Thornton Wilder's secret, as it remains the secret of every artist. A part of the explanation, however, may lie in the fact, as this interview will suggest, that not the least of his virtues is his admirable tact, his consideration for the feelings of others.

The interview took place in an apartment overlooking the Hudson River in New York City. During the conversations, which took place on the evening of December fourteenth and on the following afternoon, Mr. Wilder could watch the river lights or the river barges as he contemplated his replies.

INTERVIEWER: Sir, do you mind if we begin with a few irrelevant— and possibly impertinent—questions, just for a warm-up?

WILDER: Perfectly all right. Ask whatever comes into your head . . .

INTERVIEWER: One of our really eminent critics, in writing about you recently, suggested that among the critics you had made no enemies. Is that a healthy situation for a serious writer?

WILDER: [*After laughing somewhat ironically*] The important thing is that you make sure that neither the favorable nor the unfavorable critics move into your head and take part in the composition of your next work.

INTERVIEWER: One of your most celebrated colleagues said recently that about all a writer really needs is a place to work, tobacco, some food, and good whiskey. Could you explain to the nondrinkers among us how liquor helps things along?

WILDER: Many writers have told me that they have built up mnemonic devices to start them off on each day's writing task. Hemingway once told me he sharpened twenty pencils; Willa Cather that she read a passage from the Bible (not from piety, she was quick to add, but to get in touch with fine prose; she also regretted that she had formed this habit, for the prose rhythms of 1611 were not those she was in search of). My springboard has always been long walks. I drink a great deal, but I do not associate it with writing.

INTERVIEWER: Although military service is a proud tradition among contemporary American writers, I wonder if you would care to comment on the circumstance that you volunteered in 1942, despite the fact that you were a veteran of the First World War. That is to say, do you believe that a seasoned and mature artist is justified in abandoning what he is particularly fitted to do for patriotic motives?

WILDER: I guess everyone speaks for himself in such things. I felt very strongly about it. I was already a rather old man, was fit only for staff work, but I certainly did it with conviction. I have always felt that both enlistments were valuable for a number of reasons.

One of the dangers of the American artist is that he finds himself almost exclusively thrown in with persons more or less in the arts. He lives among them; eats among them; quarrels with them; marries them. I have long felt that portraits of the nonartist in American literature reflect a pattern, because the artists don't really frequent them. He portrays the man in the street as he remembers him from childhood, or he copies him out of other books. So one of the benefits of military service, *one* of them, is being thrown into daily contact with nonartists, a thing young American writers should consciously seek—his acquaintance should include also those who have read only *Treasure Island* and have forgotten that. Since 1800 many central figures in narratives have been, like their authors, artists or quasi-artists. Can you name three heroes in earlier literature who partook of the artistic temperament?

INTERVIEWER: Did the young Thornton Wilder resemble George Brush and in what ways?

WILDER: Very much so. I came from a very strict Calvinistic father, was brought up partly among the missionaries of China, and went to that splendid college at Oberlin at a time when the classrooms and student life carried a good deal of that pious didacticism which would now be called narrow Protestantism. And that book (*Heaven's My Destination*) is, as it were, an effort to come to terms with those influences.

The comic spirit is given to us in order that we may analyze, weigh, and clarify things in us which nettle us, or which we are outgrowing, or trying to reshape. That is a very autobiographical book.

INTERVIEWER: Why have you generally avoided contemporary settings in your work?

WILDER: I think you would find that the work is a gradual drawing near to the America I know. I began with the purely fantastic twentieth-century Rome (I did not frequent such circles there); then, Peru; then, Hellenistic Greece. I began, first with *Heaven's My Destination*, to approach the American scene. Already, in the one-act plays, I had become aware of how difficult it is to invest one's contemporary world with the same kind of imaginative life one has extended to those removed in time and place. But I always feel that the progression is there and visible; I can be seen collecting the practice, the experience, and courage to present my own times.

INTERVIEWER: What is your feeling about "authenticity"? For example, you had never been in Peru when you wrote *The Bridge of San Luis Rey*.

WILDER: The chief answer to that is that the journey of the imagination to a remote place is child's play compared to a journey into another time. I've been often in New York, but it's just as preposterous to write about the New York of 1812 as to write about the Incas.

INTERVIEWER: You have often been cited as a "stylist." As a writer who is obviously concerned with tone and exactness of expression, do you find that the writing of fiction is a painful and exhausting process, or do you write easily, quickly, and joyously?

WILDER: Once you catch the idea for an extended narration—drama or novel—and if that idea is firmly within you, then the writing brings you perhaps not so much pleasure as a deep absorption... [*Mr. Wilder reflected here for a moment and then continued*]. You see, my wastepaper basket is filled with works that went a quarter-through and which turned out to be one of those things which failed to engross the whole of me... And then for a while, there's a very agonizing period of time in which I try to explore whether that work I've rejected cannot be reoriented in such a way as to absorb me. The decision to abandon it is hard.

INTERVIEWER: Do you do much rewriting?

WILDER: I forget which of the great sonneteers said: "One line in the fourteen comes from the ceiling; the others have to be adjusted around it." Well, likewise there are passages in every novel whose first writing is pretty much the last. But it's the joint and cement, between those spontaneous passages, that take a great deal of rewriting.

INTERVIEWER: I don't know exactly how to put the next question, because I realize you have a lot of theories about narration, about how a thing should be told—theories all related to the decline of the novel, and so on. But I wonder if you would say something about the problem of giving a "history" or a summary of your life in relation to your development as a writer.

WILDER: Let's try. The problem of telling you about my past life as a writer is like that of imaginative narration itself, it lies in the effort to employ the past tense in such a way that it does not rob those events of their character of having transpired in freedom. A great deal of writing and talking about the past is unacceptable. It freezes the historical in a determinism. Today's writer smugly passes his last judgment and confers on existing attitudes the lifeless aspect of plaster-cast statues in a museum. They recount the past as though the characters knew what was going to happen next.

INTERVIEWER: Well, to begin—do you feel that you were born in a place and at a time, and to a family—all of which combined favorably to shape you for what you were to do?

WILDER: Comparisons of one's lot with others teaches us nothing and enfeebles the will. Many born in an environment of poverty, disease, and stupidity, in an age of chaos, have put us in their debt. By the standards of many people, and by my own, these dispositions were favorable—but what are our judgments in such matters? Everyone is born with an array of handicaps—even Mozart, even Sophocles—and acquires new ones. In a famous passage, Shakespeare ruefully complains that he was not endowed with another writer's "scope"! We are all equally distant from the sun, but we all have a share in it. The most valuable thing I inherited was a temperament that does not revolt against Necessity and that is constantly renewed in Hope. (I am alluding to Goethe's great poem about the problem of each man's "lot"— the *Orphische Worte.*)

INTERVIEWER: Did you have a happy childhood?

WILDER: I think I did, but I also think that that's a thing about which people tend to deceive themselves. Gertrude Stein once said "Communists are people who fancied that they had an unhappy childhood." (I think she meant that the kind of person who can persuade himself that the world would be completely happy if everyone denied himself a vast number of free decisions, is the same kind of person who could persuade himself that in early life he had been thwarted and denied all free decision.) I think of myself as having been—right up to and through my college years—a sort of sleepwalker. I was not a dreamer, but a muser and a self-amuser. I have never been without a whole repertory of absorbing hobbies, curiosities, inquiries, interests. Hence, my head has always seemed to me to be like a brightly lighted room, full of the most delightful objects, or perhaps I should say, filled with tables on which are set up the most engrossing games. I have never been a collector, but the resource that I am describing must be much like that of a collector busying himself with his coins or minerals. Yet, collectors are apt to be "avid" and competitive, while I have no ambition and no competitive sense. Gertrude also said, with her wonderful yes-saying laugh: "Oh, I wish I were a miser; being a miser must be so occupying." I have never been unoccupied. That's as near as I can get to a statement about the happiness or unhappiness of my childhood. Yet: I am convinced that except in a few extraordinary cases, one form or another of an unhappy childhood is essential to the formation of exceptional gifts. Perhaps I should have been a better man if I had had an unequivocally unhappy childhood.

INTERVIEWER: Can you see—or analyze, perhaps—tendencies in your early years which led you into writing?

WILDER: I thought we were supposed to talk about the art of the novel. Is it all right to go on talking about myself this way?

INTERVIEWER: I feel that it's all to the point.

WILDER: We often hear the phrase "a winning child." Winning children (who appear so guileless) are children who have discovered how effective charm and modesty and a delicately calculated spontaneity are in winning what they want. All children, emerging from the egocentric monsterhood of infancy ("Gimme! Gimme!" cries the Nero in the bassinet), are out to win their way—from their parents, playmates, from "life," from all that is bewildering and inexplicable in themselves. They are also out to win some expression of themselves as individuals. Some are early marked to attempt it by assertion, by slam-bang methods; others by a watchful docility; others by guile. The future author is one who discovers that language, the exploration and manipulation of the resources of language, will serve him in winning through to his way. This does not necessarily mean that he is highly articulate in persuading or cajoling or outsmarting his parents and companions, for this type of child is not usually of the "community" type—he is at one remove from the persons around him. (The future scientist is at eight removes.) Language for him is the instrument for digesting experience, for explaining himself to himself. Many great writers have been extraordinarily awkward in daily exchange, but the greatest give the impression that their style was nursed by the closest attention to colloquial speech. Let me digress for a moment: probably you won't want to use it. For a long time I tried to explain to myself the spell of

Madame de Sévigné; she is not devastatingly witty nor wise. She is simply at one with French syntax. Phrase, sentence, and paragraph breathe this effortless at-homeness with how one sees, feels, and says a thing in the French language. What attentive ears little Marie de Rabutin-Chantal must have had! Greater writers than she had such an adjustment to colloquial speech—Montaigne, La Fontaine, Voltaire—but they had things to say: didactic matter; she had merely to exhibit the genius in the language.

I have learned to watch the relation to language on the part of young ones—those community-directed toward persuasion, edification, instruction; and those engaged ("merely" engaged) in fixing some image of experience; and those others for whom language is nothing more than a practical convenience ("Oh, Mr. Wilder, tell me how I can get a wider vocabulary?").

INTERVIEWER: Well now, inasmuch as you have gone from storytelling to playwriting, would you say the same tendencies which produced the novelist, produced the dramatist?

WILDER: I think so, but in stating them I find myself involved in a paradox. A dramatist is one who believes that the pure event, an action involving human beings, is more arresting than any comment that can be made upon it. On the stage it is always *now;* the personages are standing on that razor edge, between the past and the future, which is the essential character of conscious being; the words are arising to their lips in immediate spontaneity. A novel is what *took place;* no self-effacement on the part of the narrator can hide the fact that we hear his voice recounting, recalling events that are past and over, and which he has selected—from uncountable others—to lay before us from his presiding intelligence. Even the most objective novels are cradled in the authors' emotions and the authors' assumptions about life and mind and the passions. Now the paradox lies not so much in the fact that you and I know that the dramatist equally has selected what he exhibits and what the characters will say—such an operation is inherent in any work of art—but that all the greatest dramatists, except the very greatest *one,* have precisely employed the stage to convey a moral or religious point of view concerning the action. The theater is supremely fitted to say: "Behold! These things are..." Yet most dramatists employ it to say: "This moral truth can be learned from beholding this action."

The Greek tragic poets wrote for edification, admonition, and even for our political education. The comic tradition in the theater carries the intention of exposing folly and curbing excess. Only in Shakespeare are we free of hearing axes ground.

INTERVIEWER: How do you get around this difficulty?

WILDER: By what may be an impertinence on my part. By believing that the moralizing intention resided in the authors as a convention of their times—usually, a social convention so deeply buried in the author's mode of thinking that it seemed to him to be inseparable from creation. I reverse a popular judgment: we say that Shaw wrote diverting plays to sugarcoat the pill of a social message. Of these other dramatists, I say they injected a didactic intention in order to justify to themselves and to their audiences the exhibition of pure experience.

INTERVIEWER: Is your implication then that drama should be art for art's sake?

WILDER: Experience for experience's sake—rather than for moral improvement's sake. When we say that Vermeer's *Girl Making Lace* is a work of art for art's sake, we are not saying anything contemptuous about it. I regard the theater as the greatest of all art forms, the most immediate way in which a human being can share with another the sense of what it is to be a human being. This supremacy of the theater derives from the fact that it is always "now" on the stage. It is enough that generations have been riveted by the sight of Clytemnestra luring Agamemnon to the fatal bath, and Oedipus searching out the truth which will ruin him; those circumambient tags about "don't get prideful" and "don't call anybody happy until he's dead" are incidental concomitants.

INTERVIEWER: Is it your contention that there is no place in the theater for didactic intentions?

WILDER: The theater is so vast and fascinating a realm that there is room in it for preachers and moralists and pamphleteers. As to the highest function of the theater I rest my case with Shakespeare — *Twelfth Night* as well as *Macbeth*.

INTERVIEWER: If you will forgive me, I'm afraid I've lost track of something we were talking about a while back—we were talking about the tendencies in your childhood which went into the formation of a dramatist.

WILDER: The point that I've been leading up to is that a dramatist is one who from his earliest years has found that sheer gazing at the shocks and countershocks among people is quite sufficiently engrossing without having to encase it in comment. It's a form of tact. It's a lack of presumption. That's why so many earnest people have been so exasperated by Shakespeare: they cannot isolate the passages wherein we hear him speaking in his own voice. Somewhere Shaw says that one page of Bunyan "who plants his standard on the forefront of...I-forget-what...is worth a hundred by such shifting opalescent men."

INTERVIEWER: Are we to infer from what you say that the drama ought to have no social function?

WILDER: Oh no,—there are at least two. First, the presentation of *what is*, under the direction of those great hands, is important enough. We live in *what is*, but we find a thousand ways not to face it. Great theater strengthens our faculty to face it.

Secondly, to be present at any work of man-made order, and harmony, and intellectual power—Vermeer's *Lace-Maker* or a Haydn quartet or *Twelfth Night*—is to be confirmed and strengthened in our potentialities as man.

INTERVIEWER: I wonder if you don't hammer your point pretty hard because actually you have a considerable element of the didactic in you.

WILDER: Yes, of course. I've spent a large part of my life trying to sit on it, to keep it down. The pages and pages I've had to tear up. I think the struggle with it may have brought a certain kind of objectivity into my work. I've become accustomed to readers taking widely different views of the intentions in my books and plays. A good example is George Brush, whom we were talking about before. George, the hero of a novel of mine which I wrote when I was nearly forty, is an earnest, humorless, moralizing, preachifying, interfering product of "Bible belt" evangelism. I received many letters from writers of the George Brush mentality angrily denouncing me for making fun of sacred things, and a letter from the Mother Superior of a convent in Ohio saying that she regarded the book as an allegory of the stages in the spiritual life.

Many thank me for the "comfort" they found in the last act of *Our Town;* others tell me that it is a desolating picture of our limitation to "realize" life—almost too sad to endure.

Many assured me that *The Bridge of San Luis Rey* was a satisfying demonstration that all the accidents of life were overseen and harmonized in providence; and a society of atheists in New York wrote me that it was the most artful exposure of shallow optimisms since *Candide* and asked me to address them.

A very intelligent woman to whom I offered the dedication of *The Skin of Our Teeth* refused it, saying that the play was so defeatist. ("Man goes stumbling, bumbling down the ages.") *The Happy Journey to Trenton and Camden* received its first performance, an admirable one, at the University of Chicago. Edna St. Vincent Millay happened to be in the audience. At the close of the play she congratulated me at having so well pictured that "detestable bossy kind of mother."

Most writers firmly guide their readers to "what they should think" about the characters and events. If an author refrains from intruding his point of view, readers will be nettled, but will project into the text their own assumptions and turns of mind. If the work has vitality, it will, however slightly, alter those assumptions.

INTERVIEWER: So that you have *not* eliminated all didactic intentions from your work after all?

WILDER: I suspect that all writers have some didactic intention. That starts the motor. Or let us say: many of the things we eat are cooked over a gas stove, but there is no taste of gas in the food.

INTERVIEWER: Bravo!—In one of your Harvard lectures you spoke of—I don't remember the exact words—a prevailing hiatus between the highbrow and lowbrow reader. Do you think a work could appear at this time which would satisfy both the discriminating reader and the larger public?

WILDER: What we call a great age in literature is an age in which that is completely possible: that the whole total Athenian audience took part in the flowering of Greek tragedy and Greek comedy. And so in the age of the great Spaniards. So in the age of Elizabeth. We certainly are not, in any sense, in the flowering of a golden age now; and one of the unfortunate things about the situation is this great gulf. And it would be a very wonderful thing if we see more and more works which close that gulf between the highbrows and lowbrows.

INTERVIEWER: Someone has said—one of your dramatist colleagues, I believe, I can't remember which one—that a writer only deals with one or two ideas throughout his work. Would you say your work reflects those one or two ideas?

WILDER: Yes, I think so. I only have become aware of it myself recently. Those ideas seem to have prompted my work before I realized it. Now, at my age, I am amused by the circumstance that what is now conscious with me, was for a long time latent. One of those ideas is this: an unresting preoccupation with the surprise of the gulf between each tiny occasion of the daily life and the vast stretches of time and place in which every individual plays his role.

By that I mean the absurdity of any single person's claim to the importance of his saying: "I love!" . . . "I suffer!" when one thinks of the background of the billions who have lived and died, who are living and dying, and presumably will live and die.

This was particularly developed in me by the almost accidental chance that, having graduated from Yale in 1920, I was sent abroad to study archaeology at the American Academy in Rome. We even took field trips in those days and in a small way took part in diggings. When one has swung a pickax which will reveal the curve of a street four thousand years covered over which was once an active, much traveled highway, one is never quite the same again. You look at Times Square as a place about which you imagine someday scholars saying: "There appears to have been some kind of public center here."

This preoccupation came out in my work before I realized it. Even *Our Town,* which I now see is filled with it, was not so consciously directed by me at the time. At first glance, the play appears to be practically a genre study of the picture of a village in New Hampshire. On second glance, it appears to be a meditation about the difficulty of, as the play says, "realizing life while you live it." But buried back in the text, from the very commencement of the play, is a constant repetition of the words *hundreds, thousands, millions.* It's as though the audience— no one has ever mentioned this to me, though—is looking at that town at ever greater distances through a telescope.

I'd like to cite some examples of this. Soon after the play begins the Stage Manager calls upon the professor from the geology department of the state university who says how many million years old the ground is they're on. And the Stage Manager talks about putting some objects and reading matter into the cornerstone of a new bank and covering it with a preservative so that it can be read a thousand years from now. Or as minister presiding at the wedding, the Stage Manager muses to himself about the marriages that have ever taken place— "millions of 'em, millions of 'em...Who set out to live two by two..." Finally among the seated dead, one of the dead says: "My son was a sailor and used to sit on the porch. And he says the light from that star took millions of years to arrive."

There is still more of this. So that when finally the heartbreak of Emily's unsuccessful return to life again occurs, it is against the background of the almost frightening range of these things.

Then *The Skin of Our Teeth,* which takes five thousand years to go by, is really a way of trying to make sense out of the *multiplicity* of the human race and its affections.

So that I see myself making an effort to find the dignity in the trivial of our daily life, against those preposterous stretches which seem to rob it of any such dignity; and the validity of each individual's emotion.

INTERVIEWER: I feel that there is another important theme running through your work which has to do with the nature of love. For example, there are a number of aphorisms in *The Bridge of San Luis Rey* which are often quoted and which relate to that theme. Do your views on the nature of love change in your later works?

WILDER: My ideas have not greatly changed; but those aphorisms in *The Bridge* represent only one side of them and are limited by their application to what is passing in that novel. In *The Ides of March*, my ideas are more illustrated than stated.

Love started out as a concomitant of reproduction; it is what makes new life and then shelters it. It is therefore an affirmation about existence and a belief in value. Tens of thousands of years have gone by; more complicated forms of society and of consciousness have arisen. Love acquired a wide variety of secondary expressions. It got mixed up with a power conflict between male and female; it got cut off from its primary intention and took its place among the refinements of psychic life and in the cult of pleasure; it expanded beyond the relations of the couple and the family and reappeared as philanthropy; it attached itself to man's ideas about the order of the universe and was attributed to the gods and God.

I always see beneath it, nevertheless, the urge that strives toward justifying life, harmonizing it,—the source of energy on which life must draw in order to better itself. In *The Ides of March* I illustrate its educative power (Caesar toward Cleopatra and his wife; the actress toward Marc Antonio) and its power to "crystallize" idealization in the lover (Catullus's infatuation for the destructive "drowning" Clodia— he divines in her the great qualities she once possessed). This attitude has so much the character of self-evidence for me that I am unable to weigh or even "hear" any objections to it. I don't know whether I am uttering an accepted platitude or a bit of naïve nonsense.

INTERVIEWER: Your absorbing interest in James Joyce and Gertrude Stein is pretty well known. I wonder if there are any other literary figures who are of particular interest to you.

WILDER: In present-day life?

INTERVIEWER: Well, past or present.

WILDER: I am always, as I said earlier, in the middle of a whole succession of very stormy admirations up and down literature. Every now

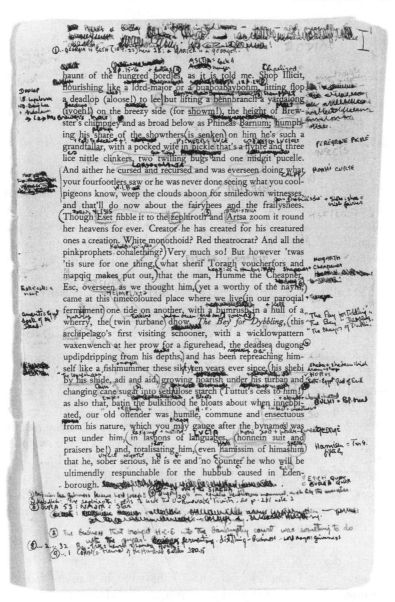

A page from Wilder's annotated copy of James Joyce's Finnegans Wake.

Courtesy of Yale Collection of American Literature, Beinecke Rare Book and Manuscript Library.

and then, I lose one; very sad. Among contemporaries, I am deeply indebted to Ezra Pound and Mr. Eliot. In the past, I have these last few years worked a good deal with Lope de Vega, not in the sense of appraisal of his total work but almost as a curious and very absorbing game—the pure technical business of dating his enormous output of plays... I could go on forever about these successive enthusiasms.

INTERVIEWER: Do you believe that a serious young writer can write for television or the movies without endangering his gifts?

WILDER: Television and Hollywood are a part of show business. If that young writer is to be a dramatist, I believe that he's tackling one of the most difficult of all métiers—far harder than the novel. All excellence is equally difficult, but considered as sheer métier, I would always advise any young writer for the theater to do everything—to adapt plays, to translate plays, to hang around theaters, to paint scenery, to become an actor, if possible. Writing for TV or radio or the movies is all part of it. There's a bottomless pit in the acquisition of how to tell an imagined story to listeners and viewers.

INTERVIEWER: If that young writer has the problem of earning a livelihood, are teaching English, or advertising, or journalism suitable vocations?

WILDER: I think all are unfavorable to the writer. If by day you handle the English language either in the conventional forms which are journalism or advertising, or in the analysis which is teaching English in school or college, you will have a double, a quadruple difficulty in finding *your* English language at night and on Sundays. It is proverbial that every newspaper reporter has a half-finished novel in his bureau drawer. Reporting—which can be admirable in itself—is poles apart from shaping concepts into imagined actions and requires a totally different ordering of mind and language. When I had to earn my living for many years, I taught French. I should have taught mathematics. By teaching math or biology or physics, you come refreshed to writing.

INTERVIEWER: Mr. Wilder, why do you write?

WILDER: I think I write in order to discover on my shelf a new book which I would enjoy reading, or to see a new play that would engross me.

INTERVIEWER: Do your books and plays fulfill this expectation?

WILDER: No.

INTERVIEWER: They disappoint you?

WILDER: No, I do not repudiate them. I am merely answering your question—they do not fulfill *that* expectation. An author, unfortunately, can never experience the sensation of reading his own work as though it were a book he had never read. Yet with each new work that expectation is prompting me. That is why the first months of work on a new project are so delightful: you see the book already bound, or the play already produced, and you have the illusion that you will read or see it as though it were a work by another that will give you pleasure.

INTERVIEWER: Then all those other motivations to which other writers have confessed play no part in your impulse to write—sharing what experience has taught you, or justifying your life by making a thing which you hope to be good?

WILDER: Yes, I suppose they are present also, but I like to keep them below the level of consciousness. Not because they would seem pretentious, but because they might enter into the work as strain. Unfortunately, good things are not made by the resolve to make a good thing, but by the application to develop fitly the one specific idea or project which presents itself to you. I am always uncomfortable when in "studio" conversation, I hear young artists talking about "truth" and "humanity" and "what is art?" and most happy when I hear them talking about pigments or the timbre of the flute in its lower range or the spelling of dialects or James's "center of consciousness."

INTERVIEWER: Is there some final statement you would wish to make about the novel?

WILDER: I'm afraid that I have made no contribution toward the intention of this series of conversations on the art of the novel. I think of myself as a fabulist, not a critic. I realize that every writer is necessarily a critic—that is, each sentence is a skeleton accompanied by enormous activity of rejection; and each selection is governed by general principles concerning truth, force, beauty, and so on. But, as I have just suggested, I believe that the practice of writing consists in more and more relegating all that schematic operation to the subconscious. The critic that is in every fabulist is like the iceberg—nine-tenths of him is underwater. Yeats warned against probing into how and why one writes; he called it "muddying the spring." He quoted Browning's lines:

> Where the apple reddens do not pry
> Lest we lose our Eden, you and I.

I have long kept a journal to which I consign meditations about the "omniscience of the novelist" and thoughts about how time can be expressed in narration, and so on. But I never reread those entries. They are like the brief canters that a man would take on his horse during the days preceding a race. They inform the buried critic that I know he's there, that I hope he's constantly at work clarifying his system of principles, helping me when I'm not aware of it, and intimating that I hope he will not intrude on the day of the race.

Gertrude Stein once said laughingly that writing is merely "telling what you know." Well, that telling is as difficult an exercise in technique as it is in honesty; but it should emerge as immediately, as spontaneously, as *undeliberately* as possible.

—RICHARD H. GOLDSTONE
Winter, 1956

LILLIAN HELLMAN

Courtesy of the Photography Collection, Harry Ransom Humanities
Research Center, The University of Texas at Austin.

Lillian Hellman was born in New Orleans on June 20 in the year 1905,
although she occasionally claimed it was 1906 or even 1907. She was
Southern to the core, but her family moved when she was a child and
she spent most of her formative years in New York. She married young
and moved first to Paris and then to Hollywood, where she worked as
a script reader. In 1930 she met the writer Dashiell Hammett, known
as Dash to intimates. Their relationship did not begin right away (she
was married and would soon return to New York), but it would eventually blossom into a great romance.

Hellman's first play, *The Children's Hour,* opened in 1934 and made
her an overnight sensation despite its controversial homoerotic
themes. It ran for 691 performances and enabled her to become in-

volved in a number of lucrative Hollywood projects that protected her when her next play, *Days to Come,* closed within a week of its opening in 1936. Success on Broadway returned with her 1939 play *The Little Foxes* (the 1941 film adaptation was also a hit), and she won the New York Drama Critics' Circle Award in 1941 for *Watch on the Rhine.*

With the Spanish Civil War under way in the mid-1930s, Hellman made a trip to Europe that turned her into an ardent Loyalist, the first of many antifascist and antitotalitarian political causes she would advocate in her long career. Her left-wing views would later draw the ire of Joseph McCarthy and the House Un-American Activities Committee (HUAC), and from the late 1940s to the 1960s she was blacklisted in Hollywood.

Although Hellman's anti-Nazi sentiments were reflected in *Watch on the Rhine,* it was with her 1944 play *The Searching Wind* (in which characters reflect on the rise of Mussolini and Hitler) that she made her political views more explicit in her work. This was followed by *Another Part of the Forest* (1946), which Hellman directed herself and intended as a continuation of the lives of the Hubbards, the central family in *The Little Foxes. The Autumn Garden,* which opened to mixed reviews in 1951, would be her last original play until 1960, when *Toys in the Attic* won her a second Drama Critics' Circle Award.

Following her celebrated HUAC testimony in 1952 and Hollywood blacklisting, Hellman dedicated herself to other people's work, including adapting Jean Anouilh's *The Lark* and editing a book of Anton Chekhov's letters. In the 1960s she began teaching and writing her memoir trilogy: *An Unfinished Woman* (1969), which won a National Book Award, *Pentimento* (1973), and the bestselling *Scoundrel Time* (1976). She died of heart failure in 1984.

———

Miss Hellman spends her summers on Martha's Vineyard in a comfortable white house at the bottom of a sandbank. There is nothing of old Cape Cod about the house, which is newly built with lots of windows and a wooden deck facing the harbor. Out of view on top of the sandbank is her old house, which she sold after Dashiell Hammett died. That one was plainer and more regional in style, with yellow painted shingles and climbing roses, and, like a Yankee farmhouse of the last century, it had a complex of boxlike rooms where guests thronged. At the far east of the old house stood a tower formed by the shell of an old windmill, and it was there that Dash lived and would retreat when company came. At the end

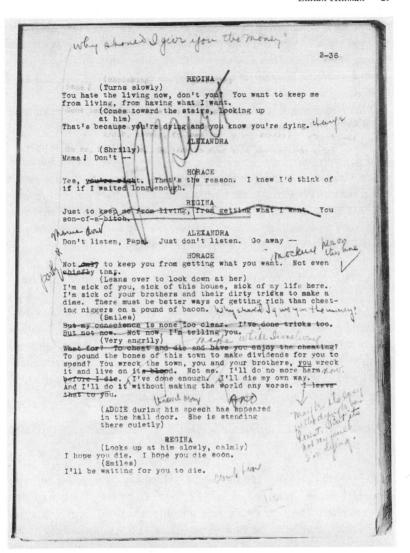

A manuscript page from The Little Foxes. Courtesy of Harry Ransom Humanities Research Center, The University of Texas at Austin.

of his life he became a recluse, talking to almost no one. He was a thin, finely built man and not tall, but when he was seen walking in delicate silence, in the cruel wasting of his illness, down a crowded sidewalk on his way to the library, unrecognized, unknown, forgotten, it was the dignity of his bearing that set him off from the summer people.

Miss Hellman spoke with us over three afternoons during a more than usually harried Labor Day weekend on Martha's Vineyard, during which she was pushing herself to finish a film script for Sam Spiegel. The conditions were not ideal, for either interviewer or subject, as there were many telephone calls, interruptions, and people passing through the room. Her voice, though, has a quality that is not easily captured on the printed page: at once angry, funny, slyly feminine, sad, affectionate, and harsh. While talking she often allows her laughter to break into her answers like an antidote to bitterness, giving a more generous dimension to her comments.

INTERVIEWER: Before you wrote plays, did you write anything else?

HELLMAN: Yes, short stories, a few poems. A couple of the stories were printed in a long-dead magazine called *The Paris Comet,* for which Arthur Kober worked. Arthur and I were married and living in Paris. Let's see, about 1928, 1929, somewhere in there. They were very lady-writer stories. I reread them a few years ago. The kind of stories where the man puts his fork down and the woman knows it's all over. You know.

INTERVIEWER: Was it Dashiell Hammett who encouraged you to write plays?

HELLMAN: No. He disliked the theater. He always wanted me to write a novel. I wrote a play before *The Children's Hour* with Louis Kronenberger called *The Dear Queen*...It was about a royal family. A royal family who wanted to be bourgeois. They kept running away to be middle class, and Dash used to say the play was no good because Louis would laugh only at his lines and I would laugh only at mine.

INTERVIEWER: Which of your plays do you like best?

HELLMAN: I don't like that question. You always like best the last thing you did. You like to think that you got better with time. But you know it isn't always true. I very seldom reread the plays. The few times I have, I have been pleasantly surprised by things that were better than I had remembered and horrified by other things I had thought were good. But I suppose *The Autumn Garden*. I suppose I think it is the best play, if that is what you mean by *like*.

INTERVIEWER: Somebody who saw you watch the opening night in Paris of Simone Signoret's adaptation of *The Little Foxes* said that through the performance you kept leaving your seat and pacing the vestibule.

HELLMAN: I jump up and down through most performances. But that particular night I was shaken by what I was seeing. I like *The Little Foxes*, but I'm tired of it. I don't think many writers like best their best-known piece of work, particularly when it was written a long time ago.

INTERVIEWER: What prompted you to go back to the theme and the characters of *The Little Foxes*? Only seven years later you wrote *Another Part of the Forest*.

HELLMAN: I always intended to do *The Little Foxes* as a trilogy. Regina in *The Little Foxes* is about forty years old, and the year is 1900. I had meant to take up with her again in about 1920 or 1925, in Europe. And her daughter, Alexandra, was to have become maybe a spinsterish social worker, disappointed, a rather angry woman.

INTERVIEWER: In the third act of *The Little Foxes* is a speech which carries the burden of the play. It says there are people who eat the earth and all the people on it, like the locusts in the Bible. And there are the people who let them do it. "Sometimes I think it ain't right to stand and watch them do it." At the end of this play Alexandra decides that she is not going to be one of those passive people. She is going to leave her mother.

HELLMAN: Yes, I meant her to leave. But to my great surprise, the ending of the play was taken to be a statement of faith in Alexandra, in her denial of her family. I never meant it that way. She did have courage enough to leave, but she would never have the force or vigor of her mother's family. That's what I meant. Or maybe I made it up afterwards.

INTERVIEWER: These wheelers and dealers in your plays—the gouging, avaricious Hubbards. Had you known many people like that?

HELLMAN: Lots of people thought it was my mother's family.

INTERVIEWER: Might you ever write that third play?

HELLMAN: I'm tired of the people in *The Little Foxes.*

INTERVIEWER: In *Regina,* the opera Marc Blitzstein based on *The Little Foxes,* the badness of Regina is most emphatic.

HELLMAN: Marc and I were close friends but we never collaborated. I had nothing to do with the opera. I never saw Regina that way. You have no right to see your characters as good or bad. Such words have nothing to do with people you write about. Other people see them that way.

INTERVIEWER: You say in your introduction that *The Children's Hour* is about goodness and badness.

HELLMAN: Goodness and badness is different from good and bad people, isn't it? *The Children's Hour*—I was pleased with the results—was a kind of exercise. I didn't know how to write a play and I was teaching myself. I chose, or Dashiell Hammett chose for me, an actual law case, on the theory that I would do better with something that was there, had a foundation in fact. I didn't want to write about myself at the age of twenty-six. The play was based on a law case in a book by William Roughead ... I changed it, of course, completely, by the time I finished. The case took place in Edinburgh in the nineteenth century, and was about two old-maid schoolteachers who ran a sort of second-rate private school. A little Indian girl, an India Indian, had been enrolled by her grandmother in the school. She brought charges of lesbianism against the two teachers. The two poor middle-aged ladies spent the rest of their lives suing, sometimes losing, sometimes winning, until they no longer had any money and no school.

INTERVIEWER: As a rule does the germ of a play come to you abstractly? Do you work from a general conception?

HELLMAN: No, I've never done that... I used to say that I saw a play only in terms of the people in it. I used to say that because I believed that is the way you do the best work. I have come now to think that it is people *and* ideas.

INTERVIEWER: Have characters invented themselves before you write them?

HELLMAN: I don't think characters turn out the way you think they are going to turn out. They don't always go your way. At least they don't go my way. If I wanted to start writing about you, by page ten I probably wouldn't be. I don't think you start with a person. I think you start with the parts of many people. Drama has to do with conflict in people, with denials... But I don't really know much about the process of creation and I don't like talking about it.

INTERVIEWER: Is there something mysterious in what a play evokes as art and the craft of writing it?

HELLMAN: Sure. That is really the only mystery because theories may work for one person and not for another. It's very hard, at least for me, to have theories about writing.

INTERVIEWER: But you had to begin with a clear idea of what the action of the play would be?

HELLMAN: Not always. Not as I got older. It was bright of Hammett to see that somebody starting to write should have a solid foundation to build on. It made the wheels go easier. When I first started to write I used to do two- or three-page outlines. Afterwards, I didn't.

INTERVIEWER: Do you think the kind of play you do—the well-made play, one which runs the honest risk of melodrama for a purpose—is going to survive?

HELLMAN: I don't know what survives and what doesn't. Like everybody else, I hope I will survive. But survival won't have anything to do with well-made or not well-made, or words like *melodrama*. I don't like labels and -isms. They are for people who raise or lower skirts because that's the thing you do for this year. You write as you write, in your time, as you see your world. One form is as good as another. There are a thousand ways to write, and each is as good as the other if it fits you, if you are any good. If you can break into a new pattern along the way, and it opens things up, and allows you more freedom, that's something. But not everything, maybe even not much. Take any form, and if you're good . . .

INTERVIEWER: Do you have to do with the casting of your plays?

HELLMAN: Yes.

INTERVIEWER: Do you feel you were well served always?

HELLMAN: Sometimes, sometimes not. *Candide* and *My Mother, My Father, and Me* were botched, and I helped to do the botching. You never know with failures who has done the harm. *Days to Come* was botched. The whole production was botched, including my botching. It was an absolute horror of a failure. I mean the curtain wasn't up ten minutes and catastrophe set in. It was just an awful failure. Mr. William Randolph Hearst caused a little excitement by getting up in the middle of the first act and leaving with his party of ten. I vomited in the back aisle. I did. I had to go home and change my clothes. I was drunk.

INTERVIEWER: Have you enjoyed the adaptations you have done of European plays?

HELLMAN: Sometimes, not always. I didn't like Anouilh's *The Lark* very much. But I didn't discover I didn't like it until I was halfway through . . . I liked *Montserrat*. I don't seem to have good luck with adaptations. I got nothing but pain out of *Candide*. That's a long story. . . . No, I had a good time on *Candide* when I was working alone. I am not a collaborator. It was a stormy collaboration. But I had a good time alone.

INTERVIEWER: *Candide* was a box-office failure, but obviously it was a success. The record is very popular.

HELLMAN: It has become a cult show. It happens. I'm glad.

INTERVIEWER: Do you think *My Mother, My Father, and Me* was a cult show?

HELLMAN: It opened during the newspaper strike, and that was fatal. Yes, I guess we were a cult show. Oddly enough, mostly with jazz musicians. The last week the audience was filled with jazz musicians. Stan Getz had come to see it and liked it, and he must have told his friends about it. I hope it will be revived because I like it. Off Broadway. I had wanted it done off-Broadway in the beginning.

INTERVIEWER: Can you comment on your contemporaries—Arthur Miller?

HELLMAN: I like *Death of a Salesman*. I have reservations about it, but I thought it was an effective play. I like best *A View from the Bridge*.

INTERVIEWER: *After the Fall?*

HELLMAN: So you put on a stage your ex-wife who is dead from suicide and you dress her up so nobody can mistake her. Her name is Marilyn Monroe, good at any box office, so you cash in on her, and cash in on yourself, which is maybe even worse.

INTERVIEWER: In an important subplot of this play a man who was once briefly a Communist names a close friend before a congressional committee.

HELLMAN: I couldn't understand all that. Miller felt differently once upon a time, although I never much liked his House Un-American Committee testimony: a little breast-beating and a little apology. And recently I went back to reread it and liked it even less. I suppose, in the play, he was being tolerant: those who betrayed their friends had a point, those who didn't also had a point. Two sides to every question and all that rot.

INTERVIEWER: And Tennessee Williams?

HELLMAN: I think he is a natural playwright. He writes by sanded fingertips. I don't always like his plays—the last three or four seem to me to have gone off, kind of way out in a conventional way. He is throwing his talent around.

INTERVIEWER: Mary McCarthy wrote in a review that you get the feeling that no matter what happens Mr. Williams will be rich and famous.

HELLMAN: I have the same feeling about Miss McCarthy.

INTERVIEWER: She has accused you, among other things, of a certain "lubricity," of an overfacility in answering complex questions. Being too facile, relying on contrivance.

HELLMAN: I don't like to defend myself against Miss McCarthy's opinions, or anybody else's. I think Miss McCarthy is often brilliant and sometimes even sound. But, in fiction, she is a lady writer, a lady magazine writer. Of course, that doesn't mean that she isn't right about me. But if I thought she was, I'd quit. I would like critics to like my plays because that is what makes plays successful. But a few people I respect are the only ones whose opinions I've worried about in the end.

INTERVIEWER: There is a special element in your plays—of tension rising into violence. In *Days to Come* and *Watch on the Rhine* there are killings directly onstage. Was there possibly, from your association with Dashiell Hammett and his work, some sort of influence, probably indirect, on you?

HELLMAN: I don't think so, I don't think so. Dash and I thought differently and were totally different writers. He frequently objected to my use of violence. He often felt that I was far too held up by how to do things, by the technique. I guess he was right. But he wasn't writing for the theater and I was.

INTERVIEWER: You have written a lot of movies?

HELLMAN: Let's see. I wrote a picture called *The Dark Angel* when I first started. I did the adaptation of *Dead End.* I did the adaptation of *The Little Foxes.* Right now I'm doing a picture called *The Chase.*

INTERVIEWER: Did you ever worry about Hollywood being a dead end for a serious writer?

HELLMAN: Never. I wouldn't have written movies if I'd thought that. When I first went out to Hollywood one heard talk from writers about whoring. But you are not tempted to whore unless you want to be a whore.

INTERVIEWER: The other night when we listened to Peter Seeger sing his folk songs you seemed nostalgic.

HELLMAN: I was moved by seeing a man of conviction again.

INTERVIEWER: We aren't making them like that anymore?

HELLMAN: Not too many. Seeger's naïveté and the sweetness, the hard work, the depth of belief I found touching. He reminded me of very different times and people. There were always x number of clowns, x number of simple-minded fools, x number of fashionables who just went along with what was being said and done, but there were also re-markable people, people of belief, people willing to live by their be-liefs. Roosevelt gave you a feeling that you had something to do with your government, something to do with better conditions for yourself and for other people. With all its foolishness the thirties were a good time and I often have regrets for it. Many people of my age make fun of that period, and are bitter about it. A few do so out of a genuine re-gret for foolish things said or foolish things done—but many do so be-cause belief is unfashionable now and fear comes with middle age.

INTERVIEWER: Do people still mention your statement before the House Un-American Activities Committee, "I cannot and will not cut my conscience to fit this year's fashions"?

HELLMAN: Yes.

INTERVIEWER: Did that put you in contempt of Congress?

HELLMAN: No, I never was in contempt. They brought no contempt charges at the end of that day. My lawyer, Joseph Rauh, was so proud and pleased. He was afraid I would be harmed because I might have waived my rights under the Fifth Amendment.

INTERVIEWER: You took the stand that you would tell the Committee all they wanted to know about you, but you weren't going to bring trouble upon innocent people no matter if they had been fooled?

HELLMAN: We sent a letter* saying that I would come and testify about myself as long as I wasn't asked questions about other people. But the Committee wasn't interested in that. I think they knew I was innocent, but they were interested in other people. It was very common in those days, not only to talk about other people, but to make the talk as interesting as possible. Friendly witnesses, so called, would often make their past more colorful than ever was the case. Otherwise you might turn out to be dull. I thought mine was a good position to take—I still think so.

INTERVIEWER: Was it something of a custom among theater people in those days, when they were going to name some old acquaintance to a committee, to call him beforehand and let him know? Just to be fair and square, as it were?

HELLMAN: Yes. They would telephone around among their friends. In several cases the to-be-injured people actually gave their permission. They understood the motive of their friends' betrayal—money, injury

---

*Following the interview is the text of this letter. The Committee rejected the proposal contained in the letter.

to a career. Oh, yes, there was a great deal of telephoning around. Kind of worse than testifying, isn't it?—the fraternity of the betrayers and the betrayed. There was a man in California who had been barred from pictures because he had been a Communist. After a while he was broke, this Mr. Smith, and his mother-in-law, who was getting bored with him—and anybody would have been bored with him—said that he could have a little piece of land. So he started to build a two-room house, and he borrowed the tools from his closest friend, his old college roommate, Mr. Jones. He had been working on his house for about seven or eight months and almost had it finished when Mr. Jones arrived to say that he had to have the tools back because, he, Mr. Jones, was being called before the Committee the next day and was going to name Mr. Smith and thought it was rather unethical for Mr. Smith to have his tools while he was naming him. I don't know whether the house ever got finished ... Clowns, they were.

INTERVIEWER: A little-known aspect of Lillian Hellman is that she was the inspiration for Dashiell Hammett's Nora Charles, the loyal wife of Nick Charles, the detective-hero of *The Thin Man*. That marriage is beautifully evoked in the book and was played by William Powell and Myrna Loy in the movies.

HELLMAN: Yes.

INTERVIEWER: Didn't it give you some gratification?

HELLMAN: It did, indeed.

INTERVIEWER: When Myrna Loy turned into her, then she became the perfect wife.

HELLMAN: Yes. I liked that. But Nora is often a foolish lady. She goes around trying to get Nick into trouble.

INTERVIEWER: And that was about you both?

HELLMAN: Well, Hammett and I had a good time together. Most of it, not all of it. We were amused by each other.

INTERVIEWER: Was it because of that book that Gertrude Stein invited you to dinner?

HELLMAN: Miss Stein arrived in America and said that there were two people that she wanted to meet. They were both in California at that minute—Chaplin and Dash. And we were invited to dinner at the house of a friend of Miss Stein; Charlie Chaplin, Dash and myself, Paulette Goddard, Miss Toklas, our host and hostess, and another man. There was this magnificent china and lace tablecloth. Chaplin turned over his coffee cup, nowhere near Stein, just all over this beautiful cloth, and the first thing Miss Stein said was, "Don't worry, it didn't get on me." She was miles away from him. She said it perfectly seriously. Then she told Dash he was the only American writer who wrote well about women. He was very pleased.

INTERVIEWER: Did he give you any credit for that?

HELLMAN: He pointed to me, but she didn't pay any attention. She wasn't having any part of me. I was just a girl around the table. I talked to Miss Toklas. We talked about food. It was very pleasant.

INTERVIEWER: Did you know Nathanael West?

HELLMAN: He managed a hotel, the Sutton Hotel. We all lived there half-free, sometimes all-free. Dash wrote *The Thin Man* at the Sutton Hotel. Pep West's uncle or cousin owned it, I think. He gave Pep a job out of kindness. There couldn't have been any other reason. Pep liked opening letters addressed to the guests. He was writing, you know, and he was curious about everything and everybody. He would steam open envelopes, and I would help him. He wanted to know about everybody.

Dash had the Royal Suite—three very small rooms. And we had to eat there most of the time because we didn't have enough money to eat anyplace else. It was awful food, almost spoiled. I think Pep bought it extra cheap. But it was the depression and I couldn't get a job. I remember reading the manuscript of *The Dream Life of Balso Snell* in the hotel. And I think he was also writing *Miss Lonelyhearts* at that time.

Dash was writing *The Thin Man*. The hotel had started out very fancy—it had a swimming pool. I spent a good deal of time in the swimming pool... I had nothing else to do with myself.

Then the Perelmans* bought a house in Bucks County. We all went down to see it. There was a dead fish in a closet. I don't know why I remember that fish. Later we would all go down for weekends, to hunt. I have a snapshot of the Perelmans and Dash and me and Pep and Bob Coates.

Even in a fuzzy snapshot you can see that we are all drunk. We used to go hunting. My memory of those hunting trips is of trying to be the last to climb the fence, with the other guns in front of me, just in case. Pep was a good shot. He used to hunt with Faulkner. So was Dash.

INTERVIEWER: Did Faulkner come around a lot in those days?

HELLMAN: Faulkner and Dash liked each other. Dash's short stories were selling, the movies were selling. So we had a lot of money, and he gave it away and we lived fine. Always, he gave it away—to the end of his life when there wasn't much, anymore. We met every night at some point for months on end, during one of Faulkner's New York visits. We had literary discussions. A constant argument about Thomas Mann. This must have taken up weeks of time.

INTERVIEWER: Was Faulkner quiet?

HELLMAN: He was a gallant man, very southern. He used to call me Miss Lillian. I never was to see him much after that period, until a few years ago when I saw him a couple of times. We remembered the days with Dash, and he said what a good time in his life that was and what a good time we had had together.

INTERVIEWER: Was any play easy to write?

HELLMAN: *The Autumn Garden* was easier than any other.

---

*S. J. Perelman was West's brother-in-law.

INTERVIEWER: At the very end of the play, the retired general, Griggs, makes one of the rare speeches in your plays that is of a remotely "philosophic" nature.

HELLMAN: Dash wrote that speech. I worked on it over and over again but it never came right. One night he said, "Go to bed and let me try." Dash comes into this interview very often, doesn't he?

INTERVIEWER: "That big hour of decision, the turning point in your life, the someday you've counted on when you'd suddenly wipe out your past mistakes, do the work you'd never done, think the way you'd never thought, have what you'd never had, it just doesn't come suddenly. You trained yourself for it while you waited—or you've let it all run past you and frittered yourself away."

HELLMAN: Yes, the basic idea was his. Dash was hipped on the subject. I think I believe that speech...I know I do...Dash worked at it far harder than I ever have, as his death proved. He wasn't prepared for death, but he was prepared for the trouble and the sickness he had, and was able to bear it, I think because of this belief, with enormous courage, and quietness.

INTERVIEWER: What is the sensation the writer has when he hears his own words from the mouth of somebody else? Of even the most gifted actor?

HELLMAN: Sometimes you're pleased and the words take on meanings they didn't have before, larger meanings. But sometimes it is the opposite. There is no rule. I don't have to tell you that speech on the stage is not the speech of life, not even the written speech.

INTERVIEWER: But do you hear dialogue spoken when you are writing it?

HELLMAN: I guess I do. Anyway, I read it to myself. I usually know in the first few days of rehearsals what I have made actors stumble over, and what can or cannot be cured.

INTERVIEWER: Do you have disputes with actors who want their lines changed?

HELLMAN: Not too many. I took a stubborn stand on the first play and now I have a reputation for stubbornness.

INTERVIEWER: Is that because you have written always to be read, even more than to be acted?

HELLMAN: Partly. But I had learned early that in the theater, good or bad, you'd better stand on what you did. In *Candide* I was persuaded to do what I didn't believe in, and I am no good at all at that game. It wasn't that the other people were necessarily wrong, I just couldn't do what they wanted. With age, I guess, I began to want to be agreeable.

INTERVIEWER: Would you mind if your plays were never produced ever again but only read?

HELLMAN: I wouldn't like it. Plays are there to be acted. I want both.

INTERVIEWER: The famous Hemingway dialogue, the best of it, turns to parody when actors speak it verbatim in adaptations of his work.

HELLMAN: That's right. It shows up, it shows up. That's just what I meant by listening to the actor. Writing for the theater is a totally different form. But then, if you want to be good and hope people will also read the plays, then it becomes a question of making sure the two forms come together. Very often in the printed form, you must recast a sentence. I do it—when I'm not too lazy—for the published version. But in minor ways, like changing the place of a verb, or punctuation. I overpunctuate for theater scripts.

INTERVIEWER: Do you think the political message in some of your plays is more important than the characters and the development?

HELLMAN: I've never been interested in political messages, so it is hard for me to believe I wrote them. Like every other writer I use myself and the time I live in. The nearest thing to a political play was *The Searching Wind*, which is probably why I don't like it much anymore. But even there I meant only to write about nice, well-born people who, with good intentions, helped to sell out a world.

INTERVIEWER: Maybe this was one play in which you were more concerned with a situation of crisis than with your characters?

HELLMAN: Yes. But I didn't know that when I was writing it. I felt very strongly that people had gotten us into a bad situation—gotten us into a war that could have been avoided if Fascism had been recognized early enough.

INTERVIEWER: What were you doing in those war years?

HELLMAN: In 1944 I was invited by the Russians to come on a kind of cultural mission. Maybe because they were producing *Watch on the Rhine* and *The Little Foxes* in Moscow.

INTERVIEWER: What were those productions like?

HELLMAN: *The Little Foxes* was an excellent production. *Watch on the Rhine* was very bad. I had thought it would be the other way around. I would go to rehearsals of *Watch on the Rhine* with Sergei Eisenstein and when I made faces or noises, he would say, "Never mind, never mind. It's a good play. Don't pay any attention to what they are doing. They can't ruin it." I saw a great deal of Eisenstein. I was very fond of him.

INTERVIEWER: When did you discover that you could no longer earn money by writing for the movies?

HELLMAN: I learned about the blacklisting by accident in 1948. Wyler and I were going to do *Sister Carrie*. Somebody, I think Mr. Balaban, told Wyler that I couldn't be hired. That unwritten, unofficial, powerful blacklist stayed in effect until two or three years ago.

INTERVIEWER: Weren't you offered clearance if you would sign something? If you made an appropriate act of contrition?

HELLMAN: Later. Shortly after the first blacklisting I was offered a contract by Columbia Pictures—a contract that I had always wanted—to direct, produce, and write, all three or any. And a great, great deal of money. But it came at the time of the famous movie conference of top Hollywood producers... They met to face the attacks of the Red-baiters and to appease them down. A new clause went into movie contracts. I no longer remember the legal phrases, but it was a lulu. I didn't sign the contract.

INTERVIEWER: What did you think about what was happening?

HELLMAN: I was so unprepared for it all, so surprised McCarthy was happening in America. So few people fought, so few people spoke out. I think I was more surprised by that than I was by McCarthy.

INTERVIEWER: People in the theater or pictures?

HELLMAN: Yes and literary people and liberals. Still painful to me, still puzzling. Recently I was asked to sign a protest about Polish writers. I signed it, it was a good protest, I thought, and went out to mail it. But I tore it up when I realized not one of the people protesting had ever protested about any of us.

INTERVIEWER: What did you think was going to happen?

HELLMAN: I thought McCarthy would last longer than he did. I thought the whole period would be worse and longer than it was. You know, I was very worried about Dash. He was a sick man and I was scared that he might go back to prison and get sicker—I lived for a long time in fear that he would go back and not get good medical treatment and be alone and—But jail hadn't worried him much or he pretended it hadn't. It amused him to act as if jail was like college. He talked about going to jail the way people talk about going to college. He used to make me angry...

INTERVIEWER: *The Maltese Falcon* was taken off the shelves of the USIS libraries when Roy Cohn and David Schine were riding high. Dashiell Hammett was called before Senator McCarthy's committee.

HELLMAN: Yes. It was on television and I watched it. They called Dash, and Dash was a handsome man, a remarkably handsome man, and he looked nice. One of the senators, I think McCarthy, said to him, "Mr. Hammett, if you were in our position, would you allow your books in USIS libraries?" And he said, "If I were you, Senator, I would not allow any libraries." A good remark. McCarthy laughed. Nobody else did, but McCarthy did...Dash had an extremely irritating habit of shrugging his shoulders. For years I would say, "Please don't shrug your shoulders." I don't know why it worried me, but it did. He was shrugging his shoulders like mad at the committee. He'd give an answer, and he'd shrug his shoulders with it. And when he was finished and got to the airport he rang me up and said, "Hey, how did you like it? I was shrugging my shoulders just for you."

INTERVIEWER: Did that period—and its effect on people—appeal to you as a subject?

HELLMAN: I've never known how to do it. It was really a clownish period. It was full of clowns talking their heads off, apologizing, inventing sins to apologize for. And other clowns, liberals, who just took to the hills. Ugly clowning is a hard thing to write about. Few people acted large enough for drama or pleasant enough for comedy.

INTERVIEWER: Then you went to England to do a movie?

HELLMAN: I used to try to explain that it wasn't as bad as they thought it was. And it wasn't. They were exaggerating it because they don't always like us very much. So much talk about Fascism here and how many people were in jail. The only time I ever met Richard Crossman, he didn't know I knew Hammett. Hammett was in jail, and Crossman said what a disgrace that was. "What's the matter with all of you, you don't lift a finger for this man? It couldn't happen here, we'd have raised a row." I told him I had lifted a finger.

INTERVIEWER: Did you ever think of living abroad as other Americans were doing?

HELLMAN: I was tempted to stay in England, but I couldn't. I like this country. This is where I belong. Anyway, I don't much like exiles. But I used to try to persuade Dash to go away, just to save his life. He had emphysema. He caught tuberculosis in the First World War and emphysema in the Second. He had never been to Europe. He used to laugh when I suggested his leaving here. He had a provincial dislike of foreigners, and an amused contempt for Russian bureaucracy. He didn't understand all of our trotting around Europe. Thought it was a waste of time.

INTERVIEWER: Did he laugh at the idea that they admired him over there?

HELLMAN: No. He liked it but it didn't interest him much. When I told him that André Gide admired him, he made a joke which you can't print in this family magazine.

INTERVIEWER: Let's be bold.

HELLMAN: All right. He said, "I wish that fag would take me out of his mouth."

INTERVIEWER: Who did he want to admire his work?

HELLMAN: Like most writers he wanted to be admired by good writers. He had started off as a pulp writer, you know, and had a wide audience—He wrote a lot for a pulp mystery magazine, *The Black Mask*. But I believe Dash took himself very seriously as a writer from the beginning.

INTERVIEWER: He helped you with your work. Did you help him with his?

HELLMAN: No, no.

INTERVIEWER: Did he show you his novels while he was writing them?

HELLMAN: *The Thin Man* and some stories, and a novel unfinished at his death. The other novels were written before I met him.

INTERVIEWER: But he worked very painstakingly with you, on your work.

HELLMAN: Oh yes, and was very critical of me. The rules didn't apply the other way. I had many problems writing *The Little Foxes.* When I thought I had got it right, I wanted Dash to read it. It was five o'clock in the morning. I was pleased with this sixth version, and I put the manuscript near his door with a note, "I hope *this* satisfies you." When I got up, the manuscript was outside my door with a note saying, "Things are going pretty well if you will just cut out the liberal black-amoor chitchat."

INTERVIEWER: He meant the Negro servants talking?

HELLMAN: Yes. No other praise, just that.

INTERVIEWER: So you knew you were all right?

HELLMAN: No, I wrote it all over again... He was generous with anybody who asked for help. He felt that you didn't lie about writing and anybody who couldn't take hard words was about to be shrugged off, anyway. He was a dedicated man about writing. Tough and generous.

INTERVIEWER: Was he always reasonably successful?

HELLMAN: Oh, no. He earned a kind of living at first, but pulp magazines didn't pay much. He was not really discovered until shortly before I met him, in 1930. He had been writing for a long time.

INTERVIEWER: He read constantly?

HELLMAN: Enormously. He had little formal education. He quit school at thirteen to work. He was the most widely read person I ever knew. He read anything, just anything. All kinds of science books, farm books, books on making turtle traps, tying knots, novels—He spent almost a year on the retina of the eye. I got very tired of retinas. And there was a period of poisonous plants and Icelandic sagas and how to take the muddy taste from lake bass. I finally made a rule that I would not listen to any more retina of the eye talk or knot talk or baseball talk or football talk.

INTERVIEWER: Do you consider yourself to be closely tied to the theater and to "theater people"?

HELLMAN: In the early days I didn't think it out, but I stayed away from them. I was frightened of competing. I felt that the further I stayed away, the better chance I had. No, I don't know too many theater people.

INTERVIEWER: A man, who has known both breeds, said that on the whole writers are even more narcissistic and nastier and more competitive than people in show biz.

HELLMAN: Hard to know the more or less. But people in the theater are usually generous with money and often with goodwill. Maybe the old troopers' world—having to live together and sharing. Writers are interesting people, but often mean and petty. Competing with each other and ungenerous about each other. Hemingway was ungenerous about other writers. Most writers are. Writers can be the stinkers of all time, can't they?

INTERVIEWER: The playwright knows dangers that are different from those the novelists know?

HELLMAN: Yes, because failure is faster in the theater. It is necessary that you not become frightened of failure. Failure in the theater is more dramatic and uglier than in any other form of writing. It costs so much, you feel so guilty. In the production of *Candide,* for the first time in my life, I guess, I was worried by all this. It was bad for me.

INTERVIEWER: Writing about the Lincoln Center Repertory in *The New York Review of Books,* Elizabeth Hardwick said that the trouble with the present theater is that it is all professionalism and is divorced from literature.

HELLMAN: Yes, of course she was right. There shouldn't be any difference between writing for the theater and writing for anything else. Only that one has to know the theater. Know it. To publish a novel or a poem one doesn't have to know print types or the publishing world. But to do a play, no matter how much one wishes to stay away from it, one has to *know* the theater. Playwrights have tried to stay away, including Shaw and Chekhov, but in the end, they were involved. Chekhov used to send letters of instructions and angry notes. A play is not only on paper. It is there to share with actors, directors, scene designers, electricians.

INTERVIEWER: Do you believe there are many talented writers working at present?

HELLMAN: Yes, but nothing like the period when I was very young, in the twenties. That was a wonderfully talented generation, the one before mine. But, you know, I think there's talent around now. Maybe not great talent, but how often does that occur anyway? It is good that we have this much. And there are signs now of cutting up. They are not always to my taste, but that doesn't matter. Cutting up is a form of belief, a negative expression of it, but belief.

INTERVIEWER: The hard professionalism in writers of that generation, like Ring Lardner, Dashiell Hammett, or Dorothy Parker, seems very unfashionable now. Young writers take themselves very seriously as highbrows and artists.

HELLMAN: The writer's intention hasn't anything to do with what he achieves. The intent to earn money or the intent to be famous or the intent to be great doesn't matter in the end. Just what comes out. It is a present fashion to believe that the best writing comes out of a hophead's dream. You pitch it around and paste it up. So sentimental.

INTERVIEWER: Sentimental or romantic?

HELLMAN: Romantic and sentimental. I am surprised, for example, at the sentimentality in much of Genet, and surprised that people are romantic enough not to see its sentimentality. I mean a sentimental way of looking at life, at sex, at love, at the way you live or the way you think. It is interesting that the "way-out" is not the sharpness of a point of view or the toughness, but just tough words and tough actions, masking the romantic. Violence, in space, is a romantic notion. Anti-bourgeois in an old-fashioned sense.

INTERVIEWER: Philip Rahv said the old idea of *épatisme* is dead. You can no longer scandalize the bourgeois. He may be vicious about defending his property; but as to morality, he is wide open to any and all nihilistic ideas.

HELLMAN: Yes, indeed. He has caught up. That is what words like "the sexual revolution" mean, I guess—the bourgeois sexual revolution. I agree with Philip. Epataying is just a sticking out of the tongue now, isn't it? The tongue or other organs.

INTERVIEWER: You have seen a lot of the contemporary theater in Europe. How does it compare with ours?

HELLMAN: The British have more talented young men and women than we have here, but I doubt if they are major talents. Genet and Ionesco are interesting men, but they are not to my taste in the theater. Beckett is the only possibly first-rate talent in the world theater. But he must grow larger, the scale's too small. We don't know much about the Russian theater. Obviously, it hasn't produced good playwrights. Certainly, not when I was there. But Russian production, directing, and acting are often wonderful. But that's a dead end. When the major talents are directors, actors, and scene designers—that's dead-end theater. Fine to see, but it ain't going nowhere. You have to turn out good new writers.

INTERVIEWER: What about the revival of Brecht?

HELLMAN: Brecht was the truest talent of the last forty or fifty years. But a great deal of nonsense has been written about Brecht. Brecht himself talked a great deal of nonsense. Deliberately, I think. He was a showman and it is showmanlike in the theater to have theories. But that doesn't matter. What a wonderful play *Galileo* is. Writers talk too much.

INTERVIEWER: What do you want to do next?

HELLMAN: I am going to edit that anthology. I had a struggle with myself because Dash would not have wanted it. He didn't want the short stories printed again. But I decided that I was going to have to forget what he wanted. Someday even the second copyrights will expire and the stories will be in public domain. I don't really know why he didn't want them reprinted—maybe because he was too sick to care. It will be a hard job. I have already started the introduction and I find it very difficult to write about so complex a man, and even I knew so little of what he was. I am not sure I can do it in the end, but I am going to have a try. But I don't know his reasons. Probably when you're sick enough you don't care much. He went through a bad time...

—JOHN PHILLIPS
—ANNE HOLLANDER
Winter–Spring, 1965

May 19, 1952

Honorable John S. Wood
Chairman
House Committee on Un-American Activities

Dear Mr. Wood:

As you know, I am under subpoena to appear before your Committee on May 21, 1952.

I am most willing to answer all questions about myself. I have nothing to hide from your Committee and there is nothing in my life of which I am ashamed. I have been advised by counsel that under the Fifth Amendment I have a constitutional privilege to decline to answer any questions about my political opinions, activities and associations, on the grounds of self-incrimination. I do not wish to claim this privilege. I am ready and willing to testify before representatives of our Government as to my own opinions and my own actions, regardless of any risks or consequences to myself.

But I am advised by counsel that if I answer the Committee's questions about myself, I must also answer questions about other people and that if I refuse to do so, I can be cited for contempt. My counsel tells me that if I answer questions about myself, I will have waived my rights under the Fifth Amendment and could be forced legally to answer questions about others. This is very difficult for a layman to understand. But there is one principle that I do understand: I am not willing, now or in the future, to bring bad trouble to people who, in my past association with them, were completely innocent of any talk or any action that was disloyal or subversive. . . .

But to hurt innocent people whom I knew many years ago in order to save myself is, to me, inhuman and indecent and dishonorable. I cannot and will not cut my conscience to fit this year's fashions, even though I long ago came to the conclusion that I was not a political person and could have no comfortable place in any political group. . . .

I am prepared to waive the privilege against self-incrimination and to tell you anything you wish to know about my views or actions if your Committee will agree to refrain from asking me to name other people. If the Committee is unwilling to give me this assurance, I will be forced to plead the privilege of the Fifth Amendment at the hearing.

A reply to this letter would be appreciated.

Sincerely yours,
Lillian Hellman

EXORCISING BECKETT

© Jerry Bauer

Of his youth in Dublin, Samuel Beckett once said, "You might say I had a happy childhood...though I had little talent for happiness." The second son of a wealthy quantity surveyor and a retired nurse, Beckett frequently claimed to have been born on Good Friday, April 13, 1906, though his birth certificate lists May 13 as the official date.

In 1928, having graduated from Trinity College first in his class in modern languages, Beckett began a two-year teaching appointment at the École Normale Supérieure in Paris. There he befriended and assisted James Joyce, taking dictation and copying down parts of what would eventually become *Finnegans Wake* (1939). He then began a three-year appointment as a lecturer at Trinity College. In 1934, during a visit to London, he began work on a short story that slowly developed into his first novel, the Joycean derivative *Murphy* (1938).

In 1937 Beckett resettled permanently in Paris. A year later, while recovering in a hospital from a stab wound he had received from a pimp to whom he had refused to give money, Beckett was visited by a piano student named Suzanne Déchevaux-Dumesnil. They began a relationship that was to last the rest of their lives. During the war Beckett and Déchevaux-Dumesnil were involved in a French Resistance group and on several occasions only narrowly missed capture by the Nazis. They escaped to the countryside and wandered for months, living as vagabonds until they came to the village of Roussillon, where they remained in hiding two and a half years. Beckett's style solidified with the novel *Watt* (1953), which he wrote to stave off mental breakdown during his time in the country. After the war Beckett was awarded a Croix de Guerre with a gold star and was presented a citation signed by Charles de Gaulle in recognition of his Resistance activities.

In the years following the war, Beckett began to write almost exclusively in French. During the fifties he composed the "trilogy" of novels *Molloy* (1951), *Malone meurt* [Malone Dies] (1951), and *L'Innommable* [The Unnamable] (1953), as well as his three major plays: *En attendant Godot* [Waiting for Godot] (1952), *Fin de partie* [Endgame] (1957), and *Krapp's Last Tape* (1958), all of which contain isolated characters, trapped in lives of repetition, who attempt and fail to make sense of their existences.

Although more than once deemed by its author a "bad play," written, he said, "as a relaxation, to get away from the awful prose I was writing at the time," *Waiting for Godot*, along with the other plays, is unquestionably what has secured Beckett's reputation in the public imagination. "The Beckett of the dramas," states the critic Harold Bloom, "will survive as long as Shakespeare and Molière, Racine and Ibsen."

Beckett received numerous awards and citations, including an honorary doctorate from Trinity College and the Prix International des Editeurs, which he shared with Jorge Luis Borges. In 1969 he received the Nobel Prize for Literature, which he accepted reluctantly though gratefully. He spent the final year of his life in a barely furnished room in a nursing home, writing until the end. He died December 22, 1989.

Ussy
17. 8. 61

Dear Dick

Thanks for letters and proofs. I'm returning these separately by air mail today. They are excellent. I think the risk of confusion negligible. "do." may stand and the risk of confusion "do", but it's too ugly. Or "sim.", as in musical scores. I wd. not object to this. But I think we may leave it.

If the *pentimento* Proof 10 (*Pause.*) too late now) throws things too much out of gear, ignore it. I think the aspect of the page would be improved if WINNIE & WILLIE were in smaller capitals. But perhaps this is not possible.

I shall look at the story again when I get back to Paris next week and then send it to you with final suggestions.

No news either of Alan's plans or of Devine's. Berlin Sept. 30 = with Gerta Drews said to be good.

Greetings to Jeannette.

yrs. ever

S/M

Besides you shd. address mail Bd. St. Jacques, never sure of its being forwarded from here and never sure of being able to stay here from one day to the next.

A letter from Beckett to Richard Seaver about Happy Days *and the story* "The Calmative," *which Seaver had recently translated.*
Courtesy of Richard Seaver.

Beckett, an intensely introspective and private man, was one of the few authors who refused to be interviewed by *The Paris Review* (Thomas Pynchon, J. D. Salinger, and Harper Lee have been others). The following feature appeared in issue 104, in the fall of 1987.

I met Beckett in 1980, when I sent him, with no introduction, a book I'd written, and to my astonishment, he read the book and replied almost at once. Six weeks later, his note having emboldened me to seek a meeting, our paths crossed in London, and he invited me to sit in on the rehearsals of *Endgame,* which he was then conducting with a group of American actors for a Dublin opening in May.

It was a happy time for him. Away from his desk, where his work, he said (I've never heard him say otherwise), was not going well at all, he was exploring a work which, though he'd written it twenty-five years before, remained among his favorites. The American group, called the San Quentin Drama Workshop because they had discovered his work—through a visiting production of *Waiting for Godot*—while inmates at San Quentin, was particularly close to his heart, and working in London he was accessible to the close-knit family that collects so often where he or his work appears. Among those who came to watch were Billie Whitelaw, Irene Worth, Nicole Williamson, Alan Schneider, Israel Horovitz, Siobhan O'Casey (Sean's daughter), three writers with Beckett books in progress, two editors who'd published him and one who wanted to, and an impressive collection of madmen and Beckett freaks who had learned of his presence via the grapevine. One lady, in her early twenties, came to ask if Beckett minded that she'd named her dog after him (Beckett: "Don't worry about me. What about the dog?"), and a wild-eyed madman from Scotland brought flowers and gifts for Beckett and everyone in the cast and a four-page letter entitled "Beckett's Cancer, Part Three," which begged him to accept the gifts as "a sincere token of my deep and long-suffering love for you," while remembering that "I also hold a profound and comprehensive loathing for you, in response to all the terrible corruption and suffering which you have seen fit to inflict upon my entirely innocent personality."

The intimacy and enthusiasm with which Beckett greeted his friends as well as newcomers like myself—acting for all the world as if I'd done him an enormous favor to come—was a great surprise for me, one of many ways in which our meetings would force me to reconsider the conception of him which I had formed during the twenty years I'd been reading and, let's be honest about it, worshiping him. Who would expect the great master of grief and disenchantment to be so expansive, so relaxed in company? Well, as it turned out, almost everyone who knew him. My surprise was founded not in his uncharacteristic behavior but in the erroneous, often bizarre misunderstandings that had gathered about him in my mind. Certainly, if there's one particular legacy that I take from our meetings it is the way in which those misunderstandings were first revealed and then corrected. In effect, Beckett's presence destroyed the Beckett myth for me, replacing it with something at once larger and more ordinary. Even today I haven't entirely understood what this correction meant to me, but it's safe to say that the paradoxical effects of Beckett incarnate—inspiring and disheartening, terrifying, reassuring, and humbling in the extreme—are nowhere at odds with the work that drew me to him in the first place.

The first surprise was the book to which he responded. Because it was journalism—an investigation of the world of neurosurgery—I had been almost embarrassed to send it, believing that he of all people would not be interested in the sort of information I'd collected. No, what I imagined he'd really appreciate was the novel that had led me to neurosurgery, a book to which I had now returned, which dealt with brain damage and presented it with an ambiguity and dark humor that, as I saw it, clearly signaled both his influence and my ambition to go beyond it. As it turned out, I had things exactly backward. For the novel, the first two chapters of which he read in London, he had little enthusiasm, but the nonfiction book continued to interest him. Whenever I saw him, he questioned me about neurosurgery, asking, for example, exactly how close I had stood to the brain while observing surgery, or how much pain a craniotomy entailed, or, one day during lunch at rehearsals: "How is the skull removed?" and "Where do they put the skull bone while they're working inside?" Though I'd often heard it said of him that he read nothing written after 1950, he remembered the names of the patients I'd mentioned and inquired as to their condition, and more than once he expressed his admiration for the surgeons. Later he did confess to me that he read very little, finding what he called "the intake" more and more "excruciating," but I doubt that he ever lost his interest in certain kinds of information, especially those which concerned the human brain. "I have long believed," he'd written me in his first response to my book, "that here in the end is the writer's best chance, gazing into the synaptic chasm."

Seventy-four years old, he was very frail in those days, even more gaunt and wizened than his photos had led me to expect, but neither age nor frailty interfered with his sense of humor. When I asked him how he was doing one morning at the theater, he replied with a great display of exhaustion and what I took to be a sly sort of gleam in his eye, "No improvement." Another day, with an almost theatrical sigh, "A little wobbly." How can we be surprised that on the subject of his age he was not only unintimidated but challenged, even inspired? Not five minutes into our first conversation he brought us round to the matter: "I always thought old age would be a writer's best chance. Whenever I read the late work of Goethe or W. B. Yeats I had the impertinence to identify with it. Now, my memory's gone, all the old fluency's disappeared. I don't write a single sentence without saying to myself, 'It's a lie!' So I know I was right. It's the best chance I've ever had." Two years later—and older—he explored the same thoughts again in Paris. "It's a paradox, but with old age, the more the possibilities diminish, the better chance you have. With diminished concentration, loss of memory, obscured intelligence—what you, for example, might call "brain damage"—the more chance there is for saying something closest to what one really is. Even though everything seems inexpressible, there remains the need to express. A child needs to make a sand castle even though it makes no sense. In old age, with only a few grains of sand, one has the greatest possibility." Of course, he knew that this was not a new project for him, only a more extreme version of the one he'd always set himself, what he'd laid out so clearly in his famous line from *The Unnamable:* "... it will be the silence, where I am, I don't know, I'll never know, in the silence you don't know, you must go on, I can't go on, I'll go on." It was always here, in "the clash," as he put it to me once, "between can't and must" that he took his stand. "How is it that a man who is completely blind, completely deaf, must see and hear? It's this impossible paradox which interests me. The unseeable, the unbearable, the inexpressible." Such thoughts of course were as familiar to me as they would be to any attentive reader of Beckett, but it was always amazing to hear how passionately—and innocently—he articulated them. Given the pain in his voice, the furrowed, struggling concentration on his face, it was impossible to believe that he wasn't unearthing these thoughts for the first time. Absurd as it sounds, they seemed less familiar to him than to me. And it was no small shock to realize this. To encounter, I mean, the author of some of the greatest work in our language, and find him, at seventy-four, discovering his vision in your presence. His excitement alone was riveting, but for me the greatest shock was to see how intensely he continued to work on the issues that had preoccupied him all his life. So much so that it didn't matter where he was or who he was with, whether he was literally "at work" or in a situation that begged for small talk. I don't think I ever had a conversation with him in which I wasn't, at some point, struck by an almost naive realization of his sincerity, as if reminding myself that he was not playing the role one expected him to play, but simply pursuing the questions most important to him. Is it possible that no one surprises us more than someone who is (especially when our expectations have been hyperbolic) exactly what we expect? It was as if a voice in me said, "My God, he's serious!" or, "So he's meant it all along!" And this is where my misunderstandings became somewhat embarrassing. Why on earth should he have surprised me? What did it say of my own sense of writing and reading or the culture from which I'd come that integrity in a writer—for this was after all the simple fact that he was demonstrating—should have struck me as so extraordinary?

Something else he said that first night in London was familiar to me from one of his published interviews, but he said this too as if he'd just come upon it, and hearing it now, I felt that I understood, for the first time, that aspect of his work which interested me the most. I'm speaking of its intimacy and immediacy, the uncanny sense that he's writing not only in a literary but an existential present tense, or more precisely, as John Pilling calls it in his book *Samuel Beckett,* an imperfect tense. The present tense of course is no rare phenomenon in modern, or for that matter, classical fiction, but unlike most writers who write *in* the present, Beckett writes *from* the present and remains constantly vulnerable to it. It is a difference of which he is acutely aware, one which distinguishes him even from a writer he admires as much as he does Kafka. As he said in a 1961 interview, "Kafka's form is classic, it goes on like a steamroller, almost serene. It seems to be threatened all the time, but the consternation is in the form. In my work there is consternation behind the form, not in the form." It is for this reason that Beckett himself is present in his work to a degree that, as I see it, no other writer managed before him. In most of his published conversations, especially when he was younger and not (as later) embarrassed to speak didactically, he takes the position that such exposure is central to the work that he considers interesting. "If anything new and exciting is going on today, it is the attempt to let Being into art." As he began to evolve a means by which to accommodate such belief, he made us realize not only the degree to which Being had been kept out of art but *why* it had been kept out, how such exclusion is, even now, the *raison d'être* of most art, and how the game changes, the stakes rising exponentially, once we let it in. Invaded by real time, narrative time acquires an energy and a fragility and, not incidentally, a truth which undermines whatever complacency or passivity the reader—not to mention the writer—has brought to the work, the assumption that enduring forms are to be offered, that certain propositions will rise above the flux, that "painkillers," which Hamm seeks in vain throughout *Endgame,* will be provided. In effect, the narrative illusion is no longer safe from the narrator's reality. "Being," as he said once, "is constantly putting form in danger," and the essence of his work is its willingness to risk such danger. Listen to the danger he risks in this sentence from *Molloy:* "A and C I never saw again. But perhaps I shall see them again. But shall I be able to recognize them? And am I sure I never saw them again?"

The untrustworthy narrator, of course, had preceded Beckett by at least a couple of centuries, but his "imperfect" tense deprives Molloy of the great conceit that most authors have traditionally granted their narrators—a consistent, dependable memory. In effect, a brain that is neither damaged, in that it doesn't suffer from amnesia, nor normal, in that it is consistent, confident of the information it contains, and immune to the assaults that time and environment mount on its continuities. But Beckett's books are not *about* uncertainty any more than they're *about* consternation. Like their author, like the Being which has invaded them, they are themselves uncertain, not only in their conclusions but their point of view. Form is offered, because as he has so often remarked, that is an obligation before which one is helpless, but any pretense that it will endure is constantly shown to be just that, pretense and nothing more. A game the author can no longer play and doesn't dare relinquish. "I know of no form," he said, "that does not violate the nature of Being in the most unbearable manner." Simply stated, what he brought to narrative fiction and drama was a level of reality that dwarfed all others that had preceded it. And because the act of writing—i.e., his own level of reality, at the moment of composition—is never outside his frame of reference, he exposes himself to the reader as no writer has before him. When Molloy changes his mind it's because Beckett has changed his mind as well, when the narrative is inconsistent it's not an aesthetic trick but an accurate reflection of the mind from which that narrative springs. Finally, what Molloy doesn't know Beckett doesn't know either. And this is why, though they speak of Joyce or Proust or other masters in terms of genius, so many writers will speak of Beckett in terms of courage. One almost has to be a writer to know what courage it takes to stand so naked before one's reader or, more important, before oneself, to relinquish the protection offered by separation from the narrative, the security and order which, in all likelihood, were what drew one to writing in the first place.

That evening, speaking of *Molloy* and the work that followed it, he told me that, returning to Dublin after the war, he'd found that his mother had contracted Parkinson's disease. "Her face was a mask, completely unrecognizable. Looking at her, I had a sudden realization that all the work I'd done before was on the wrong track. I guess you'd have to call it a revelation. Strong word, I know, but so it was. I simply understood that there was no sense adding to the store of information, gathering knowledge. The whole attempt at knowledge, it seemed to me, had come to nothing. It was all haywire. What I had to do was investigate not-knowing, not-perceiving, the whole world of incompleteness." In the wake of this insight, writing in French ("Perhaps because French was not my mother tongue, because I had no facility in it, no spontaneity") while still in his mother's house, he had begun *Molloy* (the first line of which is "I am in my mother's room"), thus commencing what was to be the most prolific period of his life. Within the first three paragraphs of his chronicle, Molloy says "I don't know" six times, "perhaps" and "I've forgotten" twice, and "I don't understand" once. He doesn't know how he came to be in his mother's room, and he doesn't know how to write anymore, and he doesn't know why he writes when he manages to do so, and he doesn't know whether his mother was dead when he came to her room or died later, and he doesn't know whether or not he has a son. In other words, he is not an awful lot different from any other writer in the anxiety of composition, considering the alternative roads offered up by his imagination, trying to discern a theme among the chaos of messages offered by his brain, testing his language to see what sort of relief it can offer. Thus, Molloy and his creator are joined from the first, and the latter—unlike most of his colleagues, who have been taught, even if they're writing about their own ignorance and uncertainty, that the strength of their work consists in their ability to say the opposite—is saying "I don't know" with every word he utters. The whole of the narrative is therefore time-dependent, neurologically and psychologically suspect, and contingent on the movement of the narrator's mind. And since knowledge, by definition, requires a subject and an object, a knower and a known, two points separated on the temporal continuum, Beckett's "I don't know" has short-circuited the fundamental dualism upon which all narrative, and for that matter, all language, has before him been constructed. If the two points cannot be separated on the continuum, what is left? No time, only the present tense. And if you must speak at this instant, using words which are by definition object-dependent, how do you do so? Finally, what is left to know if knowledge itself has been, at its very root, discredited? Without an object, what will words describe or subjugate? If subject and object are joined, how can there be hope or memory or order? What is hoped for, what is remembered, what is ordered? What is Self if knower and known are not separated by self-consciousness?

Those are the questions that Beckett has dealt with throughout his life. And before we call them esoteric or obtuse, aesthetic, philosophical, or literary, we'd do well to remember that they're not much different from the questions many of us consider, consciously or not, in the course of an ordinary unhysterical day, the questions which, before Molloy and his successors, had been excluded, at least on the surface, from most of the books we read. As Beckett wrote once to Alan Schneider, "The confusion is not my invention.... It is all around us and our only chance is to let it in. The only chance of renovation is to open our eyes and see the mess.... There will be new form, and ... this form will be of such a type that it admits the chaos and does not try to say that it is really something else."

At the time of his visit with his mother, Beckett was thirty-nine years old, which is to say the same age as Krapp, who deals with a similar revelation in his tape-recorded journals and ends (this knowledge, after all, being no more durable than any other) by rejecting it: "What a fool I was to take that for a vision!" That evening, however, as we sat in his hotel room, there was no rejection in Beckett's mind. In the next three years, he told me, he wrote *Molloy, Malone Dies, The Unnamable, Stories and Texts for Nothing,* and—in three months, with almost no revision of the first draft—*Waiting for Godot.* The last, he added, was "pure recreation." The novels, especially *The Unnamable,* had taken him to a point where there were no limits, and *Godot* was a conscious attempt to reestablish them. "I wanted walls I could touch, rules I had to follow." I asked if his revelation—the understanding, as he'd put it, that all his previous work had been a lie—had depressed him. "No, I was very excited! There was no effort in the writing. I worked all day and went out to the cafés at night."

He was visibly excited by the memory, but it wasn't long before his mood shifted, and his excitement gave way to sadness and nostalgia. The contrast between the days he had remembered and the difficulty he was having now—"racking my brains," as he put it, "to see if I can go a little farther"—was all too evident. Sighing loudly, he put his long fingers over his eyes, then shook his head. "If only it could be like that again."

So this is the other side of his equation, one which I, like many of his admirers, have a tendency to forget. The enthusiasm he had but moments before expressed for his diminishments did not protect him from the suffering those diminishments had caused. Let us remember that this is a man who once called writing "disimproving the silence." Why should he miss such futile work when it deserts him? So easy, it is, to become infatuated with the way he embraces his ignorance and absurdity, so hard to remember that when he does so he isn't posturing or for that matter "writing," that what keeps his comedy alive is the pain and despair from which it is won. The sincerity of writers who work with pain and impotence is always threatened by the vitality the work itself engenders, but Beckett has never succumbed to either side of this paradox. He has never, that is to say, put his work ahead of his experience. Unlike so many of us, who found in the Beckett vision— "Nothing is funnier than unhappiness," says Nell in *Endgame*—a comic aesthetic which had us, a whole generation of writers, I think, collecting images of absurdity as if mining precious ore, he has gazed with no pleasure whatsoever at the endless parade of light and dark. For all the bleakness of *Endgame,* it remains his belief, as one of the actors who did the play in Germany recalls, that "Hamm says no to nothingness." Exploit absurdity though he does, there is no sign, in his work or his conversation, that he finds life less absurd for having done so. Though he has often said that his real work began when he "gave up hope for meaning," he hates hopelessness and longs for meaning as much as anyone who has never read *Molloy* or seen *Endgame.*

One of our less happy exchanges occurred because of my tendency to forget this. In other words, my tendency to underestimate his integrity. This was three years later, on a cold, rainy morning in Paris, when he was talking, yet again, about the difficulties he was having in his work. "The fact is, I don't know what I'm doing. I can't even bring myself to open the exercise book. My hand goes out to it, then draws back as if on its own." As I say, he often spoke like this, sounding less like a man who'd been writing for sixty years than one who'd just begun, but he was unusually depressed that morning, and the more he talked, the more depressed I became myself. No question about it, one had to have a powerful equanimity that his grief might leave it intact. When he was inside his suffering, the force of it spreading out from him could feel like a tidal wave. The more I listened to him that morning, the more it occurred to me that he sounded exactly like Molloy. Who else but Molloy could speak with such authority about paralysis and bewilderment, in other words, a condition absolutely antithetical to authority itself? At first I kept such thoughts to myself, but finally, unable to resist, I passed them along to him, adding excitedly that, if I were forced to choose my favorite of all Beckett lines, it would be Molloy's: "If there's one question I dread, to which I've never been able to invent a satisfactory reply, it's the question, 'What am I doing?' " So complete was my excitement that for a moment I expected him to share it. Why not? It seemed to me that I'd come upon the perfect antidote to his despair in words of his own invention. It took but a single glance from him—the only anger I ever saw in his eyes—to show me how naive I'd been, how silly to think that Molloy's point of view would offer him the giddy freedom it had so often offered me. "Yes," he muttered, "that's my line, isn't it?" Not for Beckett the pleasures of Beckett. As Henry James once said in a somewhat different context: "My job is to write those little things, not read them."

One of the people who hung around rehearsals was a puppeteer who cast his puppets in Beckett plays. At a cast party one night he gave a performance of *Act Without Words* which demonstrated, with particular force, the consistency of Beckett's paradox and the relentlessness with which he maintains it. For those who aren't familiar with it, *Act Without Words* is a silent, almost Keatonesque litany about the futility of hope. A man sits beside a barren tree in what seems to be a desert, a blistering sun overhead. Suddenly, offstage, a whistle is heard and a glass of water descends, but when the man reaches for it, it rises until it's just out of reach. He strains for it, but it rises to elude him once again. Finally he gives up and resumes his position beneath the tree. Almost at once the whistle sounds again, and a stool descends to rekindle his hope. In a flurry of excitement, he mounts, stretches, grasps, and watches the water rise beyond his reach again. A succession of whistles and offerings follow, each arousing his hope and dashing it until at last he ceases to respond. The whistle continues to sound but he gives no sign of hearing it. Like so much Beckett, it's the bleakest possible vision rendered in comedy nearly slapstick, and that evening, with the author and a number of children in the audience and an ingenious three-foot-tall puppet in the lead, it had us all, children included, laughing as if Keaton himself were performing it. When the performance ended, Beckett congratulated the puppeteer and his wife, who had assisted him, offering—with his usual diffidence and politeness—but a single criticism. "The whistle isn't shrill enough."

As it happened, the puppeteer's wife was a Buddhist, a follower of the path to which Beckett himself paid homage in his early book on Proust, when he wrote, "The wisdom of all the sages, from Brahma to Leopardi...consists not in the satisfaction but in the ablation of desire." As a devotee and a Beckett admirer, this woman was understandably anxious to confirm what she, like many people, took to be his sympathies with her religion. In fact, not a few critical opinions had been mustered, over the years, concerning his debt to Buddhism, Taoism, Zen, the No theater, all of it received—as it was now received

from the puppeteer's wife—with curiosity and appreciation and absolute denial by the man it presumed to explain. "I know nothing about
Buddhism," he said. "If it's present in the play, it is unbeknownst to
me." Once this had been asserted, however, there remained the possibility of unconscious predilection, innate Buddhism, so to speak, so
the woman had another question, which had stirred in her mind, she
said, since the first time she'd seen the play. "When all is said and done,
isn't this man, having given up hope, finally liberated?" Beckett looked
at her with a pained expression. He'd had his share of drink that night,
but not enough to make him forget his vision or push him beyond his
profound distaste for hurting anyone's feelings. "Oh, no," he said quietly. "He's *finished.*"

I don't want to dwell on it, but I had a personal stake in this exchange. For years I'd been studying Zen and its particular form of sitting meditation, and I'd always been struck by the parallels between
the practice and Beckett's work. In fact, to me, as to the woman who
questioned him that evening, it seemed quite impossible that he didn't
have some explicit knowledge, perhaps even direct experience, of Zen,
and I had asked him about it that very first night at his hotel. He answered me as he answered her: he knew nothing of Zen at all. Of
course, he said, he'd heard Zen stories and loved them for their "concreteness," but other than that he was ignorant on the subject. Ignorant, but not uninterested. "What do you do in such places?" he asked.
I told him that mostly we looked at the wall. "Oh," he said, "you don't
have to know anything about Zen to do that. I've been doing it for fifty
years." (When Hamm asks Clov what he does in his kitchen, Clov
replies: "I look at the wall." "The wall!" snaps Hamm. "And what do you
see on your wall? . . . naked bodies?" Replies Clov, "I see my light
dying.") For all his experience with wall-gazing, however, Beckett
found it extraordinary that people would seek it out of their own free
will. Why, he asked, did people do it? Were they seeking tranquillity?
Solutions? And finally, as with neurosurgery: "Does it hurt?" I answered with growing discomfort. Even though I remained convinced
that the concerns of his work were identical with those of Zen, there
was something embarrassing about discussing it with him, bringing
self-consciousness to bear, I mean, where its absence was the point.
This is not the place for a discussion of Zen, but since it deals, as Beckett does, with the separation of subject and object ("No direct . . . con-

tact is possible between subject and object," he wrote in his book on Proust, "because they are automatically separated by the subject's consciousness of perception..."), the problems of Self, of Being and Nonbeing, of consciousness and perception, all the means by which one is distanced or removed from the present tense, it finds in Beckett's work a mirror as perfect as any in its own literature or scripture.

This in itself is no great revelation. It's not terribly difficult to find Zen in almost any great work of art. The particular problem, however, what made my questions seem—to me at least—especially absurd, is that such points—like many where Beckett is concerned—lose more than they gain in the course of articulation. To point out the Zen in Beckett is to make him seem didactic or, even worse, therapeutic, and nothing could betray his vision more. For that matter, the converse is also true. Remarking the Beckett in Zen betrays Zen to the same extent and for the same reasons. It is there that their true commonality lies, their mutual devotion to the immediate and the concrete, the Truth which becomes less True if made an object of description, *the Being which form excludes.* As Beckett put it once, responding to one of the endless interpretations his work has inspired, "My work is a matter of fundamental sounds. Hamm as stated, Clov as stated.... That's all I can manage, more than I could. If people get headaches among the overtones, they'll have to furnish their own aspirin."

So I did finally give up the questions, and though he always asked me about Zen when we met—"Are you still looking at the wall?"—I don't think he held it against me. His last word on the matter came by mail, and maybe it was the best. In a fit of despair I had written him once about what seemed to me an absolute, insoluble conflict between meditation and writing. "What is it about looking at the wall that makes the writing seem obsolete?" Two weeks later, when I'd almost forgotten my question, I received this reply, which I quote in its entirety:

Dear Larry,

When I start looking at walls, I begin to see the writing. From which even my own is a relief.

As ever,
Sam

Rehearsals lasted three weeks and took place in a cavernous building, once used by the BBC, called the Riverside Studios. Since it was located in a section of London with which I was not familiar, Beckett invited me that first morning to meet him at his hotel and ride out in the taxi he shared with his cast. Only three of his actors were present that day—Rick Cluchey, Bud Thorpe, and Alan Mandell (Hamm and Clov and Nagg respectively)—the fourth, Nell, being Cluchey's wife, Teresita, who was home with their son, Louis Beckett Cluchey, and would come to the theater in the afternoon. The group had an interesting history, and it owed Beckett a lot more than this production, for which he was taking no pay or royalties. Its origins dated to 1957, when Cluchey, serving a life sentence for kidnapping and robbery at San Quentin, had seen a visiting production of *Waiting for Godot* and found in it an inspiration that had completely transformed his life. Though he'd never been in a theater—"not even," he said, "to rob one"—he saw to the heart of a play which at the time was baffling more sophisticated audiences. "Who knew more about waiting than people like us?" Within a month of this performance, Cluchey and several other inmates had organized a drama group which developed a Beckett cycle—*Endgame, Waiting for Godot,* and *Krapp's Last Tape*—that they continued, in Europe and the United States, after their parole. Though Cluchey was the only survivor of that original workshop, the present production traced its roots to those days at San Quentin and the support which Beckett had offered the group when word of their work had reached him. Another irony was that Mandell, who was playing Nagg in this production, had appeared with the San Francisco Actor's Workshop in the original production at San Quentin. By now Beckett seemed to regard Rick and Teri and their son, his namesake, as part of his family, and the current production was as much a gift to them as a matter of personal or professional necessity. Not that this was uncharacteristic. In those days much of his work was being done as a gift to specific people. He'd written *A Piece of Monologue* for David Warrilow, and in the next few years he'd write *Rockaby* for Billie Whitelaw and *Ohio Impromptu* for S. E. Gontarski, a professor at Ohio State, who was advisory editor of the *Journal of Beckett Studies*. When I met him later in Paris he was struggling to write a promised piece for Cluchey at a time when he had, he said, no interest in work at all. In my opinion, this was not merely because he took no promise lightly or because at this point in his life he valued especially this sort of impetus, though both of course were true, but because the old demarcations, between the work and the life, writing and speaking, solitude and social discourse, were no longer available to him. If his ordinary social exchanges were less intense or single-minded than his work it was certainly not apparent to me. I never received a note from him that didn't fit on a 3 × 5 index card, but (as the above-mentioned note on Zen illustrates) there wasn't one, however lighthearted, that wasn't clearly Beckett writing. Obviously, this was not because of any particular intimacy between us, but because, private though he was, and fiercely self-protective, he seemed to approach every chance as if it might be his last. You only had to watch his face when he talked—or wait out one of those two- or three-minute silences while he pondered a question you'd asked—to know that language was much too costly and precarious for him to use mindlessly or as a means of filling gaps.

Wearing a maroon polo sweater, gray flannel pants, a navy blue jacket, no socks, and brown suede sneakerlike shoes, he was dressed, as Cluchey told me later, much the same as he'd been every time they'd met for the past fifteen years. As the taxi edged through London's morning rush hour, he lit up one of the cheroots he smoked and observed to no one in particular that he was still unhappy with the wheelchair they'd found for Hamm to use in this production. Amazing how often his speech echoed his work. "We'd need a proper wheelchair!" Hamm cries. "With big wheels. Bicycle wheels!" One evening, when I asked him if he was tired, his answer—theatrically delivered—was a quote from Clov: " 'Yes, tired of all our goings on.' " And a few days later, when a transit strike brought London to a standstill, and one of the actors suggested that rehearsals might not go on, he lifted a finger in the air and announced with obvious self-mockery, "Ah, but we must go on!" I'm not sure what sort of wheelchair he wanted but several were tried in the next few days until one was found that he accepted. He was also unhappy with the percussion theme he was trying to establish, two pairs of knocks or scrapes which recur throughout the play—when Nagg, for example, knocks on Nell's ashcan to rouse her, when Hamm taps the wall to assure himself of its solidity, or when Clov climbs the two steps of his ladder with four specific scrapes of his slippers. For Beckett, these sounds were a primary musical motif, a fundamental continuity. It was crucial that they echo each other. "Alan," he said, "first thing this morning, I want to rehearse your knock." Most discussions I was to hear about the play were like this, dealing in sound or props or other tangibles, with little or no mention of motivation, and none at all of meaning. Very seldom did anyone question him on intellectual or psychological ground, and when they did, he usually brought the conversation back to the concrete, the specific. When I asked him once about the significance of the ashcans which Nagg and Nell inhabit, he said, "It was the easiest way to get them on and off stage." And when Mandell inquired, that morning in the taxi, about the meaning of the four names in the play—four names which have been subject to all sorts of critical speculation, Beckett explained that Nagg and Clov were from *Nagel* and *clou,* the German and French for "nail," Nell from the English *nail,* and Hamm from the English *hammer.* Thus, the percussion motif again: a hammer and three nails. Cluchey remembered that when Beckett directed him in Germany in *Krapp's Last Tape* a similar music had been developed around the words "Ah well," which recur four times in the play, and with the sound of Krapp's slippers scraping across the stage. "Sam was obsessed with the sound of the slippers. First we tried sandpapering the soles, then layering them with pieces of metal, then brand-new solid leather soles. Finally, still not satisfied, he appeared one day with his own slippers. 'I've been wearing these for twenty years,' he said. 'If they don't do it, nothing will.' " More and more, as rehearsals went on, it would become apparent that music— "The highest art form," he said to me once. "It's never condemned to explicitness"—was his principal referent. His directions to actors were frequently couched in musical terms. "More emphasis there...it's a crescendo," or, "The more speed we get here, the more value we'll find in the pause." When Hamm directs Clov to check on Nagg in his garbage can—"Go and see did he hear me.... Both times."—Beckett said, "Don't play that line realistically. There's music there, you know." As Billie Whitelaw has noted, his hands rose and fell and swept from side to side, forming arcs like a conductor's as he watched his actors and shaped the rhythm of their lines. You could see his lips move, his jaw expanding and contracting, as he mouthed the words they spoke. Finally, his direction, like his texts, seemed a process of reduction, stripping away, reaching for "fundamental sound," transcending meaning, escaping the literary and the conceptual in order to establish a concrete immediate reality, beyond the known, beyond the idea, which the audience would be forced to experience directly, without mediation of intellect.

What Beckett said once of Joyce—"his work is not about something. It is something"—was certainly true of this production. The problem, of course, what Beckett's work can neither escape nor forget, is that words are never pure in their concreteness, never free of their referents. To quote Marcel Duchamp, himself a great friend and chess partner of Beckett's, "Everything that man has handled has a tendency to secrete meaning." And such secretion, because he is too honest to deny it, is the other side of Beckett's equation, the counterweight to his music that keeps his work not only meaningful, but (maniacally) inconclusive and symmetrical, its grief and rage always balanced with its comedy, its yearning for expression constantly humbled by its conviction that the Truth can only be betrayed by language. Rest assured that no Beckett character stands on a rug that cannot be pulled out from under him. When Didi seeks solace after Godot has disappointed them again—"We are not saints, but at least we have kept our appointment. How many people can say as much?"—Vladimir wastes no time in restoring him to his futility: "Billions."

But more than anyone else it is Hamm who gets to the heart of the matter, when he cries out to Clov in a fit of dismay, "Clov!... We're not beginning to ... to ... mean something?"

"Mean something!" Clov cries. "You and I, mean something.... Ah that's a good one!"

"I wonder ... if a rational being came back to earth, wouldn't he be liable to get ideas into his head if he observed us long enough? 'Ah good, now I see what it is, yes, now I understand what they're at!' And without going so far as that, we ourselves ... we ourselves ... at certain moments ... to think perhaps it won't all have been for nothing!"

As promised, Nagg's knock was the first order of business after we reached the theater. This is the point in the play where Nagg has made his second appearance, head rising above the rim of the ashcan with a biscuit in his mouth, while Hamm and Clov—indulging in one of their habitual fencing matches—are discussing their garden ("Did your seeds come up?" "No." "Did you scratch [the ground] to see if they have sprouted?" "They haven't sprouted." "Perhaps it's still too early." "If they were going to sprout they would have sprouted. They'll never sprout!"). A moment later, Clov having made an exit, and Hamm drifted off into a reverie, Nagg leans over to rouse Nell, tapping four times—two pairs—on the lid of her bin. Beckett demonstrated the sound he wanted, using his bony knuckle on the lid, and after Mandell had tried it six or seven times—not "Tap, tap, tap, tap," or "Tap... tap... tap... tap," but "tap, tap... tap, tap"—appeared to be satisfied. "Let's work from here," he said. Since Teri had not arrived, he climbed into the can himself and took Nell's part, curling his bony fingers over the edge of the can, edging his head above the rim, and asking, in a shaky falsetto that captured Nell better than anyone I'd ever heard in the part: "What is it, my pet? Time for love?"

As they worked through the scene, I got my first hint of the way in which this *Endgame* would differ from others I'd seen. So much so that, despite the fact that I'd seen six or seven different productions of the play, I would soon be convinced that I'd never seen it before. Certainly, though I'd always thought *Endgame* my favorite play, I realized that I had never really understood it or appreciated the maniacal logic with which it pursues its ambiguities. Here, as elsewhere, Beckett pressed for speed and close to flat enunciation. His principal goal, which he never realized, was to compress the play so that it ran in less than ninety minutes. After the above line, the next three were bracketed for speed, then a carefully measured pause established before the next section—three more lines—began. "Kiss me," Nagg begs. "We can't," says Nell. "Try," says Nagg. And then, in another pause, they crane their necks in vain to reach each other from their respective garbage cans. The next section was but a single line in length (Nell: "Why this farce, day after day?"), the next four, the next seven, and so on. Each was a measure, clearly defined, like a jazz riff, subordinated to the rhythm of the whole. Gesture was treated like sound, another form of punctuation. Beckett was absolutely specific about its shape—the manner in which, for example, Nagg's and Nell's fingers curled above the rim of their cans—and where it occurred in the text. "Keep these gestures small," he said to Cluchey, when they reached a later monologue. "Save the big one for 'All that loveliness!'" He wanted the dialogue crisp and precise but not too realistic. It seemed to me he yearned to stylize the play as much as possible, underline its theatricality, so that the actors, as in most of his plays, would be seen as clearly acting, clearly playing the roles they're doomed to play forever. The text, of course, supports such artifice, the actors often addressing each other in language which reminds us that they're onstage. "An aside, ape!" says Hamm to Clov. "Have you never heard an aside before?" Or Clov, after his last soliloquy, pausing at the edge of the stage: "This is what we call making an exit." Despite this, Beckett wanted theatrical flourish kept to a minimum. It seemed to me that he stiffened the movement, carving it like a sculptor, stripping it of anything superfluous or superficial. "Less color please," he said to Alan while they were doing Nagg and Nell together, "if we keep it flat, they'll get it better." And later, to Thorpe: "Bud, you don't have to move so much. Only the upper torso. Don't worry. They'll get it. Remember: you don't even want to be out here. You'd rather be alone, in your kitchen."

Though the play was twenty-five years old for him, and he believed that his memory had deteriorated, his memory of the script was flawless and his alertness to its detail unwavering. "That's not 'upon.' It's 'on.' " He corrected "one week" with "a week," "crawlin'" with "crawling." When Cluchey said to Thorpe, "Cover me with a sheet," Beckett snapped: "*The* sheet, Rick, *the* sheet." And when Clov delivered the line, "There are no more navigators," he corrected, "There's a pause before *navigators*." He made changes as they went along—"On 'Good God' let's leave out the 'good' "—sometimes cutting whole sections, but had no interest in publishing a revised version of the play. For all the fact that he was "wobbly," he seemed stronger than anyone else on the set, rarely sitting while he worked and never losing his concentration. As so many actors and actresses have noted, he delivered his own lines better than anyone else, and this was his principal mode of direction. When dealing with certain particular lines, he often turned away from the cast and stood at the edge of the stage, facing the wall, working out gestures in pantomime. For those of us who were watching rehearsals, it was no small thing to see him go off like this and then hear him, when he'd got what he wanted, deliver his own lines in his mellifluous Irish pronunciation, his voice, for all its softness, projecting with force to the seats at the back of the theater:

"They said to me, That's love, yes, yes, not a doubt, now you see how easy it is. They said to me, That's friendship, yes, yes, no question, you've found it. They said to me, Here's the place, stop, raise your head and look at all that beauty. That order! They said to me, Come now, you're not a brute beast, think upon these things and you'll see how all becomes clear. And simple! They said to me, What skilled attention they get, all these dying of their wounds."

To say the least, such moments produced an uncanny resonance. Unself-conscious, perfectly in character, one felt that he was not only reading the lines but writing them, discovering them now as he'd discovered them twenty-five years before. That we, as audience, had somehow become his first witness, present at the birth of his articulations. If his own present tense—the act of writing—had always been his subject, what could be more natural or inevitable than showing us this, the thoughts and meaning "secreted" and rejected, the words giving form, the form dissolving in the silence that ensued. For that was the message one finally took from such recitations, the elusiveness of the meanings he had established, the sense of the play as aging with him, unable to arrest the flow of time and absolutely resolved against pretending otherwise. Why should Hamm and Clov be spared the awareness of Molloy: "It is in the tranquillity of decomposition that I remember the long confused emotion which was my life."

Perhaps it was for this reason, that he was never far removed from what he'd written, that if an actor inquired about a line, his answers could seem almost naive. When Cluchey asked him why Hamm, after begging Clov to give him his stuffed dog, throws it to the ground, Beckett explained, "He doesn't like the feel of it." And when he was asked for help in delivering the line "I'll tell you the combination of the cupboard if you promise to finish me," he advised, "Just think, you'll tell him the combination if he'll promise to kill you." Despite—or because of—such responses, all four members of the cast would later describe the experience of his direction in language that was often explicitly spiritual. "What he offered me," said Cluchey, "was a standard of absolute authority. He gave my life a spiritual quotient." And Thorpe: "When we rehearsed, the concentration was so deep that I lost all sense of myself. I felt completely empty, like a skeleton, the words coming through me without thought of the script. I'm not a religious person, but it seemed a religious experience to me. Why? Maybe because it was order carried to its ultimate possibility. If you lost your concentration, veered offtrack for any reason, it was as if you'd sinned." Extreme though such descriptions are, I doubt that anyone who watched these rehearsals would find in them the least trace of exaggeration. More than intense, the atmosphere was almost unbearably internalized, self-contained to the point of circularity. In part, obviously, this was because we were watching an author work on his own text. In addition to this, however, the text itself—because *Endgame* is finally nothing but theater, repetition, a series of ritualized games that the actors are doomed to play forever—was precisely about the work that we were watching. When Clov asks Hamm, "What is there to keep me here?" Hamm replies, "The dialogue." Or earlier, when Hamm is asking him about his father, "You've asked me these questions millions of times." Says Hamm, "I love the old questions.... Ah, the old questions, the old answers, there's nothing like them!" If the play is finally about nothing but itself, the opportunity to see it repeated, again and again for two weeks, offered a chance to see Beckett's intention realized on a scale at once profound and literal, charged with energy but at the same time boring, deadening, infuriating. (A fact of which Beckett was hardly unaware. While they were working on the line "This is not much fun," he advised Cluchey, "I think it would be dangerous to have any pause after that line. We don't want to give people time to agree with you.") To use his own percussion metaphor, watching these rehearsals was to offer one's head up for *Endgame*'s cadence to be hammered into it. Finally, after two weeks of rehearsal, the play became musical to a hypnotic extent, less a theatrical than a meditative experience in that one could not ascribe to it any meaning or intention beyond its own concrete and immediate reality. In effect, the more one saw of it, the less it contained. To this day the lines appear in my mind without reason, like dreams or memory-traces, but the play itself, when I saw it in Dublin, seemed an anticlimax, the goal itself insignificant beside the process that had produced it. If *Waiting for Godot* is, as Vivian Mercier has written, "a play in which nothing happens, twice," it might be said of *Endgame* that it is an endless rehearsal for an opening night that never comes. And therefore that its true realization was the rehearsals we saw rather than its formal production later in Dublin. Could this be why, one reason at least, Beckett did not accompany his cast to Ireland or, for that matter, why he has never attended his own plays in the theater?

He left London the day after rehearsals ended, and I did not see him again until the following spring in Paris. At our first meeting, he seemed a totally different person, distant and inaccessible, physically depleted, extremely thin, his eyes more deeply set and his face more heavily lined than ever. He spoke from such distance and with such difficulty that I was reminded again of Molloy, who describes conversation as "unspeakably painful," explaining that he hears words "a first time, then a second, and often even a third, as pure sounds, free of all meaning." We met in the coffee shop of a new hotel, one of those massive gray skyscrapers that in recent years have so disfigured the Paris skyline. Not far from his apartment, it was his favorite meeting place because it offered a perfect anonymity. He wasn't recognized during this or any subsequent meeting I had with him there. Early on in our conversation, I got a taste of his ferocious self-protection, which was much more pronounced here, of course, where he lived, than it had been in London. "How long will you be here?" he said. "Three weeks," I said. "Good," he said. "I want to see you *once* more." Given his politeness, it was easy to forget how impossible his life would have been had he not been disciplined about his schedule, how many people must have sought him out as I had sought him out myself. What was always amazing to me was how skillful he was in letting one know, where one ranked in his priorities. Couching his decision in courtesy and gentleness, he seemed totally vulnerable, almost passive, but his softness masked a relentless will and determination. He left one so disarmed that it was difficult to ask anything of him, much less seek more time than he had offered. Though he promptly answered every letter I wrote him, it was three years before he gave me his home address, so that I would not have to write him in care of his publisher, and he has never given me a phone number, always arranging that he will call me when I come to town. Why not? Rick Cluchey told me that whenever Beckett went to Germany a documentary film crew followed him around without his permission, using a telephoto lens to film him from a distance.

As it turned out, however, there was another reason for his distance now. In London, the only unpleasant moment between us had occurred when, caught up in the excitement of rehearsals, I'd asked if I could write about him. Though his refusal, again, had been polite ("Unless of course you want to write about the work...") and I had expressed considerable regret about asking him, it would soon become clear that he had not forgotten. Even if he had, the speed with which I was firing questions at him now, nervously pressing all the issues I had accumulated since I'd seen him last, would have put him on his guard. Beckett is legendary, of course, for his hatred of interviews, his careful avoidance of media and its invasions (*The Paris Review* has tried for years, with no success, to interview him for its "Writers at Work" series), and the next time we met, he made it clear that before we continued he must know what I was after. "Listen, I've got to get this off my chest. You're not interviewing me, are you?"

We had just sat down at a restaurant to which he had invited me. The only restaurant he ever frequented, it was a classic bistro on the edge of Montparnasse where he kept his own wine in the cellar and the waiters knew his habits so well that they always took him to the same table and brought him, without his having to order, the dish he ate—filet of sole and french fries—whenever he went there. Though I had my notebook in my pocket and upon leaving him would, as always, rush to take down everything I could remember about our conversation, I assured him that I was certainly not interviewing him and had no intention of writing about him. At this point in time, there was nothing but truth in my disclaimer. (And I might add that he obviously trusted me on this score, since he gave me permission to publish this article, and as far as I can see, has never held it against me.) Since I was not yet even dimly conscious of the ambiguous, somewhat belligerent forces that led to this memoir, the notes I took were for myself alone, as I saw it, a result of the emotion I felt when I left him and the impulse, common if not entirely handsome in a writer, to preserve what had transpired between us. Taking me at my word, Beckett relaxed, poured the wine, and watched with pleasure as I ate while he picked at his food like a child who hated the dinner table. "You're not hungry?" I said. "No," he said. "I guess I'm not too interested in food anymore." And later, when I asked if he'd ever eaten in any of the Japanese restaurants that were just beginning to open in Paris: "No. But I hear they make good rice."

Considering how thin he was, I wasn't surprised to hear that the desire for food—like almost all other desires, I believe, except those which involved his work—was a matter of indifference to him. What did surprise me, as the wine allowed us to speak of things more commonplace, was the view of his domestic situation—evenings at home with his wife, and such—which emerged during the course of the evening. He told me that he'd been married for forty years, that he and

- It fascinates, so indiscreet, we see what no one is meant to see (Rugby game)—
- what do you do when not writing — gaze into space — walk —
- Joyce wrote constantly — probably at night —
- works more painful — writing or not writing — Both painful but pain is difficult
- volunteers to send TV script
- incarceration is a general condition. I told Rick prison only an extreme form. We're talking through bars now. The wall is always there.
- marriage — many near-ruptures but it gets easier as you get older —
- talking about Rick — what he can do & what he can't —

[I felt so timid with him — so often his conversation seems to be a question, asking for help, but if one ventures some suggestion (video tape) seems terribly impertinent]

- video at *Krapp* — "you can go in on the innards, etc but then you can't go back"
- reading Yeats, Dante —
- Can't write anything — but must — yes, that's it, can't & must! (as if first time) Completely impossible, hackering my hopeless mind —
- A very charming — she made two toys for me!
- I pursue paradox of "exploiting weakness" "investigating ignorance" but get nowhere —
- buys country house (40 miles from Paris) when all gray — neighbors look in on it — no friends there — goes to market for food... and drink!
- Mail a great burden — gets many many—

A page from Shainberg's notebook chronicling one of his meetings with Beckett. Courtesy of Lawrence Shainberg.

his wife had had just two addresses during all their time in Paris, that it had sometimes been difficult for them—"many near-ruptures, as a matter of fact"—but that the marriage had grown easier as they'd got older. "Of course," he added, "I do have my own door." Since I'd always thought of him as the ultimate solitary, isolated as Krapp and as cynical about sex as Molloy, I confessed that I couldn't imagine him in a situation so connubial. "Why should you find it difficult?" he said with some surprise. In fact, he seemed rather pleased with his marriage, extremely grateful that it had lasted. It was one more correction for me and, more important, I think, one more illustration of the symmetry and tension, the dialectic he maintains between his various dichotomies. Just as *can't* and *must* persist with equal force in his mind, the limitations of language no more deniable than the urgent need to articulate, the extreme loneliness which he's explored throughout his life—the utter skepticism and despair about relationships in general and sexuality in particular—has had as its counterpoint a marriage which has lasted forty years. But lest one suspect that the continuity and comfort of marriage had tilted the scales so far that the dream of succession had taken root in his mind, "No," he replied, when I asked if he'd ever wanted children, "that's one thing I'm proud of."

For all my conviction that I did not intend to write about him, I always felt a certain amount of shame when I took up my notebook after I left him. For that matter, I am not entirely without shame about what I'm writing now. One does not transcribe a man like Beckett without its feeling like a betrayal. What makes me persist? More than anything, I believe, it is something I began to realize after our meetings in Paris—that the shame I felt in relation to him had not begun with my furtive attempts to preserve him in my notebook, but rather had been a constant in our relationship long before I'd met him. To put it simply, it began to strike me that Beckett had been, since the moment I discovered *Molloy,* as much a source of inhibition as inspiration. For all the pleasure it had given me, my first reading of the trilogy had almost paralyzed me (as indeed it had paralyzed any number of other writers I knew), leaving me traumatized with shame and embarrassment about my own work. It wasn't merely that, in contrast to his, my language seemed inauthentic and ephemeral, but that he made the usual narrative games—the insulated past tense, the omniscient narrator, form which excluded reference to itself, biographical information—seem, as he put it in *Watt*, "solution clapped on problem like a snuffer on a candle." More than any other writer I knew, Beckett's work seemed to point to that which lay beyond it. It was as if, though its means were Relative, its goals were Absolute, its characters beyond time precisely because (again and again) they seemed to age before our eyes. And such accomplishment was not, it seemed to me, simply a matter of talent or genius but of a totally different approach to writing, a connection between his life and his work which I could covet but never achieve. It was this union—the joining, if you like, of "being" and "form"—that I envied in him and that caused me finally to feel that the very thought of Beckett, not to mention the presence of one of his sentences in my mind, made writing impossible. And once again: it was not merely a matter of talent. I could read Joyce or Proust or Faulkner without such problems, and I had no lack of appreciation for them. It was just that they were clearly *writers,* while Beckett was something else, a sort of meta-writer who, even as he wrote, transcended the act of writing.

Oddly enough, if there was anyone else I knew who stood in such relation to his work, it was Muhammad Ali, who seemed to laugh at boxing even as he took it to higher levels of perfection, who not only defeated but humiliated his opponents, establishing such possession of their minds that he won many fights before the first round began, because he stood outside the game in which his adversary was enclosed. One cannot play a game unless one believes in it, but Ali managed such belief without the attachment to which it usually leads. Say that he found the cusp that separates belief from attachment, concentration from fixation, and on the other hand, play from frivolity, spontaneity from formlessness. And it seems to me that Beckett has done the same. No writer has lived who took language more seriously, but none has been more eloquent about its limitations and absurdities. Like Ali, he shows us where we are imprisoned. The danger is that, in doing so, he will imprison us in his example. If some fighters tried, playing the clown, to imitate Ali, and ended by making fools of themselves in addition to being defeated, writers with Beckett too much in mind can sound worse than the weakest student in a freshman writing class. After reading Joyce or Proust, one can feel embarrassed about one's lack of music or intelligence, but in the wake of one of Beckett's convoluted, self-mocking sentences, one can freeze with horror at the thought of any form that suggests "Once upon a time," anything in fact which departs from the absolute present. But if you take that too far you lose your work in the ultimate swamp, the belief that you can capture both your subject and your object in the instant of composition: "Here I am, sitting at my desk, writing 'Here I am, sitting at my desk.' "

None of this of course is historically unprecedented. Every generation of artists has to do battle with its predecessors, and each such battle has its own unique configurations. What made it so vivid for me was that now, twenty years after that first reading, his presence affected me much as his work had. Happy though I felt to see him, however amazing I found our time together, I always left him with an acute sense that I'd come up short, failed him somehow, as if the moment had passed before I had awakened to it. As if my conversational and psychological habits had stood between us. Or more to the point, as if the *form* of my social habit had violated the nature of his *Being* in much the same way that literary form, as he'd concluded years before, violated the being it excluded. Sitting across from me in the café, his eyes fierce in their concentration, his silence so completely unapologetic, he seemed to occupy, according to my reverential opinion, a present tense—*this* space, *this* moment in time—which I could merely observe from afar. Despite—no, because of—his humility, his uncertainty, the "impotence" which, as he'd once put it, his work had set out to "exploit,"* he manifested for me, as for years he had for Rick Cluchey, a kind of ultimate authority, a sense of knowledge very near to Absolute. Neither egoism nor self-confidence—the opposite, in fact, of both— such knowledge seemed a by-product of suffering, the pain that was so evident on his face, an earned if not entirely welcome result of having explored and survived an emptiness that people of less courage, if they acknowledged it at all, considered by means of intellect alone.

Exaggerated and romantic though all this seems, I'm sure it's not entirely unjustified. Beckett is indeed an extraordinary being, a man who has traveled in realms that most people don't want to hear about, much less explore. A true writer, an artist who pursues his vision so

*"The kind of work I do," he explained to Israel Schenker in a *New York Times* interview in 1956, before he'd closed the door to media, "is one in which I'm not master of my material. The more Joyce knew the more he could. He's tending toward omniscience and omnipotence as an artist. I'm working with impotence, ignorance. I don't think impotence has been exploited in the past."

courageously and with such disregard for easy gratification that his work becomes, in the purest sense, a spiritual practice. What my responses showed, however, my idealization of him and the self-criticism it evoked, was that such authority was nothing if not a hazardous experience. Like all great wisdom, it could bring out the best or the worst in you, challenge or intimidate you, toughen you or make you self-effacing. Finally, if you were a writer, it could inspire you to listen to your own voice or trap you into years of imitating his. Like Joyce or Proust, or for that matter, any other great artist one adopts as a teacher, Beckett is an almost impossible act to follow, but more so than most, I think, because his work is so subjective, so seductive in the permissions it grants, because his apparent freedom from plot and character and his first-person present tense can draw you into a swamp in which art and self-indulgence begin to seem identical. It is so easy to think that he opens the gates for anything you're feeling or thinking at the moment you sit down at your desk. How many writers could I count who had books like mine, the one I'd shown him, the one he'd criticized because the voice was "not believable," which would not be written until the Beckett had been removed from them? The great irony is that, for all his rejection of authority and knowledge—precisely because of such rejection, in fact—Beckett is almost too much an authority, he knows too much that one must discover on one's own. If you aren't to go on imitating him, you either face the fact that there is nothing you really need to say and find yourself another vocation, or you dig for something truer in yourself, something you don't know, at the bottom of all you do. In other words, you start where he started, after meeting his mother in Dublin. The trouble is that, since most of such digging, if you're an ordinary mortal, is surely doomed to fail, it can seem as if he's taken you out of the game you're capable of playing and signed you up in one for which you've neither the courage, the talent, nor the appetite. Finally, his greatest danger—and his greatest gift—may be his simple reminder that writing is not about reiteration.

But of course there is also the other side to it, one which has explicitly to do with the nature of his vision, the "being" he allows into the work, the void he's faced, the negation he's endured, the grief he's not only experienced but transformed with his imagination. "Yes, the confusion of my ideas on the subject of death," says Molloy, "was such that I sometimes wondered, believe me or not, if it wasn't a state of being even worse than life. So I found it natural not to rush into it and, when I forgot myself to the point of trying, to stop in time." Once we'd got over our laughter and exhilaration, how were we to deal with such a statement? For Beckett, such negation had fueled the work, but for many who presumed to be his successors, it had often become an easy, a facile nihilism, less a game you lost than one you refused to play. Indeed, for some of us, true disciples, it could become one you were ashamed to play. As if, having finally been enlightened as to the absurdity of life, you were too wise to persist at its illusions, too wise to allow enthusiasm, occupy space, to feed the body you knew to be disintegrating. In effect, if you misread him well enough, Beckett could turn you into a sort of literary anorexic, make you too cool or hip, too scared, too detached and disenchanted, to take, by writing, the only food that nourished you. But the irony is that he himself, as he'd shown me in London, in our very first conversation, is anything but anorexic. That's obvious, isn't it? This man who writes, in *Molloy*, "you would do better, at least no worse, to obliterate texts than to blacken margins, to fill in the holes of words till all is blank and flat and the whole ghastly business looks like what it is, senseless, speechless, issueless misery," has published six novels and fourteen plays during his lifetime, not to mention a great body of short prose, poetry, criticism, a number of television and radio plays, and a filmscript. Just fifteen pages later in *Molloy* he writes, "Not to want to say, not to know what you want to say, and never to stop saying, or hardly ever, that is the thing to keep in mind, even in the heat of composition." Much as he can recognize the tyranny of hope or meaning, he cannot deny that there is hope and meaning within such recognition, and he cannot pretend that this hope and meaning is any less exciting or more enduring than the others. It's all part of the equation, however absurd, of being alive, and he's never rejected that condition for its alternative. After all, when Nell says, "Nothing is funnier than unhappiness," we laugh at that statement, and—if only for an instant—are less unhappy as we do so. In a sense Beckett is the great poet of negation, but what is poetry for him can easily become, if we use him incorrectly, if we make him too much an authority, or if we underestimate the integrity of his paradox, a negation so extreme and absolute that it threatens the very source of one's energy and strength.

Of course, it's not easy to speak of these things. It's always possible that his greatest gift, not only to those of us he's challenged, but the readers we might have enlisted, is the silence toward which he's pressed us. If you can't accept his example, and allow Being into your work, why add your lies to the ocean of print which is drowning the world already? In my opinion, most writers deal with his challenge in one of two ways. Either they ignore his example, go on—as I had, for example, in writing journalism—making forms that exclude Being, accepting the role of explainer, describer, or they try—as I was trying with my novel—to play his game despite the astronomical odds against any possibility of success. For those who take the latter path, the entry of Being into the form often means the entry of self-consciousness, writing about writing about writing. Too late we discover that Beckett, Molloy, Malone et al., though they may be mad, haven't a trace of neurosis or narcissism about them, that their present tense is shaped and objectified by an inherently classical, concrete mind, a sense of self which differs radically from our own. In effect, that the present tense which becomes, inevitably, an imperfect tense for them, remains a merely present—a merely reductive, a totally self-absorbed—tense for us. If you can't take the leap from present to imperfect, you remain rooted in the present. An honorable intention, of course, but if you're honest about it, you have to admit that writing and being in the present are not necessarily compatible, that in fact you're always flirting with contradiction and dishonesty. Tantalized by what amounts to a desire to write and not-write simultaneously, you may be equally loyal to form and being, but you may also be a mother who would keep her child forever in her womb. It's the sort of game in which defeat can lead to farce that's not only hypocritical but blasphemous toward the master one has pretended to revere.

———

These are just a few of the reasons, I think, I took notes when I left him, and despite my disclaimer, am writing about him now. Why? Perhaps because Beckett himself, as I said earlier, freed me from the Beckett myth. Not entirely for sure, but enough at least to help me resume a voice that differed from the one he once inspired in me. Not for nothing did he show me that he enjoyed my journalism. "Look here, Larry," he said to me once in London, "your line is witnessing."

By which I understand him to have meant: take your object and be done with it. Be content to write what you know without acknowledging every moment that you don't. So here I am, witnessing him. Maybe this is all just rationalization, but getting him down like this may be the best homage and the best revenge, the only weapon I have against the attack he mounted on my mind. I can't forget him, and I can't think of anything else to do with his example but reject it. Just as Buddhists say about their own ultimate authority, "If you meet the Buddha on the road, kill him," I say of Beckett that a writer can only proceed from him by recognizing that he is now, having taken his work to all of its ultimate conclusions, utterly emptied of possibility. As Hamm says, "All is absolute. The bigger a man is, the fuller he is.... And the emptier."

The next time we saw each other, a year later in Paris, our conversation continued, where it had begun and where it had been left, with the difficulties of writing. Because my work (the same novel) was going as badly as his, there wasn't a whole lot of joy in the air. For a moment, in fact, it became a sort of sparring match between us, agony versus agony, but then, remembering whom I was in the ring with and how much he outweighed me, I backed off. "It's not a good time at all," he sighed. "I walk the streets trying to see what's in my mind. It's all confusion. Life is all confusion. A blizzard. It must be like this for the newborn. Not much difference I think between this blizzard and that. Between the two, what do you have? Wind machines or some such. I can't write anything, but I must." He paused a moment, then suddenly brightened, once again repeating a famous Beckett line as if he'd just come upon it, "Yes, that's it! Can't and must! That's my situation!"

He spoke of a sentence that haunted him. "It won't go away, and it won't go farther: 'One night, as he sat, with his head on his hands, he saw himself rise, and go.' " Except for this, however, there was nothing. "It's like the situation I spoke of in my book on Proust. 'Not just hope is gone but desire.' " When I reminded him—quoting the line I mentioned earlier ("The wisdom of all the sages... consists not in the satisfaction but in the ablation of desire.")—that according to the book he'd remembered, the loss of desire was not an entirely unwelcome development, he replied, "Well, yes, but the writing was the only thing that made life bearable." Sighing as if in tremendous pain, he seemed to drift off for a moment. "Funny to complain about silence when one has aspired to it for so long. Words are the only thing for me and there's not enough of them. Now, it's as if I'm just living in a void, waiting. Even my country house is lonely when I'm not writing."

Occasionally, when he talked like this, there was an odd sense, absurd as it seems, that he was asking for help, even perhaps advice, but this time was different. Now seventy-eight years old, he appeared to have reached a sort of bottom-line exhaustion. He seemed smaller to me, the lines in his forehead more deeply etched, like a grid. Every gesture seemed difficult, every word a struggle. His blue eyes were shy, gentle, youthful as ever, but incredibly pained and sorrowful. I told him that sometimes I found it amazing that he went on. "Yes," he replied, "often I think it's time I put an end to it. That's all through the new work. But then again . . . there are also times when I think, maybe it's time to begin." He said there had always been so much more in the work than he'd suspected was there, and then added, in what seemed an almost unconscious afterthought, a phrase I've never forgotten, which may have summed up his work as well or better than any other: "Ambiguities infirmed as they're put down . . ."

"Which is more painful," I asked him, "writing or not writing?"

"They're both painful, but the pain is different."

He spoke a little about the different sorts of pain—the pain of being unable to write, the pain of writing itself, and—as bad as any— the pain of finishing what he'd begun. I said, "If the work is so painful when one does it and so painful when it's done, why on earth does anyone do it?"

This was one of those questions that caused him, as I've mentioned already, to disappear behind his hand, covering his eyes and bending his head toward the table for what must have been two full minutes. Then, just when I'd begun to suspect that he'd fallen asleep, he raised his head and, with an air of relief, as if he'd finally resolved a lifelong dilemma, whispered, "The fashioning, that's what it is for me, I think. The pleasure in making a satisfactory object." He explained that the main excitement in writing had always been technical for him, a combination of "metaphysics and technique." "A problem is there and I have to solve it. *Godot,* for example, began with an image—of a tree and an empty stage—and proceeded from there. That's why, when people ask me who Godot is, I can't tell them. It's all gone."

"Why metaphysics?" I said.

"Because," he said, "you've got your own experience. You've got to draw on that."

He tried to describe the work he wanted to do now. "It has to do with a fugitive 'I' [or perhaps he meant 'eye']. It's an embarrassment of pronouns. I'm searching for the non-pronounial."

" 'Non-pronounial'?"

"Yes. It seems a betrayal to say 'he' or 'she.' "

The problem of pronouns, first person versus third, which had been so much explored and illuminated throughout his work, was also the one he addressed in mine. That morning, as always, he was extremely solicitous, asking me question after question about the progress of my novel. Though the book continued to defy me, so much so that I'd begun to wonder if brain damage, as I wanted to approach it, might not be beyond the limits of art, he seemed to know exactly what I wanted to do. It wasn't surprising, of course, that the man who'd once described tears as "liquified brain" should be familiar with the subject of brain damage, but his questions were so explicit that it was difficult to believe that he hadn't considered, and rejected, the very book I wanted to write. The chapters I'd shown him in London had been written in the first person, which he had considered a mistake. "I know it's impertinent to say this, please forgive me … but this book, in my opinion, will never work in the first person." When I told him, here at the café, that I had now moved it to the third person, he nodded, but he knew that problems of point of view were never resolved with pronouns alone. "Still," he said, returning to the point he'd made when we met in London, "you need a witness, right?"

He excused himself from the table—"pardon my bladder"—but when he returned it was clear that he'd taken my book with him. "Well, do you see the end of it?"

"No," I said, "not at all."

He sighed. "It's really very difficult, isn't it?"

He sipped his coffee, then homed in on the principal issue in my book as in so much contemporary fiction—the need for objectivity and knowledge in conjunction with the need for the intimacy and immediacy of a naked subjectivity. "You need a witness and you need the first person, that's the problem, isn't it? One thing that might help … you might have a look at an early book of mine, perhaps you know it, *Mercier and Camier*. I had a similar problem there. It begins, 'I know what happened with Mercier and Camier because I was there with them all the time.' "

After I returned from Paris, I looked at *Mercier and Camier* again but found no place for his solution in the problems I had set myself. Still, I wrote an entire version of my novel in the third person, and I can say without a doubt that there were very few days I didn't feel him looking over my shoulder, whispering, "It's really very difficult, isn't it?" or when things were going worse, commenting on me as Nagg comments on Hamm, "What does that mean? That means nothing!" Halfway through, I knew it wasn't working, suspecting strongly that my only hope, despite what Beckett had said, was in the first person, but I pushed on. Certainly, it wasn't merely his recommendation that kept me going in that direction, but how can I pretend it didn't matter? When finally—a year and a half and an entire manuscript later—I turned it around and started over, in the first person, I could not, though I wrote him more than one letter about the book, bring myself to mention it to him. To my mind, the book worked, not only because it was in the first person, but because I had finally succeeded in weaning myself from him. Given all this, I felt no small trepidation when I sent him the manuscript but, as before, he read the book at once and replied with generosity and enthusiasm. There was no sign of his original disappointment and none of his position vis-à-vis my point of view. His note, as always, was confined to a 3 × 5 index card, and his scrawl, which had grown progressively worse in the years that I'd corresponded with him, was not completely legible. To my chagrin, in fact, its most important sentence was only half-accessible to me. After offering his compliments and appreciation, he concluded with a sentence that drifted off into a hopeless hieroglyphics after beginning with "And on with you now from..."

After *from* was a word which looked like *this*, but might have been *thus* or *phis*, a word which looked like *new* but might have been *man* or *ran*, a word which looked like *thought* or *bought* or *sought*, and finally a word which looked like *anew*. "And on with you now from this new thought anew"? It didn't sound like Beckett at all. I asked several friends to have a look but none could read his writing any better than I. What absurd apocryphy that a note from Beckett should conclude,

"And on with you now from [illegible] [illegible] [illegible]." Finally, unable to stand it any longer, I wrote to ask if, by some chance (after all, more than three weeks had passed since he'd written the note) he could remember what he'd written. Again he answered promptly, ending our dialogue, as I will end this memoir, with a note that was characteristic, not only in its economy and content, but in what it says about his (failing?) memory and the attitude with which he approached his correspondence:

Dear Larry,
I believe I wrote, 'And on with you now from this new nought anew.'
As ever,
Sam.

—LAWRENCE SHAINBERG
Fall, 1987

TENNESSEE WILLIAMS

Tennessee Williams celebrates his seventieth birthday at the Goodman Theatre, March 24, 1981.
Courtesy of the Goodman Theatre.

Born in Columbus, Mississippi, on March 26, 1911, as Thomas Lanier Williams, the future Tennessee was the second of three children. The first child, Rose, was almost two years Tom's senior, and her struggles with mental illness (which culminated, tragically, in one of America's first lobotomies) were a theme that reappeared often in the playwright's work. So did his father's alcoholism and long periods away from home, which left Tom to grow up in a home dominated by women.

Never much of a student, Williams had some early success as a writer of short stories and plays. In 1939 he adopted the name Tennessee and, soon after, had his first extended homosexual relationship. Fame came quickly with *The Glass Menagerie*, which opened in Chicago in late 1944 and in March 1945 on Broadway, where it won the New

York Drama Critics' Circle Award. This was followed by *A Streetcar Named Desire*, which opened in late 1947 and for which he won a Pulitzer Prize and a second Drama Critics' Award.

Williams's personal life was in an almost constant state of turmoil, but at least through the 1940s and early fifties his work didn't seem to suffer for it. Following *Summer and Smoke* (which opened in New York in 1948), *The Rose Tattoo* (1951), and *Camino Real* (1953), Williams began writing *Cat on a Hot Tin Roof*. Its opening in 1955 proved his greatest success yet, garnering him another Pulitzer and Drama Critics' Award, and it ran for nearly seven hundred performances. The play's central character, Maggie, was the latest in a line of female roles—running from Amanda in *Menagerie* through Blanche in *Streetcar*—that were so memorable and fully formed that they have, with time, shrugged off their fictional origins and come to seem almost historic figures.

Williams would go on to write many more plays, including *Suddenly Last Summer* (1958), *Sweet Bird of Youth* (1959), and *The Night of the Iguana* (1961), which were quite successful, both onstage and in their filmed versions. He struggled throughout with drugs, alcohol, and depression, and never again created anything to match the epic stature of his earlier works. He died in February 1983 at the Hotel Elysée in New York from choking on the cap of a medicine bottle.

—

Tennessee Williams was unusually happy on his seventieth birthday. He was in Chicago for a production of his new play, A House Not Meant to Stand, *at the Goodman Theater and that typically fraught process was going well. He was tanned from having spent most of the winter at his home in Key West, Florida. Dressed in a loose embroidered shirt, beige slacks, and soft canvas shoes, he looked at least a decade younger than he was.*

He began his birthday as he did every day, by waking at dawn to write. He then took a swim in the pool and opened presents and greetings from friends before sitting down with me for several hours. We began by talking about the Italian literary prize he had recently won for The Roman Spring of Mrs. Stone, *which he found somewhat puzzling because when the novel and movie first appeared the Italians had been angered by the story of a Roman gigolo romancing an older woman.*

The interview continued several weeks later in New York at his semiofficial residence, the Hotel Elysée. He had come to New York to see his sister, Rose, who was resident at a private sanitarium upstate, and to consult with his editors

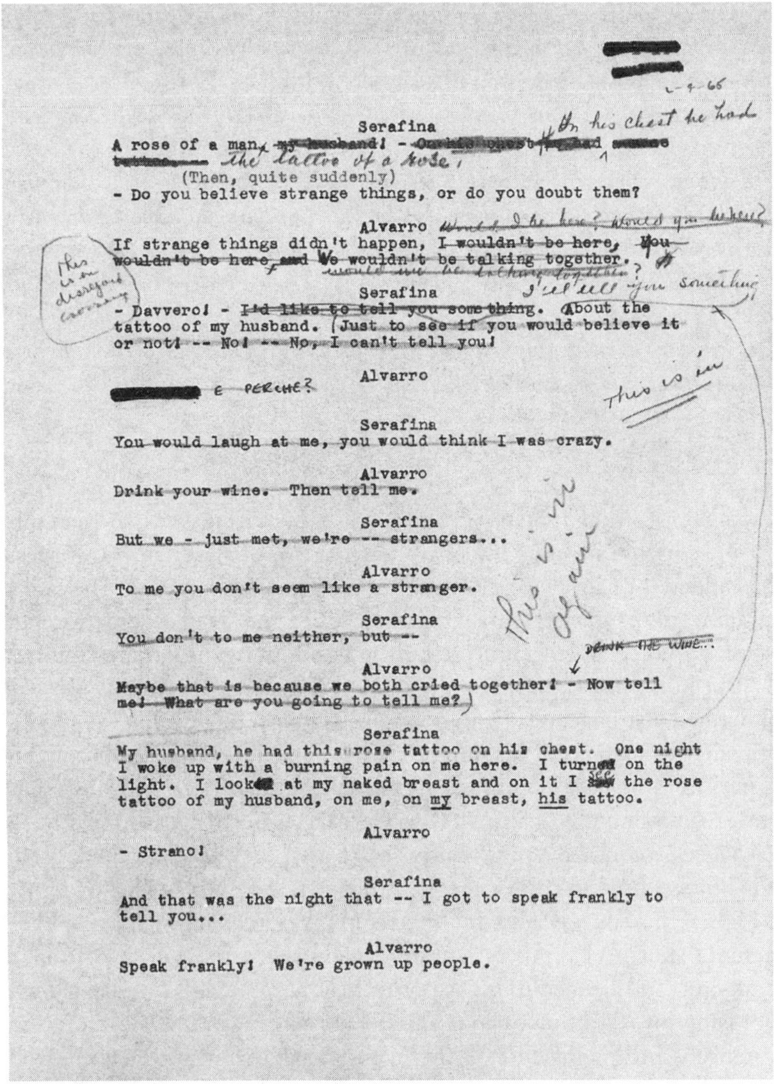

[redacted]

6-4-65

Serafina

A rose of a man, my husband! - On his chest he had a rose tattoo.

On his chest he had the tattoo of a rose.

(Then, quite suddenly)

- Do you believe strange things, or do you doubt them?

Alvarro

If strange things didn't happen, I wouldn't be here, You wouldn't be here, and We wouldn't be talking together.

Would I be here? Would you be here? Would we be talking together?

this is an disregard crossing?

Serafina

- Davvero! - I'd like to tell you some thing. About the tattoo of my husband. Just to see if you would believe it or not! -- No! -- No, I can't tell you!

I'll tell you something

Alvarro

[redacted] E PERCHE?

This is in

Serafina

You would laugh at me, you would think I was crazy.

Alvarro

Drink your wine. Then tell me.

Serafina

But we - just met, we're -- strangers...

Alvarro

To me you don't seem like a stranger.

Serafina

You don't to me neither, but --

This is in again

DRINK THE WINE...

Alvarro

Maybe that is because we both cried together! - Now tell me! What are you going to tell me?

Serafina

My husband, he had this rose tattoo on his chest. One night I woke up with a burning pain on me here. I turned on the light. I looked at my naked breast and on it I saw the rose tattoo of my husband, on me, on my breast, his tattoo.

Alvarro

- Strano!

Serafina

And that was the night that -- I got to speak frankly to tell you...

Alvarro

Speak frankly! We're grown up people.

A manuscript page from The Rose Tattoo. Courtesy of Tennessee Williams Papers, Rare Book and Manuscript Library, Columbia University.

about three forthcoming books. Additionally, Williams had three full-length plays in various preproduction stages and was negotiating with producers about a possible remake of the film version of A Streetcar Named Desire.

The night before I interviewed him in New York, Williams and I, along with the painter Vassilis Voglis, spent a night on the town that ended at a bar called Rounds, which boasts a somewhat piss-elegant decor and a clientele consisting largely of male hustlers and those who employ them. Around noon the next day, we completed the interview, although he was still tired from the night's festivities. Perhaps because of that he was more subdued than he'd been in Chicago and his answers more reflective. As a rule he dislikes talking about his work and the process by which he creates his art, but on that dreary, gray day in New York he was open to it and told me what he could about how he writes.

THE GENESIS OF WRITING

I was a born writer, I think. Yes, I think that I was. At least when I had this curious disease affecting my heart at the age of eight. I was more or less bedridden for half a year. My mother exaggerated the cause. She said I swallowed my tonsils! Years later, when I had the *Time* cover story, and she was quoted, doctors looked it up and said, "A medical impossibility!"

But I do think there was a night when I nearly died, or possibly *did* die. I had a strange, mystical feeling as if I were seeing a golden light. Elizabeth Taylor had the same experience. But I survived that night. That was a turning point, and I gradually pulled out of it. But I was never the same physically. It changed my entire personality. I'd been an aggressive tomboy until that illness. I used to beat up all the kids on the block. I used to confiscate their marbles, snatch them up!

Then that illness came upon me, and my personality changed. I became a shut-in. I think my mother encouraged me to be more of a shut-in than I needed to be. Anyway, I took to playing solitary games, amusing myself. I don't mean masturbation. I mean I began to live an intensely imaginative life. And it persisted that way. That's how I turned into a writer, I guess. By the age of twelve, I started writing.

MOTHER AND MISS ROSE

My mother—everyone calls her Miss Edwina—was essentially more psychotic than my sister Rose. Mother was put away once, you know.

She was put away long before she was old, in the early part of the decade of the fifties. I was on St. Thomas in the Virgin Islands, and she called me up.

"Tom, guess where I am?" she said.

"Why, Mother, aren't you at home?"

"No, Tom, they put me away!"

She was living alone, and I guess her fantasies got the best of her. She thought the blacks were planning an uprising in St. Louis, and they were exchanging signals by rattling the garbage pails. She called the family doctor over to tell him about these threatening aspects of life, and he took her right to the bughouse! So I left St. Thomas and sprung her.

Later, when I was in St. Louis, the phone rang and she picked it up. There was no one at the other end. After a while, she said, "*I* know who you are! I'm here waiting! *Unafraid!*"

Mother chose to have Rose's lobotomy done. My father didn't want it. In fact, he cried. It's the only time I saw him cry. He was in a state of sorrow when he learned that the operation had been performed.

I was at the University of Iowa, and they just wrote me what happened. I didn't know anything about the operation. I'd never heard of a lobotomy. Mother was saying that it was bound to be a great success. Now, of course, it's been exposed as a very bad procedure that isn't practiced anymore. But it didn't embitter me against my mother. It saddened me a great deal because my sister and I cared for each other. I cared for her more than I did my mother. But it didn't embitter me against Miss Edwina. No, I just thought she was an almost criminally foolish woman.

Why was the operation performed? Well, Miss Rose expressed herself with great eloquence, but she said things that shocked Mother. I remember when I went to visit her at Farmington, where the state sanitarium was. Rose loved to shock Mother. She had great inner resentment towards her, because Mother had imposed this monolithic puritanism on her during adolescence. Rose said, "Mother, you know we girls at All Saints College, we used to abuse ourselves with altar candles we stole from the chapel." And Mother screamed like a peacock! She rushed to the head doctor, and she said, "Do anything, *anything* to shut her up!" Just like Mrs. Venable, you know, except that Mother wasn't as cruel as Mrs. Venable, poor bitch. Whatever Mother did, she didn't know what she was doing.

She was terrified of sex. She used to scream every time she had sex with my father. And we children were terrified. We'd run out in the streets and the neighbors would take us in.

A year or so before Mother died, she believed she had a horse living with her in her room. She didn't like its presence at all, and she complained bitterly about this imaginary horse that moved into the place with her. She'd always wanted a horse as a child. And now that she finally had one, she didn't like it one bit.

At the end, she changed her name. Miss Edwina dropped the *a* from her name and became Edwin Williams. That's how she signed herself. It's strange to have a mother who at ninety-four decides to call herself Edwin.

Miss Rose smokes too much. She enters a restaurant and asks, "How many packs of Chesterfields do you have? *I'll take them all!*" Or she'll ask in a store, "How many bars of Ivory soap do you have? That all you got? Well, I need at least twenty!"

One night Rose went with me to Mrs. Murray Crane's as a dinner guest. She had a huge reticule with her. Do you know what that is? It's a huge embroidered bag. Rose was very sly, as schizophrenics often are. All during dinner, after each course, or even while people were eating, she would turn to Mrs. Crane, this stately dowager to her right, and say, "Have a cigarette, dear?" And Mrs. Crane would reply, "Oh, I don't smoke, Miss Williams. I do not smoke! And I fear that you're smoking too *much*, Miss Williams!"

Well, Miss Rose took umbrage at that. So after dinner she excused herself. There were four or five lavatories in this duplex apartment, and Rose was gone for a *remarkably* long time. When she came back her reticule was absolutely packed like Santa Claus's bag. She'd cleared the house completely out of soap and toilet paper! It was the biggest haul since the James Brothers. Needless to say, we didn't get a return engagement there.

She's very nervous, you know. When she was in Key West while you were there, she was trying not to smoke so she tried to keep herself busy. She took it upon herself to water all the trees and plants, and there are a great many. Rose would take a glass of water from the house, water a plant with it, return and fill the glass, and go out again, all day long. I find that touching, how she tries to occupy her time.

She has curious misapprehensions about things. Richard Zoerink was so kind to her. They would go walking in Key West along the water. He'd buy her an ice cream cone, something she loves. One day, I asked Rose where she'd been that afternoon, and she said that she and Richard had taken a walk along the Mediterranean Sea, and she had enjoyed the view of Italy. Lovely Miss Rose. She thinks she's Queen of England, you know. She once signed a photograph of herself to me, "Rose of England."

I love her, you know. For a person like Rose who spent many years in a state asylum, as she had to do before I got any money, living is constantly a defensive existence. The stubbornness, the saying "No!" flatly to things is almost an instinctive response. If I say to Rose, "Don't you think it's time for you to get some rest?" Her instinct is just to say, "No!"

Once in Key West some people dropped by, and they began telling some very bawdy jokes. Rose didn't approve. So she got up and stood in a corner with her hands clasped in prayer. My cousin Stell, who was taking care of her, said, "Rose, why are you standing like that?"

Rose replied, "I'm praying for their redemption!"

SUCCESS

It all began for me in Chicago in 1944. I've had some of the happiest times of my life here. We were in Chicago for three and a half months with *The Glass Menagerie*. We opened in late December, and played until mid-March. And I had a lovely time. I knew a lot of university students, you know?

So I associate the success of *Menagerie* with the Chicago critics Claudia Cassidy and Ashton Stevens. They really put it over. The opening night audience had never seen this kind of theater before, and their response was puzzlement. And I suppose the play would have died here if Claudia Cassidy and Ashton Stevens hadn't kept pushing and pushing and pushing. They compared Laurette Taylor to Duse, which was a good comparison, I think. Miss Cassidy is very elderly now, but her mind's as sharp as a whistle!

Menagerie got to New York in 1945. It was sold out three and a half months before it opened. People would stop off in New York to see it because they knew it was a new kind of theater, and they knew about

Laurette's incredible performance, though the rest of the cast was pretty run-of-the-mill.

The sudden success? Oh, it was terrible! I just didn't like it. If you study photographs taken of me the morning after the huge reception it got in New York, you'll see I was very depressed.

I'd had one eye operation, and I went into the hospital for another one I needed. Lying in the hospital, unable to move for several days, people came over and read to me, and I recovered some sense of reality.

Then, after *Menagerie*, I went to Mexico and had a marvelously happy time. I went alone. Leonard Bernstein was there. He introduced me to Winchell Mount, who gave weekly Saturday night dances. All male. And I learned how to follow! I was the belle of the ball because I could always dance well, but I gave up that career for writing.

Before the success of *Menagerie* I'd reached the very, very bottom. I would have died without the money. I couldn't have gone on any further, baby, without money when suddenly, *providentially, The Glass Menagerie* made it when I was thirty-four. I couldn't have gone on with these hand-to-mouth jobs, these jobs for which I had no aptitude, like waiting on tables, running elevators, and even being a Teletype operator. None of this stuff was anything I could have held for long. I started writing at twelve, as I said. By the time I was in my late teens I was writing every day, I guess, even after I was in the shoe business for three years. I wrecked my health, what there was of it. I drank black coffee so much, so I could stay up nearly all night and write, that it exhausted me physically and nervously. So if I suddenly hadn't had this dispensation from Providence with *Menagerie*, I couldn't have made it for another year, I don't think.

WHERE PLAYS COME FROM

The process by which the idea for a play comes to me has always been something I really couldn't pinpoint. A play just seems to materialize, like an apparition it gets clearer and clearer and clearer. It's very vague at first, as in the case of *Streetcar*, which came after *Menagerie*. I simply had the vision of a woman in her late youth. She was sitting in a chair all alone by a window with the moonlight streaming in on her desolate face, and she'd been stood up by the man she planned to marry.

I believe I was thinking of my sister because she was madly in love with some young man at the International Shoe Company who paid her court. He was extremely handsome, and she was profoundly in love with him. Whenever the phone would ring, she'd nearly faint. She'd think it was he calling for a date, you know? They saw each other every other night, and then one time he just didn't call anymore. That was when Rose first began to go into a mental decline. From that vision *Streetcar* evolved. I called it at the time, "Blanche's Chair in the Moon," which is a very bad title. But it was from that image, you know, of a woman sitting by a window that *Streetcar* came to me.

Of course, the young man who courted my sister was nothing like Stanley. He was a young executive from an Ivy League school. He had every apparent advantage. It was during the Depression years, however, and he was extremely ambitious. My father had an executive position at the time with the shoe company, and the young man had thought perhaps a marriage to Rose would be to his advantage. Then, unfortunately, my father was involved in a terrible scandal and nearly lost his job. At any rate, he was no longer a candidate for the Board of Directors. He had his ear bit off in a poker fight! It had to be restored. They had to take cartilage from his ribs, and skin off his ass, and they reproduced something that looked like a small cauliflower attached to the side of his head! So any time anybody would get into the elevator with my father, he'd scowl, and people would start giggling. That was when the young man stopped calling on Rose. He knew the giggling had gone too far and gotten into the newspapers.

The idea for *The Glass Menagerie* came very slowly, much more slowly than *Streetcar* for example. I think I worked on *Menagerie* longer than any other play. I didn't think it'd ever be produced. I wasn't writing it for that purpose. I wrote it first as a short story called "Portrait of a Girl in Glass," which is, I believe, one of my best stories. I guess *Menagerie* grew out of the intense emotions I felt seeing my sister's mind begin to go.

INFLUENCES

What writers influenced me as a young man? *Chekhov!*
As a dramatist? Chekhov!

As a story writer? Chekhov!

D. H. Lawrence, too, for his spirit, of course, for his understanding of sexuality, of life in general.

EFFECTS

When I write I don't aim to shock people, and I'm surprised when I do. But I don't think that anything that occurs in life should be omitted from art, though the artist should present it in a fashion that is artistic and not ugly.

I set out to tell the truth. And sometimes the *truth* is shocking.

LOOKING BACK

I now look back at periods of my life, and I think, was that really *me*? Was I doing those things? I don't feel any continuity in my life. It is as if my life were segments that are separate and do not connect. From one period to another it has all happened behind the curtain of work. And I just peek out from behind the curtain now and then and find myself on totally different terrain.

The first period was from the age of eleven until I left the university and went into the shoe business. I was madly in love with a girl named Hazel who was frigid. And that period in my life was marked by extreme shyness. I couldn't look at people in the face without blushing. In high school, I couldn't verbally answer questions. I could only give written answers. I couldn't produce my voice. It sounded like grunting, you know? *That* shy. I supposed it was caused by an unconscious clash in me between my sexual drives and the puritanism imposed by my mother, and the great fear my father inspired in me. He was a terrifying man. He was so unhappy that he couldn't help but be tyrannical at home. That was one period.

The next period was happy. It was after I came out in the gay world. I didn't think of it as coming out. I thought of it as a new world, a world in which I seemed to fit for the first time, and where life was full of adventure that satisfied the libido. I felt comfortable at last. And that was a happy time, but *The Glass Menagerie* ended that period and new problems developed with success.

From then through the sixties, because even during the sixties I was working more or less steadily, that was another period different from the rest. But at the end of the sixties I ended up in the bughouse because I violated Dr. Max Jacobson's instructions not to drink when I took the speed injections. Toward the end, this combination produced paranoia and affected my memory and my health. When I went to New York, I couldn't remember having met my producers before, although they'd had daily meetings with me in Key West. Finally, after Anne Meacham and I fled to Tokyo after the terrible reception of *In the Bar of a Tokyo Hotel,* I became more and more ill. I had to be assisted up stairs. When I returned home alone to Key West I was *very* ill. They were building a new kitchen on my house, and the stove was in the patio. It was still operating there while the builders worked. I was stumbling around with a Silex pan, totally disoriented, trying to get it on the stove. And I just sat down on the stove! It was an electric stove, and I inflicted third-degree burns on my body! I think Marion Vaccaro called my brother, and Dakin came down to Key West. He called Audrey Wood, and she said, "Well, put him in a hospital." But she didn't bother to say which one.

Dakin, thinking I was going to die anyway, I was in such terrible condition, had me immediately converted to Roman Catholicism so I'd be saved from hell, and then he just threw me into Barnes Hospital [St. Louis], right into the psychiatric ward, which was *incredibly* awful. They suddenly snatched away every pill I had! The injections went too. So I blacked out. It was cold turkey, baby. They tell me I had three brain concussions in the course of one long day, and a coronary. How I survived, I don't know. I think there were homicidal intentions at work there. I was in that place for three and a half months. The first month I was in the violent ward, although I was not violent. I was terrified and I crouched in a corner trying to read. The patients would have terrible fights over the one television set. Someone would put on the news, and another patient would jump up, yelling, and turn on cartoons. No wonder they were violent.

CHRISTIANITY

I was born a Catholic, really. I'm a Catholic by nature. My grandfather was an English Catholic [Anglican], very, very high church. He was higher church than the Pope. However, my "conversion" to the

Catholic Church was rather a joke because it occurred while I was taking Dr. Jacobson's miracle shots. I couldn't learn anything about the tenets of the Roman Catholic Church, which are ridiculous anyway. I just loved the beauty of the ritual in the Mass. But Dakin found a Jesuit father who was very lovely and all, and he said, "Mr. Williams is not in a condition to learn anything. I'll give him extreme unction and just pronounce him a Catholic."

I was held up in the Roman Catholic Church, with people supporting me on both sides, and I was declared a Catholic. What do you think of that? Does that make me a Catholic? No, I was whatever I was before.

And yet my work is full of Christian symbols. Deeply, deeply Christian. But it's the image of Christ, His beauty and purity, and His teachings, yes...but I've never subscribed to the idea that life as we know it, what we're living now, is resumed after our death. No. I think we're absorbed back into, what do they call it? The eternal flux? The eternal shit, that's what I was thinking.

POETRY

I'm a poet. And then I put the poetry in the drama. I put it in short stories, and I put it in the plays. Poetry's poetry. It doesn't have to be called a poem, you know.

YOUNG WRITERS

If they're meant to be writers, they will write. There's nothing that can stop them. It may kill them. They may not be able to stand the terrible indignities, humiliations, privations, shocks that attend the life of an American writer. They may not. Yet they may have some sense of humor about it, and manage to survive.

WRITING

When I write, everything is visual, as brilliantly as if it were on a lit stage. And I talk out the lines as I write.

When I was in Rome, my landlady thought I was demented. She

told Frank [Merlo], "Oh, Mr. Williams has lost his mind! He stalks about the room talking out loud!"

Frank said, "Oh, he's just writing." She didn't understand *that*.

REWRITING

In writing a play, I can get started on the wrong tangent, go off somewhere, and then have to make great deletions and begin over, not *all* the way over, but just back to where I went off on that particular tangent. This is particularly true of the surrealist play that I'm currently writing. I'm dedicating it to the memory of Joe Orton. *The Everlasting Ticket* it's called. It's about the poet laureate of Three Mile Island. I'm in the third revision of *Ticket* at the moment.

I do an enormous amount of rewriting. And when I finally let a play go, when I know it's complete and as it should be, is when I see a production of it that satisfies me. Of course, even when *I'm* satisfied with a production, the critics are not, usually. In New York especially. The critics feel I'm basically anarchistic, and dangerous as a writer.

AUDIENCE

I don't have an audience in mind when I write. I'm writing mainly for myself. After a long devotion to playwriting I have a good inner ear. I know pretty well how a thing is going to sound on the stage, and how it will play. I write to satisfy this inner ear and its perceptions. That's the audience I write for.

DIRECTORS

Sometimes I write for someone specifically in mind. You know, I always used to write for [Elia] Kazan, although he no longer works as a director. What made him a great director was that he had an infinite understanding of people on an incredible level.

At one point Kazan and Jose Quintero were rather equal in talent. That was when Quintero began at the Circle in the Square downtown and did things like *Summer and Smoke* and *Long Day's Journey into Night*. Those early things. Then he took heavily to drink.

He was living at a very fashionable address, the penthouse apartment at 1 Fifth Avenue. I remember walking with Quintero out on the terrace. I said to him, "Why are you killing yourself like this with liquor? Because you are, you know. You're drinking much too heavily." He always liked me very much. He was an extremely kind and sweet person. He said, "I know. I know. It's just that all of a sudden I got all this attention, and it made me self-conscious. It scared me. I didn't know how my work was *done.* I simply worked through intuition. Then suddenly it seemed to me as if secrets of mine were being exposed." And so he drank excessively, and now he can't drink at all.

During *The Seven Descents of Myrtle,* as they called it, although it was actually *Kingdom of Earth,* Quintero was drinking so heavily that Estelle Parsons said she couldn't take direction from him. David Merrick was producing, and he came to town. He said, "I have to fire this man. He's destroying the play." And I said, "Mr. Merrick, if you fire poor Jose I'm going to withdraw the play." So he let it come in.

You know, in those days David Merrick was a lovely man. He's been around the bend some since, but he was so nice in those days. We both went to Washington University. We were in the same drama class, I believe. In the sixties he used to come to my apartment at the Mayfair when I wouldn't go out ever. He came over there to tell me he wanted to do *Kingdom of Earth.* And I just slurred something in reply. That's how I talked in those days. He said, "It's a very funny play!" And I went *grrrowwww...* I didn't give a shit whether he put it on or not, or whether I lived through the night.

TITLES

Sometimes I'll come up with a title that doesn't sound good in itself, but it's the only title that really fits the meaning of the play. Like *A House Not Meant to Stand* isn't a beautiful title. But the house it refers to in the play is in a terrible state of disrepair, virtually leaking rainwater everywhere. That house, and therefore the title, is a metaphor for society in our times. And, of course, the critics don't like that sort of thing, nor do they dare to openly approve of it. They know who butters their bread.

Some titles come from dialogue as I write a play, or from the setting itself. Some come from poetry I've read. When I need a title I'll usually reread the poetry of Hart Crane. I take a copy of Crane's work with me when I travel. A phrase will catch my eye and seem right for what I'm writing. But there's no system to it. Sometimes a line from the play will serve as its title. I often change titles a number of times until I find one that seems right.

There is a Catholic church in Key West named Mary, Star of the Sea. That would make a lovely title for a play.

LINE CHANGES

Performers can be enormously valuable in suggesting line changes in a play, I mean if they're intelligent performers. For instance, Geraldine Page. She's very intelligent, and she's a genius at acting. Being a genius at acting, and being intelligent aren't always the same thing. She'd suggest line changes. She'd say, "I find this line difficult to read." I think most of her suggestions were good, although she's not a writer. So I'd make the changes to satisfy her. I often do that with actors, if they're intelligent and care about the play.

MARLON BRANDO

Brando came up to the Cape when I was there. There was no point in discovering him, it was so obvious. I never saw such raw talent in an individual, except for Laurette Taylor, whose talent was hardly raw. Then, before he was famous, Brando was a gentle, lovely guy, a man of extraordinary beauty when I first met him. He was very natural and helpful. He repaired the plumbing that had gone on the whack, and he repaired the lights that had gone off. And then he just sat calmly down and began to read. After five minutes, Margo Jones, who was staying with us, said, "Oh, this is the greatest reading I've ever heard, even in *Texas!*" And that's how he was cast in *Streetcar.*

WARREN BEATTY

I didn't know of Warren's work, and I thought the role in *The Roman Spring of Mrs. Stone* should be played by a Latin-type since the role's a Roman gigolo. I happened to be in Puerto Rico with Marion Vaccaro, you know, the banana queen? She and I were gambling. She was playing blackjack, and I was playing roulette. All of a sudden a waiter came up to me with a little glass of milk, on a silver platter, and said, "A gentleman has sent this to you." I said, "I don't appreciate this kind of sarcasm!" So I went on playing roulette.

After I'd lost the amount of money I allow myself to lose, I started to leave. And there standing grinning at the door was Warren Beatty.

"Tennessee, I've come to read for you," he said. He was very young then, a really handsome boy.

I said, "But why, Warren? You're not the type to play a Roman gigolo."

And he said, "I'm going to read with an accent, and without it. I've come all the way from Hollywood to read for you."

"Well, that's lovely of you." And Marion and I went to his room, and he read fabulously. With an accent, and without.

Warren has no embarrassment about anything. Whenever he sees me he always embraces me. What an affectionate, warm, lovely man. I've found actors to be lovely people, although there are a few of them who have been otherwise.

AUDREY WOOD

Ever since my split with Audrey Wood [his longtime agent] there's been a holding pattern. I think she's the dominant figure in this. I think she has stock in the concern, ICM, and she won't allow anything to happen until I'm dead, baby.

Why did I break with her? I didn't. Just the usual thing happened. An opening night. My nerves always go like spitfire then. We had a very good first preview [of *The Two-Character Play*]. The second preview we had a bunch of old, sour dames. They didn't get anything, and they hated it. It enraged me. I always lose my mind slightly when I get angry. Audrey was used to this. It happened time and time again. It shouldn't have surprised her at all. And I just turned to her after the performance and said, "You must have been pleased by this audience," because she hadn't been pleased by the enthusiastic, younger audience the night before. She got angry, and left town immediately with the greatest amount of publicity. And I realized that she had neglected me so totally during my seven years of terrible depression that any kind of professional relationship with her was no longer tenable.

I don't hold grudges. So when I encountered her some time later in the Algonquin Hotel, I stretched out my hand to touch hers. There was no way of avoiding her. She hissed like a snake! and drew back her hands as if I were a leper. Well, since then I know this woman hates me! She'd lost interest in me. I don't think you should lose interest in a person who is in deep depression. That's when your interest and concern should be most, if you're a true friend.

And I think I had a great deal to do with making her career. She'd only sold *Room Service* to the Marx Brothers before I came along and got her Bill Inge and Carson McCullers and . . . this sounds bitter, and I hold no animosity toward people. I hope I don't.

BEST FRIENDS

Carson McCullers and Jane Bowles were my best friends as writers. I think if poor Carson had not suffered this very early stroke when she'd barely turned thirty, she would have been the greatest American writer. She had recurrent illnesses, of course, each diminishing her power. It was a tragic thing to watch. It went on for ten years. I met her in Nantucket. I'd written her a fan letter about *Member of the Wedding,* I thought it was so lovely. I knew cousins of hers. And at my invitation, she came to the island to be my guest. Such an enchanting person! This was the last year before she had a stroke, the year Carson lived at 31 Pine Street in Nantucket with Pancho and me.

My other great writer friend, Jane Bowles, I first met in Acapulco in the summer of 1940, after I'd broken up with Kip. I took a trip to Mexico on one of these share-the-expense plan tours. I went down with a Mexican boy who'd married an American hooker, you know? He met her at the World's Fair. The poor girl was terrified. She was a sweet girl, but she was a hooker and he didn't know it. And she'd come to my room at night and tell me they were having terrible problems sexually. I think he was gay, you know, because all the *other* men in the car were. That's a pretty good indication! She said she wasn't getting any sex, and she thought I'd provide her with some.

I said, "I'm afraid, honey, it's not quite what I do anymore because, frankly, I'm homosexual."

"Oh, that's all right," she said, "I know female hygiene is a lot more complicated!" God, I thought that was a funny answer!

Apparently, their marriage worked out somehow. I left some of my gear in the trunk of the car, and several years later after I'd become known, after *The Glass Menagerie,* she shipped it all back to me with a very lovely note.

It was that summer in Mexico when I met Jane Bowles. I knew she was there with Paul. Poor Paul was always sick. He couldn't eat anything in Mexico. But there's very little in Mexico you *can* eat, at least not in those days. They were such a charmingly odd couple, I loved them both. Jane produced such a small body of work, but it was tremendous work. And Paul's work? I guess it's about as good as anything is now.

FRANK MERLO

I met Frankie by accident at the Atlantic House in Provincetown one summer, the summer of 1947 when I was finishing *Streetcar.* I was in the Atlantic House, and Pancho was there, Margo Jones, and Joanna Albus. We were all living in a cottage. Stella Brooks was singing at the Atlantic House, and I'd gone out on the porch at the Atlantic House to breathe the fresh air and the lovely sea mist coming in. And Frankie came out behind me, and leaned against the balcony, and I observed that beautifully sculptured body in Levi's, you know? I was rather bold, as I am at certain moments. And I just said, "Would you like to take a drive?" He grinned, and said yes. He'd come there with John La-Touche, you know, the songwriter.

So we drove out to the beach and made love. It was ecstatic, even though it was in the sand.

I didn't see him again until accidentally I ran into him in a delicatessen on Third Avenue. I was living in an apartment designed by Tony Smith on East Fifty-eighth Street. Frankie was with a young war buddy of his. And I said, "Why Frank!" And he said, "Hi, Tenn." I said, "Why haven't you called me?" And he replied, "I read about your great success, and I didn't want to seem like I was trying to hop on the bandwagon."

He and his buddy came home with me to this lovely apartment. And Frankie just stayed on. He was so close to life! I was never that close, you know. He gave me the connection to day-to-day and night-to-night living. To reality. He tied me down to earth. And I had that for fourteen years, until he died. And that was the happy period of my adult life.

TRAVEL

I'm restless. I like traveling. When Frank Merlo was living, he being Sicilian, we spent four or five, sometimes six months out of the year in Rome.

I was once asked why I travel so much, and I said, "Because it's harder to hit a moving target!"

THE COMPETITION

I don't compete with Eugene O'Neill or anyone else. My work is totally in its own category. It's more esoteric than anyone else's, except Joe Orton's. And I don't compete with Joe Orton. I love him too much.

EUGENE O'NEILL

Now O'Neill is not as good a playwright as, for instance, Albee. I don't think he's even as good as Lanford Wilson. I could give you quite a list.

I liked O'Neill's writing. He had a great spirit, and a great sense of drama, yes. But most of all it was his spirit, his *passion*, that moved me. And when *The Iceman Cometh* opened to very bad notices, very mixed notices at best in New York, I wrote him a letter. I said, in reading your play, at first I found it too long, then I gradually realized that its length, and the ponderosity of it, are what gave it a lot of its power. I was deeply moved by it, finally.

He wrote me a very nice reply and said he was always deeply depressed after an opening and that he appreciated my letter particularly. But that letter has disappeared like most of my letters.

LIQUOR

O'Neill had a terrible problem with alcohol. Most writers do. American writers nearly all have problems with alcohol because there's a great deal of tension involved in writing, you know that. And it's all right up to a certain age, and then you begin to need a little nervous support that you get from drinking. Now my drinking has to be moderate. Just look at the liver spots I've got on me!

OPENING NIGHTS

On opening nights in the old days, when I really could drink—I can't drink heavily now because of this pancreatitis I developed from over-drinking—but when I *could* drink, on opening nights I'd either have a flask on me and keep myself drunk and stand at attention in the theater, or else I'd dart out to the nearest bar and sit there until nearly before the curtain came down and then I'd head back into the theater.

Now I take openings much more calmly. If they're giving a good performance, and they usually do on opening night, I just sit and enjoy it. After the curtain, I take a red-eye flight out of town. I have a car waiting for me with the luggage in it, and scoot out to La Guardia or Kennedy and take the red-eye to Key West.

KEY WEST

It's delightful. When I first went there in 1941 it was still more de-lightful than it is now. I have one-quarter of a city block there now, you know. A swimming pool. My studio with a skylight. I have a little guesthouse in the form of a ship's cabin, with a double-decker bunk in it. And I have my gazebo, the Jane Bowles Summer House. Everything I need for a life. It's a charming, comfortable place.

HABITS OF WORK

In Key West I get up just before daybreak, as a rule. I like being com-pletely alone in the house in the kitchen when I have my coffee and ruminate on what I'm going to work on. I usually have two or three pieces of work going at the same time, and then I decide which to work on that day.

I go to my studio. I usually have some wine there. And then I care-fully go over what I wrote the day before. You see, baby, after a glass or two of wine I'm inclined to extravagance. I'm inclined to excesses be-cause I drink while I'm writing, so I'll blue-pencil a lot the next day. Then I sit down, and I begin to write.

My work is *emotionally* autobiographical. It has no relationship to the actual events of my life, but it reflects the emotional currents of my life. I try to work every day because you have no refuge but writing. When you're going through a period of unhappiness, a broken love affair, the death of someone you love, or some other disorder in your life, then you have no refuge but writing. However, when depression comes on of a near clinical nature, then you're paralyzed even at work. Immediately after the death of Frank Merlo, I was paralyzed, unable to write, and it wasn't until I began taking the speed shots that I came out of it. Then I was able to work like a demon. Could you live without writing, baby? I couldn't.

Because it's so important, if my work is interrupted I'm like a raging tiger. It angers me so. You see, I have to reach a high emotional pitch in order to work if the scene is dramatic.

I've heard that Norman Mailer has said that a playwright only writes in short bursts of inspiration while a novelist has to write six or seven hours a day. Bull! Now Mr. Mailer is more involved in the novel form, and I'm more involved in the play form. In the play form I work steadily and hard. If a play grips me I'll continue to work on it until I reach a point where I can no longer decide what to do with it. Then I'll discontinue work on it.

DRUGS

There was a very lovely young guy at New Directions named Robert MacGregor, who's dead now. He'd been a patient of Dr. Max Jacobson. He only took little pills that Jacobson gave him. I was in a state of such profound depression that he thought anything was worth trying, so he took me to Jacobson. It was through this Robert MacGregor that I had those three years of Jacobson shots that he mailed to me in the various parts of the country.

I did find Max Jacobson's shots marvelously stimulating to me as a writer. And during those last three years of the sixties, before my collapse, I did some of my best writing. People don't know it yet, but I did.

My collapse was related to the fact that I continued to drink while taking the shots. I was not supposed to. I had a bad heart. Dr. Max Jacobson never listened to my heart. Never took my pulse. Never took my blood pressure. He would just look at me. He was really sort of an alchemist. He would look at me for a long time. He had all these little vials in front of him. He'd take a drop from one, and a drop from another, and then look at me again, and take another drop or two.... Of course, the primary element was speed. And after I had a shot, I'd get into a taxi and my heart would begin to pound, and I'd immediately have to have a drink or I wouldn't be able to get home. I'd have died in the cab otherwise.

ON BEING SINGLE

I think it made it possible for me to practice my profession as a writer. You know what happened to poor Norman Mailer. One wife after another, and all that alimony. I've been spared all that. I give people money, yes. But I couldn't have afforded alimony, not to all those wives. I would've had to behead them! Being single made it possible for me to work.

HOMOSEXUALITY

I never found it necessary to deal with it in my work. It was never a pre-occupation of mine, except in my intimate, private life. In my work, I've had a great affinity with the female psyche. Her personality, her emotions, what she suffers and feels. People who say I create transvestite women are full of shit. Frankly. Just vicious shit. Personally, I like women more than men. They respond to me more than men do, and they always have. The people who have loved me, the ratio of women to men is about five to one, I would say.

I know there's a right-wing backlash against homosexuals. But at the age of seventy I no longer consider it a matter of primary concern. Not that I want anything bad to happen to other homosexuals. God knows, enough has.

I always thought homosexual writers were in the minority of writers. Nobody's yet made a correct census of the actual number of homosexuals in the population of America. And they never will be able to because there are still too many closets, some of them rather securely locked. And it's also still dangerous to be openly homosexual.

CRUISING

I enjoyed cruising, more for Donald Windham's company, than for the pickups that were made. After all, pickups are just pickups. But Windham was a delightful friend to be with. I always realized that he had a streak of bitchery in him. And that's why my letters to him had a great deal of malicious humor in them. I knew he liked that. And since I was writing to a person who enjoyed that sort of thing I tried to amuse him with those things. Of course, I didn't know he was *collecting* my letters! And I didn't know I was signing away the copyright. I'm happy the letters were published because they're beautiful, I think. I'm very unhappy that he may have shut down *London Magazine* with that lawsuit.*

There used to be a place in Times Square called the Crossroads Tavern, right near a place called Diamond Jim Brady's. The place was closing down, and on this occasion these big, drunk sailors came and picked us up. We didn't pick *them* up. I wasn't attracted to them. I didn't want to, and I felt really uneasy about the situation. But Windham was always attracted to rough sailor types.

As it happened Windham was staying at the Claridge Hotel, which doesn't exist now in the Times Square area. He had been living with a painter, Paul Cadmus. He was occupying a room with Paul Cadmus, and it was through Paul Cadmus that he met Sandy Campbell.† It had been inconvenient for Cadmus to have Donald Windham at his place one night, and so he'd gotten him a room at the Claridge. And Donald had taken the two sailors and me into Claridge's.

I got more and more suspicious because in the lobby the sailors said, "We'll go up the elevator, and you wait ten minutes, and we'll meet you in the corridor...." Or something like that. It seemed suspicious, but I was a little high, and so was Donald.

We got up to the room, and it was really a bestial occurrence. I hated every minute of it. Finally, after they ripped the phones out of the wall, they stood me against a wall with a switchblade knife while they beat Windham, knocking a tooth out, blackening both his eyes, beating him almost to death. I kept saying, "Oh, don't do that, don't hit him anymore! He's *tubercular!*"

Then they said, "Now it's your turn!" So they stood poor, bloody Windham against the wall while they beat me nearly to death. I had a

---

*When Donald Windham published *Tennessee Williams' Letters to Donald Windham: 1940–1965*, Dotson Rader wrote an essay for *London Magazine* reviewing the letters. The piece was critical of Windham. Mr. Windham responded with a lawsuit, later settled out of court.

†Sandy Campbell is Windham's friend and companion.

concussion from the beating. Next thing I knew I was at the emergency Red Cross station at the YMCA where I lived.

KIP

Kip was very honest, and I loved him and I think he loved me. He was a draft dodger from Canada. He had a passion to be a dancer, and he knew he couldn't if he went into the war. It'd be too late, he felt, when it was over, for him to study dancing. You see, he was a boy of twenty-one or twenty-two when the war happened.

I've written a play called *Something Cloudy, Something Clear* about Kip. The setting is very important in this play. It involves a bleached, un-furnished beach shack in which the writer, who represents me, but is called August, is working on a portable typewriter supported by an old crate. He sleeps on a mattress on the floor. Alongside that set is the floor of another beach house shack that's been blown away in a hurri-cane. This floor, however, forms a platform on which Kip used to dance, practicing dancing to my Victrola. The subtitle of the play is *The Silver Victrola*.

I prefer the title *Something Cloudy, Something Clear* because it refers to my eyes. My left eye was cloudy then because it was developing a cataract. But my right eye was clear. It was like the two sides of my na-ture. The side that was obsessively homosexual, compulsively inter-ested in sexuality. And the side that in those days was gentle and understanding and contemplative. So it's a pertinent title.

Now this play is written from the vantage point of 1979, about a boy I loved and who is now dead. The author (August) knows it's 1979. He knows Kip is dead, and that the girl whom Kip dances with is dead. I've invented the girl. Occasionally during the play the author onstage will make references that puzzle the boy, Kip, and the girl. But the author is the only one who realizes that it's really forty years later, and the boy and girl are dead, and he survives, still he survives. It happened in the summer of 1940, and it's a very lyrical play, probably the most lyrical play I've done in a very long while.

Kip died at the age of twenty-six. It was just after I completed my professionally abortive connection with MGM. The phone rang one day and an hysterical lady said, "Kip has ten days to live." A year before I had been told that Kip had been successfully operated on for a benign brain tumor.

He was at the Polyclinic Hospital near Times Square. You know how love bursts back into your heart when you hear of the loved one's dying.

As I entered Kip's room he was being spoon-fed by a nurse: a dessert of sugary apricots. He had never looked more beautiful. Kip's mind seemed as clear as his Slavic blue eyes.

We spoke awhile. Then I rose and reached for his hand and he couldn't find mine, I had to find his.

After Kip died his brother sent me, from Canada, snapshots of Kip posing for a sculptor and they remained in my wallet some twenty years. They disappeared mysteriously in the sixties. Well, Kip lives on in my leftover heart.

HEMINGWAY AND FITZGERALD

Hemingway had a remarkable interest in and understanding of homosexuality, for a man who wasn't a homosexual. I think both Hemingway and Fitzgerald had elements of homosexuality in them. I make quite a bit of that in my rewrite of *Clothes for a Summer Hotel*.

Have you ever read "A Simple Enquiry" by Hemingway? Well, it's about an Italian officer in the Alps during the First World War. And he's of course deprived of female companionship. He has an orderly, a very attractive young orderly. He desires the orderly. And he asks the boy, rather bluntly, "Are you interested in girls?" The boy panics for a moment, and says, "Oh, yes, I'm engaged to be married." And the boy goes out of the room, and the Italian officer says, "I wonder if that little sonofabitch was lying?"

The final line in Hemingway's *Islands in the Stream* is one man saying I love you to another. It didn't mean they'd had homosexual relations, although Gertrude Stein intimated that Hemingway had. But does it matter? I don't think it matters.

You know what he said about Fitzgerald? Hemingway said that "Fitzgerald was pretty. He had a mouth that troubled you when you first met him, and troubled you more later."

Fitzgerald played the female lead in the Princeton Triangle Club, and there's a picture of him as a woman that's more feminine than any woman could look. Fitzgerald never had an affair with anybody but his wife. There was Sheilah Graham at the end, but did he sleep with her? I doubt it. Anyway, I don't think the sexuality of writers is all that interesting. It has no effect, I can tell you that. In very few instances does it have any effect on their ability to portray either sex. I am able to write of men as well as women, and I always project myself through whichever sex I'm writing about.

FIDEL CASTRO

I met Castro only once, and that was through Hemingway. The time I met Hemingway was the time I met Castro. I was in Havana during the first year of Castro's regime. Castro would have remained a friend of the United States except for that bastard John Foster Dulles, who had this phobia about anything revolutionary. He apparently thought that Mr. Batista—a sadist who tortured students to death—was great fun.

I met Hemingway through Kenneth Tynan at the restaurant Floridita in Havana. Hemingway and I had a very pleasant meeting. He gave us both a letter of introduction to Castro. Hemingway said this was a good revolution. And if Mr. Dulles hadn't alienated Castro, it might have been.

Castro was a gentleman. An educated man. He introduced me to all the Cuban cabinet. We'd been waiting three hours on the steps for this emergency cabinet meeting to end. When he introduced us, he turned to me and said, "Oh, that *cat*!" and winked. He meant *Cat on a Hot Tin Roof,* of course. I found that very engaging.

JOHN F. KENNEDY

I met President Kennedy through Gore Vidal, at the family estate in Palm Beach before he was president. And then I met him at the White House, where he gave a great dinner party for André Malraux and invited all the literary people, the theater people.

John Kennedy was a great gentleman, a really good, gentle man. On the way to see him we were caught in terrible traffic. Gore Vidal isn't a particularly good driver, though he's a good writer at times. So we were an hour late for lunch with Mr. Kennedy, and he acted as if we were on time. His manners were so impeccable, and Jackie was a tremendous charmer, and still is, I presume, although I haven't seen her in a long time.

THE CARTER WHITE HOUSE

The first time I went there was some occasion when the film industry was being honored. At that time the Carters had not yet adjusted themselves to entertaining. He's rather abstemious, Mr. Carter, which is the one major fault I found with him. We were only allowed to have one very small glass of what was purported to be a California chablis. I downed my glass in one swallow, and then tried to figure out how to get some more. All there was was wine. No hard liquor. Nothing. But you could only have one glass. So I got ahold of Sam Spiegel, who is a very portly gentleman, and I said, "Sam, will you stand in front of the table and slip me another glass of wine surreptitiously?" So I hid behind Sam, and he snuck me several small glasses which helped to get me through the evening.

Later, when I went to the White House, the Carters had begun serving champagne. But they never did get around to hard liquor.

I think Jimmy Carter was a great humanitarian, and his second term might have been wonderful compared to what we got. I thought his human rights concern was right, and I am sorry that our government has abandoned it.

I don't think the big money people wanted Mr. Carter back in. He wasn't pliable enough.

JANE WYMAN

Jane Wyman was in the movie of *The Glass Menagerie*. She married Ronald Reagan. The no-nose girl married the no-brain man!

HOLLYWOOD

Most of my films were subjected to excessive censorship. Which is one of the reasons why I might be interested in seeing *Streetcar* done again as a film by Sidney Lumet, now that Kazan has stopped directing. But I'd have to have a great Stanley, and the only person they've mentioned so far is Sylvester Stallone, and so I'm not paying much attention to this project of remaking *Streetcar* until there's a suitable Stanley, and a really great actress to play Blanche.

In the 1940s I had a glorious time in Hollywood because I was fired almost at once from the project I was working on and they had to continue to pay me. That was in my contract. For six months they had to pay me $250 a week. This was in 1943, when $250 was equivalent to about $1,000 now, I would guess. They had to pay me whether I had an assignment or not.

First they put me on *Marriage Is a Private Affair* for Lana Turner. Well, they expressed great delight with my dialogue, and I think it was good. But they said, "You give Miss Turner too many multisyllable words!" So I said, "Well, some words *do* contain more than one syllable!" And Pandro Berman, who loved me very much—Lana Turner just happened to be his girlfriend at the time—he said to me, "Tennessee, Lana can tackle two syllables, but I'm afraid if you go into three you're taxing her vocabulary!"

Then they asked me if I'd like to write a screenplay for a child star, one named Margaret O'Brien. I said, "I'd sooner shoot myself!" By that time I knew I'd get the $250 regardless.

So I lived out in Santa Monica and had a ball until the money ran out.

ELIZABETH TAYLOR

Monty Clift was one of the great tragedies among actors, even more than Marilyn Monroe, I believe. One of the loveliest things about Elizabeth Taylor was her exceptional kindness to him. Many women were very kind to him. Katharine Hepburn. But Elizabeth particularly. She's a very dear person. She's the opposite of her public image. She's not a bitch, even though her life has been a very hell. Thirty-one operations, I believe. Pain and pain. She's so delicate, fragile really.

I saw her in Fort Lauderdale at the opening of Lillian Hellman's *The Little Foxes,* and she held that stage as if she'd always been a stage actress. But she has a little deficiency of humor. I knew she would catch it, I hoped she would. And she opened so well in Washington that I think she must have caught the humor.

I know you think Lillian Hellman's a somewhat limited playwright. But *Hellman* doesn't think so, does she? No! After the opening, when I saw Liz Taylor could act onstage, there was a huge party, with great imported champagne, the works! The director was seated next to me at my table. He said he had to get up and call Hellman.

I said, "Well, tell her I want a piece of her royalties!"

So he gave her the message, and came back to the table grinning. "Hellman said to tell you the check is in the mail!"

She's a funny woman, and a skillful playwright. Several of her plays are enormously skillful.... I've heard she has emphysema. Who *isn't* sick! They're all sick and dying!

WILLIAM INGE

Bill Inge was a tragic person. *Tragic.* The critics treated him very cruelly. They're brutal. I always thought he wrote two wonderful plays. *Come Back, Little Sheba* was a brilliant play. That's when I introduced him to Audrey Wood. And then he wrote a play in which a kid kills his mother, an enormously brilliant work. *Natural Affection,* or something like that.

I met him in St. Louis. I came back there during the run of *Menagerie* in Chicago, and he interviewed me for a paper called the St. Louis *Star-Times.* He was the drama and music critic for it. He entertained me quite a bit the week I was there. We became friends.

At the end of his life, Barbara Baxley, with whom he attempted to have a heterosexual affair, and who was very, very fond of him, called me and said that Inge was in a desperate situation in California. "He's sleeping with lots of barbiturates under his mattress. He only gets up to drink, and then he goes back to bed."

I said, "He's on a suicide course."

She said, "I know it. He commits himself voluntarily, and then lets himself out the next day."

"Who's he with?"

"His sister," she said. "I want you to call his sister and tell her that she's got to commit him."

So after consulting Maureen Stapleton, who said I should, I did call his sister and she said, "Yes, that's just how it is." She was talking in a whisper. I said, "I can hardly hear you. Why are you whispering like that?"

She answered, "Because I never know whether he's up or down."

I said, "Just listen then. Get him into a hospital. Don't have him commit himself. *You* commit him. Otherwise he's going to kill himself."

Well, a month later in Rome I read a headline in the Rome *Daily American* that Bill Inge was dead. He had asphyxiated himself by running the motor on his car in a closed garage.

Fitzgerald, Hemingway, Hart Crane, Inge...oh, the debris! The *wreckage*! Toward the end of an American writer's life it's just dreadful. Hemingway's last years were a nightmare. He tried to walk into the propeller of a plane. Fitzgerald's end was not much better, although it was less dramatic.... Once they become known, everybody wants a piece of them.

CHRISTOPHER ISHERWOOD

I met him in the forties in California. At the time he was into Vedanta, an Eastern religious thing. He was living in a monastery. They had periods of silence and meditation, you know. The night I met him, through a letter from Lincoln Kirstein, I arrived during one of these silent periods. The monk who opened the door handed me a pencil and paper to write what my business was and who I'd come to see. I wrote, "Christopher Isherwood," and they regarded me with considerable suspicion from that point on.

In this big room in the monastery, everyone was sitting in...what do they call it? The lotus position? Including Christopher. All strictly observing the vow of silence. I didn't dig the scene.

I suddenly made some reference out loud about the Krishna. I didn't know who the hell he was, I was only trying to break the silence. Christopher got up, and wrote on a piece of paper, "I'll call you tomorrow." He was very polite, and he took me to the door.

He's a superb writer, and I haven't a clue why he went through this period in a monastery. I think it was a period of unhappiness in his life. I think his love affair with Bill Caskey was breaking up, or had broken up, and he had not yet found Don Bachardy. He was intensely lonely. So he went into this monastery that had this vow of silence and poverty.

I found Chris terribly attractive, not so much in a sexual way, but as a person. Charismatic. Brilliant. And one of the greatest gentlemen I've known. So, being attracted to him, I declared myself.

Then I found out that another one of the vows they took in this place was sexual abstinence! Christopher said to me, "Tennessee, it's perfectly all right if I submit *passively* to oral intercourse, but I cannot perform it. I'd be breaking the vow!" I howled with laughter, and so did he. Then we cemented our friendship.

YEVTUSHENKO

What's happened to him? Is he still in favor with the Soviets?

When he was last in the States he asked me to have lunch with him. He ordered bottles of Château Lafite-Rothschild. And the bill was so tremendous it occupied three pages! I was stuck with it, of course. I told him he was a fucking capitalist pig!

He was accompanied by this very fat gourmand of a translator who didn't translate anything. Yevtushenko spoke perfect English and he understood English perfectly. And the alleged translator didn't understand a damn thing except how to eat and drink like a rich capitalist!

I've heard a lot of people speak against Yevtushenko. I don't know how far he can be trusted, but he's charming in his way. If you can afford it.

TRUMAN CAPOTE

I met Truman in 1948, I guess. He'd just published *Other Voices, Other Rooms.* I thought he was quite cute, slim, with this marvelously witty, slightly malicious tongue. I got mad at him after a while. He said something cruel about Frankie. Frank Merlo, Jack Dunphy, who was Truman's friend, and I, we were all traveling in my Buick Roadmaster convertible. We'd gotten as far as Naples. At a waterfront restaurant in Naples he said something quite cruel, and I said I'm not going on to Ischia with this man. After a couple of days, Frankie talked me into it. And we went anyway.

I never disliked Truman after that, I just realize that he has this impulse to be catty at times. I think it's because he's a little guy who's been picked on a lot, especially when he was growing up. You know, Truman makes the mistake of claiming he was born in New Orleans, and giving interviews, even points out the house he was born in. Everyone knows he was born in Huntsville, Alabama. Everyone in Huntsville claims him. They all know it, it's registered.

Now why does he do such things? I think it's because the poor little man likes mystery, likes to confuse people about himself. Well, Truman's a mythologist, baby, you know that. That's a polite way of saying he does fabricate. I love him too much to say he's a liar. That's part of his profession.

MY FUNNIEST ADVENTURE

I was alone in Miami. Frank [Merlo] hadn't arrived yet from New York. I was staying in Miami until he got there and took me to Key West.

It was night, and I was lonely. I walked out onto Biscayne Boulevard. There's a park along there. This young vagrant was lolling on a bench. I think he was mentally retarded, poor child. I struck up a conversation with him. He seemed not too bright, but personable. I said I was alone, would he like to accompany me to my hotel? He said he would. Well, once he got under a streetlight I saw he'd never be able to go through a hotel lobby because his clothes were so dilapidated. So I suggested that we go out by the pool where I had a cabana.

We got out there, and he suddenly jerked my wallet out of my pocket. I had only seven dollars in it, though. Then he tried to get my wristwatch off. It had a very simple clasp upon it, but he couldn't manage to get it unclasped. Finally he gave up on that. I wasn't frightened at all for some reason. I was wearing a ring with three diamonds and he couldn't get that off either. It was a tight fit. So I said, "Now this is a very silly situation. I've got hundreds of dollars upstairs in my room. You sit down here and rest, and I'll be down in a little while with a large sum of money for you." I'd realized by this time that he was a moron.

Well, I went back to my room in the hotel, locked the door, and went to bed. And at half-hour intervals all night, the phone would ring and he'd say, "I'm still waiting!" I finally said, "Baby, go see a doctor. You really think I was coming back down with a hundred dollars for you?" I liked the poor kid by that time.

It's the funniest adventure I ever had. "I'm still waiting!" He might still be.

HUMOR

You know, with advancing age I find humor more and more interesting. Black humor, especially. My present play, the one I'm working on

[*The Everlasting Ticket*], I call a Gothic comedy. My humor is Gothic in theater. I make some serious, even tragic observations about society, but I make them through the medium of comedy.

THE RICH

My feeling about the rich is not anger, really, but a feeling that they are emotionally restricted. They live in a very narrow, artificial world, like the world of Gloria Vanderbilt, who can be very unpleasant, you know. Or the Oscar de la Rentas, who are the most shocking of all. They are the Madame du Barrys of our time! You mention Oscar de la Renta to me and I turn purple with rage. They are basically very common people, you know. I know where he's from and how he started, and I know all about where she's from, too. Now they think they're the best thing since the invention of the wheel. I find them an outrageous symptom of our society, the shallowness and superficiality, the lack and fear of any depth that characterizes this age, this decade. It appalls me.

The sixties were a decade of great vitality. The civil rights movement, the movement against war and imperialism. When I said to Gore Vidal, "I slept through the sixties," I was making a bad joke. I was intensely aware of what was going on. Even in the violent ward I read the newspapers avidly. Then we had brave young people fighting against privilege and injustice. Now we have the de la Rentas.

TODAY'S COLLEGE KIDS

They aren't noticeable now. They seem to be totally reactionary, like the rich. The ones I've met rarely seem different from their parents in attitudes and values.

In the sixties, or even the early seventies, the kids I met seemed to be in revolt against the mores and social ideas of their parents. It may just be an illusion of mine, but it seems today that the children are frightened of deviating from their parents' way of life and thought. The ME-ME-ME Generation. Selfishness. A complete lack of interest in what's happening in the world. No interest in what's going on in El Salvador, this military junta supported by our government that rushes its troops into villages, pulls the peasants out, and slaughters them! American kids don't care. In Guatemala, four hundred people a day being slaughtered, although no one mentions it much. Honduras. Don't they care, this generation? We know why Allende was assassinated, how and why. All Latin America is in strife, and the ME-ME-ME Generation doesn't appear to care.

The sixties were intensely alive! We were really progressing towards a workable, just society. But then Nixon came along, and everything fell back into its old routine of plutocracy.

LECTURES

I don't give formal lectures, although they call them that. I just give formal readings. Once I went to the University of Tennessee in Knoxville with a prepared lecture. When I got there I discovered I'd left the lecture at home. So I had to get up on stage and improvise, which infuriated the professors. They were outraged! Knoxville, like other academic places, is very reactionary.

THE STATE OF THE CULTURE

Literature has taken a backseat to the television, don't you think? It really has. We don't have a culture anymore that favors the creation of writers, or supports them very well. I mean, serious artists. On Broadway, what they want are cheap comedies and musicals and revivals. It's nearly impossible to get serious work even produced, and then it's lucky to have a run of a week. They knocked Albee's *Lolita* down horribly. I've never read such cruel reviews. But I felt it was a mistake for Albee to do adaptations. He's brilliant doing his own original work. But even so, I think there's a way of expressing one's critical displeasures with a play without being quite so hard, quite so cruel. The critics are literally killing writers.

REGRETS

Oh God, yes, baby! But I can't think about them now. So many things to regret. But there are, I believe, so very *few* things that one can change in one's life. There are very few acts of volition. I don't believe in individual guilt. I don't think people are responsible for what they do. We are products of circumstances that determine what we do.

That's why I think capital punishment's an outrage. But then the population growth and the growth of crime have become so enormous there aren't enough prisons to put people in. Prisons. Killing. Yet I don't believe in individual guilt at all, and sometimes I wonder whether I even believe in collective guilt. And yet I do believe that the intelligent person, the moral individual, must avoid evil and cruelty and dishonesties. One can try to pursue a path of virtue. That remains to us, I hope.

THE NOBEL PRIZE

I'll tell you why I think I haven't gotten it.

I'd heard I'd been nominated for it several times in the fifties. But then suddenly a scandal happened. This lady, I call her the crepe de chine Gypsy, went to Stockholm. And she lured me to Stockholm by telling me she was living in a charming little hotel near the waterfront, and that I would have my own suite with a private entrance. And that I would have a fantastic time, if you know what I mean—I was at the height of my fame then—she used my name as an excuse to get all the people around that she'd wanted to meet but had no way of meeting. She later turned out to be a dominatrix! Well, she had all the press there. She was like a field marshal! "You over that way! You over there! You do not approach Mr. Williams until I give you the signal!" Barking out orders. Oh, it was just terrifying. The next morning the newspapers all came out saying Mr. Williams arrived in Stockholm preceded by a very powerful press agent! And my agent in Scandinavia, Lars Schmidt, who married Ingrid Bergman, said, "You know, you've been nominated for the Nobel Prize but now it's finished." The scandal was so awful, the press having been abused, and they associated me with this awful woman.

Well, after all, one doesn't *have* to get it. It'd be nice because it's a lot of money, isn't it? I could use that, if I could get it.

CURRENT WORK

I've been busy with the production of the new play, *A House Not Meant to Stand*. The production of a play is for me an event that eclipses everything else, even turning seventy. I love the Goodman Theater, and I'm going to work with them again. We're already making plans to move this play on to the main stage, and to do *Something Cloudy, Something Clear*, about the summer when I met Kip on the Cape, though I've added other characters besides Kip and me.

And I've got an important play, *In Masks Outrageous and Austere*. It's a line of Elinor Wylie's, from a poem by her. It goes like this: "In masks outrageous and austere/the years go by in single file;/Yet none has merited my fear,/and none has quite escaped my smile."

It happens to fit the play, which has a great deal of poetry in it and yet at the same time the situation is bizarre as hell. It's about the richest woman on earth. Babe Foxworth is her name. She doesn't know where she is. She's been abducted to Canada, on the east coast. But they don't know where they are. A village has been constructed like a movie set to deceive them. Everything is done to confine and deceive them while her husband is being investigated. Babe is really an admirable person, besides her hypersexuality, though that can be admirable. I think it is! It's a torture to her because she's married to a gay husband who's brought along his boyfriends. I think it's an extremely funny play.

ADVICE TO YOUNG PLAYWRIGHTS

What shouldn't you do if you're a young playwright? *Don't bore the audience!* I mean, even if you have to resort to totally arbitrary killing onstage, or pointless gunfire, at least it'll catch their attention and keep them awake. Just keep the thing going any way you can.

THE MONEY PEOPLE

Do you know what the most difficult aspect of playwriting is? I'll tell you. *It's dealing with the money people.* The commercial end of it is the most appalling part. The demands for changes and rewrites don't bother me if they're made by the director, and I think they're intelligent demands. But when the money people get into the act, you're in trouble.

MY MOST DIFFICULT PLAY

I think *Clothes for a Summer Hotel* was the most difficult play to write, of all my plays. Because of the documentation I had to do. I had to spend four or five months reading everything there is about Fitzgerald and Zelda. There's a huge amount of material. Finally, when it was written I had to cut an hour out of the play on the road. Jose Quintero was in very fragile health, and after every opening, he had to flee. So I had to do it without any help or advice from anybody. To cut an hour out of it. And then I had to start rewriting it. The scene the critics objected to most violently was that between Hemingway and Fitzgerald. But that's an integral part of the play because each was a central figure in the life of the other. I thought the confrontation between them indispensable. Now I've rewritten the play again, and I've built up that scene, not so much in length of playing time, but in content, making it more pointed.

ZELDA FITZGERALD

Zelda's one great love affair was with this French aviator. It was her first infidelity to Scott, and probably her only one. It was aggressive because she was being liberated by infidelity from this very possessive love that Scott had for her. And for the first time she was experiencing erotic ecstasy. She'd never experienced that with Scott. She used to complain to poor Scott that he was sexually inadequate.

She frightened the aviator by the violence of her reactions. She went around the bend because of him. She tried to kill herself, swallowing the contents of a bottle of morphine or something. The aviator was frightened away.

Zelda was also terribly anti-Semitic, like most Southern women, and a touch of it goes into the play [*Clothes*]. I think I just couldn't leave it out and do a true portrait of her. I have her make a single anti-Semitic remark in the play, which is about Sheilah Graham, whose real name is Lily Sheil.

In the theater you hardly dare use the word *Jew*, and it's really a detriment to a very fine people that they're so frightened of any criticism whatsoever, although after the Holocaust they certainly have reason to be frightened. I have no feelings of anti-Semitism, but those feelings do exist in other people, and it's difficult to present a picture of the world as it truly is without on occasion allowing a voice to those sentiments.

CHILDREN

I'm very happy I never had any children. There have been too many instances of extreme eccentricity and even lunacy in my family on all four sides for me to want to have children. I think it's fortunate I never did.

Rose, Dakin, and I are the last of two direct bloodlines, the Dakin family, and the Williams. And all three of us are childless.

HANDLING LONELINESS

It's not easy. I have a few close friends, though. And you can get by with a few. And as for sex? I don't feel I require it that much anymore. I miss having a companion very much. I'll never be without someone with me, although it'll just be someone who is fond of me and takes care of me, but it won't be a sexual thing anymore.

DEATH

Everyone's afraid of it, but I'm no more than most, I suppose. I'm beginning to reconcile myself to it. I'm *not* reconciled to dying before my work is finished, though. I have a very strong will. There were occasions in the last years or so when I might have gone out. But my will forces me to go on because I've got unfinished work.

—DOTSON RADER
Fall, 1981

EUGÈNE IONESCO

© Jerry Bauer

The preeminent practitioner of the theater of the absurd, Eugène Ionesco was born in Slatina, Romania, on November 26, 1912, the son of a Romanian father and a French mother. While Ionesco was still an infant, the family moved to France, but the marriage was not a happy one, and Ionesco's father moved back to Romania when that country entered the First World War. When Ionesco's mother returned to Romania with her children in 1925, she learned that her husband, through falsifying documents, had managed to divorce her and retain custody of the children.

At the age of eighteen, Ionesco enrolled at the University of Bucharest and began to write essays and poems. In 1934 he published a book of criticism, *Non*. He spent a few years working as a teacher before moving back to France in 1938, where, but for a few years spent in Romania during the early part of the Second World War, he remained until his death.

Ionesco's first play, *La Cantatrice chauve* [The Bald Soprano] (1950), was inspired by the repetitive and nonsensical phrases he had encountered while attempting to learn English. Experimental and surreal like all his work, the play sets out to demonstrate the insufficiency of language as a mode of communication and the insidiousness of daily life in a society bound by meaningless formalities.

Beginning in the fifties Ionesco wrote a series of plays that focused on the fortunes of a single character, a modern-day Everyman named Bérenger. In the most famous of these, *Rhinocéros* (1959), Bérenger is surrounded by people who willingly transform themselves into rhinoceroses. Inspired by Ionesco's having witnessed a friend's slow acceptance of and conversion to Nazism, the play concludes with Bérenger caught between his temptation to join the mob and his desire to retain his humanity. Bérenger is featured in three other plays: *Amédée* (1954), *Tueur sans gages* [The Killer] (1958), and *Le Roi se meurt* [Exit the King] (1962).

Ionesco wrote several volumes of essays and criticism, many of which share the vehement opposition to totalitarianism and oppression that characterize his plays. His only novel, *Le Solitaire* [The Hermit], was published in 1972.

In his final years Ionesco abandoned writing and devoted himself to painting and exhibiting his works. He died in Paris on March 28, 1994.

———

Ionesco and his Romanian wife of forty-five years, Rodica, live in an exotic top-floor apartment on the Boulevard Montparnasse above La Coupole, surrounded by a collection of books and pictures by some of Ionesco's oldest friends and colleagues, including Hemingway, Picasso, Sartre, and Henry Miller. Our interview took place in the drawing room, where Miró's portraits, Max Ernst's drawing of Ionesco's Rhinoceros, *and a selection of Romanian and Greek icons adorn the walls.*

Ionesco, a small, bald man with sad, gentle eyes, seems quite fragile at first glance—an impression that is immediately belied by his mischievous sense of humor and his passionate speech. Beside him Rodica, also slight, with dark, slanted eyes and an ivory complexion, looks like a placid Oriental doll. During the course of the interview she brought us tea and frequently asked how we were

bornée à ce conflit simple, — il n'y aurait rien en ~~pas~~
de nouveau, de vrai, de profond, — mais une
réalité grossière et schématique. Nous nous apercevons
que tout est bien plus complexe. Et dans cette
prison, un homme doit ~~mourir~~ être exécuté. On
ne voit pas ce condamné sur la scène. Il est pourtant
présent à notre conscience, infiniment obsédant. C'est
le héros de la pièce. Ou plutôt: c'est la mort
qui est ce héros. Gardiens et prisonniers ~~vivent~~ *resentful*
~~cette mort~~, ~~la revoir~~ ensemble, vivent cette mort, —
sauf le bourreau et le vieux prisonnier: il n'y a
que ces derniers qui soit déshumanisés. A part eux,
l'humanité profonde de cette oeuvre réside dans la
communion ~~vraie~~, ~~une~~ terrible de cette hantise,
cette angoisse qui est celle de tous. Une union,
au-delà de la désunion; une fraternité, presque
inconsciente mais dont l'auteur nous fait prendre
conscience, là se crée ou se révèle. Il est
évident que cette angoisse ~~est~~ propre à nous tous.
Les gardiens, les prisonniers sont très les uns et les
autres, des mortels que hantent le fait essentiel
qu'ils sont des mortels, — et la pièce touche
aux ~~ultimes~~ problèmes essentiels des hommes qui fait que
les hommes soient des hommes. Voilà un théâtre
populaire, — celui de la communion dans la
même angoisse. Impopulaire, aussi, — car
à Paris, du moins, le <u>Obituel du matin</u> n'a pas eu

A Eugène Ionesco manuscript page.

getting on. The Ionescos' steady exchange of endearments and their courtesy with each other reminded me of some of the wonderful old couples portrayed by Ionesco in many of his plays.

INTERVIEWER: You once wrote, "The story of my life is the story of a wandering." Where and when did the wandering start?

IONESCO: At the age of one. I was born near Bucharest, but my parents came to France a year later. We moved back to Romania when I was thirteen, and my world was shattered. I hated Bucharest, its society, and its mores—its anti-Semitism for example. I was not Jewish, but I pronounced my *r*'s as the French do and was often taken for a Jew, for which I was ruthlessly bullied. I worked hard to change my *r*'s and to sound Bourguignon! It was the time of the rise of Nazism and everyone was becoming pro-Nazi—writers, teachers, biologists, historians.... Everyone read Chamberlain's *Foundations of the Nineteenth Century* and books by rightists like Charles Maurras and Léon Daudet. It was a plague! They despised France and England because they were *yiddified* and racially impure. On top of everything, my father remarried and his new wife's family was very right-wing. I remember one day there was a military parade. A lieutenant was marching in front of the palace guards. I can still see him carrying the flag. I was standing beside a peasant with a big fur hat who was watching the parade, absolutely wide-eyed. Suddenly the lieutenant broke rank, rushed toward us, and slapped the peasant, saying, "Take off your hat when you see the flag!" I was horrified. My thoughts were not yet organized or coherent at that age, but I had feelings, a certain nascent humanism, and I found these things inadmissible. The worst thing of all, for an adolescent, was to be different from everyone else. Could I be right and the whole country wrong? Perhaps there were people like that in France—at the time of the Dreyfus trials, when Paul Déroulède, the chief of the anti-Dreyfusards, wrote "Chants du Soldat"—but I had never known it. The France I knew was my childhood paradise. I had lost it, and I was inconsolable. So I planned to go back as soon as I could. But first, I had to get through school and university, and then get a grant.

INTERVIEWER: When did you become aware of your vocation as a writer?

IONESCO: I always had been. When I was nine, the teacher asked us to write a piece about our village *fête*. He read mine in class. I was encouraged and continued. I even wanted to write my memoirs at the age of ten. At twelve I wrote poetry, mostly about friendship—"Ode to Friendship." Then my class wanted to make a film and one little boy suggested that I write the script. It was a story about some children who invite some other children to a party, and they end up throwing all the furniture and the parents out of the window. Then I wrote a patriotic play, *Pro Patria*. You see how I went for the grand titles!

INTERVIEWER: After these valiant childhood efforts you began to write in earnest. You wrote *Hugoliade* while you were still at university. What made you take on poor Hugo?

IONESCO: It was quite fashionable to poke fun at Hugo. You remember Gide's "Victor Hugo is the greatest French poet, alas!" or Cocteau's "Victor Hugo was a madman who thought he was Victor Hugo." Anyway, I hated rhetoric and eloquence. I agreed with Verlaine, who said, "You have to get hold of eloquence and twist its neck off!" Nonetheless, it took some courage. Nowadays it is common to debunk great men, but it wasn't then.

INTERVIEWER: French poetry is rhetorical, except for a few exceptions like Villon, Louise Labé, and Baudelaire.

IONESCO: Ronsard isn't. Nor are Gérard de Nerval and Rimbaud. But even Baudelaire sinks into rhetoric: "Je suis belle, ô mortels!" and then when you see the actual statue he's referring to, it's a pompous one! Or:

> Mon enfant, ma soeur,
> Songe à la douceur,
> D'aller là-bas vivre ensemble…

It could be used for a brochure on exotic cruises for American millionaires.

INTERVIEWER: Come on! There were no *American* millionaires in those days.

IONESCO: Ah, but there *were*! I agree with Albert Béguin, a famous critic in the thirties [author of *Dreams and the Romantic Soul*], who said that Hugo, Lamartine, Musset, et cetera... were *not* romantics, and that French romantic poetry really started with Nerval and Rimbaud. You see, the former produced versified rhetoric; they talked about death, even monologued on death. But from Nerval on, death became visceral and poetic. They didn't speak of death, they *died* of death. That's the difference.

INTERVIEWER: Baudelaire died of death, did he not?

IONESCO: All right then, you can have your Baudelaire. In the theater, the same thing happened with us—Beckett, Adamov, and myself. We were not far from Sartre and Camus—the Sartre of *La Nausée*, the Camus of *L'Étranger*—but they were thinkers who demonstrated their ideas, whereas with us, especially Beckett, death becomes a living evidence, like Giacometti, whose sculptures are walking skeletons. Beckett shows death; his people are in dustbins or waiting for God. (Beckett will be cross with me for mentioning God, but never mind.) Similarly, in my play *The New Tenant*, there is no speech, or rather, the speeches are given to the Janitor. The Tenant just suffocates beneath proliferating furniture and objects—which is a symbol of death. There were no longer words being spoken, but images being visualized. We achieved it above all by the dislocation of language. Do you remember the monologue in *Waiting for Godot* and the dialogue in *The Bald Soprano*? Beckett destroys language with silence. I do it with too much language, with characters talking at random, and by inventing words.

INTERVIEWER: Apart from the central theme of death and the black humor which you share with the other two dramatists, there is an important oneiric, or dreamlike, element in your work. Does this suggest the influence of surrealism and psychoanalysis?

IONESCO: None of us would have written as we do without surrealism and dadaism. By liberating the language, those movements paved the way for us. But Beckett's work, especially his prose, was influenced above all by Joyce and the Irish Circus people. Whereas my theater was born in Bucharest. We had a French teacher who read us a poem by Tristan Tzara one day which started, *"Sur une ride du soleil,"* to demonstrate how ridiculous it was and what rubbish modern French poets were writing. It had the opposite effect. I was bowled over and immediately went and bought the book. Then I read all the other surrealists—André Breton, Robert Desnos…I loved the black humor. I met Tzara at the very end of his life. He, who had refused to speak Romanian all his life, suddenly started talking to me in that language, reminiscing about his childhood, his youth, and his loves. But you see, the most implacable enemies of culture—Rimbaud, Lautréamont, dadaism, surrealism—end up being assimilated and absorbed by it. They all wanted to destroy culture, at least organized culture, and now they're part of our heritage. It's culture and not the bourgeoisie, as has been alleged, that is capable of absorbing everything for its own nourishment. As for the oneiric element, that is due partly to surrealism, but to a larger extent due to personal taste and to Romanian folklore—werewolves and magical practices. For example, when someone is dying, women surround him and chant, "Be careful! Don't tarry on the way! Don't be afraid of the wolf; it is not a real wolf!"—exactly as in *Exit the King.* They do that so the dead man won't stay in infernal regions. The same thing can be found in *The Tibetan Book of the Dead,* which had a great impact on me too. However, my deepest anxieties were awakened, or reactivated, through Kafka.

INTERVIEWER: Especially the Kafka of "The Metamorphosis"?

IONESCO: Yes, and of *Amerika.* Remember how his character, Karl Rossmann, goes from cabin to cabin and can't find his way? It is very oneiric. And Dostoyevsky interested me because of the way he deals with the conflict between good and evil. But all this already had happened by the time I left Bucharest.

INTERVIEWER: How did you manage to return to Paris—I believe at the age of twenty-six—and stay for good?

IONESCO: I had a degree in French literature and the French government gave me a grant to come and do a doctorate. In the meantime, I had married and was working as a teacher. My wife, Rodica, was one of the few people who thought the same as I did. Perhaps it's because she comes from that part of Romania which is very Asiatic—the people are small and have slit eyes. Now I'm becoming a racialist! Anyway, I was going to write a thesis on "The Themes of Death and Sin in French Poetry." There's the grand title again.

INTERVIEWER: Did you write it?

IONESCO: Oh no! As I researched, I noticed that the French—Pascal, Péguy, et cetera—had problems of faith, but they had no feeling for death and they *certainly* never felt guilty. What they had plenty of was the feeling of age, of physical deterioration and decay. From Ronsard's famous sonnet about aging, "*Quand vous serez bien vieille...*," to Baudelaire's *Une Charogne*, to Zola's *Thérèse Raquin* and *Nana*—it's all degradation, decomposition, and rot. But not death. Never. The feeling of death is more metaphysical. So I didn't write it.

INTERVIEWER: Is that why you also gave up dramatizing Proust, because his preoccupation with time is different from yours?

IONESCO: Precisely. Also, *Remembrance of Things Past* is too long and difficult, and what is interesting is the seventh volume, *Time Regained*. Otherwise, Proust's work is concerned with irony, social criticism, worldliness, and the passage of time, which are not my preoccupations.

INTERVIEWER: When you settled in Paris, did you try to meet the authors whose works you had read, and get into the literary world?

IONESCO: I did research at the National Library and met other students. Later, I met Breton, who came to see my play *Amédée* in 1954. I continued seeing him until his death in 1966. But he had been dropped by the literary establishment because, unlike Aragon, Éluard, and Picasso, he refused to join the Communist Party, and so he wasn't fashionable anymore.

INTERVIEWER: You also got involved with the Collège de 'Pataphysique. Could you tell me about it?

IONESCO: Quite by chance, I met a man named Sainmont, who was a professor of philosophy and the founder, or *Le Providateur général,* of the Collège de 'Pataphysique. Later I met Raymond Queneau and Boris Vian, who were the most important and active members. The Collège was an enterprise dedicated to nihilism and irony, which in my view corresponded to Zen. Its chief occupation was to devise commissions, whose job it was to create subcommissions, which in turn did nothing. There was one commission which was preparing a thesis on the history of latrines from the beginning of civilization to our time. The members were students of Dr. Faustroll, who was an invented character and the prophet of Alfred Jarry. So the purpose of the Collège was the demolition of culture, even of surrealism, which they considered too organized. But make no mistake, these people were graduates of the École Normale Supérieure and highly cultured. Their method was based on puns and practical jokes—*le canular.* There is a great tradition of puns in Anglo-Saxon literature—Shakespeare, *Alice in Wonderland*—but not in French. So they adopted it. They believed that the science of sciences is the 'Pataphysique and its dogma, *le canular.*

INTERVIEWER: How was the Collège organized, and how did one join it?

IONESCO: It was organized with great precision: there was a hierarchy, grades, a pastiche of freemasonry. Anybody could join, and the first grade was that of *Auditeur amphitéote.* After that, you became a *Regent,* and finally a *Satrap.* The satrap was entitled to be addressed as *Votre transcendence,* and when you left his presence you had to walk backwards. Our principal activity was to write pamphlets and to make absurd statements, such as, "Jean Paulhan does not exist!" Our meetings took place in a little café-restaurant in the Latin Quarter, and we discussed nothing, because we believed—and I still do—that there is no reason for anything, that everything is meaningless.

INTERVIEWER: Is that not contradictory to your religious conversion?

IONESCO: No, because we exist on several different planes, and when we said nothing had any reason we were referring to the psychological and social plane. Our God was Alfred Jarry, and, apart from our meetings, we made pilgrimages to his grave near Paris. As you know, Jarry had written *Ubu roi,* which was a parody of *Macbeth.* Much later I wrote a play based on *Macbeth* too. Anyway, the Collège gave decorations, the most important of which was *La Gidouille,* which was a large turd to be pinned on your lapel.

INTERVIEWER: How did you acquire the honor of becoming a satrap?

IONESCO: By writing *The Bald Soprano* and *The Lesson,* since the plays made fun of everything. They both had a conventional format—scenes, dialogue, characters—but no psychology.

INTERVIEWER: Did those at the Collège ever play a practical joke on you?

IONESCO: Yes. At the premiere of *The Bald Soprano,* twenty to thirty of them turned up wearing their gidouilles on their lapels. The audience was shocked at the sight of so many big turds, and thought they were members of a secret cult. I didn't produce many puns, but I did contribute to the *Cahiers du Collège de 'Pataphysique,* the Collège's quarterly magazine, with letters in Italian, Spanish, and German—all the languages I don't speak. The letters just sounded Italian, Spanish, and German. I wish I had kept some but I haven't. The chief makers of puns and canulars were Sainmont and Queneau. They invented a poet named Julien Torma, who of course never existed, and they published his works in the *Cahiers.* They even invented a biography for him, complete with a tragic death in the mountains.

INTERVIEWER: When did the Collège cease to exist?

IONESCO: When the founders and guiding spirits—Vian, Sainmont, and finally Queneau—began to die. There was an honorary president, a certain Baron Mollet, who was not a baron at all, but a madman who had once been Guillaume Apollinaire's valet. But the 'Pataphysique is not dead. It lives on in the minds of certain men, even if they are not aware of it. It has gone into "occultation," as we say, and will come back again one day.

INTERVIEWER: To get back to your work: After you dropped your thesis in favor of your own writing, why did you choose the theater and not another literary form?

IONESCO: The theater chose me. As I said, I started with poetry, and I also wrote criticism and dialogue. But I realized that I was most successful at dialogue. Perhaps I abandoned criticism because I am full of contradictions, and when you write an essay you are not supposed to contradict yourself. But in the theater, by inventing various characters, you can. My characters are contradictory not only in their language, but in their behavior as well.

INTERVIEWER: So in 1950 you appeared, or should I say erupted, on the French stage with *The Bald Soprano*. Adamov's plays were staged almost simultaneously, and two years later there was Beckett's *Waiting for Godot*—three avant-garde playwrights who, though very different in personality and output, had a great deal in common thematically and formally, and who later became known as the chief exponents of the "theater of the absurd." Do you agree with this appellation?

IONESCO: Yes and no. I think it was Martin Esslin who wrote a book with that title about us. At first I rejected it, because I thought that everything was absurd, and that the notion of the absurd had become prominent only because of existentialism, because of Sartre and Camus. But then I found ancestors, like Shakespeare, who said, in *Macbeth*, that the world is full of sound and fury, a tale told by an idiot, *signifying nothing*. Macbeth is a victim of fate. So is Oedipus. But what happens to them is not absurd in the eyes of destiny, because destiny, or fate, has its own norms, its own morality, its own laws, which cannot be flouted with impunity. Oedipus sleeps with his mummy, kills his daddy, and breaks the laws of fate. He must pay for it by suffering. It is tragic and absurd, but at the same time it's reassuring and comforting, since the idea is that if we don't break destiny's laws, we should be all right. Not so with our characters. They have no metaphysics, no order, no law. They are miserable and they don't know why. They are puppets, undone. In short, they represent modern man. Their situation is not tragic, since it has no relation to a higher order. Instead, it's ridiculous, laughable, and derisory.

INTERVIEWER: After the success of *The Bald Soprano* and *The Lesson* you became suddenly and controversially famous. Were you lionized? Did you start frequenting literary salons and gatherings?

IONESCO: Yes, I did. Literary salons don't exist any longer in Paris, but in those days there were two. The first was the salon of Madame Dézenas—a rich lady who liked literature and the arts. All sorts of celebrities came there: Stravinsky, Etiemble, young Michel Butor, Henri Michaux.... The second salon was La Vicomtesse de Noailles's. I went there once and met Jean-Louis Barrault. I remember how a ripple of excitement, a *frisson*, ran through the gathering when Aragon and Elsa Triolet were announced. "Here come the Communists!" they all said. Aragon was in a dinner jacket and Elsa was covered in jewelry. But *I* went there to drink whiskey and to meet friends, not out of worldliness.

INTERVIEWER: Do you think worldly distractions, social life and parties, dissipate a writer's concentration and damage his work?

IONESCO: Yes, to a certain extent. But there have been great writers who have been great partygoers at the same time, such as Valéry, Claudel, and Henry James. Valéry used to get up at five in the morning, work until nine, then spend the rest of the day having fun in one way or another.

INTERVIEWER: Do you think success can be damaging for a writer, not only as a distraction but because it could make him seek out easy options and compromises?

IONESCO: It depends on how you use it. I detest and despise success, yet I cannot do without it. I am like a drug addict—if nobody talks about me for a couple of months I have withdrawal symptoms. It is stupid to be hooked on fame, because it is like being hooked on corpses. After all, the people who come to see my plays, who create my fame, are going to die. But you can stay in society and be alone, as long as you can be detached from the world. This is why I don't think I have ever gone for the easy option or done things that were expected of me. I have the vanity to think that every play I have written is different from the previous ones. Yet, even though they are written in a different way, they all deal with the same themes, the same preoccupations. *Exit the King* is also *The Bald Soprano.*

INTERVIEWER: You also wrote a play called *Macbett*, which is very different from Shakespeare's *Macbeth*. What made you go for a remake of the Bard?

IONESCO: My Macbett is not a victim of fate, but of politics. I agree with Jan Kott, the Polish author of *Shakespeare, Our Contemporary*, who gives the following explanation: A bad king is on the throne, a noble prince kills him to free the country of tyranny, but ipso facto he becomes a criminal and has to be killed in turn by someone else—and on it goes. The same thing has happened in recent history: the French Revolution liberated people from the power of the aristocrats. But the bourgeoisie that took over represented the exploitation of man by man, and had to be destroyed—as in the Russian Revolution, which then degenerated into totalitarianism, Stalinism, and genocide. The more you make revolutions, the worse it gets. Man is driven by evil instincts that are often stronger than moral laws.

INTERVIEWER: This sounds very pessimistic and hopeless and seems at variance with your mystical and religious tendencies.

IONESCO: Well, there is a higher order, but man can separate himself from it because he is free—which is what we have done. We have lost the sense of this higher order, and things will get worse and worse, culminating perhaps in a nuclear holocaust—the destruction predicted in the apocalyptic texts. Only our Apocalypse will be absurd and ridiculous because it will not be related to any transcendence. Modern man is a puppet, a jumping jack. You know, the Cathars [a Christian sect of the later Middle Ages] believed that the world was not created by God but by a demon who had stolen a few technological secrets from Him and made this world—which is why it doesn't work. I don't share this heresy. I'm too afraid! But I put it in a play called *This Extraordinary*

Brothel, in which the protagonist doesn't talk at all. There is a revolution, everybody kills everybody else, and he doesn't understand. But at the very end, he speaks almost for the first time. He points his finger towards the sky and shakes it at God, saying, "You rogue! You little rogue!" and he bursts out laughing. He understands that the world is an enormous farce, a canular played by God against man, and that he has to play God's game and laugh about it. That is why I prefer the phrase "theater of derision," which Emmanuel Jacquart used for the title of his book on Beckett, Adamov, and myself, to "theater of the absurd."

INTERVIEWER: I think Esslin was dealing with the first period of your work—*The Bald Soprano, The Lesson, Jacques,* and *The Chairs.* With the introduction of your central character, Bérenger, the plays seem to change somewhat. The dislocation of language, the black humor, and the element of farce are all still there, but not to the same degree. Instead, you develop new elements of both plot and character. How did you come to choose the name Bérenger, and did the creation of this character help with the transition?

IONESCO: I wanted a very common name. Several came to my mind and I finally chose Bérenger. I don't think the name means anything, but it is very ordinary and innocuous. In the first plays the characters were puppets and spoke in the third person as *one,* not as *I* or as *you.* The impersonal one, as in "one should take an umbrella when it is raining." They lived in what Heidegger calls "the world of one." Afterwards, the characters acquired a certain volume, or weight. They have become more individualized, psychologized. Bérenger represents the modern man. He is a victim of totalitarianism—of both kinds of totalitarianism, of the Right and of the Left. When *Rhinoceros* was produced in Germany, it had fifty curtain calls. The next day the papers wrote, "Ionesco shows us how we became Nazis." But in Moscow, they wanted me to rewrite it and make sure that it dealt with Nazism and not with their kind of totalitarianism. In Buenos Aires, the military government thought it was an attack on Peronism. And in England they accused me of being a petit bourgeois. Even in the new *Encyclopaedia Britannica* they call me a reactionary. You see, when it comes to misunderstanding, I have had my full share. Yet I have never been to the Right, nor have I been a Communist, because I have experienced, personally, both forms of totalitarianism. It is those who have never lived under tyranny who call me petit bourgeois.

INTERVIEWER: The misunderstanding of your work in England and the fact that your plays have not been widely produced there or in America dates back to your quarrel with the late critic Kenneth Tynan in the early sixties.

IONESCO: That's right. I didn't much care for the angry young men whose work Tynan was backing. I thought *them* very petit bourgeois and insignificant. I found their revolutionary zeal unconvincing, their anger small and personal, and their work of little interest.

INTERVIEWER: Also, Brecht was enjoying a vogue at the time, and you were definitely not Brechtian.

IONESCO: I think that Brecht was a good producer, but not really a poet or a dramatist, except in his early plays, *The Threepenny Opera, Baal,* and a couple of others. But his committed plays don't work. I believe that, as Nabokov said, an author should not have to deliver a message, because he is not a postman.

INTERVIEWER: Sam Goldwyn said the same thing about films, "Messages should be delivered by Western Union."

IONESCO: Did he say that? I quite agree. In France everybody was Brechtian—Bernard Dort, Roland Barthes—and they wanted to rule the theater. Later, Tynan asked me to write something for his erotic revue, *Oh! Calcutta!* which I did. Then he said: "You have so much talent, you could be Europe's first dramatist." So I said, "What should I do?" and he said, "Become Brechtian." I said, "But then I would be the second, not the first."

INTERVIEWER: Now we seem to have come full circle. A Brechtian, Roger Planchon, has just produced *Journey Among the Dead,* your auto-

biographical play, and you are considered one of the greatest dramatists of our time. You have been sitting in the French Academy since
1970, next to some of the people who rejected your plays at first. I understand that the process of election to the Academy involves writing
letters and calling on each member personally, pleading your case and
asking to be elected. There are many famous rejections, like Baudelaire's heartbreaking letters to the members of the Academy, begging
them to vote for him. And Zola. It seems a humiliating process. Yet
you, a rebel, why did you go through with it?

IONESCO: I didn't. There were people who wanted me there, like René
Clair, Jean Delay, and others; and I said I would apply on the condition
that I would not have to call on people and write letters. I simply presented my letter of candidacy and I was elected by seventeen votes
against sixteen.

INTERVIEWER: How do the meetings of the Academy compare with
those of the Collège de 'Pataphysique in the old days?

IONESCO: All the members of the Academy are pataphysicians,
whether consciously, like the late René Clair, or unconsciously. Anyway, I don't go there that often, only a couple of times a year for the
elections of new members, and I always vote against them!

INTERVIEWER: Against whom?

IONESCO: Against everybody! Unfortunately, I'm such a poor in-
triguer that I have not succeeded in keeping out certain undesirable
persons, and there are people I would like to see as members who
have not yet been elected. But the elections are fun. Claudel used to
say that they were so amusing that there should be one every week.
You see, the French Academy is an association of solitaries: Jean
Delay, the inventor of modern postpsychoanalytic psychiatry; Lévi-
Strauss, the creator of modern anthropology and structuralism; Louis
de Broglie, one of the founders of modern physics; and Georges
Dumézil, a great specialist in religions. These are the most cultured
men in France, truly liberated minds and free spirits. I assure you,

only third-rate journalists denigrate the French Academy, the petit bourgeois who think they are intellectuals and who would not dream of mocking the Soviet Academy—where the members must accept all manner of indignity, pay allegiance to the Communist Party, and be censured constantly.

INTERVIEWER: You said that you didn't care much for the angry young men of the theater. What about those, like Pinter and Albee, whose works were clearly influenced by yours and Beckett's?

IONESCO: Pinter's first successful play, *The Caretaker,* was derived from Beckett and was very good. Since then, he seems to be doing what I call *du boulevard intelligent*—which is to say, he is writing clever, well-made commercial plays. In truth, these playwrights were influenced only by our language, not really by our spirit. Stoppard's play *Rosencrantz and Guildenstern Are Dead* was admirable. I also liked Albee's *The Zoo Story,* but I haven't read anything in the same vein since. Several French playwrights, Dubillard and a few others, tried their hands, but it didn't really go anywhere. What we tried to do was to put man on the stage to face himself. That is why our theater was called metaphysical. In England, where people like Edward Bond write plays in which terrible things happen, it is still on the political level. The sacred and the ritual are missing. Did I tell you that I recently went to Taiwan? It is a nice American place, and everybody speaks English. But they seem to have lost touch completely with their own traditions, their own sages, and I, not a particularly erudite amateur, had to tell them about Confucius, Buddha, Zen. In the West, also, people have lost the feeling for the sacred, *le sentiment du sacré.* We tried to bring it back by going to our sources, to the theater of antiquity. In Racine, adultery is considered a very important crime, punishable by death. In the theater of the nineteenth century, adultery is a *divertissement,* an entertainment—the *only* entertainment! So although we are considered modern, too modern, even avant-garde, *we* are the real classicists, not the writers of the nineteenth century.

INTERVIEWER: After four plays—*Amédée, The Killer, Exit the King,* and *Rhinoceros*—you dropped Bérenger. Did you think you had said enough about him?

IONESCO: I changed his name because I thought people might get bored. I called him Jean, or the Character.

INTERVIEWER: In your new play, which is a kind of oneiric biography, he is called Jean again. In the opening scene, there are two coffins, Sartre's and Adamov's, and you are standing behind them. Why did you choose those two from among all the people you have known?

IONESCO: Adamov was a great friend of mine for years, until my plays really caught on; then he turned against me. I resented him for giving in to pressure and becoming "committed," Brechtian, and pro-Communist, although he never actually joined the party. We finally broke up over some silly literary dispute. I think I accused him of stealing my dreams! With Sartre it was different. It was a case of a missed appointment, *un rendez-vous manqué,* as one journalist put it. I had loved *La Nausée,* which had influenced my only novel, *Le Solitaire* (The Hermit), but he annoyed me with his constant ideological changes. He was given solid proof of concentration camps in Russia, yet he did not publicize it because he feared it would disillusion the workers and strengthen the bourgeoisie. Towards the end, when the New Philosophers arrived on the scene, people like Foucault and Glucksmann, he told them that he was no longer a Marxist. He always had to be aligned with *le dernier cri,* the latest ideological fashion. I would have preferred him to be more obdurate, even if in error. He was called "The Conscience of Our Time"; I feel he was rather the *Un*conscience of our time—*L'inconscience.*

But he was always nice and courteous to me, and my plays were the only ones he allowed to be put on a double bill with his, so I am sad that I didn't get close to him. I had a dream about him recently: I am on a stage in front of a huge, empty auditorium, and I say, "That's it, nobody comes to see my plays anymore." Then a little man walks on-stage, and I recognize him as Sartre. He says, "Not true, look there, up in the gallery, it's full of young people." And I say to him, "Ah, Monsieur Sartre, how I would like to talk to you, at last." And he replies, "Too late . . . too late." So you see, it was a missed appointment.

INTERVIEWER: This play, *Journey Among the Dead,* has been a great success with the public as well as with the critics. It's coming to the

Comédie-Française in the spring. With that out of the way, have you started work on something else?

IONESCO: It's a play about the life and martyrdom of a modern saint, who has just been canonized by the Church—or is it beatified? Which comes first? I'm not sure. Anyway, his name was Father Maximilian Kolbe, a Pole, and he died in Auschwitz. They were going to send some prisoners to a mine, where they would die of hunger and thirst. Father Kolbe offered to go instead of a man who had a wife and children and didn't want to die. That man is still alive.

INTERVIEWER: Does it matter to you if the Church canonizes him or not? And what about the recent allegations of anti-Semitism regarding him?

IONESCO: Oh dear! It won't matter to me at all whether the Church canonizes him or not. The important thing is that such a man existed. As for his anti-Semitism, I have not heard anything. People always try to find base motives behind every good action. We are afraid of pure goodness and of pure evil. I very much doubt that such a man could have been remotely anti-Semitic.

INTERVIEWER: For this play, you already had a clear idea of the character and the plot. Do you always start with an idea?

IONESCO: It depends. Some plays start with a plan. For example, *Macbett* was a conscious parody of Shakespeare. I already had the idea for *Rhinoceros*. But I had no idea at all where plays like *The Chairs, The Lesson,* and *The Bald Soprano* would lead. I had the idea of the corpse for *Amédée,* but the rest came bit by bit.

INTERVIEWER: How do you work?

IONESCO: I work in the morning. I sit comfortably in an armchair, opposite my secretary. Luckily, although she's intelligent, she knows nothing about literature and can't judge whether what I write is good or worthless. I speak slowly, as I'm talking to you, and she takes it down. I let characters and symbols emerge from me, as if I were dreaming. I always use what remains of my dreams of the night before. Dreams are reality at its most profound, and what you invent is truth because invention, by its nature, can't be a lie. Writers who try to prove something are unattractive to me, because there is nothing to prove and everything to imagine. So I let words and images emerge from within. If you do that, you might prove something in the process. As for dictating the text to my secretary, for twenty-five years I wrote by hand. But now it is impossible for me; my hands shake and I am too nervous. Indeed, I am so nervous that I kill my characters immediately. By dictating, I give them the chance to live and grow.

INTERVIEWER: Do you correct what she has written afterward?

IONESCO: Hardly. But to get back to my new play, I tried to change the incoherent language of the previous plays into the language of dreams. I think it works, more or less.

INTERVIEWER: Do you have a favorite among your plays?

IONESCO: Until recently it was *The Chairs*, because the old man remembers a scene from his childhood, but very vaguely, like the light of a dying candle, and he remembers a garden whose gate is closed. For me that is paradise—the lost paradise. This scene is far more important to me than the end, which is more spectacular.

INTERVIEWER: We have talked about the metaphysical and ritualistic aspects of your work, but there is a comic element as well, which has greatly contributed to your popularity.

IONESCO: Georges Duhamel used to say that "humor is the courtesy of despair." Humor is therefore very important. At the same time, I can understand people who can't laugh anymore. How can you, with the carnage that is going on in the world—in the Middle East, in Africa, in South America, everywhere? There is awfully little that is conducive to mirth.

INTERVIEWER: Whatever happens in the future, your place in the literary history of our time is secure. What is your own assessment of your work?

IONESCO: I'll tell you about a dream I had recently. When I was a schoolboy in Bucharest, my father used to come into my room in the evening and check my homework. He would open my drawers and find nothing but bits of poetry, drawings, and papers. He would get very angry and say that I was a lazybones, a good-for-nothing. In my dream, he comes into my room and says, "I hear you have done things in the world, you have written books. Show me what you have done." And I open my drawers and find only singed papers, dust and ashes. He gets very angry and I try to appease him, saying, "You are right, Daddy, I've done nothing, nothing."

INTERVIEWER: Yet you go on writing.

IONESCO: Because I can't do anything else. I have always regretted having gotten involved with literature up to my neck. I would have preferred to have been a monk; but, as I said, I was torn between wanting fame and wishing to renounce the world. The basic problem is that if God exists, what is the point of literature? And if He *doesn't* exist, what is the point of literature? Either way, my writing, the only thing I have ever succeeded in doing, is invalidated.

INTERVIEWER: Can literature have any justification?

IONESCO: Oh yes, to entertain people. But that is not important. Yet, to introduce people to a different world, to encounter the miracle of being, that is important. When I write, "The train arrives at the station," it is banal, but at the same time sensational, because it is invented. Literature can also help people. Two of my translators, a Romanian and a German, were dying of cancer when they were translating *Exit the King*. They told me that they knew they were going to die, and the play helped them. Alas, it does not help me, since I am not reconciled to the idea of death, of man's mortality. So you see, I am contradicting myself a little by saying that literature can be significant. People who don't read are brutes. It is better to write than to make war, isn't it?

INTERVIEWER: So, perhaps writing has been a way of exorcising your basic anxiety about death? Or at least learning to live with it?

IONESCO: Perhaps. But my work has been essentially a dialogue with death, asking him, "Why? Why?" So only death can silence me. Only death can close my lips.

—SHUSHA GUPPY
Fall, 1984

ARTHUR MILLER

© Inge Morath

Arthur Miller was born October 17, 1915, on 112th Street in Harlem to a well-to-do Jewish family that fell out of the middle class during the Great Depression. There was little in his youth to suggest that an accomplished playwright would emerge; an unaccomplished student and late reader, the young Miller had a passion for baseball. His family's economic decline nearly cost him his chance to attend college, but he took a job in a warehouse and talked the University of Michigan into accepting him. It was then that he began writing plays, which won a few awards but did not bring him much fame. A novel, *Focus,* appeared in 1945.

Miller's first professional play was *The Man Who Had All the Luck,* which had four performances in 1944. This was an ignominious beginning, and his next play was not staged until 1947, but when it came it was a triumph. *All My Sons* was a commercial and critical success and won a New York Drama Critics' Circle Award. It was followed in quick succession by what are regarded as his greatest works: *Death of a Salesman* (1949), which won the Pulitzer Prize, *The Crucible* (1953), and *A View from the Bridge* (1955). The latter two plays addressed America's experience with McCarthyism, and a year after *Bridge* closed Miller himself was called before the House Un-American Activities Committee. He refused to name names and was sentenced to prison, although the sentence was overturned by the Supreme Court on appeal. Nine years would pass before Miller could get a new play produced in the United States.

Offstage, Miller continued to take a stand against threats to intellectual freedom and was elected international president of PEN, the writers' group, in 1965. His first marriage ended in 1956 and was followed by his second, to Marilyn Monroe. This ended as well, in 1960, but the actress's struggles formed the foundation of Miller's screenplay, *The Misfits* (which was filmed in 1960), and the breakdown of their marriage was reflected in his next play, *After the Fall* (1964).

Miller has been even more prolific in his later years, producing works such as *The American Clock* (1980), *The Ride Down Mount Morgan* (1991), and *Broken Glass* (1993). He lives in his farmhouse in Connecticut with his third wife, the photographer Inge Morath, whom he married in 1962.

———

Arthur Miller's white farmhouse is set high on the border of the roller-coaster hills of Roxbury and Woodbury, in Connecticut's Litchfield County. It is surrounded by native dogwoods, exotic katsura, Chinese scholar, tulip, and locust trees that he has raised in the years he has lived here with his wife, Inge Morath. Most of them were flowering when we arrived for our interview.

The only sound was a rhythmic hammering that echoed across the hills. Tracking the sound we came to a red barn and there found the playwright, hammer in hand, standing in the dim light amid lumber, tools, and plumbing equipment. He was a tall, rangy, good-looking man with a weathered face and sudden smile, a scholar-farmer in horn-rimmed glasses and high work shoes. Carpentry was his oldest hobby, one he began at age five, and he invited us in to judge his progress in turning the barn into a guesthouse.

We walked back to the main house, which was guarded by a suspicious basset named Hugo. Miller explained the place was unusually silent because his wife

I

> Solomon's Antiques. Solomon, buried in
> his junk, is reading the paper, drinking
> coffee from a container, smoking. Enter
> Martin.

Martin
Excuse me.

Solomon
Yes, sir.

Martin
I'm looking for a Christmas present.

Solomon
Well that depends which Christmas.

Martin
(Smiles) Well, let's say this Christmas.

Solomon (lighting a half-burned cigarette)
For this Christmas is very difficult. What're you got in mind?

Martin
(Looking around)
I don't know. I went to all the department stores, walked down
all the streets. Everything is either junk or unnecessary.

Solomon (He coughs, blows his nose) Excuse me.
My boy, you're not in the swim. Sit down, take it easy. There..
there's a nice Louis ~~the~~ Fourteen chair, sit down.

Martin
I'm exhausted.

Solomon
So is everybody. ~~im~~ The first step to wisdom is to stop. Whatever
it is, stop it. Then maybe you'll find out. For who is the present?

Martin
My wife.

Solomon
For a wife is difficult.
(Looks around points his thumb over his shoulder)
I got here a nice harp.

Martin
What the hell would she do with a harp?

Solomon
She'll have it. What do you mean?--what does she do with anything?

Martin
No, you got me wrong. I love her.

Manuscript page from an unpublished play.

was in Vermont doing a portrait of Bernard Malamud and their three-year-old daughter, Rebecca, was taking a nap. The charming glassed-in living room was eclectically decorated: white walls patterned with a Steinberg sketch, a splashy painting by their neighbor Alexander Calder, posters of early Miller plays, photographs by Ms. Morath. It also held modern furniture and antiques, figurines from a recent trip to Russia, and pottery animals atop a Spanish table, and there were plants everywhere.

Miller's study was a total contrast: a spare single-roomed structure with small louvered windows. There was a plain slab desk that he had fashioned himself, his chair, a rumpled gray daybed, a webbed chair from the thirties, and a bookshelf with half a dozen jacketless books. Tacked to the wall was a snapshot of Ms. Morath and Rebecca. The electric light was on, he confided, because he could not work by sunlight.

After adjusting the microphone, the playwright went to the daybed and, quite casually, picked up a rifle and took a shot through the open louvers at a woodchuck, which fled across the far slope. We were startled, and he smiled at our lack of composure. With that, the interview began. His tone and expression were serious, interested, and often a slight grin surfaced as he reminisced. He is a storyteller, a man with a marvelous memory and a capacity for wonder, concerned with people and ideas. We listened at our ease as he responded to our questions.

INTERVIEWER: Voznesensky, the Russian poet, said when he was here that the landscape in this part of the country reminded him of his Sigulda*—that it was a "good microclimate" for writing. Do you agree?

MILLER: Well, I enjoy it. It's not such a vast landscape that you're lost in it, and it's not so suburban a place that you feel you might as well be in a city. The distances—internal and external—are exactly correct, I think. There's a *foreground* here, no matter which way you look.

INTERVIEWER: After reading your short stories, especially "The Prophecy" and "I Don't Need You Any More," which have not only the dramatic power of your plays but also the description of place, the *foreground,* the intimacy of thought hard to achieve in a play, I wonder: is the stage much more compelling for you?

*A resort in Lithuania.

MILLER: It is only very rarely that I can feel in a short story that I'm right on top of something, as I feel when I write for the stage. I am then in the ultimate place of vision—you can't back me up any further. Everything is inevitable, down to the last comma. In a short story, or any kind of prose, I still can't escape the feeling of a certain arbitrary quality. Mistakes go by—people consent to them more—more than mistakes do on the stage. This may be my illusion. But there's another matter; the whole business of my own role in my own mind. To me the great thing is to write a good play, and when I'm writing a short story it's as though I'm saying to myself, "Well, I'm only doing this because I'm not writing a play at the moment." There's guilt connected with it. Naturally I do enjoy writing a short story, it is a form that has a certain strictness. I think I reserve for plays those things which take a kind of excruciating effort. What comes easier goes into a short story.

INTERVIEWER: Would you tell us a little about the beginning of your writing career?

MILLER: The first play I wrote was in Michigan in 1935. It was written on a spring vacation in six days. I was so young that I dared do such things, begin it and finish it in a week. I'd seen about two plays in my life, so I didn't know how long an act was supposed to be, but across the hall there was a fellow who did the costumes for the university theater and he said, "Well, it's roughly forty minutes." I had written an enormous amount of material and I got an alarm clock. It was all a lark to me, and not to be taken too seriously...that's what I told myself. As it turned out, the acts were longer than that, but the sense of the timing was in me even from the beginning, and the play had a form right from the start.

Being a playwright was always the maximum idea. I'd always felt that the theater was the most exciting and the most demanding form one could try to master. When I began to write, one assumed inevitably that one was in the mainstream that began with Aeschylus, and went through about 2,500 years of playwriting. There are so few masterpieces in the theater, as opposed to the other arts, that one can pretty well encompass all of them by the age of nineteen. Today, I don't think playwrights care about history. I think they feel that it has no relevance.

INTERVIEWER: Is it just the young playwrights who feel this?

MILLER: I think the young playwrights I've had any chance to talk to are either ignorant of the past or they feel the old forms are too square, or too cohesive. I may be wrong, but I don't see that the whole tragic arch of the drama has had any effect on them.

INTERVIEWER: Which playwrights did you most admire when you were young?

MILLER: Well, first the Greeks, for their magnificent form, the symmetry. Half the time I couldn't really repeat the story because the characters in the mythology were completely blank to me. I had no background at that time to know really what was involved in these plays, but the architecture was clear. One looks at some building of the past whose use one is ignorant of, and yet it has a modernity. It had its own specific gravity. That form has never left me; I suppose it just got burned in.

INTERVIEWER: You were particularly drawn to tragedy, then?

MILLER: It seemed to me the only form there was. The rest of it was all either attempts at it, or escapes from it. But tragedy was the basic pillar.

INTERVIEWER: When *Death of a Salesman* opened, you said to *The New York Times* in an interview that the tragic feeling is evoked in us when we're in the presence of a character who is ready to lay down his life, if need be, to secure one thing—his sense of personal dignity. Do you consider your plays modern tragedies?

MILLER: I changed my mind about it several times. I think that to make a direct or arithmetical comparison between any contemporary work and the classic tragedies is impossible because of the question of religion and power, which was taken for granted and is an a priori consideration in any classic tragedy. Like a religious ceremony, where they finally reached the objective by the sacrifice. It has to do with the community sacrificing some man whom they both adore and despise in order to reach its basic and fundamental laws and, therefore, justify its existence and feel safe.

INTERVIEWER: In *After the Fall,* although Maggie was "sacrificed" the central character Quentin survives. Did you see him as tragic or in any degree potentially tragic?

MILLER: I can't answer that, because I can't, quite frankly, separate in my mind tragedy from death. In some people's minds I know there's no reason to put them together. I can't break it—for one reason, and that is, to coin a phrase: there's nothing like death. Dying isn't like it, you know. There's no substitute for the impact on the mind of the spectacle of death. And there is no possibility, it seems to me, of speaking of tragedy without it. Because if the total demise of the person we watch for two or three hours doesn't occur, if he just walks away, no matter how damaged, no matter how much he suffers...

INTERVIEWER: What were those two plays you had seen before you began to write?

MILLER: When I was about twelve, I think it was, my mother took me to a theater one afternoon. We lived in Harlem and in Harlem there were two or three theaters that ran all the time and many women would drop in for all or part of the afternoon performances. All I remember was that there were people in the hold of a ship, the stage was rocking—they actually rocked the stage—and some cannibal on the ship had a time bomb. And they were all looking for the cannibal: it was thrilling. The other one was a morality play about taking dope. Evidently there was much excitement in New York then about the Chinese and dope. The Chinese were kidnapping beautiful, blond, blue-eyed girls who, people thought, had lost their bearings morally; they were flappers who drank gin and ran around with boys. And they inevitably ended up in some basement in Chinatown where they were irretrievably lost by virtue of eating opium or smoking some pot. Those were the two masterpieces I had seen. I'd read some others, of

154 · Playwrights at Work

course, by the time I started writing. I'd read Shakespeare and Ibsen, a little, not much. I never connected playwriting with our theater, even from the beginning.

INTERVIEWER: Did your first play have any bearing on *All My Sons,* or *Death of a Salesman*?

MILLER: It did. It was a play about a father owning a business in 1935, a business that was being struck, and a son being torn between his father's interests and his sense of justice. But it turned into a near comic play. At that stage of my life I was removed somewhat. I was not Clifford Odets: he took it head-on.

INTERVIEWER: Many of your plays have that father-son relationship as the dominant theme. Were you very close to your father?

MILLER: I was. I still am, but I think, actually, that my plays don't reflect directly my relationship to him. It's a very primitive thing in my plays. That is, the father was really a figure who incorporated both power and some kind of a moral law which he had either broken himself or had fallen prey to. He figures as an immense shadow ... I didn't expect that of my own father, literally, but of his position, apparently I did. The reason that I was able to write about the relationship, I think now, was because it had a mythical quality to me. If I had ever thought that I was writing about my father, I suppose I never could have done it. My father is, literally, a much more realistic guy than Willy Loman, and much more successful as a personality. And he'd be the last man in the world to ever commit suicide. Willy is based on an individual whom I knew very little, who was a salesman; it was years later that I realized I had only seen that man about a total of four hours in twenty years. He gave one of those impressions that is basic, evidently. When I thought of him, he would simply be a mute man: he said no more than two hundred words to me. I was a kid. Later on, I had another of that kind of a contact, with a man whose fantasy was always over-reaching his real outline. I've always been aware of that kind of an agony, of someone who has some driving, implacable wish in him which never goes away, which he can never block out. And it broods over him, it makes him happy sometimes or it makes him suicidal, but it never leaves him. Any hero, whom we even begin to think of as tragic, is obsessed, whether it's Lear or Hamlet or the women in the Greek plays.

INTERVIEWER: Do any of the younger playwrights create heroes—in your opinion?

MILLER: I tell you, I may be working on a different wavelength but I don't think they are looking at character anymore, at the documentation of facts about people. All experience is looked at now from a schematic point of view. These playwrights won't let the characters escape for a moment from their preconceived scheme of how dreadful the world is. It is very much like the old strike plays. The scheme then was that someone began a play with a bourgeois ideology and got involved in some area of experience which had a connection to the labor movement—either it was actually a strike or, in a larger sense, it was the collapse of capitalism—and he ended the play with some new positioning vis-à-vis that collapse. He started without an enlightenment and he ended with some kind of enlightenment. And you could predict that in the first five minutes. Very few of those plays could be done anymore, because they're absurd now. I've found over the years that a similar thing has happened with the so-called absurd theater. Predictable.

INTERVIEWER: In other words, the notion of tragedy about which you were talking earlier is absent from this preconceived view of the world.

MILLER: Absolutely. The tragic hero was supposed to join the scheme of things by his sacrifice. It's a religious thing, I've always thought. He threw some sharp light upon the hidden scheme of existence, either by breaking one of its profoundest laws, as Oedipus breaks a taboo, and therefore proves the existence of the taboo, or by proving a moral world at the cost of his own life. And that's the victory. We need him, as the vanguard of the race. We need his crime. That crime is a civilizing crime. Well, *now* the view is that it's an inconsolable universe. Nothing is proved by a crime excepting that some people are freer to produce crime than others, and usually they are more honest than the others. There is no final reassertion of a community at all. There isn't the kind of communication that a child demands. The best you could say is that it is intelligent.

INTERVIEWER: Then it's aware...

MILLER: It's aware, but it will not admit into itself any moral universe at all. Another thing that's missing is the positioning of the author in relation to power. I always assumed that underlying any story is the question of who should wield power. See, in *Death of a Salesman* you have two viewpoints. They show what would happen if we all took Willy's viewpoint toward the world, or if we all took Biff's. And took it seriously, as almost a political fact. I'm debating really which way the world ought to be run; I'm speaking of psychology and the spirit, too. For example, a play that isn't usually linked with this kind of problem is Tennessee Williams's *Cat on a Hot Tin Roof.* It struck me sharply that what is at stake there is the father's great power. He's the owner, literally, of an empire of land and farms. And he wants to immortalize that power, he wants to hand it on, because he's dying. The son has a much finer appreciation of justice and human relations than the father. The father is rougher, more Philistine; he's cruder, and when we speak of the fineness of emotions, we would probably say the son has them and the father lacks them. When I saw the play I thought, this is going to be simply marvelous because the person with the sensitivity will be presented with power and what is he going to do about it? But it never gets to that. It gets deflected onto a question of personal neurosis. It comes to a dead end. If we're talking about tragedy, the Greeks would have done something miraculous with that idea. They would have stuck the son with the power, and faced him with the wracking conflicts of the sensitive man having to rule. And then you would throw light on what the tragedy of power is.

INTERVIEWER: Which is what you were getting at in *Incident at Vichy*...

MILLER: That's exactly what I was after. But I feel today's stage turns away from any consideration of power, which always lies at the heart of tragedy. I use Williams's play as an example because he's that excellent that his problems are symptomatic of the time—*Cat* ultimately came down to the mendacity of human relations. It was a most accurate personalization but it bypasses the issue which the play seems to me to raise, namely the mendacity, in social relations. I still believe that when a play questions, even threatens, our social arrangement, that is when it really shakes us profoundly and dangerously, and that is when you've got to be great; good isn't enough.

INTERVIEWER: Do you think that people in general now rationalize so, and have so many euphemisms for death, that they can't face tragedy?

MILLER: I wonder whether there isn't a certain—I'm speaking now of all classes of people—you could call it a softness, or else a genuine inability to face the tough decisions and the dreadful results of error. I say that only because when *Death of a Salesman* went on again recently, I sensed in some of the reaction that it was simply too threatening. Now there were probably a lot of people in the forties, when it first opened, who felt the same way. Maybe I just didn't hear those people as much as I heard other people—maybe it has to do with my own reaction. You need a certain amount of confidence to watch tragedy. If you yourself are about to die, you're not going to see that play. I've always thought that the Americans had, almost inborn, a primordial fear of falling, being declassed—you get it with your driver's license, if not earlier.

INTERVIEWER: What about Europeans?

MILLER: Well, the play opened in Paris again only last September; it opened in Paris ten years earlier, too, with very little effect. It wasn't a very good production, I understand. But now suddenly they discovered this play. And I sensed that their reaction was quite an American reaction. Maybe it comes with having—having the guilt of wealth; it would be interesting if the Russians ever got to feel that way!

INTERVIEWER: *Death of a Salesman* has been done in Russia, hasn't it?

MILLER: Oh, many times.

INTERVIEWER: When you were in Russia recently did you form any opinion about the Russian theater public?

MILLER: First of all, there's a wonderful naïveté that they have; they're not bored to death. They're not coming in out of the rain, so to speak, with nothing better to do. When they go to the theater, it has great weight with them. They come to see something that'll change their lives. Ninety percent of the time, of course, there's nothing there, but they're open to a grand experience. This is not the way we go to the theater.

INTERVIEWER: What about the plays themselves?

MILLER: I think they do things on the stage which are exciting and deft and they have marvelous actors, but the drama itself is not adventurous. The plays are basically a species of naturalism; it's not even realism. They're violently opposed to the theater of the absurd because they see it as a fragmenting of the community into perverse individuals who will no longer be under any mutual obligation at all, and I can see some point in their fear. Of course, these things should be done if only so one can rebut them. I know that I was very moved in many ways by German expressionism when I was in school: yet there, too, something was perverse in it to me. It was the end of man, there are no people in it anymore; that was especially true of the real German stuff: it's the bitter end of the world where man is a voice of his class function, and that's it. Brecht has a lot of that in him, but he's too much of a poet to be enslaved by it. And yet, at the same time, I learned a great deal from it. I used elements of it that were fused into *Death of a Salesman.* For instance, I purposefully would not give Ben any character, because for Willy he *has* no character—which is, psychologically, expressionist because so many memories come back with a simple tag on them: somebody represents a threat to you, or a promise.

INTERVIEWER: Speaking of different cultures, what is your feeling about the French Théâtre National Populaire?

MILLER: I thought a play I saw by Corneille, *L'Illusion Comique,* one of the most exciting things I've ever seen. We saw something I never thought I could enjoy—my French is not all that good. But I had just gotten over being sick, and we were about to leave France, and I wanted to see what they did with it. It was just superb. It is one of

Corneille's lesser works, about a magician who takes people into the nether regions. What a marvelous mixture of satire, and broad comedy, and characterizations! And the acting was simply out of this world. Of course one of the best parts about the whole thing was the audience. Because they're mostly under thirty, it looked to me; they pay very little to get in; and I would guess there are between 2,500 and 3,000 seats in that place. And the vitality of the audience is breathtaking. Of course the actors' ability to speak that language so beautifully is just in itself a joy. From that vast stage, to talk quietly, and make you *feel* the voice just wafting all over the house...

INTERVIEWER: Why do you think we haven't been able to do such a thing here? Why has Whitehead's Lincoln Center Repertory Theater failed as such?

MILLER: Well, that is a phenomenon worthy of a sociological study. When I got into it, *After the Fall* was about two-thirds written. Whitehead came to me and said, "I hear you're writing a play. Can we use it to start the Lincoln Center Repertory Company?" For one reason or another I said I would do it. I expected to take a financial beating (I could hope to earn maybe 20 percent of what I normally earn with a play, but I assumed that people would say, "Well, it's a stupid but not idiotic action"). What developed, before any play opened at all, was a hostility which completely dumbfounded me. I don't think it was directed against anybody in particular. For actors who want to develop their art, there's no better place to do it than in a permanent repertory company where you play different parts and you have opportunities you've never had in a lifetime on Broadway. But the actors seemed to be affronted by the whole thing. I couldn't dig it! I could understand the enmity of commercial producers who, after all, thought they were threatened by it. But the professional people of every kind greeted it as though it were some kind of an insult. The only conclusion I can come to is that an actor was now threatened with having to put up or shut up. He had always been able to walk around on Broadway where conditions were dreadful and say, "I'm a great actor but I'm unappreciated," but in the back of his mind he could figure, "Well, one of these days I'll get a starring role and I'll go to Hollywood and get rich." This he couldn't do in a repertory theater where he signed up for several years. So the whole idea of that kind of quick success was renounced. He didn't want to face an opportunity which threatened him in this way. It makes me wonder whether there is such a profound alienation among artists that any organized attempt to create something that is not based upon commerce, that has sponsorship, automatically sets people against it. I think that's an interesting facet. I also spoke to a group of young playwrights. Now, if it had been me, I would have been knocking at the door, demanding that they read my play, as I did unsuccessfully when the Group Theatre was around. Then every playwright was banging on the door and furious and wanted the art theater to do what *he* thought they should do. We could do that because it belonged to us all—you know—we thought of the Group Theatre as a public enterprise. Well, that wasn't true at all here. Everyone thought the Lincoln Theater was the property of the directors, of Miller and Whitehead and Kazan and one or two other people. Of course, what also made it fail was, as Laurence Olivier suggested, that it takes years to do anything. But he also made the point that with his English repertory theater he got encouragement from the beginning. There were people who pooh-poohed the whole thing, and said it was ridiculous, but basically the artistic community was in favor of it.

INTERVIEWER: How about the actors themselves? Did Lee Strasberg influence them?

MILLER: I think Strasberg is a symptom, really. He's a great force, and (in my unique opinion, evidently) a force which is not for the good in the theater. He makes actors secret people and he makes acting secret, and it's the most communicative art known to man; I mean, that's what the actor's *supposed* to be doing. But I wouldn't blame the Repertory Theater failures on him, because the people in there were not Actors Studio people at all; so he is not responsible for that. But the Method is in the air: the actor is defending himself from the Philistine, vulgar public. I had a girl in my play I couldn't hear, and the acoustics in that little theater we were using were simply magnificent. I said to her, "I can't hear you," and I kept on saying, "I can't hear you." She finally got furious and said to me, in effect, that she was acting the truth, and that she was not going to prostitute herself to the audience. That was the living end! It reminded me of Walter Hampden's comment—because we had a similar problem in *The Crucible* with some actors—he said they play a cello with the most perfect bowing and the fingering is magnificent but there are no strings on the instrument. The problem is that the actor is now working out his private fate through his role, and the idea of communicating the meaning of the play is the last thing that occurs to him. In the Actors Studio, despite denials, the actor is told that the text is really the framework for his emotions; I've heard actors change the order of lines in my work and tell me that the lines are only, so to speak, the libretto for the music—that the actor is the main force that the audience is watching and that the playwright is his servant. They are told that the analysis of the text, and the rhythm of the text, the verbal texture, is of no importance whatever. This is Method, as they are teaching it, which is, of course, a perversion of it, if you go back to the beginning. But there was always a tendency in that direction. Chekhov, himself, said that Stanislavsky had perverted *The Seagull*.

INTERVIEWER: What about Method acting in the movies?

MILLER: Well, in the movies, curiously enough, the Method works better. Because the camera can come right up to an actor's nostrils and suck out of him a communicative gesture; a look in the eye, a wrinkle of his grin, and so on, which registers nothing on the stage. The stage is, after all, a verbal medium. You've got to make large gestures if they're going to be seen at all. In other words, you've got to be unnatural. You've got to say, "I am out to move into that audience; that's my job." In a movie you don't do that; as a matter of fact, that's bad movie acting, it's overacting. Movies are wonderful for private acting.

INTERVIEWER: Do you think the movies helped bring about this private acting in the theater?

MILLER: Well, it's a perversion of the Chekhovian play and of the Stanislavsky technique. What Chekhov was doing was eliminating the histrionics of his actors by incorporating them in the writing: the internal life was what he was writing about. And Stanislavsky's direction was also internal: for the first time he was trying to motivate every

Arthur Miller building a platform under his desk, 1961. © Inge Morath

move from within instead of imitating an action; which is what acting should be. When you eliminate the vital element of the actor in the community and simply make a psychiatric figure on the stage who is thinking profound thoughts which he doesn't let anyone know about, then it's a perversion.

INTERVIEWER: How does the success of Peter Weiss's *Marat/Sade* play fit into this?

MILLER: Well, I would emphasize its production and direction. Peter Brook has been trying for years, especially through productions of Shakespeare, to make the bridge between psychological acting and theater, between the private personality, perhaps, and its public demonstration. *Marat/Sade* is more an oratorio than a play; the characters are basically thematic relationships rather than human entities, so the action exemplified rather than characterized.

INTERVIEWER: Do you think the popularity of the movies has had any influence on playwriting itself?

MILLER: Yes. Its form has been changed by the movies. I think certain techniques, such as the jumping from place to place, although it's as old as Shakespeare, came to us not through Shakespeare, but through the movies, a telegraphic, dream-constructed way of seeing life.

INTERVIEWER: How important is the screenwriter in motion pictures?

MILLER: Well, you'd be hard put to remember the dialogue in some of the great pictures that you've seen. That's why pictures are so international. You don't have to hear the style of the dialogue in an Italian movie or a French movie. We're watching the film so that the vehicle is not the ear or the word, it's the eye. The director of a play is nailed to words. He can interpret them a little differently, but he has limits: you can only inflect a sentence in two or three different ways, but you can inflect an image on the screen in an infinite number of ways. You can make one character practically fall out of the frame; you can shoot it where you don't even see his face. Two people can be talking, and the man talking cannot be seen, so the emphasis is on the reaction to the speech rather than on the speech itself.

INTERVIEWER: What about television as a medium for drama?

MILLER: I don't think there is anything that approaches the theater. The sheer presence of a living person is always stronger than his image. But there's no reason why TV shouldn't be a terrific medium. The problem is that the audience watching TV shows is always separated. My feeling is that people in a group, en masse, watching something, react differently, and perhaps more profoundly, than they do when they're alone in their living rooms. Yet it's not a hurdle that couldn't be jumped by the right kind of material. Simply, it's hard to get good movies, it's hard to get good novels, it's hard to get good poetry—it's *impossible* to get good television because in addition to the indigenous difficulties there's the whole question of its being a medium that's controlled by big business. It took TV seventeen years to do *Death of a Salesman* here. It's been done on TV in every country in the world at least once, but it's critical of the business world and the content is downbeat.

INTERVIEWER: A long time ago, you used to write radio scripts. Did you learn much about technique from that experience?

MILLER: I did. We had twenty-eight and a half minutes to tell a whole story in a radio play and you had to concentrate on the words because you couldn't see anything. You were playing in a dark closet, in fact. So the economy of words in a good radio play was everything. It drove you more and more to realize what the power of a good sentence was, and the right phrase could save you a page you would otherwise be wasting. I was always sorry radio didn't last long enough for contemporary poetic movements to take advantage of it, because it's a natural medium for poets. It's pure voice, pure words. Words and silence; a marvelous medium. I've often thought, even recently, that I would like to write another radio play, and just give it to someone and let them do it on WBAI. The English do radio plays still, very good ones.

INTERVIEWER: You used to write verse drama too, didn't you?

MILLER: Oh yes, I was up to my neck in it.

INTERVIEWER: Would you ever do it again?

MILLER: I might. I often write speeches in verse, and then break them down. Much of *Death of a Salesman* was originally written in verse, and *The Crucible* was all written in verse, but I broke it up. I was frightened that the actors would take an attitude toward the material that would destroy its vitality. I didn't want anyone standing up there making speeches. You see, we have no tradition of verse, and as soon as an American actor sees something printed like verse, he immediately puts one foot in front of the other—or else he mutters. Then you can't hear it at all.

INTERVIEWER: Which of your own plays do you feel closest to now?

MILLER: I don't know if I feel closer to one than another. I suppose *The Crucible* in some ways. I think there's a lot of myself in it. There are a lot of layers in there that I know about that nobody else does...

INTERVIEWER: More so than in *After the Fall*...?

MILLER: Yes, because although *After the Fall* is more psychological it's less developed as an artifice. You see, in *The Crucible* I was completely freed by the period I was writing about—over three centuries ago. It was a different diction, a different age. I had great joy writing that, more than with almost any other play I've written. I learned about how writers felt in the past when they were dealing almost constantly with historical material. A dramatist writing history could finish a play Monday and start another Wednesday, and go right on. Because the *stories* are all prepared for him. Inventing the story is what takes all the time. It takes a year to invent the story. The historical dramatist doesn't have to invent anything, except his language, and his characterizations. Oh, of course, there's the terrific problem of condensing history, a lot of reshuffling and bringing in characters who never lived, or who died a hundred years apart—but basically if you've got the story, you're a year ahead.

INTERVIEWER: It must also be tempting to use a historical figure whose epoch was one of faith.

MILLER: It is. With all the modern psychology and psychiatry and the level of literacy higher than it ever was, we get less perspective on ourselves than at almost any time I know about. I have never been so aware of clique ideas overtaking people—fashions, for example—and sweeping them away, as though the last day of the world had come. One can sometimes point to a week or month in which things changed abruptly. It's like women's clothing in a certain issue of *Vogue* magazine. There is such a wish to be part of that enormous minority that likes to create new minorities. Yet people are desperately afraid of being alone.

INTERVIEWER: Has our insight into psychology affected this?

MILLER: It has simply helped people rationalize their situation, rather than get out of it, or break through it. In other words—you've heard it a hundred times— "Well, I am this type of person, and this type doesn't do anything but what I'm doing..."

INTERVIEWER: Do you think the push toward personal success dominates American life now more than it used to?

MILLER: I think it's far more powerful today than when I wrote *Death of a Salesman*. I think it's closer to a madness today than it was then. Now there's no perspective on it at all.

INTERVIEWER: Would you say that the girl in *After the Fall* is a symbol of that obsession?

MILLER: Yes, she is consumed by what she does, and instead of it being a means of release, it's a jail. A prison which defines her, finally. She can't break through. In other words, success, instead of giving freedom of choice, becomes a way of life. There's no country I've been to where people, when you come into a room and sit down with them, so often ask you, "What do you do?" And, being American, many's the time I've almost asked that question, then realized it's good for my soul not to know. For a while! Just to let the evening wear on and see what I think of this person without knowing what he does and how successful he is, or what a failure. We're *ranking* everybody every minute of the day.

INTERVIEWER: Will you write about American success again?

MILLER: I might, but you see, as a thing in itself success is self-satirizing; it's self-elucidating, in a way. That's why it's so difficult to write about. Because the very people who are being swallowed up by this ethos nod in agreement when you tell them, "You are being swallowed up by this thing." To really wrench them and find them another feasible perspective is therefore extremely difficult.

INTERVIEWER: In your story "The Prophecy," the protagonist says this is a time of the supremacy of personal relations, that there are no larger aims in our lives. Is this your view too?

MILLER: Well, that story was written under the pall of the fifties, but I think there's been a terrific politicalization of the people these past four or five years. Not in the old sense, but in the sense that it is no longer *gauche* or stupid to be interested in the fate of society and in injustice and in race problems and the rest of it. It now becomes aesthetic material once again. In the fifties it was *out* to mention this. It meant you were really not an artist. That prejudice seems to have gone. The Negroes broke it up, thank God! But it has been an era of personal relations—and now it's being synthesized in a good way. That is, the closer you get to any kind of political action among young people, the more they demand that the action have a certain fidelity to human nature, and that pomposity, and posing, and role taking not be allowed to strip the movement of its veracity. What they suspect most is gesturing, you know, just making gestures, which are either futile, or self-serving, or merely conscientious. The intense personal-relations concentration of the fifties seems now to have been joined to a political consciousness, which is terrific.

INTERVIEWER: Do you feel politics in any way to be an invasion of your privacy?

MILLER: No, I always drew a lot of inspiration from politics, from one or another kind of national struggle. You live in the world even though you only vote once in a while. It determines the extensions of your personality. I lived through the McCarthy time, when one saw personalities shifting and changing before one's eyes, as a direct, obvious result of a political situation. And had it gone on, we would have gotten a whole new American personality—which in part we have. It's ten years since McCarthy died, and it's only now that powerful senators dare to suggest that it might be wise to learn a little Chinese, to talk to some Chinese. I mean it took ten years, and even those guys who are thought to be quite brave and courageous just now dare to make these suggestions. Such a pall of fright was laid upon us that it truly deflected the American mind. It's part of a paranoia which we haven't escaped yet. Good God, people still give their lives for it; look what we're doing in the Pacific.

INTERVIEWER: Yet so much of the theater these last few years has had nothing to do with public life.

MILLER: Yes, it's got so we've lost the technique of grappling with the world that Homer had, that Aeschylus had, that Euripides had. And

Shakespeare. How amazing it is that people who adore the Greek drama fail to see that these great works are works of a man confronting his society, the illusions of the society, the faiths of the society. They're social documents, not little piddling private conversations. We just got educated into thinking this is all "a story," a myth for its own sake.

INTERVIEWER: Do you think there'll be a return to social drama now?

MILLER: I think there will be, if theater is to survive. Look at Molière. You can't conceive of him except as a social playwright. He's a social critic. Bathes up to his neck in what's going on around him.

INTERVIEWER: Could the strict forms utilized by Molière appear again?

MILLER: I don't think one can repeat old forms as such, because they express most densely a moment of time. For example I couldn't write a play like *Death of a Salesman* anymore. I couldn't really write any of my plays now. Each is different, spaced sometimes two years apart, because each moment called for a different vocabulary and a different organization of the material. However, when you speak of a strict form, I believe in it for the theater. Otherwise you end up with anecdotes, not with plays. We're in an era of anecdotes, in my opinion, which is going to pass any minute. The audience has been trained to eschew the organized climax because it's corny, or because it violates the chaos which we all revere. But I think that's going to disappear with the first play of a new kind which will once again pound the boards and shake people out of their seats with a deeply, intensely, organized climax. It can only come from a strict form: you can't get it except as the culmination of two hours of development. You can't get it by raising your voice and yelling, suddenly—because it's getting time to get on the train for Yonkers.

INTERVIEWER: Have you any conception of what your own evolution has been? In terms of form and themes?

MILLER: I keep going. Both forwards and backwards. Hopefully more forwards than backwards. That is to say, before I wrote my first *successful* play, I wrote, oh I don't know, maybe fourteen or fifteen other full-length plays and maybe thirty radio plays. The majority of them were nonrealistic plays. They were metaphorical plays, or symbolistic plays; some of them were in verse, or in one case—writing about Montezuma—I turned out a grand historical tragedy, partly in verse, rather Elizabethan in form. Then I began to be known really by virtue of the single play I had ever tried to do in completely realistic Ibsen-like form, which was *All My Sons.* The fortunes of a writer! The others, like *Salesman,* which are a compound of expressionism and realism, or even *A View from the Bridge,* which is realism of a sort (though it's broken up severely), are more typical of the bulk of the work I've done. *After the Fall* is really down the middle, it's more like most of the work I've done than any other play...excepting that what has *surfaced* has been more realistic than in the others. It's really an impressionistic kind of a work. I was trying to create a total by throwing many small pieces at the spectator.

INTERVIEWER: What production of *After the Fall* do you think did it the most justice?

MILLER: I saw one production which I thought was quite marvelous. That was the one Zeffirelli did in Italy. He understood that this was a play which reflected the world as one man saw it. Through the play the mounting awareness of this man was the issue, and as it approached agony the audience was to be enlarged in its consciousness of what was happening. The other productions that I've seen have all been really *realistic* in the worst sense. That is to say, they simply played the scenes without any attempt to allow the main character to develop this widened awareness. He has different reactions on page ten than he does on page one, but it takes an actor with a certain amount of brains to see that evolution. It isn't enough to feel them. And as a director Zeffirelli had an absolutely organic viewpoint toward it. The play is about someone desperately striving to obtain a viewpoint.

INTERVIEWER: Do you feel in the New York production that the girl allegedly based on Marilyn Monroe was out of proportion, entirely separate from Quentin?

MILLER: Yes, although I failed to foresee it myself. In the Italian production this never happened; it was always in proportion. I suppose, too, that by the time Zeffirelli did the play the publicity shock had been absorbed, so that one could watch Quentin's evolution without being distracted.

INTERVIEWER: What do you think happened in New York?

MILLER: Something I never thought could happen. The play was never judged as a play at all. Good or bad, I would never know what it was from what I read about it, only what it was supposed to have been.

INTERVIEWER: Because they all reacted as if it were simply a segment of your personal life?

MILLER: Yes.

INTERVIEWER: Do you think contemporary American critics tend to regard the theater in terms of literature rather than theater?

MILLER: Yes, for years theatrical criticism was carried on mainly by reporters. Reporters who by and large had no references in the aesthetic theories of the drama, except in the most rudimentary way. And off in a corner, somewhere, the professors, with no relation whatsoever to the newspaper critics, were regarding the drama from a so-called academic viewpoint. With its relentless standards of tragedy, and so forth. What the reporters had very often was a simple, primitive love of a good show. And if nothing else, you could tell whether that level of mind was genuinely interested, or not. There was a certain naïveté in the reportage. They could destroy plays which dealt on a level of sensibility that was beyond them. But by and large you got a playback on what you put in. They knew how to laugh, cry, at least a native kind of reaction, stamp their feet—they loved the theater. Since then, the reporter-critics have been largely displaced by academic critics or graduates of that school. Quite frankly, two-thirds of the time I don't know what they really feel about the play. They seem to feel that the theater is an intrusion on literature. The theater as theater—as a place where people go to be swept up in some new experience—seems to antagonize them. I don't think we can really do away with *joy:* the joy of being distracted altogether in the service of some aesthetic. That seems to be the general drift, but it won't work: sooner or later the theater outwits everybody. Someone comes in who just loves to write, or to act, and who'll sweep the audience, and the critics, with him.

INTERVIEWER: Do you think these critics influence playwrights?

MILLER: Everything influences playwrights. A playwright who isn't influenced is never of any use. He's the litmus paper of the arts. He's got to be, because if he isn't working on the same wavelength as the audience, no one would know what in hell he was talking about. He is a kind of psychic journalist, even when he's great; consequently, for him the total atmosphere is more important in this art than it is probably in any other.

INTERVIEWER: What do you think of a certain critic's statement that the success of a really contemporary play, like *Marat/Sade*, makes Tennessee Williams and his genre obsolete?

MILLER: Ridiculous. No more than that Tennessee's remarkable success made obsolete the past before him. There are some biological laws in the theater which can't be violated. It should not be made into an activated chess game. You can't have a theater based upon anything other than a mass audience if it's going to succeed. The larger the better. It's the law of the theater. In the Greek audience fourteen thousand people sat down at the same time, to see a play. Fourteen thousand people! And nobody can tell me that those people were all readers of *The New York Review of Books*! Even Shakespeare was smashed around in his time by university people. I think for much the same reasons—because he was reaching for those parts of man's makeup which respond to melodrama, broad comedy, violence, dirty words, and blood. Plenty of blood, murder, and not very well motivated at that.

INTERVIEWER: What is your feeling about Eugene O'Neill as a playwright?

MILLER: O'Neill never meant much to me when I was starting. In the thirties, and for the most part in the forties, you would have said that he was a finished figure. He was not a force anymore. *The Iceman Cometh* and *Long Day's Journey into Night*, so popular a few years ago, would not have been successful when they were written. Which is another example of the psychic journalism of the stage. A great deal depends upon when a play is produced. That's why playwriting is such a fatal profession to take up. You can have everything, but if you don't have that sense of timing, nothing happens. One thing I always respected about O'Neill was his insistence on his vision. That is, even when he was twisting materials to distortion and really ruining his work, there was an image behind it of a possessed individual, who, for good or ill, was himself. I don't think there is anything in it for a young man to learn technically; that was probably why I wasn't interested in it. He had one virtue which is not technical, it's what I call "drumming"; he repeats something up to and past the point where you say, "I know this, I've heard this ninety-three different ways," and suddenly you realize you are being swept up in something that you thought you understood and he has drummed you over the horizon into a new perception. He doesn't care if he's repeating. It's part of his insensitivity. He's a very insensitive writer. There's no finesse at all: he's the Dreiser of the stage. He writes with heavy pencils. His virtue is that he insists on his climax, and not the one you would want to put there. His failing is that so many of his plays are so distorted that one no longer knows on what level to receive them. His people are not symbolic; his lines are certainly not verse; the prose is not realistic—his is the never-never land of a quasi-Strindberg writer. But where he's wonderful, it's superb. The last play is really a masterpiece. But, to give you an example of timing: *The Iceman Cometh* opened, it happened, the same year that *All My Sons* opened. It's an interesting sociological phenomenon. That was in 'forty-seven, soon after the war. There was still in the air a certain hopefulness about the organization of the world. There was no depression in the United States. McCarthyism had not yet started. There was a kind of...one could almost speak of it as an atmosphere of goodwill, if such a term can be used in the twentieth century. Then a play comes along which posits a world *really* filled with disasters of one kind or another. A cul-de-sac is described, a bag with no way out. At that time it didn't corroborate what people had experienced. It corroborated what they were *going* to experience, and pretty soon after, it became very timely. We moved into the bag that he had gotten into first! But at the time it opened, nobody went to see *Iceman*. In a big way, nobody went. Even after it was cut, the thing took four or five hours to play. The production was simply dreadful. But nobody made any note that it was dreadful. Nobody perceived what this play was. It was described simply as the work of a sick old man of whom everybody said, "Isn't it wonderful that he can still spell?" When I went to see that play not long after it opened, there must have been thirty people in the audience. I think there were a dozen people left by the end of the play. It was quite obviously a great piece of work which was being mangled on the stage. It was obvious to me. And to a certain number of directors who saw it. Not all of them. Not all directors can tell the difference between the production and the play. I can't do it all the time, either, though *Iceman* was one where I could. But as for the critics I don't think there is anybody alive today, with the possible exception of Harold Clurman, who I would trust to know the difference between production and play. Harold can do it—not always, but a lot of the time—because he has directed a good deal.

INTERVIEWER: Could this question of timing have affected the reaction here to *After the Fall*?

MILLER: Look, *After the Fall* would have been altogether different if by some means the hero was killed, or shot himself. Then we would have been in business. I knew it at the time. As I was saying before ... there's nothing like death. Still, I just wasn't going to do it. The ironical thing to me was that I heard cries of indignation from various people, who had in the lifetime of Marilyn Monroe either exploited her unmercifully, in a way that would have subjected them to peonage laws, or mocked her viciously, or refused to take any of her pretensions seriously. So consequently, it was impossible to credit their sincerity.

INTERVIEWER: They were letting you get them off the hook.

MILLER: That's right. That's exactly right.

INTERVIEWER: And they didn't want Quentin to compromise ...

MILLER: I think Günter Grass recently has said that art is uncompromising and life is full of compromises. To bring them together is a near-impossibility, and that is what I was trying to do. I was trying to make it as much like life as it could possibly be and as excruciating—so the relief that we want would not be there: I denied the audience the relief. And of course all these hard realists betrayed their basic romanticism by their reaction.

INTERVIEWER: Do you think if you had done it in poetry that would have removed the threat more?

MILLER: Yes, I suppose so. But I didn't want to remove it. It would have seduced people in a way I didn't want to. Look, I know how to make 'em go with me . . . it's the first instinct of a writer who succeeds in the theater at all. I mean by the time you've written your third play or so you know which buttons to push; if you want an easy success there's no problem that way once you've gotten a story. People are pretty primitive—they really want the thing to turn out all right. After all, for a century and a half *King Lear* was played in England with a happy ending. I wrote a radio play about the boy who wrote that version—William Ireland—who forged Shakespeare's plays, and edited *King Lear* so that it conformed to a middle-class view of life. They thought, including all but Malone, who was the first good critic, that this was the real Shakespeare. He was an expert forger. He fixed up several of the other plays, but this one he really rewrote. He was seventeen years old. And they produced it—it was a big success—and Boswell thought it was the greatest thing he'd ever seen, and so did all the others. The only one was Malone, who on the basis of textual impossibilities—aside from the fact that he sensed it was a bowdlerization—proved that it couldn't have been Shakespeare. It's what I was talking about before: the litmus paper of the playwright: you see, Ireland sensed quite correctly what these people really wanted from *King Lear*, and he gave it to them. He sentimentalized it; took out any noxious references.

INTERVIEWER: And did it end with a happy family reunion?

MILLER: Yes, kind of like a Jewish melodrama. A family play.

INTERVIEWER: To go back to *After the Fall*. Did the style in which this play was presented in New York affect its reception?

MILLER: Well, you've hit it right on the head. You see, what happened in Italy with Zeffirelli was—I can describe it very simply: there was a stage made up of steel frames; it is as though one were looking into the back of a bellows camera—you know, concentric oblong steel frames receding toward a center. The sides of these steel frames were covered, just like a camera is, but the actors could enter through openings in these covers. They could appear or disappear on the stage at any depth. Furthermore, pneumatic lifts silently and invisibly raised the actors up, so that they could appear for ten seconds—then disappear. Or a table would be raised or a whole group of furniture, which the actors would then use. So that the whole image of all this happening inside a man's head was there from the first second, and remained right through the play. In New York the difficulty was partly due to the stage, which was open, rounded. Such a stage has virtues for certain kinds of plays, but it is stiff—there is no place to hide at all. If an actor has to *appear* stage center, he makes his appearance twenty feet off the left or right. The laborious nature of these entrances and exits is insuperable. What is supposed to "appear" doesn't appear, but lumbers onstage toward you.

INTERVIEWER: Did that Italian production have a concentration camp in the background? I remember a piece by Jonathan Miller complaining of your use of the concentration camp in New York.

MILLER: Oh yes. You see in Italy the steel frame itself *became* the concentration camp, so that the whole play in effect was taking place in the ambience of that enclosure. This steel turned into a jail, into a prison, into a camp, into a constricted mechanical environment. You could light those girders in such a way that they were forbidding—it was a great scenic idea.

INTERVIEWER: Why did you choose to use a concentration camp in the first place?

MILLER: Well, I have always felt that concentration camps, though they're a phenomenon of totalitarian states, are also the logical conclusion of contemporary life. If you complain of people being shot down in the streets, of the absence of communication or social responsibility, of the rise of everyday violence which people have become accustomed to, and the dehumanization of feelings, then the ultimate development on an organized social level is the concentration camp. Camps didn't happen in Africa, where people had no connection with the basic development of Western civilization. They happened in the heart of Europe, in a country, for example, which was probably less anti-Semitic than other countries, like France. The Dreyfus case did not happen in Germany. In this play the question is, what is there between people that is indestructible? The concentration camp is the final expression of human separateness and its ultimate consequence. It is organized abandonment... one of the prime themes of *After the Fall*.

Even in *Salesman* what's driving Willy nuts is that he's trying to establish a connection, in his case, with the world of power; he is trying to say that if you behave in a certain way, you'll end up in the catbird seat. That's your connection; then life is no longer dangerous, you see. You are safe from abandonment.

INTERVIEWER: What is the genesis of *The Crucible?*

MILLER: I thought of it first when I was at Michigan. I read a lot about the Salem witch trials at that time. Then when the McCarthy era came along, I remembered these stories and I used to tell them to people when it started. I had no idea that it was going to go as far as it went. I used to say, you know, McCarthy is actually saying certain lines that I recall the witch-hunters saying in Salem. So I started to go back, not with the idea of writing a play, but to refresh my own mind because it was getting eerie. For example, his holding up his hand with cards in it, saying, "I have in my hand the names of so-and-so." Well, this was a standard tactic of seventeenth-century prosecutors confronting a witness who was reluctant or confused, or an audience in a church which was not quite convinced that this particular individual might be guilty. He wouldn't say, "I have in my hand a list...," he'd say, "We possess the names of all these people who are guilty. But the time has not come yet to release them." He had nothing at all—he simply wanted to secure in the town's mind the idea that he saw everything, that everyone was transparent to him. It was a way of inflicting guilt on everybody, and many people responded genuinely out of guilt; some would come and tell him some fantasy, or something that they had done or thought that was evil in their minds. I had in my play, for example, the old man who comes and reports that when his wife reads certain books, *he* can't pray. He figures that the prosecutors would know the reason, that they can see through what to him was an opaque glass. Of course, he ends up in a disaster because they prosecuted his wife. Many times completely naive testimony resulted in somebody's being hanged. And it was because they originally said, "We really know what's going on."

INTERVIEWER: Was it the play, *The Crucible* itself, do you think, or was it perhaps that piece you did in *The Nation*—"A Modest Proposal"—that focused the House Un-American Activities Committee on you?

MILLER: Well, I had made a lot of statements and I had signed a great many petitions. I'd been involved in organizations, you know, putting my name down for fifteen years before that. But I don't think they ever would have bothered me if I hadn't married Marilyn. Had they been interested they would have called me earlier. And in fact I was told on good authority that the then chairman, Francis Walter, said that if Marilyn would take a photograph with him, shaking his hand, he would call off the whole thing. It's as simple as that. Marilyn would get them on the front pages right away. They had been on the front page for years, but the issue was starting to lose its punch. They ended up in the back of the paper or on the inside pages, and here they would get right up front again. These men would time hearings to meet a certain day's newspaper. In other words, if they figured the astronauts were going up, let's say, they wouldn't have a hearing that week; they'd wait until they'd returned and things had quieted down.

INTERVIEWER: What happened at the committee hearing?

MILLER: Well, I was indicted for contempt for having refused to give or confirm the name of a writer, whether I had seen him in a meeting of Communist writers I had attended some eight or ten years earlier. My legal defense was not on any of the Constitutional Amendments but on the contention that Congress couldn't drag people in and question them about anything on the congressman's mind; they had to show that the witness was likely to have information relevant to some legislation then at issue. The committee had put on a show of interest in passport legislation. I had been denied a passport a couple of years earlier. Ergo, I fitted into their vise. A year later I was convicted after a week's trial. Then about a year after that the court of appeals threw out the whole thing. A short while later the committee's chief counsel, who had been my interrogator, was shown to be on the payroll of a racist foundation and was retired to private life. It was all a dreadful waste of time and money and anger, but I suffered very little, really, compared to others who were driven out of their professions and never got back, or who did get back after eight and ten years of blacklisting. I wasn't in TV or movies so I could still function.

INTERVIEWER: Have your political views changed much since then?

MILLER: Nowadays I'm certainly not ready to advocate a tightly organized planned economy. I think it has its virtues, but I'm in deadly fear of people with too much power. I don't trust people that much anymore. I used to think that if people had the right idea they could make things move accordingly. Now it's a day-to-day fight to stop dreadful things from happening. In the thirties it was, for me, inconceivable that a socialist government could be really anti-Semitic. It just could not happen because their whole protest in the beginning was against anti-Semitism, against racism, against this kind of inhumanity; that's why I was drawn to it. It was accounted to Hitler; it was accounted to blind capitalism. I'm much more pragmatic about such things now, and I want to know those I'm against and who it is that I'm backing and what he is like.

INTERVIEWER: Do you feel whatever Jewish tradition you were brought up in has influenced you at all?

MILLER: I never used to, but I think now that while I hadn't taken over an ideology I did absorb a certain viewpoint. That there is tragedy in the world but that the world must continue: one is a condition for the other. Jews can't afford to revel too much in the tragic because it might overwhelm them. Consequently, in most Jewish writing there's always the caution, "Don't push it too far toward the abyss, because you're liable to fall in." I think it's part of that psychology and it's part of me, too. I have, so to speak, a psychic investment in the continuity of life. I couldn't ever write a totally nihilistic work.

INTERVIEWER: Would you care to say anything about what you're working on now?

MILLER: I'd better not. I do have about five things started—short stories, a screenplay, et cetera. I'm in the process of collecting my short stories. But I tell myself, "What am I doing." I should be doing a play. I have a calendar in my head. You see, the theater season starts in September, and I have always written plays in the summertime. Almost always—I did write *A View from the Bridge* in the winter. So, quite frankly, I can't say. I have some interesting beginnings but I can't see the end of any of them. It's usually that way, I plan something for weeks or months and suddenly begin writing dialogue which begins in relation to what I had planned and veers off into something I hadn't even thought about. I'm drawing down the lightning, I suppose. Somewhere in the blood you have a play, and you wait until it passes behind the eyes. I'm further along than that, but I'd rather leave it at that for now.

—OLGA CARLISLE
—ROSE STYRON
Summer, 1966

© Inge Morath

The following interview with Arthur Miller was conducted in spring 1999 at the Ninety-second Street branch of the YMHA before a packed house.

INTERVIEWER: The 1960s saw a certain radicalization aesthetically. That was the period of the Living Theater, the Open Theater, the Performance Group, and Wooster Group. I have the feeling that you never found that particularly compelling as a version of theater.

MILLER: I found myself a lot of the time being reminded of a similar outbreak of that kind of theater in the thirties when Clifford Odets and Bertolt Brecht were starting. I just felt that this was going to pass away, the way the other one did, because its emphasis was so heavily on the side of the issues rather than on the side of the characterization of people or of the human conflicts involved. They were political conflicts basically, and I felt that this was very temporary, and it was not going to endure.

INTERVIEWER: The Wooster Group tried to incorporate *The Crucible* in one of their own plays?

MILLER: The Wooster Group is a highly experimental group of actors downtown in SoHo. For *The Crucible* they were dressed like children in a nursery. I'm not quite sure what that meant! They were swinging on swings and speaking at a rate of speed that I could not follow! But I have to say, and this shows how far out I am, that I talked to young people who had seen it and were tremendously moved by this, so I decided simply to resign my job as critic because I couldn't dig it. It seemed to me absolutely *voulu*, French for "willed." They were just trying to do something different even though it was absolutely meaningless.

INTERVIEWER: *The Price*, which was the most successful play since *Death of a Salesman*, premiered in 1968. It doesn't feel like a 1968 play. It's about two brothers who come together to dispose of their father's estate, symbolized by a room full of furniture, so they spend a lot of their time looking back to the past, and this in a decade, the sixties, where the past tended to be dismissed as an irrelevance. Did you feel that that...

MILLER: That's why I wrote about it. I wanted to tell them that the past counted, that they were creatures of the past just as we all were. They had affected to negate the past, cut themselves off from it, and throw it in a wastebasket. As it turned out they were as much affected by their fathers and grandfathers. There was no way to escape it, any more than you could escape the beat of your own heart. I was on vacation in the Caribbean just before we produced *The Price,* and ran into Mel Brooks. I'd never known him before. He said, "Well, what are you doing now?" I said, "Well, I just wrote this play which we're about to put on. It's called *The Price.*" He said, "What's it about?" I said, "Well, there are these two brothers..." He said, "Stop, I'm crying!"

INTERVIEWER: Very good assessment. You began the seventies with a play which is disposed as a straight play and as a musical: *Creation of the World and Other Business,* and the musical is *Up from Paradise,* about Adam and Eve. Why? What led you to that?

MILLER: To show how man invented God. He invented God because there had to be something to stop a guy from killing his brother, and there was nothing visible in the Garden that could stop that. They needed a higher authority. Even though they invented him, pretty soon they began believing in him as a being totally independent of themselves, hoping some kind of justice would descend from Him. So it's the invention of the idea of justice, because if a brother could kill a brother then who was safe? There had to be some moral, superhuman law that would at least scare people into stopping themselves from murdering, and that's what put God in business.

INTERVIEWER: That reminds me of an earlier sixties play, *After the Fall,* which is almost about the necessity, after the Holocaust and the concentration camps, of reinventing God.

MILLER: I'm glad you mentioned that because no critic ever did! Yes, that's what it was about. There are two of my plays at least in which the play is looking into a void where there is nothing and trying to invent something to stop the world from killing itself.

INTERVIEWER: Is that also a reason why you have resisted the theater of the absurd?

MILLER: Well, I enjoyed Zero Mostel playing in Ionesco's *Rhinoceros.* One of the greatest things I ever saw in my life. He really turned himself into a rhinoceros. However, at the back of my mind always was, okay, but you've got to be very safe and very rich to really enjoy this form. You have to have grown out of the need for public order. You have to be living in a society where nobody's killing anybody. And that nagged at me, I must say. It's a spoilsport attitude because everybody was having a lot of fun being absurd. I enjoy it as much as anybody, but I'm slightly off to one side of it, saluting as it goes by.

INTERVIEWER: As the seventies went on you wrote what seems to me a very European play, European in its setting, *The Archbishop's Ceiling.*

MILLER: Maybe I'd better take a moment to describe that play. These people are in the living room of a writer in Prague in the old regime. Unlike a lot of people, he does very well under the system. He's full of contradictions because he has helped people who have gotten in trouble with the regime, and, therefore, seems to be aligned with the dissidents. On the other hand, no dissident except him seems to have this much money and the freedom to leave the country occasionally for a lecture in France or England. How does that happen, since the rest of them have no passports? So he's under suspicion in a way, but at the same time they love him because he has helped them. And meantime they think that maybe in the ceiling of his room there are microphones. He keeps having large parties in his house, and maybe he's doing this so that people will reveal themselves to the microphones in the ceiling connected to the secret police. Something like this happened in the United States in the fifties when people would talk to one another, but they weren't quite sure whether that was as far as that speech was going to go.

INTERVIEWER: This was only a few years after Watergate and the bugging of the White House by the President of the United States.

MILLER: That's a very good example: imagine Nixon getting people to talk to him about what they really felt about life and issues, knowing that at all times he was betraying them!

INTERVIEWER: Betrayal is a theme in many of your plays, isn't it? Willy Loman betrays his wife, John Proctor does likewise in *The Crucible*, a rather major betrayal of faith and trust.

MILLER: The guy in *After the Fall* says, "Why is betrayal the only truth that sticks?" I can't answer that altogether, but after all, the Bible begins with a betrayal, doesn't it? Cain has betrayed his brother by killing him. I think the old rabbis who put that Bible together understood this, that betrayal hangs over so much that men do, and from its threat comes the need for justice. It's the challenge to us all, to humanity, to keep faith, and I think it goes right down through our literature and certainly the religious ideas of the world. It's involved in a lot of my work.

INTERVIEWER: People come out of *Death of a Salesman* often crying. If you said to them that you'd watched them laughing while in their seats, they would deny it. And yet humor is part of it, isn't it?

MILLER: The whole thing is very sad, but the fact is I did a lot of laughing when I was writing the play because some of Willy Loman's ideas are so absurd and self-contradictory that you have to laugh about them; the audience in fact does, but they don't remember it, thank God! If they remembered it, they wouldn't be as moved as they are. Basically, it's the laughter of recognition, I believe.

INTERVIEWER: You moved on in the direction of what was first a television film and then a play, *Playing for Time*, your adaptation of Fania Fenelon's book, an account of her experience in a concentration camp playing in an orchestra. The concentration camp and the Holocaust are daunting subjects to approach.

MILLER: I was full of doubts because in one sense nobody can write about that subject, certainly nobody who hasn't been there, but I couldn't accept the alternative. You can't confront something like that with silence. We already know there's a considerable group of people who deny the thing ever happened, incredibly enough, so how do you remain silent in the face of that? In fact, I don't think there is a possibility of any art ever encompassing that monstrosity. At the time that I decided to do this there was very little attention being given to the Holocaust. It seemed to have completely slipped away at that particular moment.

INTERVIEWER: Do you think there's a sense in which the Holocaust had already entered your work, I don't mean in *After the Fall* and *Incident at Vichy* but in *The Crucible*, this sense of the irrational…

MILLER: When I learned about the Holocaust, it stopped me cold. I had been brought up in the twenties and thirties to imagine that the Germans were the most cultivated people in Europe and maybe the world. My grandfather, who was born in Poland but had spent some time in Vienna as a tailor, used to say when Hitler came into power, "Well, he won't last six months. The Germans are too intelligent for this idiot." It was the Russians who were stupid. Poles were stupid. The French were hopeless because they had no interest in anybody but French people! He looked to the Germans to help. The Germans were the most non-anti-Semitic people in Europe. So when they went down that route, then you felt anybody could. It was a devastating piece of news for me. It entered my work through my bones. The idea of confronting this kind of unreason and having no response possible to it is probably the most dramatic event imaginable because it leaves the human being utterly alone with his pain. To survive this psychologically is the work of a great spirit, and this kind of stubborn resistance went into *The Crucible* because there were people in Massachusetts at the time who did survive it spiritually.

INTERVIEWER: In 1984 you were one of a group of writers from around the world who went to the then Soviet Union and had a meeting with Gorbachev, which was one of the first signs that something was happening. What can you remember of that meeting?

MILLER: I had gotten a phone call from a writer I had met in Europe, and he said, "I'm in Kirghizia…" I said, "Congratulations! What do you want from me?" He said, "I want you to come here." I said, "Kirghizia?" He said, "Yes, we're going to have a meeting here." I said, "Don't. I'm finished with meetings. I don't want any more meetings." He said, "No, this has nothing to do with the government." I said, "That's impossible. You're in Russia!" He said, "Yes, but something's happening in Russia." Gorbachev had been in power a couple of months. Anyway, a lot of French, Germans, and Italians and so on met in this place. Jimmy Baldwin came and a couple of other Americans. We sat around talking. Then a message came: Would you like to come to meet Mr. Gorbachev in Moscow? So we did that, about fourteen of us. What was interesting to me was that he was saying, "The past is not a guide anymore in the sense that we used to think of it; Marx never knew anything about the atom bomb, so we have to start from reality instead of from theories." And I had a little private moment with him, I asked, "Are you a Communist?" He said, "I'm a Leninist; I'm not a Stalinist, and I think we have to start a whole new approach to Marxism." Well, I thought this was pretty hot news, and when I got back to America, I told a friend of mine, Harrison Salisbury, a retired editor of *The New York Times,* who lived down the road. He said, "Jesus, you've got to write this. This is big news." Well, I wrote a piece. I had taken notes of that occasion, which I never do, but I knew that this was an unusual historical moment, and I wrote up exactly what had been said, and he sent it down to his buddies at *The New York Times,* and nobody would print it. They couldn't believe it, so he sent it to *The Washington Post.* They wouldn't print it either. That's when I learned that we have a party line. The party line was that the Russian government was Stalinist, incapable of any change, that the whole thing was some kind of a gag. And that's how we ended up looking at a Soviet Union that was literally falling to pieces, and refusing to believe it. Because the line was that they had the atom bomb, they had all these airplanes, they had the biggest army in the world, they *had* to be powerful! Here I'd just left a man who was saying, in effect, "We are lost. We don't know where the hell we're going." That's what the substance of his speech to us was, and I couldn't get a major paper to publish it.

INTERVIEWER: There's a bit of your conversation which sticks with me because he asked you what the function of the artist was, and you said the artist's function is to speak truth to power, but does power ever listen to the artist's truth?

MILLER: I can't think of many occasions. No. Power is power. The reason it's power is because it doesn't listen. If it listened, it wouldn't be power. It'd be just one of us, and we don't have any power. I mean, I just told them exactly what the man had said. What I added it up to mean was that he was philosophically, spiritually at sea. He didn't know where the hell he was going. He was calling himself a Leninist. Well, it's meaningless. *The New York Times* always knows what's happening. So six months or so later when the fact became undeniable, came out that Gorbachev didn't know where he was going, ideology was set aside and we were allowed to read the obvious. Anyway, end of chapter.

INTERVIEWER: You began the decade of the nineties, which has proved to be amazingly prolific as far as you're concerned, with a play called *The Ride Down Mount Morgan,* about a bigamist who believes that he can get away with almost everything without consequences. It seems very much a play coming out of the Reagan period. Is that how you felt it to be or not?

MILLER: I don't see it that way. The play is testing whether there needs to be any restraint on human instinct and why. Why can't we all do exactly what we want to do? In certain people, the sexual impulse is overwhelming. Need I mention names! So what's wrong with the bigamist since that's his honest truth. His truth is the expression of the sexual instincts. Apart from the damage that it might do to the individual, is there any wider application of this question? His problem is he marries two of them at the same time. They don't know it. And it goes great for about ten years until he has an accident on a highway, and the cops call his first wife because it's with her that the car is registered, but he's on his way to the second wife, and the two women meet in the hospital lobby. The question is, well, what's wrong with this? And that's what the play is about. It's Reaganism only in the sense that the character is letting it all hang out: he's wanting to be everything to everybody, the man totally freed of obligation. But I have an old quarrel with morality.

INTERVIEWER: It's a play that you recently revised. How often does that happen?

MILLER: Very rarely. I had a very difficult time with that play. I couldn't get it right. Last week I was cleaning up my studio to try to bring some order to this chaos, and I found about fifteen different versions with sub-versions, two large boxes with manuscripts in them, collected over the past, fifteen years! It took all this time to get it right. It's a very difficult question: where do you come down? Do you simply condemn the guy out of hand, knowing that these impulses exist in most people? That means you condemn the human race. Do you condone the thing? Well, you can't do that either because of the pain that it causes other people and the social chaos it could justify. That's a hard thing to write, but I got as close to it as I think it can get.

INTERVIEWER: Are the changes major or is it simply tinkering?

MILLER: There is much variation from play to play. Some just spill out, some are more reluctant, some never emerge at all. I revise in order—generally—to further unearth theme as new connections are discovered. You want to find the center of the web where all the threads meet.

INTERVIEWER: That recent play of yours, *Broken Glass,* existed in multiple drafts. It won the Olivier Award in Britain as best play of the year. It's set in the time of *Kristallnacht* though it takes place in this country. Can you think of what the trigger was that led you back to 1938 in 1994?

MILLER: I'm not sure that I can. It's a play about a woman who around the time of the Nazi explosion in Germany wakes one morning and is paralyzed. She can't walk—a perfectly healthy woman. They can't figure out what it is. They give it the general name of hysteria, but she's not an hysterical kind of a person. It's an investigation of a whole personal as well as political situation that brought this upon her. She's not a political person, but she's living in that time when the menace of Fascism was alive in the world, and, through various means, she is affected by it.

INTERVIEWER: In your play *Golden Years,* written in the late thirties, which is about Cortés's conquest of Mexico, you wrote about two hundred Spaniards simply mesmerizing and paralyzing...

MILLER: That's right, isn't it?

INTERVIEWER: So paralysis in the face of power is obviously in your sensibility. I remember rehearsals of *Broken Glass* were going on while Sarajevo was being shelled.

MILLER: I hadn't thought of that. Well, that's what we generally feel when we read about places like Sarajevo or Bosnia or whatever. You feel paralyzed. In her case she was really paralyzed; she couldn't walk.

INTERVIEWER: The most recent play we've seen in New York is *Mr. Peters' Connection,* which starred Peter Falk. Peter is an ex-pilot looking back over his life and the life of his society, his city, his culture, trying to find out what the connections were. Now is this Arthur Miller, eighty-three, looking back over a life and trying to see where it finally fitted...

MILLER: It really came out of conversations with an actual pilot. It isn't me at all. I mean, it's me in the sense I wrote it. It's a guy who's done everything: bombing places, delivering fighter planes to Murmansk during World War II, being the chief operating officer of Eastern Airlines for years, and sitting there at the age of seventy-eight, up in Connecticut, and trying to figure out what it all comes to. I use the line that he told me when he said, "You know, I pick up a paper and there's advertisements for breast enlargement: $4,500." He says, "You know, our house where myself and four brothers and two sisters were raised cost $5,500, and now we have breast enlargement for $4,500! How do you put that together?" He says, "Then we have penile enlargement. It's the same price!" That wonderful bewilderment on the part of a very experienced man is what set that play off. He's trying to reach out and bring together the strands of experience as he's moving down the streets of New York City. He can look at a building and remember the building that was taken down in order to build this one. But he can also remember the building that was taken down for the building that preceded this building! And he says, "So what does that mean?" He's walking around with the layers of New York City in his gut and trying to come to some image that will help him digest the whole mess.

INTERVIEWER: Looking for the connections between people, between the past and the present...trying to find some kind of coherence which is, I suppose, one of the functions of theater or, indeed, art is to find some order beneath the level of the incoherent and chance and the arbitrary.

MILLER: It's a one-act stab in the darkness.

INTERVIEWER: What about the exact genesis of any given work. It would seem it's always a concept. Is it ever more specific—an image, a snatch of conversation...?

MILLER: By this time any language capable of being performed can be called a play. But if one demands a crisis followed by a climax, issues raised and to some degree resolved, then a concept would probably be required. Some writers start with concept—some with objective meaning to an action; others begin with a character, a line even, or perhaps a physical setting. For myself, a play arrives at an almost palpable architectural form, but its discovery is gradual and can begin anywhere.

INTERVIEWER: Does a character tend to change, establish an identity that seems a departure from what you originally had in mind?

MILLER: Characters, like real people, tend to deceive and deflect attempts to penetrate their motives, so as you go along you pick up hints. It's all a lot like getting to know somebody.

INTERVIEWER: How easy is it to divide a work into the requisite number of acts? Does one have to add padding to gain a few minutes? Do you think of closing lines to an act and then work toward them?

MILLER: Act breaks are mysterious; the action seems to want to fall at some point. One should realize, too, that fashion has something to do with this. Until somewhere around 1947 in New York (Europe may have been different), almost all plays were in three acts, the first pre-senting the issues or conflict; the second ending at a crisis; the third at the climax and resolution. As society's claims on the individual fell into doubt, so did the very notion of a plot or even a continuous story and all became sheer experience, moments of interest, one or another description of a moral chaos. *Salesman* and *Streetcar* come to mind among the earliest two-acters.

INTERVIEWER: Why are you drawn to theater at the end of this mil-lennium? After all, the theater is now dwarfed by giant screens. It's deafened by Dolby stereo. The electronic media appear to blot it out. It's expensive. It's very often awkward and uncomfortable to get to. Sometimes it's not very good! Why stay with theater?

MILLER: Well, in the first place, I've been doing it all my life. But I do think it's the simplest way for one citizen to address other citizens. It is the least complicated, the most naked means for a society to address it-self. It's far simpler than any filmic system. It needs nothing but a board and a man to stand on it, so that's very attractive to me. The fact that the rest is getting bigger and bigger, Disney and the rest of it, makes me feel even more attracted to the fact that it's taking place in a hall only this big, and only in this place on the planet and not in 1,700 different theaters, some of which have two or three thousand seats! I like the fact that it's intimate and that it is direct, and above all, I sup-pose, I like the fact that the writer controls it. I don't think there are very many people who decide to go to a movie because so-and-so wrote it. Which is another egotistical reason to be writing plays! But it's also that the word in the theater is the great thing. The word in the movies barely enters the scene, very little to do with anything. It's the image. So, for those reasons I choose to stay with this old-fashioned, probably dying art. But I don't think it's dying. In fact, as I go around the country, there are more and more young people who want to be in it, be part of it, for the reasons I've just said.

INTERVIEWER: Do you have a routine for writing?

MILLER: I wish I had a routine for writing. I get up in the morning, and I go out to my studio, and I write. And then I tear it up! And that's the routine, really. Then, occasionally, something sticks. And then I follow that. The only image I can think of is a man walking around with an iron rod in his hand during a lightning storm, and that's about it.

INTERVIEWER: Do you go to opening nights? Is that an easy experience?

MILLER: By that time one knows the answer. I go to buck up the actors.

—CHRISTOPHER BIGSBY
Fall, 1999

NEIL SIMON

Courtesy of Neil Simon

One of America's most popular and prolific playwrights, Neil Simon was born in Bronx, New York City, on July 4, 1927. He grew up in the Manhattan neighborhood of Washington Heights and attended the all-boys DeWitt Clinton High School.

After studying briefly at New York University as an engineering student, Simon joined the Army Air Force Reserve, which stationed him in Colorado. A week later the Second World War ended and, following his discharge, Simon moved back to New York, where he worked as a mail room clerk for Warner Bros. He soon got a job in radio, however, and with his brother Danny began writing comedy for Goodman Ace and for Robert W. Lewis's *The Little Show*.

In the 1950s the Simons moved over to television, working for *The Phil Silvers Arrow Show, The Tallulah Bankhead Show,* and Sid Caesar's *Your Show of Shows,* where they were staff writers with, among others, Mel Brooks and Woody Allen. Increasingly dissatisfied with the demands being made by network and advertising executives, Simon and his brother wrote their first play, *Come Blow Your Horn* (1960). It ran for eighty-four weeks on Broadway, and its success allowed Simon to leave television for good.

Simon's first solo effort at playwriting, *Barefoot in the Park,* was produced on Broadway in 1965. It ran for over 1,500 performances. Following that success, he continued to compose at an astonishing rate— a new play appeared on Broadway nearly every year between 1966 (*The Odd Couple*) and 1988 (*Rumors*)—but his work was not fully taken seriously by critics until the appearance of his autobiographical trilogy, *Brighton Beach Memoirs* (1982), *Biloxi Blues* (1984), and *Broadway Bound* (1986). Set in New York in the 1930s and '40s, the plays trace the development of Simon's alter ego, Eugene Jerome, who grows up in a cramped house during the Depression, joins the Army for a brief time, and eventually forms a collaborative writing team with his brother. *Biloxi Blues* earned Simon a Tony Award in 1985. Critical acclamation for Simon's work increased with the premiere in 1991 of *Lost in Yonkers,* which was awarded a Pulitzer Prize, a Drama Desk Award, and a Tony.

Many of Simon's more than thirty screenplays—*The Odd Couple* (1968) and *Chapter Two* (1979) among them—have been adaptations of his stage work, but he has also written original works for the screen, including *Murder by Death* (1976) and *The Odd Couple II* (1998).

Proposals, Simon's thirtieth play in thirty-six years, premiered in 1997.

———

These pages are the winnowing of sixteen hours of taped conversation in Simon's office on the second floor of a Spanish colonial apartment building in the Beverly Hills flats—several miles, a thousand vertical feet, and a dozen social strata below the Bel Air hilltop home Simon shares with his wife, Diane, and their daughter, Bryn.

The writer's no-nonsense work space, impersonal in its laid-back Southern Californian setting, is conspicuously empty (no secretary, no phone calls, no distractions) but intensely personal in the memorabilia that have, as Simon explains, "sort of gravitated" there over the years.

Toomey (Cont'd)

.....Answer when your name is called. The answer to that question is "Ho";.. Ho! yes, not here, not anywhere, not in or any other unacceptable form of reply, except the aforementioned "Ho", am I understood?.... Wykowski, Joseph T.

Wykowski

Ho!

Toomey

Selridge, Roy W.

Selridge

Ho!

Toomey

Carney, Donald J.

Carney

Ho!

Toomey

Epstein, Arnold B.

Epstein

Ho Ho!

Toomey
(looks at him)

..Are there two Arnold Epsteins in this company?

Epstein

No, Sergeant.

Toomey

Then just gimme one Goddam Ho.

Epstein

Yes, Sergeant.

Toomey

Epstein, Arnold B.

Epstein

Ho!

A manuscript page from Biloxi Blues.

*Halfway through the tour of the apartment, Simon stopped abruptly and re-
marked, in apparent surprise, on how many of the room's furnishings date from
the house on Manhattan's East Sixty-second Street where he lived with his first
wife, Joan: chairs, tables, photographs, paintings—some painted by Joan, a
framed letter from her written in cryptic Joycean prose and signed "Klarn." The
baseball paraphernalia on display reflects another side of Simon's life. His sub-
stantial collection of antique caps and autographed balls, with a recent emphasis
on Bobby Bonilla, would knock the kneesocks off the playwright's baseball-mad
alter ego, Eugene Jerome.*

*There are the usual theatrical souvenirs and a few unusual ones: a telegram
from the president of Columbia University informing Simon of his Pulitzer
Prize for* Lost in Yonkers, *a Neil Simon* Time *magazine cover, a poster from
the Moscow production of* Biloxi Blues, *signed by the cast, "Dear Neil Simon,
We love you and your plays. We had worked on this performance with enjoy."*

*"Doc" Simon, so called from his childhood habit of mimicking the family doc-
tor, is tall and fit, despite the chronic back problems that have curtailed his tennis playing in recent years. We sat at a massive, polished tree-stump coffee table
covered with the tools of his trade: pens neatly stacked (by the cleaning woman, he
hastened to say), scripts, finished and unfinished, books, and the long pads on
which he writes. We laughed frequently as we discussed his plays, opinions, and
past. Even when the talk turned as serious as some of his recent scripts, the face
that peered over the tree stump like a Bronx leprechaun bore two indelible Simon
trademarks: the eyes of an insatiably curious and slightly guarded child, shielded
by horn-rimmed glasses, and a faint, constant, enigmatic smile.*

INTERVIEWER: Lillian Hellman once said she always began work on a
play with something very small—a scene, or even two vague lines of
dialogue whose meaning was utterly unknown to her. What starts *you*,
what makes you think there's a play there?

SIMON: As many plays as I've written—twenty-seven, twenty-eight—
I can't recollect a moment when I've said, "This would make a good
play." I never sit down and write bits and pieces of dialogue. What I
might do is make a few notes on who's in the play, the characters I
want, where it takes place, and the general idea of it. I don't make any
outlines at all. I just like to plunge in. I'll start right from page one because I want to hear how the people speak. Are they interesting
enough for me? Have I captured them? It goes piece by piece, brick by

brick. I don't know that I have a play until I've reached thirty, thirty-five pages.

INTERVIEWER: Have you ever started thematically?

SIMON: I *think* about thematic plays, but I don't believe I write them. Nothing really takes shape until I become specific about the character and the dilemma he's in. *Dilemma* is the key word. It is always a dilemma, not a situation. To tell the truth, I really don't know what the theme of the play is until I've written it and the critics tell me.

INTERVIEWER: Every playwright, every director, every actor, speaks about conflict. We're all supposed to be in the conflict business. When you speak of dilemma, are you talking about conflict?

SIMON: Yes. In *Broadway Bound* I wanted to show the anatomy of writing comedy—with the older brother teaching Eugene, which was the case with my brother Danny and me. Stan keeps asking Eugene for the essential ingredient in comedy, and when Eugene can't answer, Stan says, "Conflict!" When he asks for the *other* key ingredient, and Eugene can only come up with, "*More* conflict?" Stan says, "The key word is *wants*. In every comedy, even drama, somebody has to want something and want it bad. When somebody tries to stop him—that's conflict." By the time you know the conflicts, the play is already written in your mind. All you have to do is put the words down. You don't have to outline the play, it outlines itself. You go by sequential activity. One thing follows the other. But it all starts with that first seed, conflict. As Stan says, it's got to be a very, very strong conflict, not one that allows the characters to say, "Forget about this! I'm walking out." They've got to stay there and fight it out to the end.

INTERVIEWER: You said that it isn't until you get to page thirty-five that you know whether or not you've got a play. Are there times when you get to page thirty-five and decide the conflict isn't strong enough, and the play disappears to languish forever in a drawer?

SIMON: I've got infinitely more plays in the drawer than have seen the lights of the stage. Most of them never come out of the drawer, but oc-

casionally one will, and it amazes me how long it has taken to germi-
nate and blossom. The best example would be *Brighton Beach Memoirs.* I
wrote the first thirty-five pages of the play and gave it to my children,
Nancy and Ellen, and Marsha, my wife at the time. They read it and
said, "This is incredible. You've got to go on with it." I showed it to my
producer, Manny Azenberg, and to Gordon Davidson, and they said,
"This is going to be a great play." I knew the play was a turn in style for
me, probing more deeply into myself, but maybe the pressure of the
words "great play" scared me, so I put it away. Periodically, I would
take it out and read it, and I wouldn't know how to do it. After nine
years I took it out one day, read the thirty-five pages, picked up my pen
and the pad I write on, and finished the play in six weeks. I have the
feeling that in the back of your mind there's a little writer who writes
while you're doing other things, because I had no trouble at that point.
Obviously, what had happened in the ensuing years in my life made
clear to me what it should be about. Somewhere in the back of my
head I grew up, I matured. I was ready to write that play. Sometimes it
helps to have some encouragement. Once I was having dinner with
Mike Nichols, and he asked, "What are you doing?" I said, "I'm working on a play about two ex-vaudevillians who haven't worked together
or seen each other in eleven years, and they get together to do an *Ed
Sullivan Show.*" He said, "That sounds wonderful. Go back and finish
it." So I did. It was as though a critic had already seen the play and said,
"I love it." But there are many, many plays that get to a certain point
and no further. For years I've been trying to write the play of what
happened to me and the seven writers who wrote Sid Caesar's *Your
Show of Shows.* But I've never got past page twenty-two because there
are seven conflicts rather than one main conflict. I've been writing
more subtext and more subplot lately—but in this situation *everybody*
was funny. I didn't have somebody to be serious, to anchor it. I always
have to find the anchor. I have to find the Greek chorus in the play, the
character who either literally talks to the audience or talks to the audience in a sense. For example, Oscar in *The Odd Couple* is the Greek
chorus. He watches, he perceives how Felix behaves, and he comments
on it. Felix then comments back on what Oscar is, but Oscar is the one
who is telling us what the play is about. More recently, in the Brighton
Beach trilogy, I've been *literally* talking to the audience, through the
character of Eugene, because it is the only way I can express the

writer's viewpoint. The writer has inner thoughts, and they are not always articulated on the stage—and I want the audience to be able to get inside his head. It's what I did in *Jake's Women*. In the first tryout in San Diego the audience didn't know enough about Jake because all he did was react to the women in his life, who were badgering him, trying to get him to open up. We didn't know who Jake was. So I introduced the device of him talking to the audience. Then he became the fullest, richest character in the play, because the audience knew things I never thought I would reveal about Jake—and possibly about myself.

INTERVIEWER: Will you return to the *Show of Shows* play?

SIMON: I do very often think about doing it. What was unique about that experience was that almost every one of the writers has gone on to do really major things: Mel Brooks's whole career...Larry Gelbart...Woody Allen...Joe Stein, who wrote *Fiddler on the Roof*... Michael Stewart, who wrote *Hello, Dolly*...it was a group of people only Sid Caesar knew how to put together. Maybe it was trial and error because the ones who didn't work fell out, but once we worked together it was the most excruciatingly hilarious time in my life. It was also one of the most painful because you were fighting for recognition, and there was no recognition. It was very difficult for me because I was quiet and shy, so I sat next to Carl Reiner and whispered my jokes to him. He was my spokesman, he'd jump up and say, "He's got it! He's got it!" Then Carl would say the line, and I would hear it, and I'd laugh because I thought it was funny. But when I watched the show on a Saturday night with my wife, Joan, she'd say, "That was your line, wasn't it?" and I'd say, "I don't remember." What I *do* remember is the screaming and fighting—a cocktail party without the cocktails, everyone yelling lines in and out, people getting very angry at others who were slacking off. Mel Brooks was the main culprit. We all came in to work at ten o'clock in the morning, but he showed up at one o'clock. We'd say, "That's it. We're sick and tired of this. Either Mel comes in at ten o'clock or we go to Sid and do something about it." At about ten to one, Mel would come in with a straw hat, fling it across the room, and say "Lindy made it!" and everyone would fall down hysterical. He didn't need the eight hours we put in. He needed four hours. He is, maybe, the most uniquely funny man I've ever met. That inspired me. I wanted to be around those people. I've fooled around with this idea for a play. I even found a title for it, *Laughter on the Twenty-third Floor,* because I think the office was on the twenty-third floor. From that building we looked down on Bendel's and Bergdorf Goodman and Fifth Avenue, watching all the pretty girls go by through binoculars. Sometimes we'd set fire to the desk with lighter fluid. We should have been arrested, all of us.

INTERVIEWER: If you ever get past page twenty-two, how would you deal with Mel and Woody and the others? Would they appear as themselves?

SIMON: No, no, no! They'd all be fictitious. It would be like the Brighton Beach trilogy, which is semiautobiographical.

INTERVIEWER: It feels totally autobiographical. I assumed it was.

SIMON: Everyone does. But I've told interviewers that if I meant it to be autobiographical I would have called the character Neil Simon. He's not Neil. He's Eugene Jerome. That gives you greater latitude for fiction. It's like doing abstract painting. You see your own truth in it, but the abstraction is the art.

INTERVIEWER: When did you realize there was a sequel to *Brighton Beach Memoirs?*

SIMON: It got a middling review from Frank Rich of *The New York Times,* but he said at the end of it, "One hopes that there is a chapter two to *Brighton Beach.*" I thought, he's asking for a sequel to a play that he doesn't seem to like!

INTERVIEWER: Are you saying Frank Rich persuaded you to write *Biloxi Blues?*

SIMON: No, but I listened to him saying, "I'm interested enough to want to know more about this family." Then, Steven Spielberg, who had gone to see *Brighton Beach,* got word to me, suggesting the next play should be about my days in the army. I was already thinking about that, and I started to write *Biloxi Blues,* which became a play about Eugene's rites of passage. I discovered something very important in the writing of *Biloxi Blues.* Eugene, who keeps a diary, writes in it his belief that Epstein is homosexual. When the other boys in the barracks read the diary and assume it's true, Eugene feels terrible guilt. He's realized the responsibility of putting something down on paper, because people tend to believe everything they read.

INTERVIEWER: *The Counterfeiters* ends with the diary André Gide kept while he was writing the book, and in it he says he knows he's writing well when the dialectic of the scene takes over, and the characters seize the scene from him, and he's become not a writer but a *reader.* Do you sometimes find that your characters have taken the play away from you and are off in their own direction?

SIMON: I've *always* felt like a middleman, like the typist. Somebody somewhere else is saying, "This is what they say now. This is what they say next." Very often it is the characters themselves, once they become clearly defined. When I was working on my first play, *Come Blow Your Horn,* I was told by fellow writers that you must outline your play, you must know where you're going. I wrote a complete, detailed outline from page one to the end of the play. In the writing of the play, I didn't get past page fifteen when the characters started to move away from the outline. I tried to pull them back in, saying, "Get back in there. This is where you belong. I've already diagrammed your life." They said, "No, no, no. This is where I want to go." So, I started following them. In the second play, *Barefoot in the Park,* I outlined the first two acts. I said, "I'll leave the third act a free-for-all, so I can go where I want." I never got through that outline either. In *The Odd Couple,* I outlined the first act. After a while I got tired of doing even that. I said, "I want to be as surprised as anyone else." I had also read a book on playwriting by John van Druten, in which he said, "Don't outline your play, because then the rest of it will just be work. It should be joy. You should be discovering things the way the audience discovers them." So, I stopped doing it.

INTERVIEWER: Gide writes about being surprised by the material coming up on the typewriter. He finds himself laughing, shocked, sometimes dismayed...

SIMON: Sometimes I start laughing—and I've had moments in this office when I've burst into tears. Not that I thought the audience might do that. The moment had triggered a memory or a feeling that was deeply hidden. That's catharsis. It's one of the main reasons I write the plays. It's like analysis without going to the analyst. The play becomes your analysis. The writing of the play is the most enjoyable part of it. It's also the most frightening part because you walk into a forest without a knife, without a compass. But if your instincts are good, if you have a sense of geography, you find that you're clearing a path and getting to the right place. If the miracle happens, you come out at the very place you *wanted* to. But very often you have to go back to the beginning of the forest and start walking through it again, saying, "I went that way. It was a dead end." You cross out, cross over. You meet new friends along the way, people you never thought you'd meet. It takes you into a world you hadn't planned on going to when you started the play. The play may have started out to be a comedy, and suddenly you get into a place of such depth that it surprises you. As one critic aptly said, I wrote *Brighton Beach Memoirs* about the family I *wished* I'd had instead of the family I *did* have. It's closer to *Ah, Wilderness!* than my reality.

INTERVIEWER: When did you realize that *Brighton Beach Memoirs* and *Biloxi Blues* were part of a trilogy?

SIMON: I thought it seemed odd to leave the Eugene saga finished after two plays. Three is a trilogy—I don't even know what two plays are called. So, I decided to write the third one, and the idea came immediately. It was back to the war theme again, only these were domestic wars. The boys were having guilts and doubts about leaving home for a career writing comedy. Against this played the war between the parents. I also brought in the character of the socialist grandfather who was constantly telling the boys, "You can't just write jokes and make people laugh." Against this came Blanche from the first play, *Brighton Beach,* trying to get the grandfather to move to Florida to take care of his aging, ill wife. To me, setting people in conflict with each other is like what those Chinese jugglers do, spinning one plate, then another, then another. I wanted to keep as many plates spinning as I could.

INTERVIEWER: What exactly do you mean when you call the Brighton Beach trilogy semiautobiographical?

SIMON: It means the play may be based on incidents that happened in my life—but they're not written the way they happened. *Broadway Bound* comes closest to being really autobiographical. I didn't pull any punches with that one. My mother and father were gone when I wrote it, so I did tell about the fights, and what it was like for me as a kid hearing them. I didn't realize until someone said after the first reading that the play was really a love letter to my mother! She suffered the most in all of it. She was the one that was left alone. Her waxing that table didn't exist in life, but it exists symbolically for *me*. It's the abstraction I was talking about.

INTERVIEWER: Speaking of abstraction, there's something mystifying to audiences—and other writers—about what the great comedy writers do. From outside, it seems to be as different from what most writers are able to do as baseball is from ballet. I'm not going to ask anything quite as fatuous as "What is humor?" but I *am* asking—is it genetic, is it a mind-set, a quirk? And, most important, can it be learned—or, for that matter, taught?

SIMON: The answer is complex. First of all, there are various styles and attitudes towards comedy. When I worked on *Your Show of Shows,* Larry Gelbart was the wittiest, cleverest man I'd ever met, Mel Brooks the most outrageous. I never knew what I was. I *still* don't know. Maybe I had the best sense of construction of the group. I only know some aspects of my humor, one of which involves being completely literal. To give you an example, in *Lost in Yonkers,* Uncle Louie is trying to explain the heartless grandmother to Arty. "When she was twelve years old, her old man takes her to a political rally in Berlin. A horse goes down and crushes Ma's foot. Nobody ever fixed it. It hurts every day of her life, but I never once seen her take even an aspirin." Later, Arty says to his older brother, "I'm afraid of her, Jay. A horse fell on her when she was a kid, and she hasn't taken an aspirin yet." It's an almost exact repetition of what Louie told him and this time it gets a huge laugh. That mystifies me. In *Prisoner of Second Avenue,* you knew there were terrible things tormenting Peter Falk. He sat down on a sofa that had stacks of pillows, like every sofa in the world, and he took one pillow after the other and started throwing them angrily saying, "You pay $800 for a sofa, and you can't sit on it because you got ugly little pillows shoved up your back!" There is no joke there. Yet, it was an enormous laugh—because the audience identified. That, more or less, is what is funny to me: saying something that's instantly identifiable to everybody. People come up to you after the show and say, "I've always thought that, but I never knew anyone *else* thought it." It's a shared secret between you and the audience.

INTERVIEWER: You've often said that you've never consciously written a joke in one of your plays.

SIMON: I try never to think of jokes as jokes. I confess that in the early days, when I came from television, plays like *Come Blow Your Horn* would have lines you could lift out that would be funny in themselves. That to me would be a "joke," which I would try to remove. In *The Odd Couple* Oscar had a line about Felix, "He's so panicky he wears his seat belt at a drive-in movie." That could be a Bob Hope joke. I left it in because I couldn't find anything to replace it.

INTERVIEWER: Have you ever found that a producer, director, or actor objected to losing a huge laugh that you were determined to cut from the play?

SIMON: An actor, perhaps, yes. They'll say, "But that's my big laugh." I say, "But it hurts the scene." It's very hard to convince them. Walter Matthau was after me constantly on *The Odd Couple,* complaining not about one of his lines, but one of Art Carney's. He'd say, "It's not a good line." A few days later, I received a letter from a doctor in Wilmington. It said, "Dear Mr. Simon, I loved your play, but I find one line really objectionable. I wish you would take it out." So, I took the line out and said, "Walter, I've complied with your wishes. I got a letter from a prominent doctor in Wilmington who didn't like the line..." He started to laugh, and then I realized, "You son of a bitch, *you're* the doctor!" And he was. Those quick lines, the one-liners attributed to me for so many years—*I* think they come purely out of character, rather than out of a joke. Walter Kerr once came to my aid by saying, "to be or not to be" is a one-liner. If it's a dramatic moment no one calls it a one-liner. If it gets a laugh, suddenly it's a one-liner. I think one of the complaints of critics is that the people in my plays are funnier than they would be in life, but have you ever seen *Medea*? The characters are a lot more dramatic in that than they are in life.

INTERVIEWER: You've also said that when you began writing for the theater you decided to try to write comedy the way dramatists write plays—writing from the characters out, internally, psychologically...

SIMON: Yes. What I try to do is make dialogue come purely out of character, so that one character could never say the lines that belong to another character. If it's funny, it's because I'm telling a story about characters in whom I may find a rich vein of humor. When I started writing plays I was warned by people like Lillian Hellman, "You do not mix comedy with drama." But my theory was, if it's mixed in life, why can't you do it in a play? The very first person I showed *Come Blow Your Horn* to was Herman Shumlin, the director of Hellman's *The Little Foxes*. He said, "I like the play, I like the people, but I don't like the older brother." I said, "What's wrong with him?" He said, "Well, it's a comedy. We have to like everybody." I said, "In *life* do we have to like everybody?" In the most painful scene in *Lost in Yonkers*, Bella, who is semiretarded, is trying to tell the family that the boy she wants to marry is also retarded. It's a poignant situation, and yet the information that slowly comes out—and the way the family is third-degreeing her—becomes hilarious, because it's mixed with someone else's pain. I find that what is most poignant is often most funny.

INTERVIEWER: In the roll-call scene in *Biloxi Blues* you riff for several pages on one word, one *syllable:* "Ho." It builds and builds in what I've heard you call a "run."

SIMON: I learned from watching Chaplin films that what's most funny isn't a single moment of laughter but the moments that come on top of it, and on top of *those*. I learned it from the Laurel and Hardy films too. One of the funniest things I ever saw Laurel and Hardy do was try to undress in the upper berth of a train—together. It took ten minutes, getting the arms in the wrong sleeves and their feet caught in the net, one terrible moment leading to another. I thought, there could be no greater satisfaction for me than to do that to an audience. Maybe "Ho" also came from sitting in the dark as a kid, listening to Jack Benny's running gags on the radio. In *Barefoot in the Park,* when the telephone man comes up five or six flights of stairs, he arrives completely out of breath. When Paul makes *his* entrance, *he's* completely out of breath. When the mother makes her entrance, *she's* completely out of breath. Some critics have written, "You milk that out-of-breath joke too much." My answer is, "You mean because it's happened three times, when they come up the fourth time they shouldn't be out of breath anymore?" It's *not* a joke, it's the natural thing. Like "Ho." Those boys are petrified on their first day in the army, confronted by this maniac sergeant.

INTERVIEWER: Do you pace the lines so the laughs don't cover the dialogue or is that the director's job? Do you try to set up a rhythm in the writing that will allow for the audience's response?

SIMON: You don't know where the laughs are until you get in front of an audience. Most of the biggest laughs I've ever had I never knew were big laughs. Mike Nichols used to say to me, "Take out all the little laughs because they hurt the big ones." Sometimes the little laughs aren't even *meant* to be laughs. I mean them to further the play, the plot, the character, the story. They're written unwittingly... strange word to pick. I cut them, and the laugh pops up somewhere else.

INTERVIEWER: When did you first realize you were funny?

SIMON: It started very early in my life—eight, nine, ten years old— being funny around the other kids. You single out one kid on your block or in the school who understands what you're saying. He's the only one who laughs. The other kids only laugh when someone tells them a joke: "Two guys got on a truck..." I've never done that in my life. I don't like telling jokes. I don't like to hear someone say to me, "Tell him that funny thing you said the other day." It's repeating it. I have no more joy in it. Once it's said, for me it's over. The same is true once it's written—I have no more interest in it. I've expelled whatever it is I needed to exorcise, whether it's humorous or painful. Generally, painful. Maybe the humor is to cover the pain up, or maybe it's a way to share the experience with someone.

INTERVIEWER: Has psychoanalysis influenced your work?

SIMON: Yes. Generally I've gone into analysis when my life was in turmoil. But I found after a while I was going when it *wasn't* in turmoil. I was going to get a college education in human behavior. I was talking not only about myself; I was trying to understand my wife, my brother, my children, my family, anybody—including the analyst. I can't put everything in the plays down to pure chance. I want them to reveal what makes people tick. I tend to analyze almost everything. I don't think it started because I went through analysis. I'm just naturally that curious. The good mechanic knows how to take a car apart; I love to take the human mind apart and see how it works. Behavior is absolutely the most interesting thing I can write about. You put that behavior in conflict, and you're in business.

INTERVIEWER: Would you describe your writing process? Since you don't use an outline, do you ever know how a play will end?

SIMON: Sometimes I think I do—but it doesn't mean that's how the play *will* end. Very often you find that you've written past the end, and you say, "Wait a minute, it ended *here*." When I started to write *Plaza Suite* it was going to be a full three-act play. The first act was about a wife who rents the same suite she and her husband honeymooned in at the Plaza Hotel twenty-three years ago. In the course of the act the wife finds out that the husband is having an affair with his secretary, and at the end of the act the husband walks out the door as champagne and hors d'oeuvres arrive. The waiter asks, "Is he coming back?" and the wife says, "Funny you should ask that." I wrote that and said to myself, "That's the end of the play, I don't want to *know* if he's coming back." That's what made me write three one-act plays for *Plaza Suite*. I don't *like* to know where the play is going to end. I purposely won't think of the ending because I'm afraid, if I know, even subliminally, it'll sneak into the script, and the audience will know where the play is going. As a matter of fact, I never know where the play is going in the *second act.* When *Broadway Bound* was completed, I listened to the first reading and thought, there's not a moment in this entire play where I see the mother happy. She's a miserable woman. I want to know *why* she's miserable. The answer was planted in the beginning of the play: the mother kept talking about how no one believed she once danced with George Raft. I thought, the boy should ask her to talk about George Raft, and as she does, she'll reveal everything in her past.

INTERVIEWER: The scene ends with the now-famous moment of the boy dancing with the mother the way Raft did—*if* he did.

SIMON: Yes. People have said, "It's so organic, you had to have known you were writing to that all the time." But I *didn't* know it when I sat down to write the play. I had an interesting problem when I was writing *Rumors.* I started off with just a basic premise: I wanted to do an elegant farce. I wrote it right up to the last two pages of the play, the denouement in which everything has to be explained—and I didn't know what it was! I said to myself, "Today's the day I have to write the explanation. All right, just think it out." I *couldn't* think it out. So I said, "Well then, go sentence by sentence." I couldn't write it sentence by sentence. I said, "Go word by word. The man sits down and tells the police the story. He starts off with, 'It was six o'clock.' " That much I could write. I kept going until everything made sense. That method takes either insanity or egocentricity—or a great deal of confidence. It's like building a bridge over water without knowing if there's land on the other side. But I do have confidence that when I get to the end of the play, I will have gotten so deeply into the characters and the situation I'll find the resolution.

INTERVIEWER: So you never write backwards from a climactic event to the incidents and scenes at the beginning of the play that will take you to it?

SIMON: Never. The linkages are done by instinct. Sometimes I'll write something and say, "Right now this doesn't mean very much, but I have a hunch that later on in the play it will mean something." The thing I always do is play back on things I set up without any intention in the beginning. The foundation of the play is set in those first fifteen or twenty minutes. Whenever I get in trouble in the second act, I go back to the first act. The answers always lie there. One of the lines people have most often accused me of working backwards from is Felix Unger's note to Oscar in *The Odd Couple*. In the second act, Oscar has reeled off the laundry list of complaints he has about Felix, including "the little letters you leave me." Now, when Felix is leaving one of those notes, telling Oscar they're all out of cornflakes, I said to myself, "How would he sign it? I know he'd do something that would annoy Oscar." So I signed it "Mr. Unger." Then I tried "Felix Unger." Then I tried "F.U." and it was as if a bomb had exploded in the room. When Oscar says, "It took me three hours to figure out that F.U. was Felix Unger," it always gets this huge laugh.

INTERVIEWER: Felix Unger also appears in *Come Blow Your Horn*. I wanted to ask why you used the name twice.

SIMON: This will give you an indication of how little I thought my career would amount to. I thought *The Odd Couple* would probably be the end of my career, so it wouldn't make any difference that I had used Felix Unger in *Come Blow Your Horn*. It was a name that seemed to denote the prissiness of Felix, the perfect contrast to the name of Oscar. Oscar may not sound like a strong name, but it did to me—maybe because of the *k* sound in it.

INTERVIEWER: So you subscribe to the *K*-theory expressed by the comedians in *The Sunshine Boys*—*K* is funny.

SIMON: Oh, I do. Not only that, *k* cuts through the theater. You say a *K*-word, and they can hear it.

INTERVIEWER: Let's talk about the mechanics of writing, starting with where you write.

SIMON: I have this office. There are four or five rooms in it, and no one is here but me. No secretary, no one, and I've never once in the many years that I've come here ever felt lonely, or even alone. I come in and the room is filled with—as corny as it might sound—these characters I'm writing, who are waiting each day for me to arrive and give them life. I've also written on airplanes, in dentists' offices, on subways. I think it's true for many writers. You blank out whatever is in front of your eyes. That's why you see writers staring off into space. They're not looking at "nothing," they're visualizing what they're thinking. I never visualize what a play will look like onstage, I visualize what it looks like in *life*. I visualize being in that room where the mother is confronting the father.

INTERVIEWER: What tools do you use? Do you use a 1928 Underwood the way real writers are supposed to? Or a computer? You mentioned using a pad and pencil...

SIMON: I wrote my early plays at the typewriter because it was what writers looked like in *His Girl Friday*.

INTERVIEWER: Lots of crumpled pages being flung across the room?

SIMON: Yes. But my back started to get so bad from bending over a typewriter eight hours a day, five or six days a week that I couldn't do it anymore, so I started to write in pads. Then a curious thing happened. I was in England and found that they have pads over there with longer pages and thinner spaces between the lines. I liked that because I could get much more on a single page. At a single glance I could see the rhythm of the speeches. If they're on a smaller page with wide spaces you don't get a sense of the rhythm. You have to keep turning. So, I write in these pads. Sometimes I write on both sides of the page, but I always leave myself lots of room to make notes and cross things out. I'll write about three pages, then go to the typewriter and type that out. Then the next day I'll read those three pages again and maybe not like them, and go back to the notebook—write it out, make changes, and then retype it. The typing is boring for me, but I can't use a word processor. It feels inhuman. It seems to me that every script comes out of a computer looking like it was written by the same person. My typewriter has its own characteristics, its own little foibles. Even there, I black out parts and write marginal notes. I'd like it to be neat, but I don't like to send it to a professional typist because they invariably correct my purposely made grammatical errors. I try to write the way people speak, not the way people *should* speak.

INTERVIEWER: When you're writing dialogue, do you write it silently or speak it aloud?

SIMON: I never *thought* I spoke the lines until my family told me I did. They said they could walk by and tell if it was going well or not by the rhythm of it. I guess I want to see if I'm repeating words, and, because I write primarily for the stage, I want to make sure the words won't be tripping badly over some tongues.

INTERVIEWER: Do you play the parts, I mean, *really* play them and get into them?

SIMON: Yes. When I wrote the Sergeant Bilko show my father asked me naively, "Do you just write Sergeant Bilko's lines or do you write the other lines too?" When you write a play, maybe even a novel, you become *everybody.* It may seem like I only write the lines spoken by the character who is like Neil Simon, but, in *Lost in Yonkers,* I'm also the grandmother—and Bella. And to do that you have to *become* that person. That's the adventure, the joy, the release that allows you to escape from your own boundaries. To be Grandma every other line for a couple of pages takes you into another being. It's interesting how many people ask, "Was this your grandmother?" I say, "No, I didn't have a grandmother like that," and they say, "Then how do you know her?" I know what she *sounds* like. I know what she *feels* like. The boys describe it when they say, "When you kiss her it's like kissing a cold prune." I describe her in a stage direction as being a very tall, buxom woman. But she doesn't necessarily have to be tall and buxom. She just has to appear that way to the boys. You can't really use that as physical description, but it will convey something to the actress.

INTERVIEWER: And to the actors playing the two boys.

SIMON: Yes. Those directions are very important.

INTERVIEWER: Family seems to be more than a predilection or interest, it is a near obsession with you. Even if you're writing about a couple, in comes an extended family of friends or the blood-related aunts, uncles, cousins, fathers, and mothers with which your plays abound. Is that because family has played such an important role, for good and ill, in your life?

SIMON: Well, for one thing, it's a universal subject. For example, when *Come Blow Your Horn* was playing, the theater doorman, a black man in his sixties, was standing in the back of the theater, laughing his head off. I went over to him after the play and asked, "Why were you laughing so much?" He said, "That's my family up there." I don't write social and political plays, because I've always thought the family was the microcosm of what goes on in the world. I write about the small wars that eventually become the big wars. It's also what I'm most comfortable with. I am a middle-class person, I grew up in a middle-class neighborhood. I try now and then to get away from the family play, but it amazes me that I've spent the last thirty-one years writing plays primarily about either my family or families very close to it. Maybe the answer is that at some point along the way you discover what it is you do best, and writing about the family unit and its extensions is what I do best.

INTERVIEWER: Your introduction to the first published collection of your work is called "The Writer as Schizophrenic." The word *observer* comes up repeatedly in your conversation, your interviews, and, especially, in your plays. Have you always seen yourself as an outsider, an observer?

SIMON: Yes, that started very early, when my parents would take me to visit family. They'd offer me a cookie or a piece of fruit, but no one *spoke* to me, because they knew I had nothing to contribute. I wasn't offended. I just thought it was the accepted norm. And that led me to believe that I was somehow invisible. On radio shows like *The Shadow,* there *were* invisible people. And movies were coming out—*The Invisible Man,* with Claude Rains. To me, invisible seemed the greatest thing you could be! If I could have one wish, it was to be invisible. First of all, you could go to any baseball game you wanted to. Free. You could go into any girl's house and watch her get undressed! But it works another way too. It means there's no responsibility. You don't have to integrate, to contribute. This becomes a part of your personality.

INTERVIEWER: Does that detachment apply to your personal relationships as pervasively as to your work?

SIMON: I'm not quite sure who I am besides the writer. The writer is expressive, the other person can sit in a room and listen and not say anything. It's very hard for me to get those two people together. In the middle of a conversation or a confrontation, I can suddenly step outside it. It's like Jekyll turning into Mr. Hyde without the necessity of taking the potion. It's why the Eugene character speaks to the audience in the trilogy: because, in a sense, he is invisible. The other characters in the play don't see him talking to the audience. They go right about their business. As I wrote it, I thought: I'm now living my perfect dream—to be invisible.

INTERVIEWER: In *Barefoot in the Park,* Corie says, "Do you know what you are? You're a watcher. There are watchers in the world, and there are doers, and the watchers sit around watching the doers do."

SIMON: In all three of my marriages I've been accused of this separation. "You're not listening to me. You're not looking at me." When you asked about where I write, I said anywhere. I just stare into space. That's happened when I was talking to my wife. I could be looking at her and not thinking about what she's saying. It's rude. It's selfish, I guess. But it's what happens; some other thought has taken its place. One of the worst and most frightening examples of that was the first time I was ever on television. I went on the Johnny Carson show. I was standing behind that curtain, hearing them give my credits. Then they said, "And here he is, the prolific playwright, Neil Simon." I walked out and froze. I thought, my God, I'm out here, I've got to deliver something, I've got to be humorous, that's what they expect of me. I sat down opposite Johnny Carson, and he asked his first question, which was fairly lengthy. After the first two words I heard *nothing.* I only saw his lips moving. I said to myself, "I've got all this time not to do anything. In other words, while his lips are moving I'm all right." So, my mind just wandered. I was looking around, saying, "Well, forty million people are watching me, I wonder if my brother's going to watch this, what's he going to think of it?" When Johnny's lips stopped, I was on.

But I had no answer because I'd never heard the question. So, I said something like, "That reminds me of something, Johnny," and went into something completely irrelevant that fortunately was funny, and we just seemed to move on with the conversation. It happens while I'm speaking to students at a college or university. I'll be talking. I'll look over the room and see one face not interested, and I'm gone, I'm lost. I wish I were out there, sitting among the invisible, but I'm up there having to deliver. The demands of coming up with something every minute are very difficult. In a sense, being in this office, I am invisible because I can stop. When I'm writing, there's no pressure to come up with the next line. I always need that escape hatch, that place to go that's within myself. I've tried coming to terms with it. I feel, as long as it doesn't bother someone else, I'm happy with it. When it *does* bother someone else, then I'm in trouble.

INTERVIEWER: And your characters share this watcher/doer problem?

SIMON: Felix in *The Odd Couple* isn't a watcher—or a doer. He's stuck. He's reached a certain point in his life and developed no further. *Most* of my characters are people who are stuck and can't move. The grandmother in *Lost in Yonkers* has been stuck for the last seventy years. The mother in *Broadway Bound*—she's *really* stuck.

INTERVIEWER: I remember George in *Chapter Two* saying, "I'm stuck, Jennie...I'm just stuck someplace in my mind, and it's driving me crazy." Going back to *Barefoot in the Park,* Corie's pretty hard on your surrogate Neil when she tells him he's not a doer. But, come to think of it, what could be more venturesome and brave—or foolhardy—than the real Neil opening a play on Broadway and exposing it to the critics and the audience?

SIMON: It *is* the most frightening thing in the world—and it was almost a matter of life and death for Joan and me with *Come Blow Your Horn.* If it had failed I would have been forced to move to California and become a comedy writer in television. But I don't worry about it anymore, and I think not being fearful of what's going to happen has allowed me to write so much. If I *do* worry, I say I won't do the play, because that means I don't think it's that good.

INTERVIEWER: Is the opposite true? Can you anticipate a hit?

SIMON: I never think of the plays as being hits when I write them. Well, I thought *Rumors,* of all plays, would be a really good commercial comedy if I wrote it well. I thought *The Odd Couple* was a black comedy. I never thought it was going to be popular, ever.

INTERVIEWER: It's your most popular play, isn't it? All over the world.

SIMON: Yes. And I thought it was a grim, dark play about two lonely men. I thought *The Sunshine Boys* wouldn't be a popular play, but it was very well received. *Chapter Two* was another one I doubted, because when you touch on a character's guilt, you touch on the *audience's* guilt, and that makes them uncomfortable. Yet the play turned out to be very successful because it was a universal theme. *Lost in Yonkers* is an enormous success, but I thought I was writing the bleakest of plays. What I liked about it was that I thought it was Dickensian: two young boys left in the hands of dreadful people. What I was afraid of was that I would hear words like *melodrama.*

INTERVIEWER: You heard "Pulitzer Prize." There are several plays that don't seem to fit in your canon. In plays like *The Good Doctor, Rumors, Fools,* and *God's Favorite* you seem to have a different agenda, there's a different relationship between you and the play than the one you've described. Could that explain their lack of critical and popular success?

SIMON: I wrote *The Good Doctor* soon after I learned my wife had a year and a half to live. She didn't know that. On the advice of the doctors, I'd elected not to tell her, and I wanted to keep on working, so it would seem to her that everything was normal. I was reading Chekhov's short stories and decided, just for practice, to translate one of them into my own language, my own humor. I knew it was a diversion. After a performance, a woman grabbed me in the foyer and said, "This is not Neil Simon!" *Fools* was an experiment that didn't work. *God's Favorite* is an absurdist black comedy about Job that was written as an outcry of anger against Joan's death. My belief in God had vanished when this beautiful young girl was dying. I wasn't Archibald

MacLeish. I thought it would be pretentious for me to try to write something like a dramatic *J.B.* So, I wrote it as a black comedy, and it did help me get through that period. Sometimes you write a play just for the sake of working at it. It's my craft. I'm allowed to go in any direction I want. I hate being pushed into certain places. Walter Kerr once wrote that he thought I was successful because I didn't listen to what was in fashion in the theater and went my own way at my peril, and that sometimes I suffered for it, and at other times I broke through. With *Lost in Yonkers* I suddenly heard from critics who said, "This is a new voice for Neil Simon. We want you to go deeper and deeper into this area." At the same time other critics complained, "I don't like this as much. It's not as funny as the old plays." They wanted *Barefoot in the Park* and *The Odd Couple.* I could have spent my whole life writing the *Barefoot in the Park*s and *Odd Couple*s, which I certainly don't denigrate, because I love them—but, where would I have gone with my life? I would have been standing still, grinding out the same story time after time after time. What I've done, I think, is take the best of me and the best of my observations and try to deepen them to re-form them and re-flesh them. At some point along the way you discover what it is you do best. Recently I've been reading Samuel Beckett's biography. When he was about forty-four years old, he said he wanted to write monologue. It was his way of expressing himself to the world. *He* was shy, too. In a sense, I think many of my plays are dramatized monologues. It's like sitting around the fire and telling you the story of my life and my father and my mother and my cousins and my aunts. In *Lost in Yonkers* I know I'm *one* of those two boys, probably the younger one. Who that grandmother is, who Aunt Bella is, with her adolescent mind, I don't know.

INTERVIEWER: You seem to be saying that *Lost in Yonkers* is even less autobiographical than the Brighton Beach trilogy.

SIMON: I'd say *Lost in Yonkers* isn't autobiographical at all. You asked me earlier whether I write thematic plays. I don't, but I have a feeling that in *Lost in Yonkers* there was a theme within me that was crying to get out, a common denominator that got to everybody. In the last fifteen, twenty years, a phrase has come into prominence that didn't exist in my childhood: dysfunctional family. My mother's and father's constant breakups seemed to show little concern for my brother and me. It was like coming from *five* broken families. That pain lingers. Writing plays is a way of working out your life. That's why I can never conceive of stopping, because I would stop the investigation of who I am and what I am.

INTERVIEWER: You have the reputation of being a tireless, even an eager, rewriter. How much of the rewriting is done during the first drafts of the play, and how much do you rewrite after the play has gone into rehearsal?

SIMON: I would say that I do no fewer than three to four major rewrites on a play before we go into rehearsal. I write the play, put it aside, take it out six months later, read it. By then I've forgotten everything about the play. It's as though someone had sent it to me in the mail and I'm reading it for the first time. I can tell right away what I don't and do like. That becomes a very easy rewrite: you just get rid of the stuff you don't like. Then we start auditions for actors, so I keep hearing the words every day. After a while I can't stand some of them, and I start to rewrite, so, in later auditions, the actors get a better script to read. I finally say it's the last draft before we go into rehearsal, and we have a reading of the play in a room with just the producer, director, and a few of the other people who will work on the play, one month before rehearsal. At that reading we have the entire cast, so now I know what it's going to sound like. Based on that reading, I'll do another major rewrite. It's rare that I would ever do what they do in musicals: "Why don't we switch scene four and scene two?" I write in a linear way, so that everything falls apart if you take anything out. Sometimes, if even a few sentences come out of the play, something suffers for it later on. Once the play opens out of town, the most important rewriting begins, based on not only the audience's and the out-of-town critics' reactions, but the reactions of ourselves, the actors, and some people we've invited to see the play and comment. I also listen—if I can, to the audience's comments on the way out of the theater. That becomes harder now that I've lost my invisibility.

INTERVIEWER: How do you remain objective with all those voices in your ear?

SIMON: Mostly it's my own intuition. I bring in rewrites no one has asked for. I'll suddenly come in with five pages, and the director and the actors will say, "You didn't like the other stuff?" I'll say, "I think this is better." If you bring in seven pages, maybe three will work. That's a big percentage. You're way ahead of the game. An analogy for it would be if you were in college and took a test, and your grade came back. You got a sixty-three on the test, and they say, "Come back tomorrow. You'll be given exactly the same test. There'll be no new questions." Well, you're going to get an eighty-four on the second test. You'll have had chances to fix it. That's what happens to a play. Day by day, it gets better and better. In the case of *Jake's Women,* in the first production a couple of years ago, there were a lot of things wrong. It was miscast, I had a director I was unfamiliar with who didn't really understand my process. We opened with a play that was about a sixty-two on a possible grade of a hundred. I brought the play up to about a seventy-eight. As we got toward the end of the run, just prior to going to New York, I thought, you can't get by in New York with a seventy-eight. You need at least a ninety-six or ninety-seven. So, I said to everyone, let's just pull it. And we did. I thought it was dead forever, because I'd put so much into it and wasn't able to save it. Two years later I took another crack at it and did a major rewrite in which, as I've told you, I had Jake speak to the audience. The play took a whole new turn. I thought it was finally up in the ninety-percent bracket.

INTERVIEWER: If a play is truly flawed, how much can you do to improve it?

SIMON: Well, in the case of something like *The Gingerbread Lady,* which *was* a flawed play, the producer was going to put up a closing notice in Boston. Maureen Stapleton, who was starring in the play, came to me and said, "If you close this play I'll never speak to you again." She said, "This is a potentially wonderful play. It needs work but don't walk away from it!" I thought, what a reasonable thing to say, because all it amounted to was more of my time. The producer said he wanted to close, to save me "from the slings and arrows of the critics in New York." I said, "I can take the slings and arrows. I've had enough success up to now. I'll *learn* from this one." What finally made up my mind, after reading three terrible reviews in Boston, was, while waiting at the airport for my plane, I picked up *The Christian Science Monitor,* and the review was a letter addressed to me. It said, "Dear Neil Simon, I know you're probably going to want to close this play, but I beg of you, don't do it. This is potentially the best play you have written. You're going into a whole new genre, a whole new mode of writing. Don't abandon it." So, I called the producer and said, "Please don't close the play. Let's run in Boston and see what happens." Then, I didn't want to get on a plane and arrive in New York an hour later; I wanted a four-hour trip on a train, so I could start the rewrite. By the time I got to New York I had rewritten fifteen pages of the play. I stayed in New York for a week and came back with about thirty-five new pages. And we went to work. The play was never a major success, but we did have a year's run, and sold it to the movies. Maureen Stapleton won the Tony Award, and Marsha Mason, who played the lead in the film version, got an Oscar nomination. So, something good came out of persevering.

INTERVIEWER: Your plays have become darker in the last several years. Is this a sign of maturity or a wish to be taken seriously, since comedy generally isn't as highly regarded as so-called serious plays?

SIMON: Maybe the plays matured because *I* matured. I *do* want to be taken more seriously, yet I want to hear the laughter in the theater. The laughs are very often the same gratification to the audience as letting themselves cry. They're interchangeable emotions.

INTERVIEWER: Most of the darker plays take place in your childhood. Does that mean that your childhood was dark, or that your view of your childhood and perhaps of the world has darkened as you've matured?

SIMON: My view of my childhood was always dark, but my view of the world has darkened considerably. The darkness in my plays reflects the way the world is *now.* The darkness in the plays, strangely enough, seems more beautiful to me. I think anything that is truthful has beauty in it. Life without the dark times is unrealistic. I don't want to write unrealistically anymore.

INTERVIEWER: What do you consider your strongest suit as a writer? And what in your view is your weakest suit?

SIMON: I think my blue suit is my weakest.

INTERVIEWER: I knew it would come to this.

SIMON: I think my greatest weakness is that I can't write outside of my own experience. I'm not like Paddy Chayefsky, who could go off and do six months of research and then write something extremely believable. I'd *like* to write about Michelangelo, but I don't *know* Michelangelo. I don't know what his life was like. I wish I could extend myself, but I don't think that's going to happen. I might play around with it from time to time. Those are the ones that wind up in the drawer.

INTERVIEWER: If you ever have a fire sale of the contents of that drawer, call me. What would you say is your particular strength?

SIMON: I think it's construction. Maybe what I write is outmoded today, the "well-made play"—a play that tells you what the problem is, then shows you how it affects everybody, then resolves it. Resolution doesn't mean a happy ending—which I've been accused of. I don't think I write happy endings. Sometimes I have *hopeful* endings, sometimes optimistic ones. I try never to end the play with two people in each other's arms—unless it's a musical. When I was writing three-act plays, a producer told me the curtain should always come down on the beginning of the fourth act. A play should never really come to an end. The audience should leave saying, "What's going to happen to them now?" As the plays progressed, some people wanted darker endings. Some critics even said the ending of *Lost in Yonkers* wasn't dark enough. But I can't write a play as dark and bleak and wonderful as *A Streetcar Named Desire.* I fall in some gray area. There is so much comedy within the dramas or so much drama within the comedies.

INTERVIEWER: In her interview for *The Paris Review,* Dorothy Parker said she got her character names from the telephone book and obituary columns. Do you have a system for naming *your* characters?

SIMON: There was a time I used to take baseball players' names. The famous ones were too obvious, so you had to take names like Crespi. There was a guy named Creepy Crespi who played for the St. Louis Cardinals. Crespi would be a good name, although I've never used it.

INTERVIEWER: It's got a nice *k* sound in it.

SIMON: Yes. I try to name the character the way the character looks to me. I spend more time on the titles of plays than on the names of the characters. What I've tried to do over the years is take an expression from life that has a double entendre in it, for example, the musical *Promises, Promises,* so that every time people speak the words it sounds like they're talking about your play. Or *The Odd Couple*—people sometimes say, "They're sort of an odd couple." If you mention an odd couple now, you think of the play. I've seen the words maybe a thousand times in newspapers since, and it seems as if I originated the term, which, of course, I didn't. *Come Blow Your Horn* comes from the nursery rhyme. *Barefoot in the Park* came from what the play was about. There's a line in the play that comes from my life, when Joan used to say to me, "Stop being a fuddy-duddy. Let's go to Washington Square Park and walk barefoot in the grass." *Chapter Two* was, literally, the second chapter of my life, after my wife Joan died, and I married Marsha. *Prisoner of Second Avenue* was a good title for a play about a man who loses his job and is left to live in that little apartment on Second Avenue while his wife goes to work. He has nothing to do but walk around the room till he knows exactly how many feet each side is— so he's literally a prisoner. *The Gingerbread Lady* is a bad title. I liked the title and then had to make up a phrase about the gingerbread lady to make it fit. The film title was better: *Only When I Laugh. The Star-Spangled Girl* was a better title than a play. I liked *Last of the Red Hot Lovers.* It seemed familiar. It comes from Sophie Tucker's slogan, "Last of the Red Hot Mamas." *Lost in Yonkers*—I love the word Yonkers, and I wanted to put the play in a specific place. I said to myself, "*What* in Yonkers?" These boys are lost, Bella is lost, this family is *all* lost...in Yonkers. *Jake's Women* is literally about a man named Jake and three women. Again, there's the *k* sound in Jake.

INTERVIEWER: Let's talk about stage directors. How much can a director help a play? Or, conversely, hurt it?

SIMON: Well, in the early days, I worked principally with Mike Nichols. He was after me day and night. "This scene isn't good enough. Work on this. Fix this." He'd call me at two or three in the morning, to the point where I'd say, "Mike, give me a chance, leave me alone. You're on my back all the time." But I always knew he was right. I wasn't that experienced a playwright. The way I work now—with Gene Saks—the conversation is generally short. He might say to me, "There's something wrong with this scene." I'll say, "I know what you mean. Let me go home and work on it." I'm much less influenced by the director now than I was before. I depend on the director in terms of *interpretation* of the play. With the Brighton Beach trilogy and *Lost in Yonkers*, I watched with clenched fists and teeth as Gene was directing, thinking, that's wrong, it's all wrong what he's doing. Then, suddenly, I *saw* what he was doing, and said, "Oh God! He has to go step by step to get to this place, trying all his things, the way *I* would try them at the writer's table."

INTERVIEWER: How much do actors influence you? Is it ever the case that the personality of an actor influences you to remold the character to the actor, playing into what you now perceive to be the actor's strength?

SIMON: I might do that. But what I try to do in terms of rewriting is always to benefit the *character*, not the actor. There's something an actor sometimes says that drives me crazy: "I would never do that." I say, you're *not* doing this, the *character* is. The one thing I almost always look for is the best actor, not the funniest actor. I rarely, rarely cast a comedian in a play. The best comedian I ever had in a play was George C. Scott. He was funnier than anybody in the third act of *Plaza Suite* because he was playing King Lear. He knew the essence of comedy is not to play "funny." I remember, at the first reading of *Barefoot in the Park*, the whole cast was laughing at every line in the play. When we finished the reading, Mike Nichols said, "Now forget it's a comedy. From here on we're playing *Hamlet*."

INTERVIEWER: I notice in the printed plays that you use ellipses, italics, and all caps. I assume the ellipses are meant to tell the actors when you want them to pause, the italics are meant to give emphasis, and that all caps ask for added emphasis, even volume.

SIMON: Yes. They are a first indication to the actor and the director. Some of those emphases change enormously in the rehearsal period, but I also have to worry about what's going to be done in stock and amateur and European productions, so I hope it's a guide to what I meant. *The Prisoner of Second Avenue* opens in the dark. All we see is a cigarette, as Mel Edison comes in. The part was played by Peter Falk. He sat down on the sofa, took a puff of the cigarette, and in the dark we heard, "Aaaahhhhhhhh." I don't know how you're going to be able to spell that, but it's got a lot of *h*s in it—a *lot* of them. It got a huge laugh because the audience heard two thousand years of suffering in that "Aaaahhhhhhhh." When Peter left and other actors played the part, they would go, "Ahh." There weren't enough *h*s, and the line wasn't funny. People tell me that when they study my work in acting class, the teachers have to give them the sounds, the nuances, the way the lines are said. I guess Shakespeare can be said a thousand different ways, but in certain kinds of lines—for example, that run on "Ho" in *Biloxi Blues*—everything depends on the timing of it. I've always considered all of this a form of music. I wish I could write tempo directions, like *allegro* and *adagio*. That's why I put dots between words or underline certain words, to try to convey the sense of music, dynamics, and rhythm.

INTERVIEWER: Do the critics ever help you, shedding light on your work, regardless of whether they're praising or damning it?

SIMON: Walter Kerr gave me one of the best pieces of criticism I've ever had. In the first line of his review of *The Star-Spangled Girl*, he said, "Neil Simon didn't have an idea for a play this year, but he wrote it anyway." That was exactly what had happened. Elliot Norton was very helpful to me in Boston with *The Odd Couple*. His title of the opening night review was, "Oh, for a Third Act." He wasn't going to waste his time telling everyone how good the first two acts were. His job, he felt, was to make me make the third act better. And his suggestion to me was to bring back the Pigeon sisters. I said, "Good idea," brought back the Pigeon sisters, and the play worked. More important than the reviews, it's the audience that tells you whether or not you've succeeded. A week prior to the opening of the play you know if it's going to work or not. If ninety percent of the critics say it doesn't work, well, you already knew that without having to read the reviews. On the other hand, the opening night of *Little Me,* Bob Fosse and I were standing in the back of the theater. The producers had allowed a black-tie audience to come from a dinner to the theater. They'd eaten, they'd had drinks, they all knew each other—that's the worst audience you can get. About three-quarters of the way through the first act, a man got up, so drunk he could hardly walk, and staggered up the aisle looking for the men's room. As he passed Bob and me, he said, "This is the worst piece of crap I've seen since *My Fair Lady!*" Go figure out what *that* means.

INTERVIEWER: Maybe the reason comedies like *Barefoot in the Park, The Odd Couple,* and *The Sunshine Boys* are sometimes underrated is quite simply that the audience is laughing at them—rather than worrying, weeping, learning—or doing any of the other virtuous things an audience is reputed to be doing at a drama. However, I think most writers would agree that it is relatively easy to make people cry and very, very hard to make them laugh.

SIMON: Billy Wilder, whom I respect enormously, once confided in me, "Drama's a lot easier than comedy." He found some of the brilliant dramas he wrote, like *Sunset Boulevard,* much easier to write than the comedies. Comedies are relentless, especially a farce like *Some Like It Hot. Rumors* was the most difficult play I ever wrote because not only did every moment of that play have to further the story, complicate it, and keep the characters in motion—*literal* motion, swinging in and out of doors—but the audience had to laugh at every *attempt* at humor. You don't have five minutes where two people can sit on a sofa and just say, "What am I doing with my life, Jack? Am I crazy? Why don't I get out of this?" You can do that in a drama. You can't do it in a farce.

INTERVIEWER: Do you make it a point to see the plays of other playwrights?

SIMON: When I was in my late teens and early twenties, I went to the theater a lot. There was always a Tennessee Williams play to see or a great English play. It was such an education. I learned more from bad plays than from good ones. Good plays are a mystery. You don't know what it is that the playwright did right. More often than not you see where a work fails. One of the things I found interesting was that a lot of comedy came from drunks on the stage. If a character was drunk he was funny. I thought, wouldn't it be great to write characters who are as funny as drunks, but are not drunk. In other words, bring out the *outrageousness* of them, and the only way you can do that is to put them in such a tight corner that they have to say what's really on their minds. That's where the humor comes from.

INTERVIEWER: Are you a good audience for other people's work? Do you laugh in the theater? I know some writers who are just not good audiences. Would you call yourself a good audience?

SIMON: I'd call myself a *great* audience. I'm appreciative of good work, no matter what its form—comedy, drama, musical. I saw *Amadeus* four times. *A Streetcar Named Desire* I could see over and over. When I'm in England I go to some of the most esoteric English plays, plays that never even come over here, and I'm just amazed at them. I've recently caught up with the works of Joe Orton. I love Tom Stoppard's plays *Jumpers* and *Travesties,* and I admire the work of Peter Shaffer. If it's good theater, yes, I'm the best audience. I'm out there screaming.

INTERVIEWER: Comedy has changed in a very noticeable way in the last thirty years. Subjects and language that were taboo are now almost obligatory. Do you think that indicates progress?

SIMON: I like the fact that one can touch on subjects one wouldn't have dealt with in years gone by. The things that Lenny Bruce got arrested for you can find on any cable station today. Television situation comedy doesn't seem as funny to me as what Chaplin and Buster Keaton did without words. There are a few good comedians, but by and large I don't think comedy is a lot better today.

INTERVIEWER: You seem to exercise a certain constraint over the language of your plays. Even *Biloxi Blues* doesn't use the kind of profanity and obscenity I remember from my days at that same airfield.

SIMON: I think to say *fuck* once in an entire play is much more shocking than to say it sixty times. Four of the last five plays I've written took place in the thirties and forties, when profanity wasn't used onstage—or in the home. The fifth play, *Rumors,* is contemporary, and it's *filled* with profanity. But I don't need profanity. I love language, and I'd rather find more interesting ways to use it than take the easy way out.

INTERVIEWER: Every playwright has fingerprints. You've mentioned thinking of your plays in musical terms, and one fingerprint of yours seems to be the "aria." At a certain point in almost every one of your plays a character in extremis launches into an extended list of all the catastrophes that are happening to him. In *Come Blow Your Horn,* Alan says, "You're using my barber, my restaurants, my ticket broker, my apartment, and my socks. How's it going, kid? Am I having fun?" In *Plaza Suite* the father explodes, "You can take all the Eislers, all the hors d'oeuvres and go to Central Park and have an eight-thousand-dollar picnic! I'm going down to the Oak Room with my broken arm, with my drenched, rented, ripped suit and I'm going to get blind!" Are you aware of doing that?

SIMON: Yes, it's a fingerprint. You'll notice that those arias always come near the end of the play. The character has reached the point where he can't contain himself anymore, and everything comes spurting out, like a waterfall, a cascade of irritations. Just mentioning one of them wouldn't be funny, but to mention *all* the irritations wraps up a man's life in one paragraph.

INTERVIEWER: The words you use to describe your comedy are words that are generally associated not with comedy at all, but with tragedy. You've talked about catharsis and your characters exploding when they can't bear the pain anymore.

SIMON: Yes. That's why I don't find television comedy very funny—because it's hardly ever about anything important. I think the weight-icr comedy is, the funnier it is. To me, Chaplin's films are master-pieces. Remember him running after a truck with the red warning flag that has fallen off it?

INTERVIEWER: And he doesn't see hundreds of rioting radicals falling enthusiastically in behind him...

SIMON: So he gets busted and goes to jail as their leader.

INTERVIEWER: Maybe when the record is written a hundred years from now it will turn out that all our comedy writers, from Chaplin and Keaton to you and Woody Allen, were writing tragedies. What's the cliché? Comedy is tragedy plus time. How fine is the line between tragedy and comedy?

SIMON: It's almost invisible. I think Mel Brooks is one of the funniest people in the world, but when he makes a picture like *Spaceballs*, he's telling us, "This is foolishness. No one is in danger," so the audience knows it's too inconsequential to laugh at. But when he does a picture like *High Anxiety* or *Young Frankenstein* there's something at stake. He's taken a frightening idea and twisted it, so we're able to laugh at it.

INTERVIEWER: Here comes a difficult question...

SIMON: As long as it doesn't have to do with math.

INTERVIEWER: I don't know a writer who wouldn't say that—or a musician who isn't *good* at math. Because music is mathematical, I guess.

SIMON: But so are plays. As surely as two plus two is four, the things you write in the play must add up to some kind of logical figure. In *Broadway Bound,* when Stan is teaching Eugene the craft of comedy, Eugene says, "It's just a comedy sketch. Does it have to be so logical? We're not drawing the plans for the Suez Canal," and Stan says, "Yes we are. It's not funny if it's not believable."

INTERVIEWER: Well, now that we've covered math and logic, here's the difficult question. You write repeatedly about an uptight man and a liberating woman: is that because it's a reflection of your relationship with the women in your life—or because you feel it's a common and important theme?

SIMON: The answer is quite simple. It's because I'm an uptight man who's been married to three liberated women. Joan was the first liberated woman I ever met and the most unconventional. She introduced me to more ways of looking at life than I'd ever dreamed of. She was more adventuresome than I'd ever been. She would jump from a plane in a parachute, and I'm the uptight man who would say, "You're crazy." Marsha was the same way. She was a feminist and had me marching in parades with a flag, yelling for women's rights. It's not that I didn't believe in women's rights, but I'm not an activist. Diane is an environmentalist, an ecologist, and also a fighter for the rights of women. Go over all the plays. With the exception of *The Odd Couple* and *The Sunshine Boys*, you'll find that the women are not only stronger but more interesting characters than the men. Again, the men are usually the Greek chorus. That's me sitting there, little Neil, born Marvin, observing the world—verbally, from a very safe place, which is what the man does in *Barefoot in the Park*, which is what he does in *Chapter Two*, in almost every play.

INTERVIEWER: In the theater, in films, rugged men usually liberate unfulfilled women. From what you say, your plays reverse that convention.

SIMON: Yes. I never feel threatened by women. I have enormous respect for them. I would also usually rather be with them than with men. I'm not much of a male bonder. I have male friends, obviously. I belong to tennis clubs. But in a social situation, I'd generally rather talk to a woman because it's like a play: you're getting the opposite point of view. You talk to a man, you're getting your own point of view. It becomes redundant. But when you're with a woman, that's when the sparks fly, that's when it's most interesting.

INTERVIEWER: Plays these days are usually in two acts rather than three, and you are using more and shorter scenes. Is that the result of changes in stage technology? Are you being influenced by film?

SIMON: I think I've been influenced by films, which have been influenced by television and commercials. Today you can see a one-minute commercial with about forty setups in it. There's a need to pace things differently because the audience's attention span has grown shorter. *Biloxi Blues* was the first major example of that because I had fourteen set changes. What also helped speed things along was that I started writing plays with larger casts, so there were many more entrances and exits. Also, having a narrator makes big time leaps possible. I *am* influenced by new technologies and techniques, but that doesn't mean I'm following the fashions. It just means that I'm moving to another phase in my career—I'm becoming less literal and more abstract.

INTERVIEWER: You've mentioned finding your characters waiting for you every time you walk into your office. Dickens complained that he hated to end his books because he didn't want to say good-bye to the characters he'd been living with.

SIMON: That's why I don't go back to see my plays again, because they belong to someone else—to the actors and the audience. That process happens in a series of events. First, you finish writing the play, and everyone reads it. Then you go into rehearsal. Day by day, it slowly becomes the director's and the actors'. They're still asking me questions. I'm still participating. I'm still the father of these children. They get onstage, and soon the play is finished. They no longer need me! I feel locked out, I'm not part of them. After the play opens, I'm almost embarrassed to go backstage, because it's the place that belongs to the director and the actors. I'm just the man who introduced the characters to them. It's a very, very sad feeling for me. What happens eventually—it may sound cold—is that I disown them. I have no interest in seeing the plays again. In fact, it's painful, especially when a play has run for a long time and new actors have come in to replace the original cast. When I walk into that theater, it's as if I were picking up my family album, and turning the pages to see my mother and father and aunt and cousins—and I say, "This isn't my family!" So, you give it up and go on to the next play.

INTERVIEWER: And the next. And the next.

SIMON: Every time I write a play it's the beginning of a new life for me. Today as I listen to you read excerpts from these plays and talk about them, it makes me feel nostalgic about how wonderful those days were—but I'm enjoying *these* days of writing, even though I see that the sun is setting.

—JAMES LIPTON
Winter, 1992

EDWARD ALBEE

Courtesy of Edward Albee

Edward Albee was born March 12, 1928, probably in Virginia, and was adopted two weeks later by Reed and Frances Albee, his biological parents having given him up. He grew up amid the splendor of the Albees' Larchmont, New York, home, where servants, tutors, and chauffeured limousines were fixtures of daily life. His relationship with his adoptive mother soured as he grew older, and eventually he was compelled to leave home for good. In time he would be removed from his mother's will.

Albee attended a number of boarding schools and studied for a year and a half at Trinity College, in Hartford, Connecticut, before briefly returning home and finally moving to New York City in 1950. There he worked at a number of increasingly frustrating odd jobs until he was thirty, when he quit his position as a messenger boy for Western Union and wrote his first play, *The Zoo Story* (1958), in just three weeks. The one-act play premiered in Berlin in 1959 and was produced four months later in New York on a double bill with Samuel Beckett's *Krapp's Last Tape* (1958).

In 1962, having written three more short works, Albee wrote his first full-length play, *Who's Afraid of Virginia Woolf?* which received the New York Drama Critics' Circle Award and two Tony Awards, and played for 644 performances on Broadway. It was made into a successful movie by Mike Nichols in 1966, and while the screenplay was not credited to Albee, his text remained virtually intact in the film. Albee's stage adaptations of other authors' works, including Carson McCullers's *The Ballad of the Sad Café* (1963) and James Purdy's *Malcolm* (1966), were less successful.

Albee received a Pulitzer Prize in 1967 for his original play *A Delicate Balance* (1966). A second, for *Seascape,* was awarded in 1975. He received honorary doctoral degrees from Emerson College (1967) and his alma mater, Trinity College (1974). Following a series of critically unsuccessful plays in the 1980s, Albee wrote the acclaimed *Three Tall Women* (1991), his first overtly autobiographical work, whose main character he based on his mother. It earned him his third Pulitzer and the New York Drama Critics' Circle Award.

———

The interview happened on a scalding, soggy-aired Fourth of July in a sunny room in Albee's small, attractive country house in Montauk, Long Island. By comparison with his luxuriously appointed house in New York City's Greenwich Village, the country place is dramatically modest. With the exception of a handsome, newly built tennis court (in which the playwright takes a disarmingly childlike pleasure and pride), and an incongruously grand Henry Moore sculpture situated high on a landscaped terrace that commands a startling view of the sea, the simplicity of the place leaves one with the curious impression that news of the personal wealth his work has brought has not quite reached the playwright in residence at Montauk. Still, it is in his country house that he generally seems most at ease, natural, at home.

Albee was dressed with a mildly ungroomed informality. He was as yet unshaved for the day, and his neo-Edwardian haircut was damply askew. He appeared, as the climate of the afternoon demanded, somewhat uncomfortable.

Tobias:

(Recollection) The cat that I had.

Agnes (~~Someone~~):

Hm?

Tobias:

The cat that I had....when I was --well, a year or so before I <u>met</u> you. She was very old: I'd had her since I was **very young**; she must have been fifteen, or more. An alley cat. She didn't like people very much, I think; at least she'd ....<u>absent</u> herself. She wouldn't run, or hide; she wasn't skittish, or, or hysterical. When people came....she'd....pick up and walk away. She liked <u>me</u>: or, rather, when I was alone with her I could see she was content: she'd sit on my lap, or near me, or on the basin when I shaved, or sleep on my clothes if I left them somewhere. She was....content, I guess; I don't know if she was happy, but she was content. We'd not had other animals --my family, and I'd taken her to college with me, and into the city, and she was....well, as much a fixture as....my good gold watch, my favorite bathrobe. She was <u>there</u>. We didn't play, you understand: she was getting on, and she'd never been....frisky --like some-- and half the time I doubt I knew she was around --consciously. It was her absence I would have noticed. **AND I LIKED HER VERY MUCH.**

Agnes (~~Someone~~):

Yes.

Tobias:

And how **the thing** happened I don't really know. She....one day she....well, one day I realized she no longer liked me. No, that's not right: one day I **realized** realized she **must have** stopped liking me some time before. I was very busy --very social, I guess, away weekends, nights out, parties where I lived, lots of people in....I spent less time alone; I used my place less than I just lived in it. But one evening I <u>was</u> alone, home, and I was suddenly aware of her absence, not **just** that she wasn't in the room with me, but that she hadn't been,

A manuscript page from A Delicate Balance.

The interviewer and subject have been both friends and composer-writer collaborators for about eighteen years. But Albee's barbed, poised, and elegantly guarded public press style took over after the phrasing of the first question—though perhaps it was intermittently penetrated during the course of the talk.

INTERVIEWER: One of your most recent plays was an adaptation of James Purdy's novel *Malcolm*. It had as close to 100 percent bad notices as a play could get. The resultant commercial catastrophe and quick closing of the play apart, how does this affect your own feeling about the piece itself?

ALBEE: I see you're starting with the hits. Well, I retain for all my plays, I suppose, a certain amount of enthusiasm. I don't feel intimidated either by the unanimously bad press that *Malcolm* got, or the unanimously good press that some of the other plays have received. I haven't changed my feeling about *Malcolm*. I liked doing the adaptation of Purdy's book. I had a number of quarrels with the production, but then I usually end up with quarrels about all of my plays. With the possible exception of the little play *The Sandbox*, which takes thirteen minutes to perform, I don't think anything I've done has worked out to perfection.

INTERVIEWER: While it doesn't necessarily change your feeling, does the unanimously bad critical response open questions in your mind?

ALBEE: I imagine that if we had a college of criticism in this country whose opinions more closely approximated the value of the works of art inspected, it might; but as often as not, I find relatively little relationship between the work of art and the immediate critical response it gets. Every writer's got to pay some attention, I suppose, to what his critics say because theirs is a reflection of what the audience feels about his work. And a playwright, especially a playwright whose work deals very directly with an audience, perhaps he should pay some attention to the nature of the audience response—not necessarily to learn anything about his craft, but as often as not merely to find out about the temper of the time, what is being tolerated, what is being permitted.

INTERVIEWER: Regarding adaptations in general, can you think of any by American playwrights that you admire at all?

ALBEE: No, I can't think of any that I admire. I've done adaptations for two reasons; first, to examine the entire problem of adaptation—to see what it felt like; and second, because I admired those two books—*The Ballad of the Sad Café* and *Malcolm*—very much and thought they belonged on the stage; I wanted to see them on the stage, and felt more confident, perhaps incorrectly, in my own ability to put them on the stage than in most adaptors'.

INTERVIEWER: One of the local reviewers, after *Malcolm* came out, referred to it as Edward Albee's "play of the year," rather as if to suggest that this is a conscious goal you've set for yourself, to have a play ready every year.

ALBEE: Do you remember the Thurber cartoon of the man looking at his police dog and saying, "If you're a police dog, where's your badge?" It's the function of a playwright to write. Some playwrights write a large number of plays, some write a small number. I don't set out to write a play a year. Sometimes, I've written two plays a year. There was a period of a year and a half when I only wrote half a play. If it depresses some critics that I seem prolific, well, that's their problem as much as mine. There's always the danger that there are so damn many things that a playwright can examine in this society of ours—things that have less to do with his artistic work than have to do with the critical and aesthetic environment—that perhaps he does have to worry about whether or not he is writing too fast. But then also, perhaps he should worry about getting as many plays on as possible before the inevitable ax falls.

INTERVIEWER: What do you mean by the inevitable ax?

ALBEE: If you examine the history of any playwright of the past twenty-five or thirty years—I'm not talking about the comedy boys, I'm talking about the more serious writers—it seems inevitable that almost everyone has been encouraged until the critics feel that they have built them up beyond the point where they can control them; then it's time to knock them down again. And a rather ugly thing starts happening: the playwright finds himself knocked down for works that quite often are just as good or better than the works he's been praised for previously. And a lot of playwrights become confused by this and they start doing imitations of what they've done before, or they try to do something entirely different, in which case they get accused by the same critics of not doing what they *used* to do so well.

INTERVIEWER: So, it's a matter of not being able to win either way.

ALBEE: Actually, the final evaluation of a play has nothing to do with immediate audience or critical response. The playwright, along with any writer, composer, painter in this society, has got to have a terribly private view of his own value, of his own work. He's got to listen to his own voice primarily. He's got to watch out for fads, for what might be called the critical aesthetics.

INTERVIEWER: Why do you think the reviews were so lacerating against *Malcolm*—a play that might simply have been dismissed as not being very good.

ALBEE: It seemed to me the critics loathed something. Now whether they loathed something above and beyond the play itself, it's rather dangerous for me to say. I think it's for the critics to decide whether or not their loathing of the play is based on something other than the play's merits or demerits. They must search their own souls, or whatever.

INTERVIEWER: When you say that the play was badly produced—

ALBEE: I didn't like the way it was directed particularly. It was the one play of mine—of all of them—that got completely out of my hands. I let the director take over and dictate the way things should be done. I did it as an experiment.

INTERVIEWER: What do you mean as an experiment?

ALBEE: As a playwright, one has to make the experiment finally to see whether there's anything in this notion that a director can contribute creatively, as opposed to interpretively.

INTERVIEWER: Do you believe that a director has any creative vitality of his own?

ALBEE: Well, that's a very "iffy" question, as President Roosevelt used to say. I imagine as an axiom you could say that the better the play the less "creativity" the director need exert.

INTERVIEWER: Have you ever had the experience of finding out that the director's way was a certain enlightenment?

ALBEE: I can't answer that honestly, because something very curious happens. In rehearsals I get so completely wrapped up with the reality that's occurring onstage that by the time the play has opened I'm not usually quite as aware of the distinctions between what I'd intended and the result. There are many ways of getting the same result.

INTERVIEWER: Well, you talk about keeping complete control of your plays. Let's say that you'd envisioned in your own mind a certain scene being done a certain way.

ALBEE: I'm not terribly concerned about which characters are standing on the right-hand side of the stage.

INTERVIEWER: That's not the point I'm trying to make. In the preparation of the early Kazan-Williams successes, Williams was in constant conflict with Kazan, and yet Kazan would come up with the one thing that would finally make the play work.

ALBEE: Do we know that it was better than Williams's original idea?

INTERVIEWER: According to his own alleged view of it, yes.

ALBEE: Some writers' view of things depends upon the success of the final result. I'd rather stand or fall on my own concepts. But there is a fine line to be drawn between pointing up something or distorting it. And one has always got to be terribly careful, since the theater is made up of a whole bunch of prima donnas, not to let the distortions occur. I've seen an awful lot of plays that I'd read before they were put into production and been shocked by what's happened to them. In the attempt to make them straightforward and commercially successful, a lot of things go out the window. I'm just saying that in the theater, which is a sort of jungle, one does have to be a little bit careful. One mustn't be so rigid or egotistical to think that every comma is sacrosanct. But at the same time there is the danger of losing control and finding that somebody else has opened a play and not you.

INTERVIEWER: Why did you decide to become a playwright? You wrote poems without notable success, and then suddenly decided to write a play, *The Zoo Story.*

ALBEE: Well, when I was six years old I decided not that I was *going* to be, but with my usual modesty, that I *was* a writer. So I started writing poetry when I was six and stopped when I was twenty-six because it was getting a little better, but not terribly much. When I was fifteen I wrote seven hundred pages of an incredibly bad novel—it's a very funny book I still like a lot. Then, when I was nineteen I wrote a couple hundred pages of another novel, which wasn't very good either. I was still determined to be a writer. And since I was a writer, and here I was thirty years old and I wasn't a very good poet and I wasn't a very good novelist, I thought I would try writing a play, which seems to have worked out a little better.

INTERVIEWER: With regard to *Zoo Story*—was its skill and power and subsequent success a surprise and revelation to you?

ALBEE: A lot interests me—but nothing surprises me particularly. Not that I took it for granted that it was going to be skillful and powerful. I'm not making any judgment about the excellence or lack of it in the play. But it did not come as a *surprise* to me that I'd written it. You must remember I've been watching and listening to a great number of people for a long time. Absorbing things, I suppose. My only reaction was, "Aha! So this is the way it's going to be, is it?" That was my reaction.

INTERVIEWER: The biggest news about you at the moment, I expect, would be the success of the film *Virginia Woolf.* The Production Code approval came hard, but apparently you approved of it yourself.

ALBEE: When the play was sold to the movies I was rather apprehensive of what would happen. I assumed they would put Doris Day in it, and maybe Rock Hudson. And I was even a little apprehensive about the actual casting. Especially Elizabeth Taylor. I wasn't apprehensive about the idea of Richard Burton being in the film, but it did seem to be a little odd that Elizabeth Taylor, who is in her early thirties, would be playing a fifty-two-year-old woman.

INTERVIEWER: At one time you were apprehensive about Mike Nichols, the director.

ALBEE: I was curious as to why they chose a man who'd never made a film before and had made his reputation directing farces on Broadway, why they chose *him* as a director to turn a serious play into a movie. I think I learned the answer: being innocent to the medium he doesn't know how to make the usual mistakes. I had a number of other reasons for apprehension. One always knows what is done to a script when it goes to Hollywood. When I saw the film in Hollywood about two or three months before it was released, I was startled, and enormously taken with the picture, partially through relief I imagine. But more than that, I discovered that no screenplay had been written, that the play was there almost word for word. A few cuts here and there. A few oversimplifications.

INTERVIEWER: Oversimplifications?

ALBEE: Yes, I'll go into those in a minute. Ernest Lehman, who is credited with the screenplay, did write about twenty-five words. I thought they were absolutely terrible. So really there wasn't a screenplay, and that delighted me. It was a third of the battle, as far as I was concerned. So that was my first delight—that the play was photographed word for word. I'm not saying it was photographed action for action. The camera didn't stay thirty-five feet from the actors and it wasn't done in one set, it moved around a good deal. It behaves and acts very much like a film. In fact, it *is* a film. There are some shots, close-ups, lots of things you can't do on the stage. Then my second delight, after finding that the play was intact, was to appreciate that the director, Mike Nichols, understood not only the play, my intentions (pretty much, again with a couple of oversimplifications), but also seemed to understand the use of the camera and the film medium, all this in his first time around. Third, I was happy that Elizabeth Taylor was quite capable of casting off the beautiful young woman image and doing something much more than she usually does in films. And the rest of the cast was more or less fine too, Dennis and Segal. I have a few quarrels with their interpretations, but they're so minor compared to what could have happened. I found that it made an awfully good picture.

INTERVIEWER: The play as a film seems to be generally better understood by film reviewers than it was by drama critics. Is it possible that these oversimplifications you're talking about, that you blame Mike Nichols for, or somebody, are responsible for the fact that the play comes over more clearly?

ALBEE: I suppose if you simplify things, it's going to make it easier to understand. But without placing blame, I'd say there *was* an oversimplification, which I regret to a certain extent. For example, whenever something occurs in the play on both an emotional and intellectual level, I find in the film that only the emotional aspect shows through. The intellectual underpinning isn't as clear. In the film I found that in the love-hate games that George and Martha play, their intellectual enjoyment of each other's prowess doesn't show through anywhere nearly as strongly as it did in the play. Quite often, and I suppose in most of my plays, people are doing things on two or three levels at the same time. From time to time in the movie of *Who's Afraid of Virginia Woolf?* I found that a level or two had vanished. At the end of the film, for example, with the revelation about the nonexistent child and its destruction, the intellectual importance of the fiction isn't made quite as clearly as it could be. In the film it's nowhere near as important as the *emotional* importance to the characters. In my view, the two of them have got to go hand in hand. But this is quibbling, you see. It's a really very good film. There are a few things that I wish hadn't happened— that enormous error in accepting somebody's stupid idea of taking the action away from the house to the roadhouse. That's the one area of the film where somebody decided to broaden it out for film terms. Yet it was the one part of the film, curiously enough, that all the film critics thought was the most stagy.

INTERVIEWER: Incidentally, when did the title "Who's Afraid of Virginia Woolf?" occur to you?

ALBEE: There was a saloon—it's changed its name now—on Tenth Street, between Greenwich Avenue and Waverly Place, that was called something at one time, now called something else, and they had a big mirror on the downstairs bar in this saloon where people used to scrawl graffiti. At one point back in about 1953, 1954 I think it was— long before any of us started doing much of anything—I was in there having a beer one night, and I saw "Who's Afraid of Virginia Woolf?" scrawled in soap, I suppose, on this mirror. When I started to write the play it cropped up in my mind again. And of course, who's afraid of Virginia Woolf means who's afraid of the big *bad* wolf . . . who's afraid of living life without false illusions. And it did strike me as being a rather typical university, intellectual joke.

INTERVIEWER: With the filming of *Who's Afraid of Virginia Woolf?* the oft-repeated evaluation of it as a play about four homosexuals who are, for the sake of convention, disguised as heterosexuals recurs. I cannot recall any public statement or comment being made by you on this interpretation of the play.

ALBEE: Indeed it is true that a number of the movie critics of *Who's Afraid of Virginia Woolf?* have repeated the speculation that the play was written about four homosexuals disguised as heterosexual men and women. This comment first appeared around the time the play was produced. I was fascinated by it. I suppose what disturbed me about it was twofold: first, nobody has ever bothered to ask *me* whether it was true; second, the critics and columnists made no attempt to document the assertion from the text of the play. The facts are simple: *Who's Afraid of Virginia Woolf?* was written about two heterosexual couples. If I had wanted to write a play about four homosexuals, I would have done so. Parenthetically, it is interesting that when the film critic of

Newsweek stated that he understood the play to have been written about four homosexuals, I had a letter written to him suggesting he check his information before printing such speculations. He replied, saying, in effect, two things: first, that we all know that a critic is a far better judge of an author's intention than the author; second, that seeing the play as being about four homosexuals was the only way that he could live with the play, meaning that he could not accept it as a valid examination of heterosexual life. Well, I'm sure that all the actresses from Uta Hagen to Elizabeth Taylor who've played the role of Martha would be absolutely astonished to learn they've been playing men.

I think it is the responsibility of critics to rely less strenuously on, to use a Hollywood phrase, "what they can live with," and more on an examination of the works of art from an aesthetic and clinical point of view. I would be fascinated to read an intelligent paper documenting from the text that *Who's Afraid of Virginia Woolf?* is a play written about four homosexuals. It might instruct me about the deep slag pits of my subconscious.

I believe it was Leslie Fiedler, in an article in *Partisan Review,* who commented that if indeed *Who's Afraid of Virginia Woolf?* did deal with four disguised homosexuals, the "shock of recognition" on the part of the public is an enormously interesting commentary on the public. To put it most briefly, *Who's Afraid of Virginia Woolf?* was *not* written about four homosexuals. One might make one more point: had *Who's Afraid of Virginia Woolf?* been a play about four homosexuals disguised as heterosexuals, the only valid standard of criticism which could be employed would be whether such license of composite characterization was destructive to the validity of the work of art. Again we come to the question of the critics' responsibility to discuss the work of art not on arbitrary Freudian terms, but on aesthetic ones. Only the most callow or insecure or downright stupid critic would fault Proust's work, for example, for the transposition that he made of characters' sexes. It would be rather like faulting Michelangelo's sculptures of the male figure because of that artist's reputed leanings. So, if a play should appear, next year, say, which the critics in their wisdom see as a disguised homosexual piece, let them remember that the ultimate judgment of a work of art, whether it be a masterpiece or a lesser event, must be solely in terms of its artistic success and not on Freudian guesswork.

INTERVIEWER: It's been said by certain critics that your plays gener ally contain no theme. Others say that you've begun to wear the same theme thin; and still others say that with each play you bravely attack a new theme.

ALBEE: I go up to my room about three or four months out of the year and I write. I don't pay much attention to how the plays relate themat- ically to each other. I think that's very dangerous to do, because in the theater one is self-conscious enough without planning ahead or won- dering about the thematic relation from one play to the next. One hopes that one is developing, and writing interestingly, and that's where it should end, I think.

INTERVIEWER: You've spoken frequently to the effect that your in- volvement with music has influenced your writing for the theater. Can you elaborate on that in any way?

ALBEE: I find it very difficult. I've been involved in one way or another with serious music ever since childhood. And I do think, or rather I *sense* that there is a relationship—at least in my own work—between a dramatic structure, the form and sound and shape of a play, and the equivalent structure in music. Both deal with sound, of course, and also with idea, theme. I find that when my plays are going well, they seem to resemble pieces of music. But if I had to go into specifics about it, I wouldn't be able to. It's merely something that I feel.

INTERVIEWER: Which contemporary playwrights do you particularly admire? Which do you think have influenced you especially, and in what ways?

ALBEE: The one living playwright I admire without any reservation whatsoever is Samuel Beckett. I have funny feelings about almost all the others. There are a number of contemporary playwrights whom I admire enormously, but that's not at all the same thing as being influ- enced. I admire Brecht's work very much. I admire a good deal of Ten- nessee Williams. I admire some of Genet's works. Harold Pinter's work. I admire Cordell's plays very much, even though I don't think they're very good. But on the matter of influence, that question is difficult. I've read and seen hundreds of plays, starting with Sophocles right up to the present day. As a playwright I imagine that in one fashion or another I've been influenced by every single play I've ever experienced. Influence is a matter of selection—both acceptance and rejection.

INTERVIEWER: In a number of articles, mention is made of the influence on you—either directly or by osmosis—of the theater of cruelty. How do you feel about the theater of cruelty, or the theories of Artaud generally?

ALBEE: Let me answer it this way. About four years ago I made a list, for my own amusement, of the playwrights, the contemporary playwrights, by whom critics said I'd been influenced. I listed twenty-five. It included five playwrights whose work I didn't know, so I read these five playwrights and indeed *now* I suppose I can say I have been influenced by them. The problem is that the people who write these articles find the inevitable similarities of people writing in the same generation, in the same century, and on the same planet, and they put them together in a group.

INTERVIEWER: The point was that the influence may not have been directly through Artaud, but perhaps, as I said, by osmosis.

ALBEE: I've been influenced by Sophocles and Noël Coward.

INTERVIEWER: Do you aspire to being more than a playwright... to being a sort of complete man of the theater? You've involved yourself in the production of plays by other writers; you've toyed with the idea of doing a musical; you've written a libretto for opera; you've been an articulate interpreter of the American theater as an institution; and even a public critic of professional drama critics. In retrospect, do you feel that you may have overextended yourself in any of these areas?

ALBEE: I've certainly done myself considerable damage, though not as an artist, by attacking the critics, because they can't take it. As for involving myself with the production of other people's plays, I consider that to be a responsibility. The playwrights unit we've been running,

Playwrights 66, encourages thirty or thirty-five writers. The plays we've put on in the off-Broadway theater, the Cherry Lane, and other places, are primarily plays that I wanted to see: other people weren't putting them on, so we did. It seems to me that if one finds oneself with the cash it's one's responsibility to do a thing like that. There's certainly no self-aggrandizement. I have done adaptations because I wanted to. I don't like the climate in which writers have to work in this country and I think it's my responsibility to talk about it.

INTERVIEWER: Do you feel that in your own particular case, on the basis of a single big-time commercial hit, that you have been raised to too high a position? For your own creative comfort.

ALBEE: I really can't answer that. I have no idea. As a fairly objective judgment I do think that my plays as they come out are better than most other things that are put on the same year. But that doesn't make them very good necessarily. The act of creation, as you very well know, is a lonely and private matter and has nothing to do with the public area... the *performance* of the work one creates. Each time I sit down and write a play I try to dismiss from my mind as much as I possibly can the implications of what I've done before, what I'm going to do, what other people think about my work, the failure or success of the previous play. I'm stuck with a new reality that I've got to create. I'm working on a new play now. I don't believe that I'm being affected by the commercial success of *Who's Afraid of Virginia Woolf?* to make this one more commercial; I don't think I'm being affected by the critical confusion over *Tiny Alice* to make this one simpler. It's a play. I'm trying to make it as good a work of art as I possibly can.

INTERVIEWER: To talk a little about *Tiny Alice*, which I guess is your most controversial play—during your widely publicized press conference on the stage of the Billy Rose Theater, you said the critical publicity had misled the audiences into thinking of the play as a new game of symbol hunting... which was at least to some degree responsible for the play's limited run. Still, you have also said that if audiences desert a play, it is either the fault of the playwright or the manner in which it was presented. With a year to reflect on the matter, how do you feel about all this now as it pertains to *Tiny Alice*?

ALBEE: I feel pretty much what I said on the stage. I keep remembering that the preview audiences, before the critics went to *Tiny Alice*, didn't have anywhere near the amount of trouble understanding what the play was about; that didn't happen until the critics *told* them that it was too difficult to understand. I also feel that *Tiny Alice* would have been a great deal clearer if I hadn't had to make the cuts I did in the third act.

INTERVIEWER: In view of the experience you had with *Tiny Alice*, the critical brouhaha and the different interpretations and the rest of it, if you were to sit down and write that play again, do you think it would emerge in any terribly different way?

ALBEE: It's impossible to tell. A curious thing happens. Within a year after I write a play I forget the experience of having written it. And I couldn't revise or rewrite it if I wanted to. Up until that point, I'm so involved with the experience of having written the play, and the nature of it, that I can't see what faults it might have. The only moment of clear objectivity that I can find is at the moment of critical heat— of self-critical heat when I'm actually writing. Sometimes I think the experience of a play is finished for me when I finish writing it. If it weren't for the need to make a living, I don't know whether I'd have the plays produced. In the two or three or four months that it takes me to write a play, I find that the reality of the play is a great deal more alive for me than what passes for reality. I'm infinitely more involved in the reality of the characters and their situation than I am in everyday life. The involvement is terribly intense. I find that in the course of the day when I'm writing, after three or four hours of intense work, I have a splitting headache, and I have to stop. Because the involvement, which is both creative and self-critical, is so intense that I've got to stop doing it.

INTERVIEWER: If one can talk at all about a general reaction to your plays, it is that as convincing and brilliant as their beginnings and middles might be, the plays tend to let down, change course, or simply puzzle at the end. To one degree or another this complaint has been registered against most of them.

ALBEE: Perhaps because my sense of reality and logic is different from most people's. The answer could be as simple as that. Some things that make sense to me don't make the same degree of sense to other people. Analytically, there might be other reasons—that the plays don't hold together intellectually; that's possible. But then it mustn't be forgotten that when people don't like the way a play ends, they're likely to blame the play. That's a possibility too. For example, I don't feel that catharsis in a play necessarily takes place during the course of a play. Often it should take place afterwards. If I've been accused a number of times of writing plays where the endings are ambivalent, indeed, that's the way I find life.

INTERVIEWER: Do *The Zoo Story* and *Virginia Woolf* both begin and continue through the longest part of their length on an essentially naturalistic course, and then somewhere toward the end of the play veer away from the precisely naturalistic tone?

ALBEE: I think that if people were a little more aware of what actually is beneath the naturalistic overlay they would be surprised to find how early the unnaturalistic base had been set. When you're dealing with a symbol in a realistic play, it is also a realistic fact. You must expect the audience's mind to work on both levels, symbolically and realistically. But we're trained so much in pure, realistic theater that it's difficult for us to handle things on two levels at the same time.

INTERVIEWER: Why did you pick the names George and Martha? As in Washington? What did you make of Arthur Schlesinger's discovery that with those names you'd obviously written a parallel of the American sociopolitical dilemma?

ALBEE: There are little local and private jokes. Indeed, I did name the two lead characters of *Virginia Woolf* George and Martha because there is contained in the play—not its most important point, but certainly contained within the play—an attempt to examine the success or failure of American revolutionary principles. Some people who are historically and politically and sociologically inclined find them. Now in one play—*Virginia Woolf* again—I named a very old Western Union man "Little Billy"—"Crazy Billy" rather. And I did that because as *you* might recall, Mr. Flanagan, you used to deliver telegrams for Western Union, and you are very old and your name is Billy. Things like that— lots of them going on in the plays. In *Zoo Story,* I named two characters Peter and Jerry. I know two people named Peter and Jerry. But then the learned papers started coming in, and of course Jerry is supposed to be Jesus... which is much more interesting, I suppose, to the public than the truth.

INTERVIEWER: Going back to those "levels of understanding," in *Virginia Woolf* the audience questioned the credibility of George and Martha's having invented for themselves an imaginary son.

ALBEE: Indeed. And it always struck me very odd that an audience would be unwilling to believe that a highly educated, sensitive, and intelligent couple, who were terribly good at playing reality and fantasy games, *wouldn't* have the education, the sensitivity, and the intelligence to create a realistic symbol for themselves. To use as they saw fit.

INTERVIEWER: Recognizing the fact that it was a symbol?

ALBEE: *Indeed* recognizing the fact that it was a symbol. And only occasionally being confused, when the awful loss and lack that made the creation of the symbol essential becomes overwhelming—like when they're drunk, for example. Or when they're terribly tired.

INTERVIEWER: What you're saying is something which I guess is not really too commonly understood. You're suggesting that George and Martha have at no point deluded themselves about the fact that they're playing a game.

ALBEE: Oh, never. Except that it's the most serious game in the world. And the nonexistent son is a symbol and a weapon they use in every one of their arguments.

INTERVIEWER: A symbolic weapon rather than a real weapon. In the midst of the very real weapons that they do use.

ALBEE: Indeed yes. Though they're much too intelligent to make that confusion. For me, that's why the loss is doubly poignant. Because they are not deluded people.

INTERVIEWER: I see. Then what you're trying to suggest now is that the last act of *Virginia Woolf* is in no way less naturalistic than the first two acts.

ALBEE: I don't find that the play veers off into a less naturalistic manner at all.

INTERVIEWER: Well, if not into a less naturalistic one, certainly into a more ritualistic, stylized one. With the Requiem Masses and all that.

ALBEE: Well, going into Latin, indeed. But that's a conscious choice of George's to read the Requiem Mass which has existed in Latin for quite a number of years. I like the sound of the two languages working together. I like the counterpoint of the Latin and the English working together.

There's one point that you've brought up that annoys me. It really annoys the hell out of me. Some critics accuse me of having a failure of intellect in the third act of *Who's Afraid of Virginia Woolf?* merely because *they* didn't have the ability to understand what was happening. And that annoys the hell out of me.

INTERVIEWER: I can see that it would. A critic recently wrote the following paragraph, "Mr. Albee complained with *Tiny Alice* that people asked questions and would not let the play merely occur to them. He complains of those critics who judge a play's matter and do not restrict themselves to its manner. Both of these statements tend to a view much in vogue—that art consists principally of style, an encounter between us and the figurative surface of a work. This view reduces ideas to decoration, character to pageant, symbol and feeling to a conveyor belt for effects. It is to shrink art to no more than a sensual response, one kind or another of happening. To some of us this modish view is nihilistic, not progressive." Now the critic in question has come fairly close to defining a theory that might be got out of, say, Susan Sontag's

Against Interpretation or her essay on style. I wonder how closely the critic's interpretations of your remarks—of the remarks, I guess, that you made most specifically at the *Tiny Alice* press conference—are true to your own understanding of them.

ALBEE: Well, this critic is a sophist. What he's done is to misinterpret my attitudes, Miss Sontag's attitudes, and the attitudes of most respectable creative people. What I said is that I thought it was not valid for a critic to criticize a play for its matter rather than its manner—that what was constituted then was a type of censorship. To give an extreme example, I was suggesting that if a man writes a brilliant enough play in praise of something that is universally loathed, that the play, if it is good and well enough written, should not be knocked down because of its approach to its subject. If the work of art is good enough, it must not be criticized for its theme. I don't think it can be argued. In the thirties a whole school of criticism bogged down intellectually in those agitprop, social-realistic days. A play had to be progressive. A number of plays by playwrights who were thought very highly of then—they were very bad playwrights—were highly praised because their themes were intellectually and politically proper. This intellectual morass is very dangerous, it seems to me. A form of censorship. You may dislike the intention enormously but your judgment of the artistic merit of the work must not be based on your view of what it's about. The work of art must be judged by how well it succeeds in its intention.

INTERVIEWER: In other words, what you're saying is that a critic should separate what he takes to be the thematic substance of a play from the success or lack of success that the author brings to its presentation.

ALBEE: It's that simple. And critics who do otherwise are damn fools and dangerous, even destructive people. I don't think it can be argued.

INTERVIEWER: You have said that it is through the actual process of writing that you eventually come to know the theme of your play. Sometimes you've admitted that even when you have finished a play you don't have any specific idea about its theme. What about that?

ALBEE: Naturally, no writer who's any good at all would sit down and put a sheet of paper in a typewriter and start typing a play unless he knew what he was writing about. But at the same time, writing has got to be an act of discovery. Finding out things about what one is writing about. To a certain extent I imagine a play is completely finished in my mind—in my case at any rate—without my knowing it, before I sit down to write. So in that sense, I suppose, writing a play is *finding out* what the play is. I always find that the better answer to give. It's a question I despise, and it always seems to me better to slough off the answer to a question which I consider to be a terrible invasion of privacy—the kind of privacy that a writer must keep for himself. If you intellectualize and examine the creative process too carefully, it can evaporate and vanish. It's not only terribly difficult to talk about, it's also dangerous. You know the old story about the—I think it's one of Aesop's Fables, or perhaps not, or a Chinese story—about the very clever animal that saw a centipede that he didn't like. He said, "My God, it's amazing and marvelous how you walk with all those hundreds and hundreds of legs. How do you do it? How do you get them all moving that way?" The centipede stopped and thought and said, "Well, I take the left front leg and then I—" and he thought about it for a while, and he couldn't walk.

INTERVIEWER: How long does the process of reflection about a play go on?

ALBEE: I usually think about a play anywhere from six months to a year and a half before I sit down to write it out.

INTERVIEWER: Think it through, or—

ALBEE: Think *about* it. Though I'm often accused of never thinking anything through, I think about it. True, I don't begin with an *idea* for a play—a thesis, in other words, to construct the play around. But I know a good deal about the nature of the characters. I know a great deal about their environment. And I more or less know what is going to happen in the play. It's only when I sit down to write it that I find out exactly what the characters are going to say, how they are going to move from one situation to another. Exactly how they are going to behave within the situation to produce the predetermined result.... If I didn't do it that way, I wouldn't be able to allow the characters the freedom of expression to make them three-dimensional. Otherwise, I'd write a treatise, not a play. Usually the way I write is to sit down at a typewriter after that year or so of what passes for thinking, and I write a first draft quite rapidly. Read it over. Make a few pencil corrections, where I think I've got the rhythms wrong in the speeches, for example, and then retype the whole thing. And in the retyping I discover that maybe one or two more speeches will come in. One or two more things will happen, but not much. Usually what I put down first is what we go into rehearsal with; the majority of the selections and decisions have gone on before I sit down at the typewriter.

INTERVIEWER: Could you describe what sort of reflection goes on? Do whole scenes evolve in your mind, or is the process so deep in your subconscious that you're hardly aware of what's going on?

ALBEE: I discover that I am thinking about a play, which is the first awareness I have that a new play is forming. When I'm aware of the play forming in my head, it's already at a certain degree in development. Somebody will ask, well what do you plan to write after the next play? And I'll suddenly surprise myself by finding myself saying, oh, a play about this, a play about that—I had never even thought about it before. So obviously a good deal of thinking has been going on, whether *subconscious* or *unconscious* is the proper term here I don't know. But whichever it is, the majority of the work gets done there. And that period can go on for six months or in the case of *The Substitute Speaker*, which is a play that I hope to be able to write this coming summer, it's a process that has been going on for three and a half years. Occasionally I pop the play up to the surface—into the conscious mind to see how it's coming along, to see how it is developing. And if the characters seem to be becoming three-dimensional, all to the good. After a certain point, I make experiments to see how well I *know* the characters. I'll improvise and try them out in a situation that I'm fairly sure *won't* be in the play. And if they behave quite naturally, in this improvisatory situation, and create their own dialogue, and behave according to what I consider to be their own natures, then I suppose I have the play far enough along to sit down and write it.

INTERVIEWER: Is that when you know that a play has gone through this "subconscious" process and is ready to come out?

ALBEE: Not necessarily. It's when I find myself typing.

INTERVIEWER: That's not an answer.

ALBEE: It really is. There's a time to go to the typewriter. It's like a dog—the way a dog before it craps wanders around in circles—a piece of earth, an area of grass, circles it for a long time before it squats. It's like that—figuratively circling the typewriter getting ready to write, and then finally one sits down. I think I sit down to the typewriter when it's time to sit down to the typewriter. That isn't to suggest that when I do finally sit down at the typewriter, and write out my plays with a speed that seems to horrify all my detractors and half of my well-wishers, that there's no work involved. It *is* hard work, and one *is* doing all the work oneself. Still, I know playwrights who like to kid themselves into saying that their characters are so well formed that *they* just take over. *They* determine the structure of the play. By which is meant, I suspect, only that the unconscious mind has done its work so thoroughly that the play just has to be filtered through the conscious mind. But there's work to be done—and discovery to be made. Which is part of the pleasure of it. It's a form of pregnancy I suppose, and to carry that idea further, there are very few people who are pregnant who can recall specifically the moment of conception of the child—but they discover that they are pregnant, and it's rather that way with discovering that one is thinking about a play.

INTERVIEWER: When you start, do you move steadily from the opening curtain through to the end, or do you skip around, doing one scene, then another? What about curtain lines? Is there a conscious building toward the finale of each act?

ALBEE: For better or for worse, I write the play straight through—from what I consider the beginning to what I consider the end. As for curtain lines, well, I suppose there are playwrights who do build toward curtain lines. I don't think I do that. In a sense, it's the same choice that has to be made when you wonder when to start a play. And when to end it. The characters' lives have gone on before the moment you chose to have the action of the play begin. And their lives are going to go on after you have lowered the final curtain on the play, unless you've killed them off. A play is a parenthesis which contains all the material you think has to be contained for the action of the play. Where do you end that? Where the characters seem to come to a pause … where they seem to want to stop—rather like, I would think, the construction of a piece of music.

INTERVIEWER: You think of yourself then as an intuitive playwright. What you're saying in effect now is that superimposing any fixed theme on your work would somehow impose limitations on your subconscious imaginative faculties.

ALBEE: I suspect that the theme, the nature of the characters, and the method of getting from the beginning of the play to the end is already established in the unconscious.

INTERVIEWER: If one worked expressly by intuition then doesn't the form get out of control?

ALBEE: When one controls form, one doesn't do it with a stopwatch or a graph. One does it by sensing, again intuitively.

INTERVIEWER: After writing a play in this sort of intuitive way, do you end by accepting its overall structure (which must also be something of a revelation to you), or do you go back and rewrite and revise with the idea of giving it cogent shape?

ALBEE: I more or less trust it to come out with shape. Curiously enough, the only two plays that I've done very much revision on were the two adaptations—even though the shape of them was pretty much determined by the original work. With my own plays, the only changes, aside from taking a speech out here, putting one in there (if I thought I dwelled on a point a little too long or didn't make it explicit enough), are very minor; but even though they're very minor—having to do with the inability of actors or the unwillingness of the director to go along with me—I've always regretted them.

INTERVIEWER: Your earlier work, from *The Zoo Story* to *Virginia Woolf,* brought you very quick and major international celebrity, even though today at—thirty-eight—

ALBEE: Thirty-seven.

INTERVIEWER: When this is published it will be thirty-eight—you would otherwise be regarded as a relatively young growing writer. Do you feel this major renown, for all the doubtless pleasure and financial security it has given you, is any threat to the growth of the young playwright?

ALBEE: Well, there are two things that a playwright can have. Success or failure. I imagine there are dangers in both. Certainly the danger of being faced with indifference or hostility is discouraging, and it may be that success—acceptance if it's too quick, too lightning quick—can turn the heads of some people.

INTERVIEWER: I was thinking less in terms of what the personal effect on you would be. In terms of what you said before, there seems to be a certain pattern that's acted out in the American theater, if not exclusively in the American theater, of elevating new playwrights to enormous prestige, and then after a certain time lapse, arrived at arbitrarily, the need comes to cut them down to size.

ALBEE: Well, the final determination is made anywhere from twenty-five to one hundred years after the fact anyway. And if the playwright is strong enough to hold on to reasonable objectivity in the face either of hostility or praise, he'll do his work the way he was going to anyway.

INTERVIEWER: Since I guess it's fairly imbecilic to ask a writer what he considers to be his best work or his most important work, perhaps I could ask you this question: which of all of your plays do you feel closest to?

ALBEE: Well, naturally the one I'm writing right now.

INTERVIEWER: Well, excepting that.

ALBEE: I don't know.

INTERVIEWER: There's no one that you feel any special fondness for?

ALBEE: I'm terribly fond of *The Sandbox*. I think it's an absolutely beautiful, lovely, perfect play.

INTERVIEWER: And as for the play you're writing now...

ALBEE: *A Delicate Balance*, which I am writing now. *The Substitute Speaker*, next, and then in some order or another, three short plays, plus a play about Attila the Hun.

INTERVIEWER: You say three short plays. Do you hold forth any prospect of going off-Broadway with anything?

ALBEE: Well, considering the way the critical reaction to my plays has been going in the past few years, I may well be there shortly.

INTERVIEWER: I was thinking out of choice rather than necessity.

ALBEE: I'm talking about that, too.

—WILLIAM FLANAGAN
Fall, 1966

HAROLD PINTER

Courtesy of Express Newspapers/Archive Photos

Harold Pinter, Britain's most significant postwar playwright, was born October 10, 1930, in Hackney, a small, working-class neighborhood near London's East End. As a student at the Hackney Downs Grammar School, he acted in plays and wrote poems and essays. Hoping to become a professional actor, he accepted a grant to study at the Royal Academy of Dramatic Art, but left after two unhappy terms.

In 1950 he began publishing poetry under the name Harold Pinta while finding work as a bit-part actor for the BBC Home Service radio programs. He resumed his training at the Central School of Speech and Drama and spent eighteen months in Ireland as a member of a touring theater company. Upon his return to London he appeared during Donald Wolfit's 1953 classical season at the King's Theatre in Hammersmith.

In 1957 a friend of Pinter's asked him to write a play for Bristol University's drama department. *The Room*, finished in four days, was the result. A year later Pinter's second play, *The Birthday Party*, was produced in the West End, where it closed, to disastrous reviews, after only one week. *A Slight Ache*, the first of Pinter's many radio and television pieces, was broadcast on the BBC in 1959.

Pinter's first major success for the stage came the following year, with *The Caretaker* (1960). His third full-length play and masterpiece, *The Homecoming*, was produced in 1965. The story of an estranged son who brings his wife home to meet his family, it contains all the earmarks of Pinter's work: a deep sense of menace, the threat of violence, the characters' inability to connect with one another. It won a Tony Award, the Whitbread Anglo-American Theater Award, and the New York Drama Critics' Circle Award.

Since *Betrayal* (1978), Pinter's stage plays, including *A Kind of Alaska* (1982), *Victoria Station* (1982), and *Mountain Language* (1989), have all been shorter works. Among his many adaptations for film are four of his own plays, as well as F. Scott Fitzgerald's *The Last Tycoon* (1974) and John Fowles's *The French Lieutenant's Woman* (1981), for which Pinter received an Academy Award nomination.

In recent years Pinter has been more active as a director than as a playwright, overseeing David Mamet's *Oleanna* in its 1993 London premiere, several works by Simon Gray, and the first production of his own most recent play, *Ashes to Ashes* (1996), which, though containing for some too many elements familiar from his earlier work, was generally well received. In 1996 Pinter received the Laurence Olivier Award for a lifetime's achievement in theater.

———

Harold Pinter recently moved into a five-story 1820 Nash house facing Regent's Park in London. The view from the floor-through top floor, where he installed his office, overlooks a duck pond and a long stretch of wooded parkland; his desk faces this view, and in late October, when the interview took place, the changing leaves and the hazy London sun constantly distracted him as he thought over questions or began to give answers. The size and comfort of the office are impressive, with a separate room nearby for his secretary and a small bar equally nearby for the beer and Scotch which he drinks steadily during the day, whether working or not. Bookshelves line one half of the area, and a velvet chaise lounge faces the small rear garden. On the walls are a series of Feliks Topolski sketches of London the-

I'll chop your spine off

```
F. - I'll knock your nut off, ~~sonny jim.~~ My word of honour.
      I'll have you for catsmeat. / you talk to me like that, son.
      Talking to your filthy lousy father like that.
3. - You know what, youre getting demented.

                        p.
      What do you think of Second Wind [for] in the fourth race ?
F. - Second Wind ? What race ?
3. - The fourth.
F. - Dont stand a chance.
3. - Sure he does.
F. - Not a chance.
3. - Thats all you know.

                                        p
F. - He talks to me about horses.

                                        p.
3. - I'll tell you one thing, its about time you learned to cook.
F. - Yes ?
3. - ~~That's what I want to say~~ I want to ask you something. That
      dinner we had before, whats the name of it ? Wjst do you
      call it ?
                        p.
      Why dont you buy a dog ? Youre a dog cook. Honest. You
      think youre cooking for a lot of dogs.
F. - If you dont like it get out.
3. - I am going out. I'm going out to buy myself a proper
      dinner.
F. - ~~Go. Go.~~ Leave me alone.
3. - Yes, but I'm not going until I decide the exact moment I
      want to go, you see. ~~You dont tell me to do anything, Dad.~~
      I go when I like. I come back when I like. ~~You wouldnt be
      here only because of me. Whose money keeps you here ?
      If it wasnt for me and Joey~~ xxxxxxxxxxxxxxxxxxxxxxxx
      you know where youd be ? Who gives you the monet to do the
      ~~cooking ?~~  Get it ? you dont ever come into it .
F. - Its my house. you ou stkife .
3. - Dont make me laugh. You're dead if I say so.
F. - ~~Yes xxx yes you ... let you ... he wont let you~~ ...
3. - ~~Joey x You dont think so?~~  F. Get burnt. ~~Damn.~~   Burn.
                        gets up.
      Here, Daddy, you going to use your stick on me ? Dont use
      your stick on me, Daddy. I havent done nothing wrong.
      Dont clout me with that stick Dad.
                        silence. 3. wraps his paper, puts it in
                        his pocket. ~~Dear. Joey comes in. Uncle Sam.~~
                        xxxxxxxxxxxxxxxxxxxxxxxxxxx .
      Eh, Dad, I forgot. One thing. Been meaning to ask you.
      That night ... that night you .. got me .. with mum ...
      what was it like ? When I was just a glint in your naughty
      old eye. you had me in mind, did you ?
F. - ~~Cut yourself to pieces.~~ Stuff your face into glass xxxx
      ~~Into broken glass.~~
```

Handwritten annotations:

Choke.
Suffocate .

F. I know what you do every night.
I know all about stinking
filthy tykes:
I know all about tykes.

F - Drownin your own bastard blood.

Shove it into a plate of glass.

Is that it a fact that you had me in mind,
or is it a fact that I was the last thing
you had in mind.

A manuscript page from The Homecoming.

ater scenes; a poster of the Montevideo production of El Cuidador; *a small financial balance sheet indicating that his first West End production,* The Birthday Party *(1958), earned £260 in its disastrous week's run; a Picasso drawing; and his citation when he was named to the Order of the British Empire last spring. "The year* after *the Beatles," he emphasizes.*

He was not working on any writing projects when the interview took place, and questions about his involuntary idleness (many questions came back to it without meaning to) were particularly uncomfortable for him. His own work is alternatively a source of mystery, amusement, joy, and anger to him; in looking it over he often discovered possibilities and ambiguities which he'd not noticed or forgotten. One felt that if he'd only rip out his telephone and hang black curtains across the wide windows he'd be much happier, though he insists that the "great boredom one has with oneself" is unrelated to his environment or his obligations.

Pinter speaks in a deep, theater-trained voice, which comes rather surprisingly from him, and indeed is the most remarkable thing about him physically. When speaking he almost always tends to excessive qualifications of any statement, as if coming to a final definition of things were obviously too impossible. One gets the impression—as one does with many of the characters in his plays— of a man so deeply involved with what he's thinking that roughing it into speech is a painful necessity.

INTERVIEWER: When did you start writing plays, and why?

PINTER: My first play was *The Room,* written when I was twenty-six. A friend of mine called Henry Woolf was a student in the drama department at Bristol University at the time when it was the only drama department in the country. He had the opportunity to direct a play, and as he was my oldest friend he knew I'd been writing, and he knew I had an idea for a play, though I hadn't written any of it. I was acting in Rep at the time, and he told me he had to have the play the next week to meet his schedule. I said this was ridiculous, he might get it in six months. And then I wrote it in four days.

INTERVIEWER: Has writing always been so easy for you?

PINTER: Well, I had been writing for years, hundreds of poems and short pieces of prose. About a dozen had been published in little magazines. I wrote a novel as well; it's not good enough to be published, really, and never has been. After I wrote *The Room,* which I didn't see performed for a few weeks, I started to work immediately on *The Birthday Party.*

INTERVIEWER: What led you to do that so quickly?

PINTER: It was the process of writing a play which had started me going. Then I went to see *The Room,* which was a remarkable experience. Since I'd never written a play before, I'd of course never seen one of mine performed, never had an audience sitting there. The only people who'd ever seen what I'd written had been a few friends and my wife. So to sit in the audience—well, I wanted to piss very badly throughout the whole thing, and at the end I dashed out behind the bicycle shed...

INTERVIEWER: What other effect did contact with an audience have on you?

PINTER: I was very encouraged by the response of that university audience, though no matter what the response had been I would have written *The Birthday Party,* I know that. Watching first nights, though I've seen quite a few by now, is never any better. It's a nerve-racking experience. It's not a question of whether the play goes well or badly. It's not the audience reaction, it's *my* reaction. I'm rather hostile toward audiences—I don't much care for large bodies of people collected together. Everyone knows that audiences vary enormously, it's a mistake to care too much about them. The thing one should be concerned with is whether the performance has expressed what one set out to express in writing the play. It sometimes does.

INTERVIEWER: Do you think that without the impetus provided by your friend at Bristol you would have gotten down to writing plays?

PINTER: Yes, I think I was going to write *The Room.* I just wrote it a bit quicker under the circumstances, he just triggered something off. *The Birthday Party* had also been in my mind for a long time. It was sparked off from a very distinct situation in digs when I was on tour. In fact the other day a friend of mine gave me a letter I wrote to him in nineteen-fifty something, Christ knows when it was. This is what it says, "I have filthy insane digs, a great bulging scrag of a woman with breasts rolling at her belly, an obscene household, cats, dogs, filth, tea-strainers, mess, oh bullocks, talk, chat rubbish shit scratch dung poison, infantility, deficient order in the upper fretwork, fucking roll on ..." Now the thing about this is *that* was *The Birthday Party*—I was in those digs, and this woman was Meg in the play, and there was a fellow staying there in Eastbourne, on the coast. The whole thing remained with me, and three years later I wrote the play.

INTERVIEWER: Why wasn't there a character representing you in the play?

PINTER: I had—I have—nothing to say about myself, directly. I wouldn't know where to begin. Particularly since I often look at myself in the mirror and say, "Who the hell's that?"

INTERVIEWER: And you don't think being represented as a character onstage would help you find out?

PINTER: No.

INTERVIEWER: Have your plays usually been drawn from situations you've been in? *The Caretaker*, for example.

PINTER: I'd met a few, quite a few, tramps—you know, just in the normal course of events, and I think there was one particular one ... I didn't know him very well, he did most of the talking when I saw him. I bumped into him a few times, and about a year or so afterward he sparked this thing off ...

INTERVIEWER: Had it occurred to you to act in *The Room*?

PINTER: No, no—the acting was a separate activity altogether. Though I wrote *The Room, The Birthday Party*, and *The Dumb Waiter* in 1957, I was acting all the time in a repertory company, doing all kinds of jobs, traveling to Bournemouth and Torquay and Birmingham. I finished *The Birthday Party* while I was touring in some kind of farce, I don't remember the name.

INTERVIEWER: As an actor, do you find yourself with a compelling sense of how roles in your plays should be performed?

PINTER: Quite often I have a compelling sense of how a role should be played. And I'm proved—equally as often—quite wrong.

INTERVIEWER: Do you see yourself in each role as you write? And does your acting help you as a playwright?

PINTER: I read them all aloud to myself while writing. But I don't see myself in each role—I couldn't play most of them. My acting doesn't impede my playwriting because of these limitations. For example, I'd like to write a play—I've frequently thought of this—entirely about women.

INTERVIEWER: Your wife, Vivien Merchant, frequently appears in your plays. Do you write parts for her?

PINTER: No. I've never written any part for any actor, and the same applies to my wife. I just think she's a very good actress and a very interesting actress to work with, and I want her in my plays.

INTERVIEWER: Acting was your profession when you first started to write plays?

PINTER: Oh, yes, it was all I ever did. I didn't go to university. I left school at seventeen—I was fed up and restless. The only thing that interested me at school was English language and literature, but I didn't have Latin and so couldn't go on to university. So I went to a few drama schools, not studying seriously; I was mostly in love at the time and tied up with that.

INTERVIEWER: Were the drama schools of any use to you as a playwright?

PINTER: None whatsoever. It was just living.

INTERVIEWER: Did you go to a lot of plays in your youth?

PINTER: No, very few. The only person I really liked to see was Donald Wolfit in a Shakespearean company at the time. I admired him tremendously; his Lear is still the best I've ever seen. And then I was reading, for years, a great deal of modern literature, mostly novels.

INTERVIEWER: No playwrights—Brecht, Pirandello...

PINTER: Oh certainly not, not for years. I read Hemingway, Dostoyevsky, Joyce, and Henry Miller at a very early age, and Kafka. I'd read Beckett's novels, too, but I'd never heard of Ionesco until after I'd written the first few plays.

INTERVIEWER: Do you think these writers had any influence on your writing?

PINTER: I've been influenced *personally* by everyone I've ever read— and I read all the time—but none of these writers particularly influenced my writing. Beckett and Kafka stayed with me the most—I think Beckett is the best prose writer living. My world is still bound up by other writers—that's one of the best things in it.

INTERVIEWER: Has music influenced your writing, do you think?

PINTER: I don't know how music can influence writing; but it has been very important for me, both jazz and classical music. I feel a sense of music continually in writing, which is a different matter from having been influenced by it. Boulez and Webern are now composers I listen to a great deal.

INTERVIEWER: Do you get impatient with the limitations of writing for the theater?

PINTER: No. It's quite different; the theater's much the most difficult kind of writing for me, the most naked kind, you're so entirely restricted. I've done some film work, but for some reason or other I haven't found it very easy to satisfy myself on an original idea for a film. *Tea Party*, which I did for television, is actually a film, cinematic, I wrote it like that. Television and films are simpler than the theater— if you get tired of a scene you just drop it and go on to another one. (I'm exaggerating, of course.) What *is* so different about the stage is that you're just *there*, stuck—there are your characters stuck on the stage, you've got to live with them and deal with them. I'm not a very inventive writer in the sense of using the technical devices other play-wrights do—look at Brecht! I can't use the stage the way he does, I just haven't got that kind of imagination, so I find myself stuck with these characters who are either sitting or standing, and they've either got to walk out of a door, or come in through a door, and that's about all they can do.

INTERVIEWER: And talk.

PINTER: Or keep silent.

INTERVIEWER: After *The Room*, what effect did the production of your next plays have on your writing?

PINTER: *The Birthday Party* was put on at the Lyric, Hammersmith in London. It went on a little tour of Oxford and Cambridge first, and was very successful. When it came to London it was completely massacred by the critics—absolutely slaughtered. I've never really known why, nor am I particularly interested. It ran a week. I've framed the statement of the box-office takings: 260 pounds, including a first night of 140 pounds and the Thursday matinee of two pounds six shillings—there were six people there. I was completely new to writing for the professional theater, and it was rather a shock when it happened. But I went on writing—the BBC were very helpful. I wrote *A Slight Ache* on commission from them. In 1960 *The Dumb Waiter* was produced, and then *The Caretaker*. The only really bad experience I've had was *The Birthday Party*; I was so green and gauche—not that I'm rosy and confident now, but comparatively... Anyway, for things like stage design I didn't know how to cope, and I didn't know how to talk to the director.

INTERVIEWER: What was the effect of this adversity on you? How was it different from unfavorable criticism of your acting, which surely you'd had before?

PINTER: It was a great shock, and I was very depressed for about forty-eight hours. It was my wife, actually, who said just that to me, "You've had bad notices before," et cetera. There's no question but that her common sense and practical help got me over that depression, and I've never felt anything like that again.

INTERVIEWER: You've directed several of your plays. Will you continue to do so?

PINTER: No. I've come to think it's a mistake. I work much as I write, just moving from one thing to another to see what's going to happen next. One tries to get the thing... *true.* But I rarely get it. I think I'm more useful as the author closely involved with a play: as a director I think I tend to inhibit the actors, because however objective I am about the text and try not to insist that *this is what's meant,* I think there is an obligation on the actors too heavy to bear.

INTERVIEWER: Since you are an actor, do actors in your plays ever approach you and ask you to change lines or aspects of their roles?

PINTER: Sometimes, quite rarely, lines are changed when we're working together. I don't at all believe in the anarchic theater of so-called creative actors—the actors can do that in someone else's plays. Which wouldn't, however, at all affect their ability to play in mine.

INTERVIEWER: Which of your plays did you first direct?

PINTER: I codirected *The Collection* with Peter Hall. And then I directed *The Lover* and *The Dwarfs* on the same bill at the Arts. *The Lover* didn't stand much of a chance because it was my decision, regretted by everyone—except me—to do *The Dwarfs,* which is apparently the most intractable, impossible piece of work. Apparently ninety-nine people out of a hundred feel it's a waste of time, and the audience hated it.

INTERVIEWER: It seems the densest of your plays in the sense that there's quite a bit of talk and very little action. Did this represent an experiment for you?

PINTER: No. The fact is that *The Dwarfs* came from my unpublished novel, which was written a long time ago. I took a great deal from it, particularly the kind of state of mind that the characters were in.

INTERVIEWER: So this circumstance of composition is not likely to be repeated?

PINTER: No. I should add that even though it is, as you say, more dense, it had great value, great interest for me. From my point of view, the general delirium and states of mind and reactions and relationships in the play—although terribly sparse—are clear to me. I know all the things that aren't said, and the way the characters actually look at each other, and what they mean by looking at each other. It's a play about betrayal and distrust. It does seem very confusing and obviously it can't be successful. But it was good for me to do.

INTERVIEWER: Is there more than one way to direct your plays successfully?

PINTER: Oh, yes, but always around the same central truth of the play—if that's distorted, then it's bad. The main difference in interpretation comes from the actors. The director can certainly be responsible for a disaster, too—the first performance of *The Caretaker* in Germany was heavy and posturized. There's no blueprint for any play, and several have been done entirely successfully without me helping in the production at all.

INTERVIEWER: When you are working on one, what is the key to a good writer-director relationship?

PINTER: What is absolutely essential is avoiding all defensiveness between author and director. It's a matter of mutual trust and openness. If that isn't there, it's just a waste of time.

INTERVIEWER: Peter Hall, who has directed many of your plays, says that they rely on precise verbal form and rhythm, and when you write "pause" it means something other than "silence," and three dots are different from a full stop. Is his sensitivity to this kind of writing responsible for your working well together?

PINTER: Yes, it is, very much so. I do pay great attention to those points you just mentioned. Hall once held a dot and pause rehearsal for the actors in *The Homecoming*. Although it sounds bloody pretentious it was apparently very valuable.

INTERVIEWER: Do you outline plays before you start to write them?

PINTER: Not at all. I don't know what kind of characters my plays will have until they ... well, until they *are*. Until they indicate to me what they are. I don't conceptualize in any way. Once I've got the clues I follow them—that's my job, really, to follow the clues.

INTERVIEWER: What do you mean by clues? Can you remember how one of your plays developed in your mind—or was it a line by line progression?

PINTER: Of course I can't remember exactly how a given play developed in my mind. I think what happens is that I write in a very high state of excitement and frustration. I follow what I see on the paper in front of me—one sentence after another. That doesn't mean I don't have a dim, possible overall idea—the image that starts off doesn't just engender what happens immediately, it engenders the possibility of an overall happening, which carries me through. I've got an idea of what *might* happen—sometimes I'm absolutely right, but on many occasions I've been proved wrong by what does actually happen. Sometimes I'm going along and I find myself writing, "C. comes in," when I didn't know that he was going to come in; he *had* to come in at that point, that's all.

INTERVIEWER: In *The Homecoming*, Sam, a character who hasn't been very active for a while, suddenly cries out and collapses several minutes from the end of the play. Is this an example of what you mean? It seems abrupt.

PINTER: It suddenly seemed to me right. It just came. I knew he'd have to say something at one time in this section and this is what happened, that's what he said.

INTERVIEWER: Might characters therefore develop beyond your control of them, changing your idea—even if it's a vague idea—of what the play's about?

PINTER: I'm ultimately holding the ropes, so they never get too far away.

INTERVIEWER: Do you sense when you should bring down the curtain, or do you work the text consciously toward a moment you've already determined?

PINTER: It's pure instinct. The curtain comes down when the rhythm seems right—when the action calls for a finish. I'm very fond of curtain lines, of doing them properly.

INTERVIEWER: Do you feel your plays are therefore structurally successful? That you're able to communicate this instinct for rhythm to the play?

PINTER: No, not really, and that's my main concern, to get the structure right. I always write three drafts, but you have to leave it eventually. There comes a point when you say that's it, I can't do anything more. The only play which gets remotely near to a structural entity which satisfies me is *The Homecoming*. *The Birthday Party* and *The Caretaker* have too much writing... I want to iron it down, eliminate things. Too many words irritate me sometimes, but I can't help them, they just seem to come out—out of the fellow's mouth. I don't really examine my works too much, but I'm aware that quite often in what I write, some fellow at some point says an awful lot.

INTERVIEWER: Most people would agree that the strength in your plays lies in just this verbal aspect, the patterns and force of character you can get from it. Do you get these words from people you've heard talking—do you eavesdrop?

PINTER: I spend *no* time listening in that sense. Occasionally I hear something, as we all do, walking about. But the words come as I'm writing the characters, not before.

INTERVIEWER: Why do you think the conversations in your plays are so effective?

PINTER: I don't know, I think possibly it's because people fall back on anything they can lay their hands on verbally to keep away from the danger of knowing, and of being known.

INTERVIEWER: What areas in writing plays give you the most trouble?

PINTER: They're all so inextricably interrelated I couldn't possibly judge.

INTERVIEWER: Several years ago, *Encounter* had an extensive series of quotations from people in the arts about the advisability of Britain joining the Common Market. Your statement was the shortest anyone made, "I have no interest in the matter and do not care what happens." Does this sum up your feeling about politics, or current affairs?

PINTER: Not really. Though that's exactly what I feel about the Common Market—I just don't care a damn about the Common Market. But it isn't quite true to say that I'm in any way indifferent to current affairs. I'm in the normal state of being very confused—uncertain, irritated, and indignant in turns, sometimes indifferent. Generally I try to get on with what I can do and leave it at that. I don't think I've got any kind of social function that's of any value, and politically there's no question of my getting involved because the issues are by no means simple—to be a politician you have to be able to present a simple picture even if you don't see things that way.

INTERVIEWER: Has it ever occurred to you to express political opinions through your characters?

PINTER: No. Ultimately, politics do bore me, though I recognize they are responsible for a good deal of suffering. I distrust ideological statements of any kind.

INTERVIEWER: But do you think that the picture of personal threat which is sometimes presented on your stage is troubling in a larger sense, a political sense, or doesn't this have any relevance?

PINTER: I don't feel myself threatened by *any* political body or activity at all. I like living in England. I don't care about political structures—they don't alarm me, but they cause a great deal of suffering to millions of people.

I'll tell you what I really think about politicians. The other night I watched some politicians on television talking about Vietnam. I wanted very much to burst through the screen with a flamethrower and burn their eyes out and their balls off and then inquire from them how they would assess this action from a political point of view.

INTERVIEWER: Would you ever use this anger in a politically oriented play?

PINTER: I have occasionally out of irritation thought about writing a play with a satirical point. I once did, actually, a play that no one knows about. A full-length play written after *The Caretaker.* Wrote the whole damn thing in three drafts. It was called *The Hothouse* and was about an institution in which patients were kept: all that was presented was the hierarchy, the people who ran the institution; one never knew what happened to the patients or what they were there for or who they were. It was heavily satirical and it was quite useless. I never began to like any of the characters, they really didn't live at all. So I discarded the play at once. The characters were so purely cardboard. I was intentionally—for the only time, I think—trying to make a point, an explicit point, that these were nasty people and I disapproved of them. And therefore they didn't begin to live. Whereas in other plays of mine every single character, even a bastard like Goldberg in *The Birthday Party*, I care for.

INTERVIEWER: You often speak of your characters as living beings. Do they become so after you've written a play? While you're writing it?

PINTER: Both.

INTERVIEWER: As real as people you know?

PINTER: No, but different. I had a terrible dream, after I'd written *The Caretaker*, about the two brothers. My house burned down in the dream, and I tried to find out who was responsible. I was led through all sorts of alleys and cafés and eventually I arrived at an inner room somewhere and there were the two brothers from the play. And I said, so you burned down my house. They said don't be too worried about it, and I said I've got everything in there, everything, you don't realize what you've done, and they said it's all right, we'll compensate you for it, we'll look after you all right—the younger brother was talking—and thereupon I wrote them out a check for fifty quid... *I* gave *them* a check for fifty quid!

INTERVIEWER: Do you have a particular interest in psychology?

PINTER: No.

INTERVIEWER: None at all? Did you have some purpose in mind in writing the speech where the older brother describes his troubles in a mental hospital at the end of Act Two in *The Caretaker*?

PINTER: Well, I had a purpose in the sense that Aston suddenly opened his mouth. My purpose was to let him go on talking until he was finished and then... bring the curtain down. I had no ax to grind there. And the one thing that people have missed is that it isn't necessary to conclude that everything Aston says about his experiences in the mental hospital is true.

INTERVIEWER: There's a sense of terror and a threat of violence in most of your plays. Do you see the world as an essentially violent place?

PINTER: The world *is* a pretty violent place, it's as simple as that, so any violence in the plays comes out quite naturally. It seems to me an essential and inevitable factor.

I think what you're talking about began in *The Dumb Waiter,* which from my point of view is a relatively simple piece of work. The violence is really only an expression of the question of dominance and subservience, which is possibly a repeated theme in my plays. I wrote a short story a long time ago called "The Examination," and my ideas of violence carried on from there. That short story dealt very explicitly with two people in one room having a battle of an unspecified nature, in which the question was one of who was dominant at what point and how they were going to be dominant and what tools they would use to achieve dominance and how they would try to undermine the other person's dominance. A threat is constantly there: it's got to do with this question of being in the uppermost position, or attempting to be. That's something of what attracted me to do the screenplay of *The Servant,* which was someone else's story, you know. I wouldn't call this violence so much as a battle for positions, it's a very common, every-day thing.

INTERVIEWER: Do these ideas of everyday battles, or of violence, come from any experiences you've had yourself?

PINTER: Everyone encounters violence in some way or other. It so happens I did encounter it in quite an extreme form after the war, in the East End, when the Fascists were coming back to life in England. I got into quite a few fights down there. If you looked remotely like a Jew you might be in trouble. Also, I went to a Jewish club, by an old railway arch, and there were quite a lot of people often waiting with broken milk bottles in a particular alley we used to walk through. There were one or two ways of getting out of it—one was a purely physical way, of course, but you couldn't do anything about the milk bottles—*we* didn't have any milk bottles. The best way was to talk to them, you know, sort of "Are you all right?" "Yes, I'm all right." "Well, that's all right then, isn't it?" And all the time keep walking toward the lights of the main road.

Another thing: we were often taken for Communists. If you went by, or happened to be passing, a Fascist's street meeting, and looked in any way antagonistic—this was in Ridley Road market, near Dalston Junction—they'd interpret your very being, especially if you had books under your arms, as evidence of your being a Communist. There was a good deal of violence there, in those days.

INTERVIEWER: Did this lead you toward some kind of pacifism?

PINTER: I was fifteen when the war ended. There was never any question of my going when I was called up for military service three years later: I couldn't see any point in it at all. I refused to go. So I was taken in a police car to the medical examination. Then I had two tribunals and two trials. I could have gone to prison—I took my toothbrush to the trials—but it so happened that the magistrate was slightly sympathetic, so I was fined instead, thirty pounds in all. Perhaps I'll be called up again in the next war, but I won't go.

INTERVIEWER: Robert Brustein has said of modern drama, "The rebel dramatist becomes an evangelist proselytizing for his faith." Do you see yourself in that role?

PINTER: I don't know what he's talking about. I don't know for what faith I could possibly be proselytizing.

INTERVIEWER: The theater is a very competitive business. Are you, as a writer, conscious of competing against other playwrights?

PINTER: Good writing excites me, and makes life worth living. I'm never conscious of any competition going on here.

INTERVIEWER: Do you read things written about you?

PINTER: Yes. Most of the time I don't know what they're talking about; I don't really read them all the way through. Or I read it and it goes—if you asked me what had been said, I would have very little idea. But there are exceptions, mainly nonprofessional critics.

INTERVIEWER: How much are you aware of an audience when you write?

PINTER: Not very much. But I'm aware that this is a public medium. I don't want to *bore* the audience, I want to keep them glued to what happens. So I try to write as *exactly* as possible. I would try to do that anyway, audience or no audience.

INTERVIEWER: There is a story—mentioned by Brustein in *The Theater of Revolt*—that Ionesco once left a performance of Genet's *The Blacks* because he felt he was being attacked, and the actors were enjoying it. Would you ever hope for a similar reaction in your audience? Would you react this way yourself?

PINTER: I've had that reaction—it's happened to me recently here in London, when I went to see *US,* the Royal Shakespeare Company's anti–Vietnam War production. There was a kind of attack—I don't like being subjected to propaganda, and I detest soapboxes. I want to present things clearly in my own plays, and sometimes this does make an audience very uncomfortable, but there's no question about causing offense for its own sake.

INTERVIEWER: Do you therefore feel the play failed to achieve its purpose—inspiring opposition to the war?

PINTER: Certainly. The chasm between the reality of the war in Vietnam and the image of what *US* presented on the stage was so enormous as to be quite preposterous. If it was meant to lecture or shock the audience I think it was most presumptuous. It's impossible to make a major theatrical statement about such a matter when television and the press have made everything so clear.

INTERVIEWER: Do you consciously make crisis situations humorous? Often an audience at your plays finds its laughter turning against itself as it realizes what the situation in the play actually is.

PINTER: Yes, that's very true, yes. I'm rarely consciously writing humor, but sometimes I find myself laughing at some particular point which has suddenly struck me as being funny. I agree that more often than not the speech only *seems* to be funny—the man in question is actually fighting a battle for his life.

INTERVIEWER: There are sexual undertones in many of these crisis situations, aren't there? How do you see the use of sex in the theater today?

PINTER: I do object to one thing to do with sex: this scheme afoot on the part of many "liberal-minded" persons to open up obscene language to general commerce. It should be the dark secret language of the underworld. There are very few words—you shouldn't kill them by overuse. I have used such words once or twice in my plays, but I couldn't get them through the Lord Chamberlain. They're great, wonderful words, but must be used very sparingly. The pure publicity of freedom of language fatigues me, because it's a demonstration rather than something said.

INTERVIEWER: Do you think you've inspired any imitations? Have you ever seen anything in a film or theater which struck you as, well, Pinteresque?

PINTER: That word! These damn words and that word Pinteresque particularly—I don't know what they're bloody well talking about! I think it's a great burden for me to carry, and for other writers to carry...Oh, very occasionally I've thought listening to something, hello, that rings a bell, but it goes no further than that. I really do think that writers write on...just write, and I find it difficult to believe I'm any kind of influence on other writers. I've seen very little evidence of it, anyway; other people seem to see more evidence of it than I do.

INTERVIEWER: The critics?

PINTER: It's a great mistake to pay any attention to *them*. I think, you see, that this is an age of such overblown publicity and overemphatic pinning down. I'm a very good example of a writer who can write, but I'm not as good as all that. I'm just a writer; and I think that I've been overblown tremendously because there's a dearth of really fine writing, and people tend to make too much of a meal. All you can do is try to write as well as you can.

INTERVIEWER: Do you think your plays will be performed fifty years from now? Is universality a quality you consciously strive for?

PINTER: I have no idea whether my plays will be performed in fifty years, and it's of no moment to me. I'm pleased when what I write makes sense in South America or Yugoslavia—it's gratifying. But I certainly don't strive for universality—I've got enough to strive for just writing a bloody play!

INTERVIEWER: Do you think the success you've known has changed your writing?

PINTER: No, but it did become more difficult. I think I've gone beyond something now. When I wrote the first three plays in 1957 I wrote them from the point of view of *writing* them; the whole world of putting on plays was quite remote—I knew they could never be done in the Reps I was acting in, and the West End and London were somewhere on the other side of the moon. So I wrote these plays completely unself-consciously. There's no question that over the years it's become more difficult to preserve the kind of freedom that's essential to writing, but when I do write, it's there. For a while it became more difficult to avoid the searchlights and all that. And it took me five years to write a stage play, *The Homecoming,* after *The Caretaker.* I did a lot of things in the meantime, but writing a stage play, which is what I really wanted to do, I couldn't. Then I wrote *The Homecoming,* for good or bad, and I felt much better. But *now* I'm back in the same boat—I want to write a play, it buzzes all the time in me, and I can't put pen to paper. Something people don't realize is the great boredom one has with oneself, and just to see those words come down again on paper, I think oh Christ, everything I do seems to be predictable, unsatisfactory, and hopeless. It keeps me awake. Distractions don't matter to me—if I had something to write I would write it. Don't ask me why I want to keep on with plays at all!

INTERVIEWER: Do you think you'd ever use freer techniques as a way of starting writing again?

PINTER: I can enjoy them in other people's plays—I thought the *Marat/Sade* was a damn good evening, and other very different plays like *The Caucasian Chalk Circle* I've also enjoyed. But I'd never use such stage techniques myself.

INTERVIEWER: Does this make you feel behind the times in any way?

PINTER: I *am* a very traditional playwright—for instance I insist on having a curtain in all my plays. I write curtain lines for that reason! And even when directors like Peter Hall or Claude Régy in Paris want to do away with them, I insist they stay. For me everything has to do with shape, structure, and overall unity. All this jamboree in "Happenings" and eight-hour movies is great fun for the people concerned, I'm sure...

INTERVIEWER: Shouldn't they be having fun?

PINTER: If they're all having fun I'm delighted, but count me out completely, I wouldn't stay more than five minutes. The trouble is I find it all so *noisy,* and I like quiet things. There seems to be such a jazz and jaggedness in so much modern art, and a great deal of it is inferior to its models: Joyce contains so much of Burroughs, for example, in his experimental techniques, though Burroughs is a fine writer on his own. This doesn't mean I don't regard myself as a contemporary writer: I mean, I'm *here.*

—LAWRENCE M. BENSKY
Fall, 1966

TOM STOPPARD

© Jerry Bauer

Tom Stoppard was born Tomas Straussler on July 3, 1937, in Zlin, Czechoslovakia (now Gottwaldov, Czech Republic). His father, a doctor for a shoe manufacturing company, was transferred by his office to Singapore while Tomas was still an infant. When his wife and children were relocated to India during the war, Dr. Straussler remained in Singapore, where he was killed during the Japanese invasion in 1941. In 1946 Stoppard's mother married Kenneth Stoppard, a British Army major who had been serving in India. The family returned to England and settled eventually in Bristol.

When he was seventeen, Stoppard left school and began writing news reports, gossip columns, and film and theater reviews for a series of Bristol newspapers. In 1960 he began working as a freelance writer and wrote his first play, *A Walk on the Water,* which was produced for television and radio before finally appearing on the stage, in 1968, as *Enter a Free Man.*

In 1963 Stoppard moved to London and began working for the magazine *Scene.* Later that year, during his sojourn to Berlin as a guest of the Ford Foundation, he wrote what would become his break-through play, *Rosencrantz and Guildenstern Are Dead* (1966), a revisitation of Shakespeare's *Hamlet* as seen through the eyes of the Danish prince's ill-fated former schoolmates. Met with almost universal acclaim, the play contains much of what would become Stoppard's stock-in-trade: exploration of serious themes through comedy, structural complexity, and sophisticated wordplay. *Rosencrantz and Guildenstern Are Dead* was produced at the Edinburgh Festival in 1966 and a year later appeared in London and New York, where it earned a New York Drama Critics' Circle Award and a Tony. Stoppard's adaptation of the work for the screen, which he directed himself, won the Grand Prize at the 1990 Venice Film Festival.

In 1976 Stoppard won a second Tony Award for *Travesties* (1974), a work inspired by the playwright's discovery that Vladimir Lenin, James Joyce, and Tristan Tzara had all lived in Zurich at the same time. Like the 1984 Tony Award–winning *The Real Thing* (1982), *Travesties* makes use of one of Stoppard's favored forms: the play within a play.

Stoppard has, in addition to his works for the stage, written over two dozen original pieces for television and radio, including *Professional Foul* (1977), *Artist Descending a Staircase* (1972), and *Indian Ink* (1995). His screenplay adaptations—J. G. Ballard's *Empire of the Sun* (1987) and John le Carré's *The Russia House* (1989) among them—have been critical and popular successes. In 1998 he won an Academy Award for an original work, the coauthored *Shakespeare in Love.*

———

Tom Stoppard lives with his second wife, Dr. Miriam Stoppard, well-known in her own right for her books and television programs, in a house built in 1722 set amid acres of fields and woodlands. The house has been attributed to John James, to Nicholas Hawksmoor, and to John Vanbrugh, but Stoppard prefers to think it was Vanbrugh on the grounds that he was also a playwright. Stoppard has four sons, two of them by his first marriage, and he is close to them all: "My family and my work, that's it," he says.

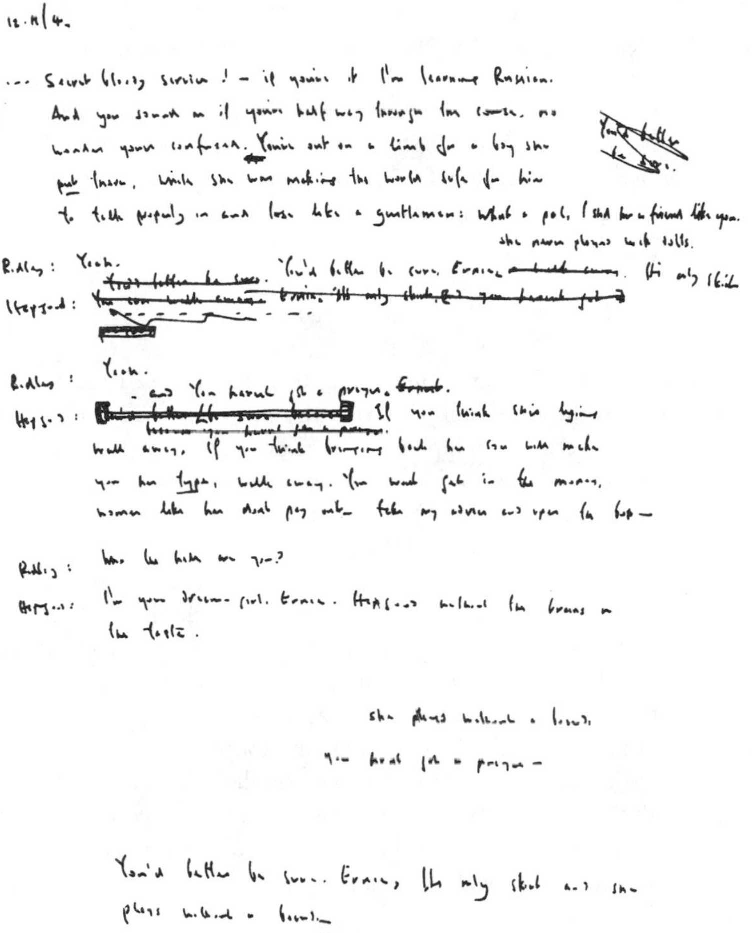

A manuscript page from Hapgood.

At the time of this interview, Stoppard was near the end of rehearsals for his new play, Hapgood, *which has since opened in London and settled in for what seems a long and happy run. For the duration of the rehearsals Stoppard had rented a furnished apartment in central London in order to avoid commuting, and although he had said, "I would never volunteer to talk about my work and myself for more than ninety seconds," he was extremely generous with his time and attention. Stoppard is tall and exotically handsome; he speaks with a very slight lisp.*

INTERVIEWER: How are the rehearsals going?

STOPPARD: So far they are conforming to pattern, alas! I mean I am suffering from the usual delusion that the play was ready before we went into production. It happens every time. I give my publisher the finished text of the play so that it can be published not too long after the opening in London, but by the time the galleys arrive they're hopelessly out of date because of all the changes I've made during rehearsals. This time I gave them *Hapgood* and told them that it was folly to pretend it would be unaltered, but I added, "I think it won't be as bad as the others." It turned out to be worse. Yesterday I realized that a chunk of information in the third scene ought to be in the second scene, and it's like pulling out entrails: as in any surgery there's blood. As I was doing it I watched a documentary about Crick and Watson's discovery of the structure of DNA—the double helix. There was only one way all the information they had could fit but they couldn't figure out what it was. I felt the same. So the answer to your question is that the rehearsals are going well and enjoyably, but that I'm very busy with my pencil.

INTERVIEWER: What provokes the changes? Does the transfer from your imagination to the stage alter your perception? Or do the director and the actors make suggestions?

STOPPARD: They make a few suggestions which I am often happy to act upon. In the theater there is often a tension, almost a contradiction, between the way real people would think and behave, and a kind of imposed dramaticness. I like dialogue which is slightly more brittle than life. I have always admired and wished to write one of those 1940s film scripts where every line is written with a sharpness and economy which is frankly artificial. Peter Wood, the director with whom I've worked for sixteen years, sometimes feels obliged to find a humanity, perhaps a romantic ambiguity, in scenes which are not written like that but which, I hope, contain the possibility. I like surface gloss, but it's all too easy to get that right for the first night only to find that *that* was the best performance of the play; from then on the gloss starts cracking apart. The ideal is to make the groundwork so deep and solid that the actors are continually discovering new possibilities under the surface, so that the best performance turns out to be the last one. In my plays there are usually a few lines which Peter loathes, for their slickness or coldness, and we have a lot of fairly enjoyable squabbles which entail some messing about with the text as we rehearse. In the case of *Hapgood* there is a further problem which has to do with the narrative mechanics, because it's a plotty play, and I can't do plots and have no interest in plots.

INTERVIEWER: Yet you have produced some complex and plausible plots. So why the aversion?

STOPPARD: The subject matter of the play exists before the story and it is always something abstract. I get interested by a notion of some kind and see that it has dramatic possibilities. Gradually I see how a pure idea can be married with a dramatic event. But it is still not a play until you invent a plausible narrative. Sometimes this is not too hard— *The Real Thing* was fairly straightforward. For *Hapgood* the thing that I wanted to write about seemed to suit the form of an espionage thriller. It's not the sort of thing I read or write.

INTERVIEWER: What was the original idea that made you think of an espionage thriller?

STOPPARD: It had to do with mathematics. I am not a mathematician but I was aware that for centuries mathematics was considered the queen of the sciences because it claimed certainty. It was grounded on some fundamental certainties—axioms—which led to others. But then, in a sense, it all started going wrong, with concepts like non-euclidean geometry—I mean, looking at it from Euclid's point of view. The mathematics of physics turned out to be grounded on *un*certainties, on probability and chance. And if you're me, you think—there's a play in that. Finding an idea for a play is like picking up a shell on a beach. I started reading about mathematics without finding what I was looking for. In the end I realized that what I was after was something which any first-year physics student is familiar with, namely quantum mechanics. So I started reading about that.

INTERVIEWER: It is said that you research your plays thoroughly.

STOPPARD: I don't think of it as research. I read for interest and enjoyment, and when I cease to enjoy it I stop. I didn't research quantum mechanics but I was fascinated by the mystery which lies in the foundation of the observable world, of which the most familiar example is the wave/particle duality of light. I thought it was a good metaphor for human personality. The language of espionage lends itself to this duality—think of the double agent.

INTERVIEWER: You seem to think the success of the play has so much to do with its production. Do you, therefore, get involved with the lighting, costumes, et cetera?

STOPPARD: It is obvious that a given text (think of any classic) can give rise to a satisfying event or an unsatisfying one. These are the only relative values which end up mattering in the theater. A great production of a black comedy is better than a mediocre production of a comedy of errors. When the writing is over, the event is the thing. I attend the first rehearsal of a new play and every rehearsal after that, as well as discussions with designers, lighting designers, costume designers... I like to be there, even though I'm doing more listening than talking. When *Hapgood* was being designed, I kept insisting that the shower in the first scene wouldn't work unless it was in the middle of the upper stage, so that Hapgood could approach us facing down the middle. Peter and Carl insisted that the scene wouldn't work unless the main entrance doors were facing the audience. They were quite right, but so was I. We opened out of town with the shower in the wings, and it didn't work at all, so we ended up having to find a way to have both the doors and the shower in view of the audience. The look of the thing is one thing. The sound of it is more important. David Lean was quoted as saying somewhere that the hardest part of making films is knowing how fast or slow to make the actors speak. I suddenly saw how *horribly* difficult that made it to make a film. Because you can't change your mind. When you write a play, it makes a certain kind of noise in your head, and for me rehearsals are largely a process of trying to reproduce that noise. It is not always wise to reproduce it in every instance, but that's another question. The first time I met Laurence Olivier, we were casting *Rosencrantz and Guildenstern*. He asked me about the Player. I said the Player should be a sneaky, snakelike sort of person. Olivier looked dubious. The part was given, thank God, or Olivier, to Graham Crowden, who is about six foot four and roars like a lion. Olivier came to rehearsal one day. He watched for about fifteen minutes, and then, leaving, made one suggestion. I forget what it was. At the door he turned again, twinkled at us all and said, "Just the odd pearl," and left.

INTERVIEWER: Is it a very anxious moment for you, working up to the first night?

STOPPARD: Yes. You are trying to imagine the effect on people who know nothing about what is going on and whom you are taking through the story. In a normal spy thriller you contrive to delude the reader until all is revealed in the denouement. This is the exact opposite of a scientific paper, in which the denouement—the discovery—is announced at the beginning. *Hapgood* to some extent follows this latter procedure. It is not a whodunit because we are told who has done it near the beginning of the first act, so the story becomes *how* he did it.

INTERVIEWER: Did you draw on some famous spies, like Philby or Blunt, for your characters?

STOPPARD: Not at all. I wasn't really interested in authenticity. John le Carré's *A Perfect Spy* uses the word *joe* for an agent who is being run by somebody, and I picked it up. I have no idea whether it is authentic or invented by le Carré.

INTERVIEWER: What happens on the first night? Do you sit among the audience or in a concealed place at the back? And what do you do afterwards?

STOPPARD: The first *audience* is more interesting than the first night. We now have previews, which makes a difference. Actually, my play *The Real Inspector Hound* was the first to have previews in London, in 1968. Previews are essential. The idea of going straight from a dress rehearsal to a first night is frightening. It happened with *Rosencrantz and Guildenstern* and we got away with it, but for *Jumpers* we had several previews by the end of which I had taken fifteen minutes out of the play. I hate first nights. I attend out of courtesy for the actors and afterwards we all have a drink and go home.

INTERVIEWER: How does the London theater world differ from New York?

STOPPARD: Theater in New York is nearer to the street. In London you have to go deep into the building, usually, to reach the place where theater happens. On Broadway, only the fire doors separate you from the sidewalk and you're lucky if the sound of a police car doesn't rip the envelope twice a night. This difference means something, I'm not quite sure what. Well, as Peter Brook will tell you, the theater has its roots in something holy, and perhaps we in London are still a little holier than thou. The potential rewards of theater in New York are really too great for its own good. One bull's-eye and you're rich and famous. The rich get more famous and the famous get richer. You're the talk of the town. The taxi drivers have read about you and they remember you for a fortnight. You get to be photographed for *Vogue* with new clothes and Vuitton luggage, if that's your bag. If it's a new play, everyone owes the writer, they celebrate him—the theater owners, the producers, the actors. Even the stage doorman is somehow touched by the wand. The sense of so much depending on success is very hard to ignore, perhaps impossible. It leads to disproportionate anxiety and disproportionate relief or disappointment. The British are more phlegmatic about these things. You know about British phlegm. The audiences, respectively, are included in this. In New York, expressions of appreciation have succumbed to galloping inflation—in London only the Americans stand up to applaud the actors, and only American audiences emit those high-pitched barks which signify the highest form of approval. But if you mean the difference between what happens on stage in London and New York, there isn't much, and there's no difference between the best. Cross-fertilization has evened out what I believe used to be quite a sharp difference between styles of American and British acting, although it is probably still a little harder to find American actors with an easy command of rhetoric, and British actors who can produce that controlled untidiness which, when we encountered it a generation ago, seemed to make acting lifelike for the first time.

INTERVIEWER: I have heard that in New York people sit up and wait for the *New York Times* review, which makes or breaks a show. It is not like that in London, but do you worry all night until the reviews come out the next day?

STOPPARD: Certainly I'm anxious. One is implicated in other people's fortunes—producers, directors, actors—and one wants the play to succeed for their sake as much as for one's own. If there is a favorable consensus among the reviewers, you accept it as a reasonable judgment. If you get mixed reviews, you are heartened by those who enjoyed it and depressed by the rejections. What one is anxious about is the judgment on the event rather than the play. None of us would have worked so hard if we didn't believe in the play, and so we don't need a critic to tell us whether we liked it, but whether we succeeded in putting it across. For the text is only one aspect of an evening at the theater; often the most memorable moments have little to do with the words uttered. It is the totality—to use the jargon—which is being judged. A favorable judgment means that on that occasion the play has worked, which does not mean that it always will.

INTERVIEWER: Do critics matter as much?

STOPPARD: In the long term, not at all. In the short term they give an extra push, or conversely give you more to push against; but favorable reviews won't save a play for long if the audiences don't like it, and vice versa. The play has to *work*.

INTERVIEWER: I would like to know what you mean by *work*.

STOPPARD: It has to be truthful. The audience must believe. But the play is also a physical mechanism. Getting that mechanism to work takes an awful lot of time and preoccupation. The way music comes in and out, lights vary, et cetera. When you've got all that right you can get back to the text. Otherwise, the fact that it seems right on paper won't help you.

INTERVIEWER: Do you change things according to what the reviews say?

STOPPARD: No. But I change things according to what happens to the play, and what I think of it. Sometimes one is involved in a revival and one wants to change things because one has changed oneself, and what used to seem intriguing or amusing might now strike one as banal. Any revival in which I am involved is liable to change.

INTERVIEWER: It has been said that Kenneth Tynan was the last critic who had a definite point of view and was bold enough to express it, thereby influencing the direction of the theater. So perhaps critics do make a difference?

STOPPARD: Ken had enthusiasms. Some lasted longer than others and while he had them he pushed them. But you have to read critics critically and make the necessary adjustment according to what you know about them. When I was a critic—on my local paper in Bristol and later for a magazine in London—I floundered between pronouncing what I hoped were magisterial judgments and merely declaring my own taste. If I might quote myself from a previous interview—"I was not a good critic because I never had the moral character to pan a friend. I'll rephrase that—I had the moral character never to pan a friend."

INTERVIEWER: But Tynan introduced into England what one associates with French intellectual life—a kind of intellectual terrorism, when suddenly one author or school is "in" and another "out," and woe betide he who disagrees! He destroyed people like Terence Rattigan and Christopher Fry and all those he called "bourgeois" playwrights, and you had to love Osborne and Brecht or else! But I recently saw Rattigan's *Separate Tables* and thought it very good indeed, infinitely better than some of the plays Ken had praised and made fashionable.

STOPPARD: Which shows that he didn't destroy them. However, I know what you mean, and one or two of my close friends thoroughly disapproved of Ken. But I hope they know what I mean when I stick up for him. The first time I met Ken was when I was summoned to his tiny office when the National Theatre offices consisted of a wooden hut on waste ground, and I was so awed by being in a small room with him that I began to stutter. Ken stuttered, as you know. So we sat stuttering at each other, mainly about his shirt, which was pale lemon and came from Turnbull and Asser in Jermyn Street. This was in the late summer of 1966, when we wore roll-neck shirts.

INTERVIEWER: You have been praised for your eloquence, your use of language—your aphorisms, puns, epigrams—as if you invented them, wrote them down, and put them into your characters' mouths. Do you?

STOPPARD: No. They tend to show up when I need them. But perhaps it is significant that very often a particular line is more or less arbitrarily attached to a particular character. I can take a line from one character and give it to another. As I just told you, there was something in the third scene of *Hapgood* which I had to put in the second scene. But the dialogue was not between the same two people—only one of them was the same. So the lines of a female character became those of a male, and it made no difference. In *Night and Day* I had to invent an African dictator, but there was no way I could do it unless he was the only African dictator who had been to the London School of Economics. You don't have to be African or a dictator to make those observations about the British press. I rely heavily on an actor's performance to help individualize a character.

INTERVIEWER: Do you act out all the characters as you write?

STOPPARD: Sometimes. I walk around the room speaking the dialogue.

INTERVIEWER: Once you've got the idea and devised the narrative, do you take notes while you're reading up on the subject?

STOPPARD: Not really. Sometimes, over the course of several months, I might cover a page with odds and ends, many of which might find their way into the play. But I don't write down in notebooks, nor jot down what I overhear—nothing like that.

INTERVIEWER: In the course of writing the play, do you get surprises, because for example, you don't know what a character is going to do next, or how the story will end?

STOPPARD: Absolutely.

INTERVIEWER: What about the order of the play, the number of acts and scenes?

STOPPARD: I don't work out the whole plot before I begin, just the general outline. The play alters as you write it. For example, in *Jumpers* the end of the first act in my scheme turned out to be the end of the second act, followed by only an epilogue. *Hapgood* was in three acts and is now in two. The reason for the change is partly intrinsic and partly circumstantial. Managements prefer two-act plays because they think that audiences like only one interval, and Peter thought it would be better for the play. It shows how pragmatic the theater is, perhaps the most pragmatic art form, apart from advertising. For example, the male secretary, Maggs, used to be Madge, a woman. But when we came to choose the understudies we realized that if the secretary were male he could understudy so-and-so. It turned out to be better for the play also, because then Hapgood is the only woman surrounded by all these men. But at first it was a question of casting.

INTERVIEWER: Having got your outline, do you proceed from the beginning to the end chronologically?

STOPPARD: Yes I do. I write plays from beginning to end, without making stabs at intermediate scenes, so the first thing I write is the first line of the play. By that time I have formed some idea of the set but I don't write that down. I don't write down anything which I can keep in my head—stage directions and so on. When I have got to the end of the play—which I write with a fountain pen; you can't scribble with a typewriter—there is almost nothing on the page except what people say. Then I dictate the play, ad-libbing all the stage directions, into a tape machine, from which my secretary transcribes the first script.

INTERVIEWER: What are the pitfalls on the way? Things that might get you stuck?

STOPPARD: It is not like playing the violin—not difficult in that way. The difficulties vary at different stages. The first is that you haven't got anything you wish to write a play about. Then you get an idea, but it might be several ideas that could belong to two or three plays. Finally, if you are lucky, they may fit into the same play. The next difficulty, as I said before, is to translate these abstract ideas into concrete situations. That is a very long and elaborate period. Another difficulty is knowing when to start; it's chicken-and-egg—you don't know what you're going to write until you start, and you can't start until you know. Finally, in some strange, quantum-mechanical way, the two trains arrive on the same line without colliding, and you can begin. The following stage is not exactly pleasant but exciting and absorbing—you live with the fear that "it" may go away. There is a three-month period when I don't want to say good morning to anyone lest I miss the thought that would make all the difference.

INTERVIEWER: Once the play begins to take shape, what do you feel?

STOPPARD: Tremendous joy. Because whenever I finish a play I have no feeling that I would ever have another one to write.

INTERVIEWER: Do you disappear from home to write?

STOPPARD: I disappear into myself. Sometimes I go away for a short period, say a week, to think and concentrate, then I come back home to carry on.

INTERVIEWER: Where do you work and when?

STOPPARD: I have a very nice long room, which used to be the stable. It has a desk and lots of paper, et cetera. But most of my plays are written on the kitchen table at night, when everybody has gone to bed and I feel completely at peace. During the day, somehow I don't get much done; although I have a secretary who answers the phone, I always want to know who it is, and I generally get distracted.

INTERVIEWER: Do you have an ideal spectator in mind when you write?

STOPPARD: Perhaps I do. Peter Wood has quite a different spectator in mind, one who is a cross between Rupert Bear and Winnie the Pooh. He assumes bafflement in order to force me to explain on a level of banality. If I had an ideal spectator it would be someone more sharp-witted and attentive than the average theatergoer whom Peter thinks of. A lot of changes in rehearsals have to do with reconciling his spectator with mine.

INTERVIEWER: You have said that all the characters talk like you. Does that mean that you have trouble creating female characters? You once said, "There is an area of mystery about women which I find difficult to penetrate." Yet the eponymous character of your new play, *Hapgood*, is a woman.

STOPPARD: I wonder when I said that! It is not what I feel now. When I said I wasn't interested by plot or character I meant that they are not the point for me. Before writing *Night and Day* I thought, I'm sick of people saying there are no good parts for women in my plays, so I'll do one. It turned out not to be just about a woman, and I thought, well, one day I'll do a Joan of Arc. But I never think, I'm writing for a woman so it had better be different.

INTERVIEWER: How important are curtain lines?

STOPPARD: Very important, because they define the play's shape, like the spans of a bridge. It's like architecture—there is a structure and a conscious architect at work. Otherwise you could decide to have an interval at 8:30, and whatever was being said at that moment would be your curtain line. It wouldn't do.

INTERVIEWER: You said that you have worked with Peter Wood for sixteen years, but are you always closely involved with your plays' productions?

STOPPARD: In this country, yes. In America I was involved with the production of *The Real Thing,* which was directed by Mike Nichols. But who knows what's going on elsewhere? You are pleased the plays are being done and hope for the best.

INTERVIEWER: You have been accused of superficiality; some people say that your plays are all linguistic pyrotechnics, dazzling wordplay, intelligent punning, but that they don't have much substance. How do you react to that charge?

STOPPARD: I suppose there is a certain justice in it, insofar as if I were to write an essay instead of a play about any of these subjects it wouldn't be a profound essay.

INTERVIEWER: Nowadays fame has become a thing in itself. In French the word is *gloire,* which is nicer because it denotes achievement; it has connotations of glory. But fame doesn't: you can be famous just for being famous. Now that you are, do you still feel excited by it, or do you think it isn't that important?

STOPPARD: Oh, I like it. The advantages are psychological, social, and material. The first because I don't have to worry about who I am—I am the man who has written these plays. The social advantages appeal to half of me because there are two of me: the recluse and the fan. And the fan in me is still thrilled to meet people I admire. As for the material side, I like having some money. The best way to gauge wealth is to consider the amount of money which you can spend *thoughtlessly*—a casual purchase which simply doesn't register. The really rich can do it in Cartier's; I'm quite happy if I can do it in a good bookshop or a good restaurant.

INTERVIEWER: What about the company of your peers. Harold Pinter?

STOPPARD: The first time I met Harold Pinter was when I was a journalist in Bristol and he came down to see a student production of *The Birthday Party*. I realized he was sitting in the seat in front of me. I was tremendously intimidated and spent a good long time working out how to engage him in conversation. Finally, I tapped him on the shoulder and said, "Are you Harold Pinter or do you just look like him?" He said, "What?" So that was the end of that.

INTERVIEWER: Going back to your work, *Jumpers* was about moral philosophy, and in it you attacked logical positivism and its denial that metaphysical questions are valid...

STOPPARD: Ah, but remember that I was attacking a dodo—logical positivism was over by the time I wrote the play. I was amused to see Freddy [Sir Alfred] Ayer being interviewed on television. The interviewer asked him what were the defects of logical positivism, and Freddy answered, "I suppose its main defect was that it wasn't true." The play addressed itself to a set of attitudes which people didn't think of as philosophical but which in fact were. At the same time, it tried to be a moral play, because while George has the right ideas, he is also a culpable person; while he is defending his ideas and attacking the opposition, he is also neglecting everyone around him and shutting out his wife who is in need, not to mention shooting his hare and stepping on his tortoise.

INTERVIEWER: In the play you say that the Ten Commandments, unlike tennis rules, can't be changed, implying that there are fundamental moral principles which are eternally valid because of their transcendental provenance—their foundation in religion. Do you believe that?

STOPPARD: Yes, I do.

INTERVIEWER: Are you religious?

STOPPARD: Well, I keep looking over my shoulder. When I am asked whether I believe in God, my answer is that I don't know what the question means. I approve of belief in God and I try to behave as if there is one, but that hardly amounts to faith. I don't know what religious certainty would consist of, though many apparently have it. I am uneasy with religious ceremonials, because I think intellectually, and the case for God is not an intellectual one. However, militant humanism grates on me much more than evangelism.

INTERVIEWER: I would like to ask you about your early influences. What about the angry young men and the kitchen-sink school of the fifties, or Beckett, whom you are quoted as saying had the greatest impact on you?

STOPPARD: There were good plays and not-so-good plays. I was moved by and interested by John Osborne's *Look Back in Anger,* Beckett's *Waiting for Godot, The Birthday Party* by Pinter, *Next Time I'll Sing to You* ... I mean when I was starting to write plays. I'd be wary of calling them influences. I don't write the way I write because I liked them, I liked them because of the way I write, or despite it.

INTERVIEWER: So if we forget about "influence," who are the writers you admire and go back to?

STOPPARD: I had a passion for Hemingway and Evelyn Waugh, and I think I will always return to them, apart from anyone else.

INTERVIEWER: Does it annoy you that people compare you to George Bernard Shaw?

STOPPARD: I don't think they do very much. I find the comparison embarrassing, by which I mean flattering. Shaw raises conversation to the power of drama, and he does it for three acts. I sometimes do it for three pages, though the tone is very different; but my theatrical impulses are flashier. The result can be exhilarating when things go right, and pathetic when things go wrong. Anyway, one's admirations don't have much to do with the way one likes to write. I've been going around for years saying that Alan Bennett is one of the best playwrights we've had this century, and he does exactly what I don't do and can't do; he makes drama out of character study. The fact that his jokes are very good helps but he's really a social anthropologist who prefers to report in the form of plays. Incidentally, I think Bennett's comparative lack of recognition among the academically minded has most to do with a snobbishness about television—where much of his best work appears. David Mamet is another great enthusiasm of mine, and another writer who has almost nothing in common with me.

INTERVIEWER: What actually led you to write plays? Could you describe the genesis of your plays other than *Hapgood* and *Jumpers*?

STOPPARD: I started writing plays because everybody else was doing it at the time. As for the genesis of plays, it is never the story. The story comes just about last. I'm not sure I can generalize. The genesis of *Travesties* was simply the information that James Joyce, Tristan Tzara, and Lenin were all in Zurich at the same time. Anybody can see that there was some kind of play in that. But what play? I started to read Richard Ellmann's biography of Joyce, and came across Henry Carr, and so on and so on. In the case of *Night and Day*, it was merely that I had been a reporter, that I knew quite a lot about journalism, and that I should have been writing another play about *something* and that therefore it was probably a good idea to write a play about journalists. After that, it was just a case of shuffling around my bits of knowledge and my prejudices until they began to suggest some kind of story. I was also shuffling a separate pack of cards which had to do with sexual attractions. Quite soon I started trying to integrate the two packs. And so on.

INTERVIEWER: There's another aspect of your work which I would like to talk about, that is adaptations of other playwrights' plays. Are the two activities very different?

STOPPARD: Yes, they are. I don't do adaptations because I have a thing about them, but to keep busy. I write a play every three or four years and they don't take that long—perhaps a year each.

INTERVIEWER: Does someone do the literal translation for you from the original language first?

STOPPARD: Yes, since I don't read any other languages. I have done two plays by Arthur Schnitzler, *Dalliance* and *Undiscovered Country*, one by Molnár, *Rough Crossing,* and a play by Johann Nestroy which became *On the Razzle.*

INTERVIEWER: Do you tinker with the original text?

STOPPARD: There is no general rule. *Undiscovered Country* was pretty faithful. I thought of Schnitzler as a modern classic, not to be monkeyed about with. But you're not doing an author a favor if the adaptation is not vibrant. So in the end I started "helping," not because Schnitzler was defective but because he was writing in 1905 in Vienna. When you are writing a play you use cultural references by the thousands, and they all interconnect like a nervous system. In the case of *Dalliance,* Peter Wood started with the idea that the third act should be transferred to the wings of the opera. He did it beautifully and it worked very well. The number of critics who suddenly turned out to be Schnitzler purists was quite surprising. As for *On the Razzle,* that had a wonderful plot—which wasn't Nestroy's own anyway—and I invented most of the dialogue. The Molnár play was set in an Italian castle and I put it on an ocean liner called the *Italian Castle.* And I also made up nearly all the dialogue. So you can see there's a difference between "translation" and "adaptation."

INTERVIEWER: So far your adaptations have been of plays. Have you ever thought of adapting a novel, or a book of testimony, into a play or a series of plays? For example, Primo Levi's *If This Is a Man,* or Nadezhda Mandelstam's *Hope Against Hope?* I mention these because I know you admire them as much as I do.

STOPPARD: I think Nadezhda Mandelstam's books are two of the greatest books written in this century. But what would be the point of turning them into plays?

INTERVIEWER: To make them accessible to a larger audience, the way Olivia Manning's *The Balkan Trilogy* was resurrected and became a bestseller after it was shown on television as a six-part series.

STOPPARD: It would be admirable if it made people turn to the Mandelstam books. I quite agree that television would be the way to do it.

INTERVIEWER: Let's talk about another of your activities—writing filmscripts. You have never written an original one. Why not?

STOPPARD: Because I don't have any original ideas to spare.

INTERVIEWER: What if someone gave you the idea?

STOPPARD: That is possible, but it would be pure accident if you gave me the right one. The reason is that all you know about me is what I have written so far; it has nothing to do with what I want to do next because I don't know, either.

INTERVIEWER: What is the difference between writing a play and writing a filmscript?

STOPPARD: The main difference is that in films the writer serves the director, and in the theater the director serves the writer—broadly speaking.

INTERVIEWER: Now for the first time you are going to direct your own film version of *Rosencrantz and Guildenstern*. Are you looking forward to it?

STOPPARD: The reason why I agreed to do it myself was that the producers gave me a list of twenty possible directors and I couldn't see why any of them should or should not do it, since I had no idea what each would wish to do. So I suggested myself, because it was the line of least resistance, and also because I am the only director willing to commit the necessary violence to the play—I've thrown masses of it out, and I've added things.

INTERVIEWER: You are friendly with Czech playwrights, like Václav Havel and others. Do you feel any special affinity with them as a result of your own Czech origin?

STOPPARD: This whole Czech thing about me has gotten wildly out of hand. I wasn't two years old when I left the country and I was back one week in 1977. I went to an English school and was brought up in English. So I don't feel Czech. I like what Havel writes. When I first came across his work, I thought *The Memorandum* was a play I'd have liked to have written, and you don't think that of many plays. And when I met him I loved him as a person. I met other writers there I liked and admired, and I felt their situation keenly. But I could have gotten onto the wrong plane and landed in Poland or Paraguay and felt the same about writers' situations there.

INTERVIEWER: I wanted to ask you about radio plays, because you started out writing some, and before *Rosencrantz* had a number of them produced on the radio. It is always astonishing that despite television, radio is still so popular, especially for plays. What are your feelings about radio—its technique, possibilities, and differences from other dramatic forms?

STOPPARD: Radio plays are neither easier nor harder. I'm supposed to be writing one now, and the hard part is simply finding a play to write. The pleasant part will be writing it. There is nothing much to be said about radio technique except what is obvious—scene setting through dialogue and sound effects. I'd like to write a radio play which consisted entirely of sound effects but I suppose it would be rather a short one.

INTERVIEWER: After you have seen *Hapgood* through, what are you going to do?

STOPPARD: I would like to write a very simple play, perhaps with two or three people in one setting. A literature play rather than an event play. Getting *Hapgood* ready was exhausting and frustrating—it has as many scene changes, light cues, sound cues, et cetera, as a musical. I'd like to write a play where all the time and the energy can be devoted to language, thought process, and emotion.

INTERVIEWER: It is often said that a writer's output is the product of a psychosis, of self-examination. Is there any indication of this in your case?

STOPPARD: You tell me!

INTERVIEWER: What is the most difficult aspect of playwriting?

STOPPARD: Structure.

INTERVIEWER: And the easiest?

STOPPARD: Dialogue.

INTERVIEWER: What about the curtain lines? Do they come first and then you work your way towards them, or do they arrive in the natural progression of writing the dialogue?

STOPPARD: Curtain lines tend to be produced under the pressure of the preceding two or three acts, and usually they seem so dead right, to me anyway, that it really is as if they were in the DNA, unique and inevitable.

INTERVIEWER: What are some of your favorite curtain lines—and not necessarily those in your own plays?

STOPPARD: "The son of a bitch stole my watch" [from *The Front Page*]—I quote from memory—and "You that way; we this way" [from *Love's Labour's Lost*].

INTERVIEWER: Not to put you to the test, but can you provide a curtain line for this interview?

STOPPARD: "That's all, folks."

—SHUSHA GUPPY
Winter, 1988

JOHN GUARE

© Sara Barrett

John Guare was born in Manhattan on February 5, 1938, and grew up in Queens, which he considers a borough of failed dreams. He was, as he put it, "just a subway ride to the heart of the action. [But] fourteen minutes on the Flushing line is a very long distance." He attended Catholic schools and then went to Georgetown University, graduating in 1961. He earned an M.A. in English from Yale and ended up in the Air Force Reserve. He wrote a few plays for the New Dramatists' Committee, then headed off into the world, at one point hitching from Paris to Cairo.

Guare's career in theater began in the mid-1960s at New York's legendary Caffé Cino, which at the time was the focal point of the exper-

imental off-off-Broadway theater scene. He was also among the original members of the Eugene O'Neill Theater Center in Waterford,
Connecticut, and their innovative summer playwrights' festival would
come to define the way American theaters develop new plays. While
abroad he had written the first act of *The House of Blue Leaves*, and it
opened (with Guare himself acting the lead role) in 1966 at the O'Neill
Center. Four years and many drafts later, the play had its New York
opening and won the 1971 New York Drama Critics' Circle Award; it
would later win four Tony Awards in a revival at Lincoln Center in
1986.

In 1968 Guare won an Obie Award for a one-act play, *Muzeeka*,
which he followed with another one-act, *CopOut*, in 1969. He then
collaborated with Mel Shapiro in a musical adaptation of *Two Gentlemen of Verona*, for which he also wrote the lyrics. It won the 1972
Drama Critics' Circle Award and a Tony Award for best musical. As
playwright-in-residence at the New York Shakespeare Festival,
Guare wrote a number of plays, including *Landscape of the Body* and
Marco Polo Sings a Solo. His screenplay for Louis Malle's *Atlantic City*
won many film critics' awards as well as an Oscar nomination.

Following the triumphant revival of *The House of Blue Leaves*, Lincoln Center produced Guare's *Six Degrees of Separation*, which was
based on the true story of a black con man. It won the Drama Critics'
Circle Award in 1991 and was in production at theaters around the
world through the mid-1990s. His next play, *Four Baboons Adoring the
Sun*, opened in 1992 and was also produced at Lincoln Center. His
most recent play is *Chaucer in Rome*.

Guare has taught at Yale, Harvard, and New York Universities and
was elected a member of the American Academy and the Institute of
Arts and Letters in 1989.

———

*John Guare's rambling Greenwich Village apartment is comfortably worn and
packed to the ceilings with books and photographs, with a nineteenth-century
church steeple visible outside the window. The interview took place in 1992, soon
after* Four Baboons Adoring the Sun *opened at Lincoln Center. Guare had just
finished a screenplay for Martin Scorsese based on the life of George Gershwin.*

*There was little peace during the interview. Guare's assistant, Mary Pat
Walsh, gave advice to houseguests who came in and out. The phone rang inces-*

                                    HALCY
My excellent Duke.

                                    WAYNE
          After you.   *[handwritten: Pu (PU]*
                                                  [handwritten: Those Highway, just late]
                                    HALCY   *[handwritten: motorway: Sich.]*
          After you.   *[handwritten: home within Sich.]*

WAYNE AND HALCY SMILE AT EACH OTHER AND BOW.
PHILIP AND PENNY HAPPILY FOLLOW THEM AND THEIR CHILDREN OFF.
[handwritten marginalia]
                              MESSENGER #2 (SINGS)
          You must always stop at a cafe by the sea
          You must bask in the sun by this lunatic, crazily blue sea.
          You must watch your kids play
          The eternal game of Ringalevio!!!!
          See them running in and out of the water
          See them throwing an orange frisbee
          ALL the while you drink Bellinis!
          What are Bellinis?   *[handwritten: / MESSEger as we]*
          Champagne and fresh white peaches!

PENNY AND PHILIP RETURN, ARM IN ARM, PEACEFUL. THEY WATCH THEIR
CHILDREN IN THE DISTANCE AND DRINK BELLINIS.
[handwritten marginalia]
                                    PHILIP
          Can't tell who's yours.

                                    PENNY   *[handwritten: PL: Separate ...]*
          Can't tell who's mine.

WAYNE AND HALCY APPEAR. THE HARPISCHORD PLAYS TREMOLO.

                                    PENNY
          I heard the murmuring first.   It wasn't a babble like
          babbling brook.   But it had the quality of clear water
          running over glittery stones.

                                    PHILIP
          Can't tell who's yours. Can't tell who's mine - it's all
          going to be fine - · but then I heard it too - I heard-
          what? -the sound of exotic birds clawing the earth--

                                    WAYNE
           ---to marry an Etruscan.

                                    HALCY
          Mel is a wonderful man. Just does not possess
          one drop of Etruscan blood. I love him. Our
          kids. The most wonderful kids. I'm happy.
[handwritten marginalia: discover or recall / off-od Exp!]

A manuscript page from Four Baboons Adoring the Sun.

santly and dogs barked. Even when the interview continued at Lincoln Center, the feeling of life beating at Guare's door persisted, as did the sense that he enjoys, or perhaps relies on, the clamor.

INTERVIEWER: Why do I always feel there's something blasphemous about your work?

GUARE: I don't know why you feel that way. Are you all right?

INTERVIEWER: There's something dangerous about your work. A Jacobean undercurrent.

GUARE: Hold on!

INTERVIEWER: All right, let's start with this then: you once told me that you thought of playwriting as simply another job in the theater.

GUARE: To stay around any place you love, you have to have a job. In college at Georgetown in the fifties, I got my first theater job checking coats at the National, which was Washington's main theater. I sold orange drinks there at intermission and felt personally responsible for the entire audience's receptivity to what was going on onstage. I ushered at the Shubert in New Haven during graduate school when plays en route to Broadway still went out of town to try out. I worked backstage at summer stock doing jobs from garbage man, to strapping on Herbert Marshall's wooden leg, to fixing Gloria Swanson's broken plumbing in her dressing room with her yelling at me as I worked the plunger. I ran the light board for her show, which involved bringing up all the stage lights surreptitiously when she came onstage so the audience would subliminally think, gee, isn't everything brighter when she's around? I was supposed to do it very quietly. It was an old light board and very squeaky. I'd bring the lights up one point—and it squeaked. I don't know what the audience felt when they heard that sound—when she came on and left the stage. It was called a star bump. Knowing lore like that made me feel there was a secret freemasonry to the theater. Then I toured as an advance man for a summer stock package, setting up the show each week in a different theater before moving on to the next. Even with *Six Degrees of Separation* I felt part of my job as playwright was to go backstage two or three times every week during the run to check the backstage temperature—who's unhappy, who's not speaking, whose costumes are wearing out. You must keep people happy backstage because that affects what's onstage. During a run, the playwright feels like the mayor of a small town filled with noble creatures who have to get out there and make it brand new every night. When a production works, it's unlike any other joy in the world.

INTERVIEWER: So you chose the theater life early on.

GUARE: My parents started taking me to plays early. Plays have a celebratory nature that no other form has. Theater always meant celebration, a birthday, a reward for good grades. I felt at home in a theater. I loved being part of an audience. All the rules: the audience has to see the play on a certain date at a certain time in a certain place in a certain seat. You watched the stage in unison with strangers. The theater had intermissions where you could smoke cigarettes in the lobby and imagine you were interesting. The theater made everybody in the audience behave better, as if they were all in on the same secret. I found it amazing that what was up on that stage could make these people who didn't know each other laugh, respond, gasp in exactly the same way at the same time.

INTERVIEWER: What was the first play you saw?

GUARE: *Annie Get Your Gun.* Ethel Merman.

INTERVIEWER: I have a theory that there are two kinds of people in the theater ... those who started out because they went to see *Annie Get Your Gun* or those who went into it because they read Antonin Artaud.

GUARE: I was reading Artaud during *Annie Get Your Gun.* A girl, Jane, in our grammar school class was actually in *Annie Get Your Gun,* and she'd be off Wednesdays for matinees. On holidays, Sister Donalda, the very stern superior, would come to our class and ask Jane to come forward and sing Sister's favorite song; Jane would step to the front of the class and belt out "You Can't Get a Man with a Gun."

INTERVIEWER: So you've always been stagestruck?

GUARE: In the blood. My mother's family was in show business. Her two uncles toured in vaudeville with a bill of sixteen plays they cobbled together from 1880 to 1917 with titles like *Pawn Ticket 210, The Old Toll House,* and *Girl of the Garrison.* Lines like the old man coming forward and saying, "Twenty-five years ago this very night my son left home taking the money he did not know was rightfully his. Oh, if I could only see him again." *(flickering outside the window)* "Oh, the same lightning! The same thunder!" *(knock knock)* "Who can that be!"

My grandfather was a cop in Lynn, Massachusetts. In a raid on a Lynn cathouse they found a very small child left by one of the arrested girls. He brought the baby home; he turned out to be five years old and a midget. Little Billy was taken into the act by the uncles for the good reason that he was a great little hoofer and song shouter. The act broke up when little Billy left to join the George M. Cohan Review of 1918; dressed as a tiny soldier, he was one of the cast who introduced *Over There.* My mother's real brother, who was known in our family as Big Bill, became an agent for stars like W. C. Fields, Al Jolson, and Will Rogers. Big Bill was called "Square Deal" Grady by Damon Runyon for the "creative" contracts he made with his clients. He was head of casting at MGM from 1934 to 1956. I never saw Big Bill much but his presence and power to discover people figured heavily in my dream life. In fact, the monologue that opens the second act of *The House of Blue Leaves* happened exactly as described: Big Bill was on a major MGM talent hunt searching for an unknown child to play Huckleberry Finn. To escape all these kids, he came to see us. I decided fate had sent him to me: *I* would be Huck. I packed my bags and went mad and auditioned. He quickly left thinking he'd been set up by my parents. My mother cried. It was horrible. I gave up all dreams of acting at age eight. Playwriting seemed a lot safer.

INTERVIEWER: Did you ever want to write anything else? A novel?

GUARE: In college I was editor of the literary magazine and wrote sensitive short stories overly inspired by Flaubert. Our English teacher actually knew Katherine Anne Porter; he showed her a short story I had written. She told him she would pay $1,500 for the first sentence:

"After Pinky vomited, Ingrid Aldamine sat up in bed." She liked the rhythm. She didn't mention anything about the rest. However, if I could write one sentence that an actual famous writer would comment on—wow! Those few crumbs were enough for me. But no more stories. I felt I was betraying a higher calling by writing mere short stories or novels. I believed plays to be on a higher and rarer plane. I still do. Novelists were only a couple of hundred years old. Playwrights were thousands of years old. If I was going to be a writer, it had to be plays.

INTERVIEWER: When did you actually discover this?

GUARE: In 1949, I was eleven. My pal, Bobby, and I read a story in *Life* magazine about two boys spending their summer vacation making a movie of Tom Sawyer. We had no camera but Bobby had a garage. I immediately wrote three plays. Between shanghaiing kids on the block and rounding up puppets, we got together a cast. We then called *Life* magazine to alert them to this great story. "Time-Life," the operator said. "We have this great story of two boys spending their summer vacation..." "Time-Life, to whom do you wish to speak?" "No, you see, these two boys..." Click!

INTERVIEWER: The operator obviously didn't have a good nose for a story.

GUARE: We lowered our sights and called the local Long Island paper. "Two boys are putting on plays and—wait! We're giving all the proceeds to the orphans of Long Beach!" "Oh yeah?" they said. On the last day of our performances, a big black car pulled up to Bobby's garage. A photographer took our pictures; they published a story about an eleven-year-old playwright. For my twelfth birthday, my parents gave me a portable typewriter because I was a playwright; I still use it.

INTERVIEWER: What happened to the orphans of Long Beach?

GUARE: Oh, they were all given lifetime passes to the beach.

INTERVIEWER: Do you think of yourself as a regional writer?

GUARE: Yes. From the region of New York.

INTERVIEWER: Have you always lived in the city?

GUARE: Yes and no. In 1950, when I was twelve, my father suffered an angina. He had to take at least a year off from work so he, my mother, and I lived most of the time in Ellenville, in upstate New York, with his elderly aunt, who was also quite sick, mentally and physically. It was the McCarthy time. Since the grammar school in Ellenville neither pledged allegiance to the flag nor said the Our Father, the nuns in Jackson Heights in New York City agreed with my parents that it would be better for me not to go to school at *all* rather than enroll in an obvious Commie den. So I stayed enrolled at St. Joan of Arc in Jackson Heights, but I had all this time by myself in Ellenville. Television had not yet come to Ellenville, which was in the low part of a valley. All I did was read. And read. And I wrote. And I walked and walked, lived in my own world, my soul protected from the red menace. I'm the only person I know who benefited from the McCarthy period. In 1950 a play I read about, again in *Life* magazine (obviously my link to the world), opened on Broadway. It was called *The Wisteria Trees.* Joshua Logan had taken *The Cherry Orchard* and set it down south. What a good idea! It made me read *The Cherry Orchard.* What a great play! I knew about Tennessee Williams, again from a story in *Life.* I even saw the movie of *A Streetcar Named Desire* up there in Ellenville at the Shadowland Theater. I started reading Chekhov's plays and loved *Three Sisters.* I remembered what Joshua Logan had done with *The Wisteria Trees.* Hmmm. I typed out the first act of my play on my new official playwright's typewriter—every time those girls moaned for "Moscow," I typed in "New Orleans," hearing the aching, yearning voice of Kim Stanley, whom I knew from television in New York. That was playwriting. Neurotic, misunderstood Southerners trying to get to New Orleans.

INTERVIEWER: It must have been a good lesson, copying out *Three Sisters.*

GUARE: It taught me about typing. I learned more about basic play structure poring over the original cast albums of shows ... the brainstorm that the second song was usually the "want" song. And how in *Guys and Dolls* the need for a spot for the oldest established permanent floating crap game in New York was technically no different than those three sisters yearning to get to Moscow. The *need* made the story. Creating the arc and completing it.

INTERVIEWER: How long did that period of off-and-on hooky last?

GUARE: Until I went to Catholic high school in Brooklyn. I took a long subway ride each day to Williamsburg, which was simultaneously an old Hasidic and a brand-new Latino community. I learned how to conjugate Latin verbs and do euclidean geometry standing up in a packed morning rush hour. The training of doing homework in a crowded subway is good preparation for working in the theater, where rehearsal is the place you do your rewriting—nightmarishly public, even if it's just the cast and crew. I also went to more and more plays. The best thing I ever saw was Tyrone Guthrie's production of *Tamburlaine the Great*. I still haven't seen anything like Anthony Quayle striding over a map of the world. A body hoisted to the top of the Winter Garden stage and down below a phalanx of archers shooting arrows into it. Marlowe was better than anybody.

INTERVIEWER: You wrote plays in college.

GUARE: A play a year. The songs in *House of Blue Leaves* written by the failed songwriter were my successes in a college musical in 1960 that started out as a musical of *The Great Gatsby* but ended up as a version of *Singin' in the Rain,* called *The Thirties Girl.*

INTERVIEWER: You went to the Yale School of Drama...

GUARE: ...where I read every play in the library and talked about plays and wrote plays, ushered at the Shubert and learned how plays were rewritten and rerehearsed; then I'd see them in New York and see how sometimes the rewriting had harmed them.

INTERVIEWER: You studied playwriting. You've taught it. What can you learn from those classes?

GUARE: In a good playwriting course you learn which playwright you write like. And why you admire that writer.

INTERVIEWER: Do all writers become peers?

GUARE: Yes. If you can't be arrogant in drama school, where can you be? You learn to approach, say, Chekhov as a peer. How does he deal with entrances and exits? You study how Chekhov gets somebody off-stage: you see how he takes a simple exit in *Uncle Vanya,* in which Sonya leaves to ask permission to play the piano and builds to Sonya's sudden return—"He says no"—a heartstopping moment that sums up a life.

INTERVIEWER: And after Chekhov?

GUARE: Irish writers. F. Scott Fitzgerald. I was bowled over by the fact that Lady Gregory's first play was *Colman and Guaire.* It was a sign.

INTERVIEWER: Why Irish?

GUARE: Because I'm Irish. One hundred percent on both sides.

INTERVIEWER: There's a line in *The House of Blue Leaves* where one character says to Bananas, "What else was I going to name a little Italian girl?" I always assumed you were Italian.

GUARE: That was my attempt to disguise the real stuff in the play.

INTERVIEWER: Parenthesis. Once and for all. How do you pronounce your name? I've heard it "Gor." "Gar."

GUARE: "Grrr." In Ireland it's pronounced somewhere between "Gworra" and "Gorra," but when they came to Vermont, they flattened it out into a sound that rhymes with *bare, blare, care, dare, fare, glare, hare, mare,* et cetera, et cetera. I was once answering questions after a talk, and a woman asked, "Mr. Gwa-ray, would you talk about the meaning..." I interrupted her. "Excuse me, but it's pronounced Guare." She said, very grand, "I pronounce it Gwa-ray."

INTERVIEWER: Back to the Irish.

GUARE: I saw every performance of a college production of *The Importance of Being Earnest*, and so I wrote a play in emulation of Wilde. I wrote an additional act to *Plough and the Stars* because O'Casey didn't go far enough. Shaw—*Heartbreak House* is the best. Williams's *Orpheus Descending* opened in Washington my freshman year, and I went to the first performance. A latecomer fell noisily down the steep balcony stairs during the first act; I yelled out, "It's Orpheus descending!" and everybody laughed. Oh, if only I could be European or Southern and not cursed with the nothingness of my surroundings!

INTERVIEWER: O'Neill?

GUARE: O'Neill won a Nobel so he was like a European. It's hard to learn from somebody like O'Neill. He's great in spite of his flaws. His genius has nothing to teach others except to keep writing all your life, and maybe at the end you'll write a few masterpieces.

INTERVIEWER: Shakespeare?

GUARE: We can only learn one lesson from Shakespeare and that's that there are no stage directions. It never says, "JULIET (*in a melancholy yet noble, quixotic way*)." The emotions and the intentions must be firmly embedded right in the lines.

INTERVIEWER: And the more moderns?

GUARE: I was very taken with Auden and Isherwood's *Ascent of F6* because it took place scaling a mountain. I only knew plays in living rooms. I hated our living room. Through reading F. Scott Fitzgerald and reading about him, I learned about his friend on the Riviera, Philip Barry, also an Irish-American. I liked the destructive lives they led and the glamorous wish-fulfillment worlds of *Holiday* and *The Philadelphia Story*. I wished I lived in their living rooms with no financial necessities. I liked the rhythm and artificiality of high comedy. And I liked Barry's plays for their mood changes. They could suddenly go pensive. For learning purposes, they seemed more manageable than O'Neill.

INTERVIEWER: More manageable?

GUARE: Barry wrote not only boulevard plays like *Holiday* or *Paris Bound*, but far more instructive, nobly failed experiments like *Hotel Universe* or *Here Come the Clowns*. I did a thesis on him and learned about the nineteenth-century form *comédie larmoyante*, "tearful comedy"... noble and brave and smiling through the tears and flattering the audience. Take the closing lines of *The Philadelphia Story:* "You look like a goddess." "Yes, but I feel like a human being." And how *comédie larmoyante* grew into the well-made plays of Sardou and Scribe and then how that was turned on its ear by Ibsen, whose plays did everything *not* to make you comfortable.

INTERVIEWER: What else did you learn?

GUARE: Moss Hart said the audience will give you all their attention in the play's first fifteen minutes; but in the sixteenth minute they will decide whether to go on the journey you want them to take. That first fifteen minutes draws up the contract of your agreement with the audience. You can subvert it or play with it, but you must set up the premises for the evening, whether the play is *Mother Courage* or *Getting Gertie's Garter*—well, maybe not *Getting Gertie's Garter*. I once gave a course at Yale on only the first fifteen minutes of a play. *The Homecoming. The Cherry Orchard. What the Butler Saw*. The information the audience receives in that opening movement, that musical statement, allows us to enter the world of that play.

INTERVIEWER: How important are other aspects of the stage to a playwright?

GUARE: While I was a student at Yale in 1962, I took courses in set design, lighting, and costume from Donald Oenslager and Ernest Bevan. I needed to learn the light in which a play must live. I wasn't any good at the technical bits, but that wasn't the point. I learned the work processes and the range of possibilities of the design people with whom the playwright shares the stage. They provide the visual entry into the playwright's world. The playwright is the person responsible for everything on that stage. If the play doesn't work because of a miscast actor or because of a bad set, or it's misdirected, it's the play that will take the brunt. *Anything* that happens on that stage is playwriting. So the playwright better know the actors available, the directors, the designers, all of whom deal with the life being created onstage. I once saw a comedy in rehearsal, funny and knockdown, but not until it got onstage did we all realize that the costumes, which had looked so witty on paper, had been constructed in a very heavy fabric that disguised and covered the actors' bodies and dephysicalized them. It was too late and too expensive to change anything. The costumes went on. They got raves. The play was a bust. So the playwright has to look at paintings, listen to music, to say, yes that's the effect I want my plays to have.

INTERVIEWER: Craft.

GUARE: Yes. I love the part of playwriting that is a craft to be learned continually, the -*wright* part, like *shipwright* or *wheelwright*, or *cartwright*. Whether Aeschylus or George S. Kaufman, a playwright is a writer who understands the technical aspects of knowing how to deliver exposition, how to get a character on and offstage, where to place the intermission, how to bring down a curtain. How to have all the characters' stories end up simultaneously. That's craft, and craft can be taught by emulation. You figure out how your playwright of the moment accomplishes those facts of the theater. You learn to study those playwrights technically, the way a musician does a score, breaking the work down to learn how its composer achieved certain effects. And then, having learned a technique, one can use it oneself.

INTERVIEWER: Strindberg says somewhere the final effect is all.

GUARE: Yes. Learning how to drive your work to that uncluttered final point is a craft. You learn there's no such thing as a perfect play unless it's *Life Is a Dream* by Pedro Calderón de la Barca.

INTERVIEWER: What other plays?

GUARE: When I was a kid, I saw a play that had a profound effect on me—*Time Remembered* by Jean Anouilh, with Richard Burton, Susan Strasberg, and Helen Hayes, of all people. It was a straight play that had a pit orchestra—a literal melodrama for which Vernon Duke wrote a wonderful score; it created such an air of magic. I saw it out of town, and I remember Helen Hayes being great. I went every night. Then it came to New York and sort of flattened out. It didn't get very good reviews; I went to see it. Dull, very dull. There was something missing from it. I later read an interview with Helen Hayes that said when she was in Washington, she'd never been more scared in her life. She didn't understand one thing she was doing onstage. She didn't understand the play. She was in a panic every night. Then in Boston, dreading going on, she was waiting in her dressing room when she heard a harpsichord being played on the radio that soothed her, and she said, "Oh, that's what my character is, I'm a harpsichord." So, I said to myself, oh, *that's* the trouble, she became a harpsichord. I learned that it's better to create panic on the stage because panic is alive. That was a great revelation to me, that experience with *Time Remembered*.

Dürrenmatt's *The Visit* also had a profound effect on me. To have a play draw you in with humor and then make you crazy and send you out mixed up! When I got to Feydeau, Strindberg, Pinter, Joe Orton, and the "dis-ease" they created, I was home. Pinter's plays had the rhythm of high comedy trapped in the wrong surroundings; I identified with that. I loved the strictures of farce, besides liking the sound of an audience laughing. I loved Feydeau's one rule of playwriting: Character A: My life is perfect as long as I don't see Character B. Knock knock. Enter Character B. And Feydeau's hysteria opened the door to Strindberg.

I always liked plays to be funny and early on stumbled upon the truth that farce is tragedy speeded up. Filling up that hunger. Get to Moscow. Get into an adult world. The want becomes a need. The need becomes a hunger and because you're speeding it up so much . . .

INTERVIEWER: . . . it becomes ridiculous.

GUARE: Exactly. The intensity puts it on the edge. The top keeps spinning faster until it can only explode, and if you've got a stageful of people at that psychic, manic state and an audience in tune with them, then something dangerous might happen out of that hysteria. You want to move the audience into a new part of themselves.

INTERVIEWER: Speaking of Irish, what about Beckett?

GUARE: Beckett's a great writer but a bad influence. Young writers used to think that tramps speaking non sequiturs was playwriting. As a teacher, you want to stop people from writing pastiches of Beckett and thinking that's playwriting. You want them to learn how to admire him, but to know the aim of playwriting is not to become a ventriloquist in someone else's voice.

INTERVIEWER: What about your voice?

GUARE: You have to keep working to find your voice, then have the grace or good sense to recognize it as your voice and then learn how to use it.

INTERVIEWER: How is being a playwright different from being a novelist?

GUARE: A playwright is a writer who only has ninety-nine pieces of paper to tell his tale. You've got to get your story told in approximately two hours. If it's too long you have to learn how to cut without destroying the intention of your work. People think playwriting is just somebody supplying the words. No. Theater is the place where you learn all your lessons in a crowd. Imagine a novelist watching five hundred people simultaneously reading a draft of a novel and then making adjustments based on their immediate responses. Also, you had better know the audience with whom you want to draw up the contract. Peter Brook gave a seminar at La Mama and someone asked him what the prime aesthetic problem was in the theater. He said, "Oh, that's easy. When once you've discovered the laugh, it's how do you keep the laugh."

INTERVIEWER: You've had the most traditional route to becoming a playwright. You didn't run off to sea ...

GUARE: No. I went to California after I graduated in 1963. That last year at Yale I wrote a play called *Did You Write My Name in the Snow?* which was seen by people from MCA. I got the offer of a job as a writing trainee at Universal Studios. My uncle finally spoke to me again, the first time since the *Huckleberry Finn* fiasco. Impressed that I had a master's from Yale and that Universal was interested in me, he got me a job—as a trainee at MGM. Wow! Which job to take! Luckily, I got my draft notice and spent six months in the Air Force. During that time an aunt in San Francisco asked me to come see her. She was very disappointed in me. What was this about going to work in the movies? What happened to my dreams of being a playwright? I said I had to make a living; eventually I would get back to writing plays. She said I knew nothing about life and I'd get swallowed up. She had planned to leave me ten thousand dollars. Now, she would give the sum to me if I left California, went back to New York, wrote plays, went to Europe, sent her postcards. If I didn't do this, she would leave the money to a dog charity. So I headed back to New York, lived in a rented room in Brooklyn. Off Broadway was beginning—our version of Paris in the twenties. I saw remarkable plays at the Caffé Cino by Lanford Wilson and H. M. Katoukas, who walked around the Village with a parakeet tied to each finger of his hands. Ten parakeets flying all around him. The Caffé was run by a burly Sicilian, Joe Cino, who worked in a steam laundry from 7:00 A.M. to 4:00 P.M., then went to his kingdom, his paradise, a café on Cornelia Street decorated with a crush of twinkling Christmas tree lights, religious statues, Kewpie dolls, and blowups of Jean Harlow and Maria Callas, a kind of insane storefront attic. I brought two plays to Cino. He said, sorry we're only doing plays by Aquarians. I sputtered that I *was* an Aquarius! He looked at my driver's license. February 5. He weighed my plays in his beefy hands, then checked his astrological charts. "You go into rehearsal in two weeks, run for two weeks with a possibility of an extension for a third." I don't know what would have happened to me if I had been a Gemini.

INTERVIEWER: It makes about as much sense as most producers' philosophies.

GUARE: My father came to the Cino to see my play. He was shocked that we passed the hat for money afterwards. A Yale graduate and here

I was passing the hat on Cornelia Street! He had an idea. Write a hit *musical,* then come back to the Cino when you won't have to pass the hat. I told him to get lost. Yet another stupid idea. At about that same time, Edward Albee earned himself eternal playwright sainthood. Out of the profits from *Who's Afraid of Virginia Woolf?* he and his producers took a lease on a theater on Van Dam Street, and every week for six months of the year from 1963 to 1969 they produced a new play. The plays were not reviewed. Audiences just showed up at the theater to see what was there. They were very exciting times. I once wrote a play called *A Day for Surprises* on a Thursday, and it opened the next Monday.

INTERVIEWER: When did the O'Neill Theater Center come into play?

GUARE: The O'Neill changed everything for me. In 1965, questionnaires were sent around to various theaters and agents to name promising playwrights, and they picked twenty names, mine among them. They brought us up to Waterford, Connecticut, to ask us what playwrights wanted. Well, their plays performed of course, to meet other actors, a theater community, a place to learn what designers do and meet directors...give ourselves more tools to work with. That first group included Lanford Wilson, Sam Shepard, and Leonard Melfi. After a long weekend they returned us to New York and dropped us off in Times Square. We all felt we'd never hear from them again, that it was just an artsy version of the Fresh Air Fund. So I forgot about it. I went on living very frugally on my aunt's legacy for four years. I went to Europe, got a job in London, which was then a miracle of great acting and theater: Olivier's *Othello,* Pinter's *Homecoming.* Then I hitched from Paris to Egypt.

INTERVIEWER: Your aunt, did you send her postcards?

GUARE: I had made a bargain. Sure did.

INTERVIEWER: Did you write on that trip?

GUARE: I got to Cairo at the end of 1965. My parents sent me news clippings of the day the Pope came to New York. Their long letter told me that while I might be seeing the world I didn't know *what* I had missed by not being in New York that magical day—a Pope voluntarily leaving Rome for the first time ever to fly across an ocean to plead for peace, and I could miss *that!* Sitting in Cairo, reading what that day meant to them back on Queens Boulevard, I saw my life and all our dreams and where those dreams had taken us, and I realized I had a subject. I started writing *The House of Blue Leaves.* I read that letter, and everything that had happened to me in my life became accessible. I heard the sound of my life. I was no longer a secret Southern writer. I heard New York for the first time.

INTERVIEWER: By then the O'Neill Theater Center was in operation.

GUARE: The center was having its first official summer in Waterford, in 1966. In those days they would choose a playwright and assign him or her a date to read a play. I had the first act of *House of Blue Leaves,* and I played the lead—well, read it. I liked the people who were up there—Bobby Lewis, Alan Schneider, Jose Quintero, Lloyd Richards. I liked the sense of community and festivity. It was all very receptive and intelligent and hip. I found an audience it was great fun to write for. I had a *place* to write for. I learned about keeping at the business of doing new work in front of audiences, working with actors, learning the way *they* work, finding the kind of actors who understand the rhythms of your work. That's all a theater company is really: a group of talented people who laugh at the same jokes. You have to learn about design. What kind of visuals your work needs to register. And the audience—you have to keep listening to the audience, not to see what they want, but rather to learn how to make them respond the way you want. The first days at the O'Neill made all this alive.

INTERVIEWER: So you had the first act of a play ...

GUARE: Because of the response at the O'Neill to the first act of *House of Blue Leaves,* I got a grant to go back to New Haven as a fellow during Robert Brustein's first year at the Yale Drama School. A TV network gave money and movie cameras to Yale so playwrights could learn how to make movies. Sam Shepard, Ken Brown, who wrote *The Brig,* Barbara Garson, who wrote *MacBird,* Megan Terry, and I were the first group. What a remarkable year! Robert Lowell was in residence. Jonathan Miller. Irene Worth. Arnold Weinstein. André Gregory. Ron Leibman. Linda Lavin. Bill Bolcom. I wrote *Muzeeka* about all those undergraduates I saw around me, so free and happy but wondering what in adult life would allow them to keep their spirit and freedom. How do we keep any ideals in this particular society? Vietnam was starting to become a specter that wouldn't go away.

INTERVIEWER: You didn't go back to the O'Neill after 1968.

GUARE: By 1969 the O'Neill realized that no one would ever leave. So the emphasis changed, and you had to submit a play to be chosen. The play was chosen rather than the playwright.

INTERVIEWER: You had a play done on Broadway.

GUARE: *CopOut*. It opened and closed. What I expected from *CopOut* I don't know. The actress—Linda Lavin played the role nobly—had to flee the stage, be shot, and fall dead at the theater doors so the audience would have to step guiltily over her corpse in order to leave the theater. She only avoided being trampled on for a few days. I was depressed because the reviews were scathing: "not a review, an obituary" was the tone. I went on the maiden voyage of the *QEII* because maybe an iceberg would hit it; I went up to the Arctic Circle to escape the pain. All this while, we were having backers' auditions for *House of Blue Leaves*. The first act was written in one sitting, but it took me nearly five years to write the second act. I knew what the events would be, but I lacked the technical skill to handle nine people onstage, to make the material do what I wanted it to do. But finally we thought we were ready. A friend from the O'Neill, John Lahr, told me about a director from the Guthrie Theater named Mel Shapiro. I saw his work at Lincoln Center on a Václav Havel play; I loved it. We got a wonderful cast, went into rehearsal. *Blue Leaves* was a success. We won the Obie and the New York Drama Critics' prize, and my picture was on the cover of the *Saturday Review of Literature*. Then Joe Papp asked Mel to direct *Two Gentlemen of Verona*. The production toured around the city parks on a truck in the summer of 1971. Because of the work we had done on farce structure for *Blue Leaves*, Mel asked me if I would cut and shape

Two Gentlemen into ninety minutes. Galt MacDermot was the resident composer that summer. By the time we opened, we had a musical that became a great success and moved from Central Park to Broadway, where it won the Tony Award. So I had a play and a musical on at the same time in New York. I was asked to do more musicals. I knew I should get back to the business of being a playwright. I didn't know quite what to do. I was in a panic. I had no new projects, having spent so much time with *Blue Leaves* and then *Two Gentlemen.* Then I remembered what my father had said.

INTERVIEWER: Write a musical hit and back to Cino.

GUARE: The Cino had ended with Cino's tragic, drug-induced suicide. But maybe it was time to get out of New York and start new Cinos. So a few of us, including Mel Shapiro, moved up to Nantucket and started a theater where we did *Marco Polo Sings a Solo.* I wrote fifteen drafts of that play. Then I realized that I shouldn't spend so much time trying to make something perfect.

INTERVIEWER: Rewriting is an art.

GUARE: Garson Kanin once said, "Isn't it funny that not many people know how to write a play but everybody knows how to rewrite a play." That's what you have to be careful about: to whom you listen and whom you close out. And also, strangely, how to keep the radar open just in case somebody, some stranger, does throw something good at you. Answers are easy. Formulating the problem; that's the art. But finally you have to realize there are certain times when, as Valéry says, a work of art isn't finished, it's just abandoned. You have to cut bait and move on to the next work.

INTERVIEWER: Going to Nantucket meant leaving the main source of your work—New York.

GUARE: That's one of the reasons I started writing the *Lydie Breeze* plays—literally to stop looking around my city, New York, and to draw water out of a different well, a well that was also mine. Living in Nantucket got me in touch with the New England part of my past—my mother was from Lynn, Massachusetts, and my father's family is from Gloucester, Massachusetts, and Montpelier, Vermont. If you die in Montpelier, you'll get buried from Guare's Funeral Parlor. My father's grandfather had been a ship captain in Gloucester. My parents were born in the 1890s, and I wanted to imagine myself back in that time and write out of that. A pre-Freudian time. I wanted to make sense out of family myths, overheards and recriminations and family legends and half-understood events that happened before I was born in 1938. When my parents were battling at night, I'd hear my mother say to my father, "Your grandfather might have been a slave driver, but you're not turning me into one of his slaves." And I'd put my hands over my ears and stay under the covers. Years later, I wondered what they were talking about, what did that mean? That time in Nantucket awakened a lot of that lost past in me; I was very grateful because a whole new imaginative life began once I got to Nantucket. That's all we wanted to do—arrange our lives to make our unconscious usable.

INTERVIEWER: I believe that there are four plays from this Nantucket well, three of them done.

GUARE: I wrote *Lydie Breeze* first, but that's chronologically the last. To explain the past of the characters, I wrote another play called *Gardenia*, which dealt with these people at the end of the Civil War. Then I wanted to write the magical time when these people all met during the war. That play is called *Women and Water.*

INTERVIEWER: And the fourth?

GUARE: It'll come. It'll come.

INTERVIEWER: *Six Degrees of Separation* is about to close at Lincoln Center after an eighty-week run, and next week you go into rehearsal with a new play, *Four Baboons Adoring the Sun,* also at Lincoln Center, directed by Sir Peter Hall.

GUARE: At the moment I'm the luckiest of playwrights. I belong to a theater.

INTERVIEWER: Why do you say "at the moment" so ominously?

GUARE: Isn't that the law of the theater? Not to mention life.

INTERVIEWER: What is the definition of a successful play for a playwright?

GUARE: One that generates a new play. That's all you can hope for. To get on to the next play.

INTERVIEWER: Is there always a next play in mind?

GUARE: There'd better be. On a plane coming back from London in 1972, I got in a panic because I had no new work and said to myself, before this plane lands I'm going to have the first act of something. I don't care what it is. I can't land without having another play to work on. I wrote the first act of *Marco Polo Sings a Solo*. I promised myself that I would never get in a situation again where a project ended, and I had nothing to go on to. If it's a success you're stuck with a terrible thing: oh my God, how am I going to repeat that? Or, if it's a failure: how do I get back in the saddle again? I like to keep a number of projects going at the same time, so the day after opening I've got something in some midstate to get to and not have to start from scratch.

INTERVIEWER: Do you work every day?

GUARE: I literally get sick if I don't. I like to work, I like to get up in the morning and go to work.

INTERVIEWER: What does it mean to be a playwright in America?

GUARE: You could give two hundred answers to that. One would involve masochism. Another one: how to avoid suicide and despair. You try to find a way to support yourself that doesn't crush your life. You try to find the best people to work with.

INTERVIEWER: What's your process of writing a play? How does it begin for you?

GUARE: Each play has its own rules.

INTERVIEWER: *Landscape of the Body*. How did that come about?

GUARE: I lived over by the river in Greenwich Village in the seventies. It was a creepy time because of a lot of murders going on there. One morning I went to a coffee shop up the street and saw four tough kids, aged eleven or twelve, sitting in the booth. Two boys. Two girls. The boys had their sleeves rolled up to show the enrapt girls their forearms covered with an awful lot of gold wristwatches. They leaned forward like conspirators, whispering, giggling, bragging. I couldn't get close enough to hear the words. I went home and wrote down what I imagined they were saying. Later that week, I got knocked down by a speed bike. The cyclist, masked in goggles, screamed over me, "You asshole! You broke the chain on my bike!" The membrane between life and death seemed so tenuous that it's hard to tell the difference. The collision must have unlocked some buried fantasy because I went home and wrote the play very quickly. It was narrated very merrily by a dead porn star; I wrote a lot of Broadway-style songs for her because they were fun to write.

INTERVIEWER: Do they all happen this quickly?

GUARE: No! With *Muzeeka,* for example, what was crazy was that I couldn't *begin* it. The typical trouble is with endings. Not this play. I knew what I didn't want the beginning to be, but I didn't know what it should be. It needed something lyrical. And it had to have weight, but nothing would come. I was living temporarily over a tobacco shop in New Haven. I went to my parents' apartment in New York to get some stored clothes and found a suitcase containing notebooks from two years before when I'd hitchhiked from Paris to Egypt. I opened the journals out of nostalgic curiosity. I read an entry made while hitching out of Rome, caught in a torrential downpour, running for shelter into what turned out to be the Etruscan Museum, staying there a few gleeful hours writing a long riff about wishing I'd been born an Etruscan. After that, I dropped the journal and stopped writing. But where the Etruscan entry broke off was exactly where my play picked up! The 1965 entry fit like a jigsaw into place as the 1967 beginning. Unaware, I had begun writing this play two years before, but hadn't known it until that chance discovery of the notebooks, which I just as easily could have lost or never found. Without making it sound too much like Santa's workshop, I realized the full impact of how our subconscious or unconscious never stops, how we have to keep track of everything. Because we don't know what is going to be of value to us. So, out of fear, I began keeping a journal that I now refer to over and over. In Copenhagen I found this solidly bound 250-page notebook that fits easily into the pocket. I fill up four in a year, then send away for more. I have this vision that one day I will reach into my drawer and feel it's the last volume. When I reach page 250, I'll write in "The End" and keel over.

INTERVIEWER: What volume are you up to now?

GUARE: Volume 82.

INTERVIEWER: Eighty-two times 250? That's roughly 16,000 pages.

GUARE: Sixteen thousand indecipherable pages. Korean hieroglyphics. Once I was on the downtown bus writing in my book, and a woman next to me tapped me and said, "Excuse me. What language are you writing in?"

INTERVIEWER: Are they for publication? Like the Cheever journals?

GUARE: They're not confessional. They're workout books I use every day to keep the buzz going, the buzz that writing gives you, to stop the moss from growing over the brain and blocking that subconscious part, to stop the constant death-desire to self-censor. If I don't have anything to write about that day, I copy passages out of what I'm reading. The papers. A novel. Any writer is a sculptor who makes his own clay and then has to protect that clay in hopes of transformation. The journals are autobiographical. They're about what happens. What did Jean Rhys say? "I am my own novel." I'm my own play.

INTERVIEWER: In spite of these journals your work doesn't seem autobiographical. *House of Blue Leaves. Rich and Famous. Bosoms and Neglect.*

GUARE: In the journals I can happily be my own hero and victim. But when you translate that journal material into a play, you begin building a new world; and the "I" becomes just another citizen of that world to be treated with the same objective scrutiny, irony, and disdain. Besides, I don't like autobiographical work where you can tell which character is the author because he or she is the most sensitive, the most misunderstood, the most sympathetic. Everybody including yourself should be fair game.

INTERVIEWER: Do you write with endings in mind?

GUARE: No. If you knew where you were going why would you bother writing? There'd be nothing to discover. I can still remember throwing up when I realized what the ending of *The House of Blue Leaves* would be—that after the songwriter realized the true worth of his work he would have to kill his wife because she saw him as he was.

INTERVIEWER: Can you say something about the kind of actors you'd prefer to see in your plays?

GUARE: I love actors who are performers, who are clowns—meaning they are willing to make fools of themselves, to stride that brink of panic. I feel that Stanislavsky—at least the way he's been interpreted through the Method in America—has been the enemy of performance; I'm not interested in that style of naturalism. How we *escape* naturalism always seems to be the key. Naturalism is great for television and the small screen. Theatrical reality happens on a much higher plane. People on a stage are enormous, there to drive us crazy. I love actors who can do that.

INTERVIEWER: How do you pick a director?

GUARE: I once asked Lanford Wilson this and he said, "Easy. I ask the potential director to tell me the story of my play, and if his story matches up with my story then perhaps we can work together."

INTERVIEWER: What's that letter you keep up there on the wall?

GUARE: It's a Xerox of a letter by William Inge to Jean Kerr. I keep it up there the way St. Jerome kept a skull in front of him, to remind me of the realities of theater. Jean Kerr wrote Inge soliciting funds for a playwriting group. Inge replied, "Isn't helping new dramatists a little like helping people into Hell?"

INTERVIEWER: Did you know Inge?

GUARE: In 1965 I got a job at Falmouth as William Inge's assistant on a new pre-Broadway play. I needed to learn how a play was physically put together by a professional playwright. I never even asked if Inge was any good, but he'd had success and had connected mightily with audiences in the past. *Picnic. Bus Stop.* If I didn't like his work, the fault was mine. After the opening of the play, *Family Things, Etc.,* later called *Where's Daddy?* the critic from the Boston paper had Inge on his TV show as a guest. He read Inge his review of the show with the camera on Inge's face. The review was unbelievably cruel and unexpected. Inge returned to Falmouth, went into his room, and never worked on the play again. He committed suicide two years later. I learned if one is going to be a playwright one must develop armor to deal with such horrific occupational hazards.

INTERVIEWER: There's a line in *Rich and Famous* where the young playwright reads his review and says, "They don't print this in every copy of the paper, do they?" How do you deal with reviews?

GUARE: I deal with reviews by not reading reviews, and that's a truth. My wife reads them and gives me the gist of them so I know what the quality of my life will be the next year. Get that teaching job.

INTERVIEWER: What's the difference between writing for the movies and writing for the theater?

GUARE: The Dramatists Guild. And how it protects the playwright. In the theater, the playwright holds the copyright—actually owns the play and only leases the right to its use for a specific length of time to the producer. In the movies, the producer holds the copyright. The writer is always only a hired hand. In the movies, the writer is paid up front. In the theater, the writer takes his or her chances. There is a profound difference in knowing the playwright can forgo that contractual right if he or she wishes, but it's there to use.

INTERVIEWER: What sort of experience have you had in the movies?

GUARE: It's not that working in movies is whore work, and the theater is purity. It all comes down to the people you work with. I admire Louis Malle and had a wonderful time working with him. When *Atlantic City* was finished, we looked at each other and said, that's exactly what we meant. I've been lucky. I've worked only with people I admired. When the producers of *Atlantic City* balked at my being on the set every day, Louis Malle gave the classic answer: "If you have someone here for the hair, why not somebody for the words?" Writing for the movies is like working on a musical. You have to recognize and accept the collaborative aspects before you start. You have to recognize what work the camera will do, what work you must not do. You underwrite a scene in the movies. The camera will pick up textures of reality that in a play would be the business of words.

INTERVIEWER: What's the main obligation of a playwright?

GUARE: I think it's to break the domination of naturalism and get the theater back to being a place of poetry, a place where language can reign. Theater poetry is not just highfalutin language you spray on the event like Fry's *Venus Observed*. Theater poetry is response to the large event, events that force the poetry. It took me a very long time to realize the mythic size of Ibsen, to see that the mechanics of plot in an Ibsen play function the same way that fate does in Greek tragedy. Truth does not exist merely in the actor feeling the heat of the teacup. Behavioral naturalism belongs to television acting and movie acting. Theater acting should be closer to Cyrano de Bergerac or Falstaff or Edmund the Bastard. Or Ethel Merman. It's about finding truth on the large scale with the recognition of the actor as performer. In real life we're all such performers. Naturalism wants to reduce us. Naturalism always seems to be the most unnatural thing. I really respect the opera notebooks of Stanislavsky where he writes about Mimi having to find her truth on the specific note called for in Puccini's music—not when she decides to feel it.

INTERVIEWER: And novels?

GUARE: A novelist writes a manuscript, gives it to the agent or the editor, who sends it back and forth until the publisher accepts it, and one day the author finds the book in stores. But a play—a playwright has not only that wonderful, brutal period of solitude writing the play, but then the day comes when you're ready to show your work to the theater's equivalent of a publisher, the producer, and the theater's equivalent of an editor, the director. You begin working with the designers who will provide the visual entry that introduces the audience to the world you've made. You start casting and choosing actors—a process much like the painter choosing the necessary tubes of paint and what consistency and what color they should be. Ahh! With a new shade an entire world opens up.

INTERVIEWER: Do you see a theme to your work?

GUARE: Don't make it sound like English 101. Each play is a part of the one long play that is a playwright's life. I know the way each play came out of the previous play. People don't have radical shifts of consciousness in the course of their lifetimes. I can look at a play I wrote at 2:00 A.M. in 1963 the night before I went into the Air Force—*The Loveliest Afternoon of the Year*—and say, isn't that funny. I'm still dealing with the issues in that play—identity, faith, the desperation it takes people to get through their lives, the lunatic order we try to put on the chaos of life, and, technically, how to get the play out of the kitchen sink and hurl it into the Niagara Falls of life.

INTERVIEWER: Now about those Jacobeans...

—ANNE CATTANEO
Winter, 1992

SAM SHEPARD

Archive Photos

"The poet laureate of America's emotional Badlands" (*Newsweek*), Sam Shepard was born Samuel Shepard Rogers VII, November 5, 1943, on a southern Illinois army base where his father was stationed. After a period of frequent moving from base to base, the Rogers family settled on a ranch in California, where they raised sheep and grew avocados. Shepard spent a few years in a local junior college studying agricultural science, but his father's descent into alcoholism and the accompanying deterioration of the family scene caused him to flee. He joined a touring theatrical group and, despite having only a few months' acting to his credit, headed to New York to embark on a career in theater. Once there, in the emerging world of avant-garde theater on the Lower East Side, he quickly found an interest in writing.

His reputation was built with a series of short plays for off- and off-off-Broadway theater, including *Chicago* (1965), *Icarus's Mother* (1965), *Red Cross* (1966), *La Turista* (1967), and *Forensic and the Navigators* (1967), all of which won Obie Awards. Their characteristic, somewhat jarring combination of visual and verbal imagery was due in part to the young Shepard's having written hastily, and to his early suspicion that revision violated a work's integrity. Around that time Shepard met the writer-director Joseph Chaikin, with whom he would collaborate during the seventies and eighties.

In 1971 Shepard moved with his wife of two years, O-Lan Johnson Dark, and their infant son to England, where he composed a number of well-received medium-length plays, including *The Tooth of Crime* (1972) and *Geography of a Horse Dreamer* (1974). In 1974 he returned to California and began writing the plays that have secured his reputation—*Curse of the Starving Class* (1978), *Fool for Love* (1983), and the Pulitzer Prize–winning *Buried Child* (1978). In 1983 Shepard divorced his wife and began a relationship with the actress-producer Jessica Lange.

Shepard made his feature-film debut as an actor in 1978, playing an affluent farmer in *Days of Heaven*. In 1984 he received an Academy Award nomination for his portrayal of Chuck Yeager in *The Right Stuff*. Although he has continued to receive numerous invitations to act, Shepard has limited himself to only a few roles, claiming, "The work just isn't that much fun."

He received the Golden Palm Award at the 1984 Cannes Film Festival for his screenplay to Wim Wenders's *Paris, Texas*. In 1986 he directed the original production of his play *A Lie of the Mind*, which won the New York Drama Critics' Circle Award.

———

This interview was conducted over several days in the living room of a Manhattan apartment by the East River. For the last meeting Sam Shepard arrived at the end of a late-afternoon snowstorm, his leather jacket unbuttoned in spite of the bad weather. He immediately became distracted by an out-of-tune Steinway in the corner, then returned to the couch for a discussion of his recently completed yearlong retrospective at New York's Signature Theatre. He said he had been exhausted by the theater's rehearsals, by a trip to London the previous week, and by a hectic schedule of public readings. Nevertheless, at the end of the meeting he de-

path.

Nat Henkins, our clarinet player, was not into the wild ~~baby~~ **thing**
It just didn't interest him for some reason
animal ~~obsession~~ like me and Mitchell. In fact, the only thing *(were)*
The Dorsey Brothers & that ilk.
that seemed to twirl Nat's ticket ~~was~~ 40's Big Band music. He

modeled himself after the young Benny Goodman, parting his hair
with Pomeade &
down the middle ~~and~~ slicked back, wore black rimmed glasses and
shirt
kept his top button buttoned at all times. He also read sheet

music fluently which kept me and Mitchell somewhat in a state

of awe and admiration, although privately we thought he was a

dipshit. ~~prude.~~ Nat looked the most out of place pulling a wolf pup off

the railroad tracks. His body never looked fully committed to
task.
the ~~action.~~ Neither did his clothes. He would rest too long

between pulls and spend a lot of time wiping the palms of his

hands on his pants leg and staring vacantly down the tracks

before grabbing the chain again and joining us in the struggle.
His hands were extremely white & long-fingered.
The groans he made were full of complaint rather than effort

and this started to piss me and Mitchell off. We could sense

Nat's half-heartedness and lack of urgency. Mitchell's voice

was punctuated by gasps for air as he leaned against the weight

of the baby wolf. "You understand, Nat, that the fruit train
You
is gonna' be blasting through here in about fifteen minutes? *understand that don't you?"* ~~Mitchell said.~~

"It never blasts through," Nat said, "That's an exager—
It's a law.
ation. They're not allowed to blast through towns. Besides,

I don't see why you don't just turn him loose. Wolf's not gonna'

just stand there and let himself get smashed by a fruit train.

He's not that stupid."

Mitchell stopped pulling and stood up straight, staring

A manuscript page from the story "Wild to the Wild" in Cruising Paradise.

clined to be driven back to his midtown hotel, saying he would rather walk back through Central Park instead.

Like many writers, Shepard is easy to imagine as one of the characters of his own work. In person, he is closer to the laconic and inarticulate men of his plays than to his movie roles. Self-contained, with none of the bearing of an actor, he retains a desert California accent and somehow seems smaller than one expects.

INTERVIEWER: The West figures predominantly as a mythology in many of your plays. You grew up there, didn't you?

SHEPARD: All over the Southwest, really—Cucamonga, Duarte, California, Texas, New Mexico. My dad was a pilot in the Air Force. After the war he got a Fulbright fellowship, spent a little time in Colombia, then taught high school Spanish. He kind of moved us from place to place.

INTERVIEWER: Do you think you'll ever live in the West again?

SHEPARD: No, I don't think so. The California I knew, old rancho California, is gone. It just doesn't exist, except maybe in little pockets. I lived on the edge of the Mojave Desert, an area that used to be farm country. There were all these fresh-produce stands with avocados and date palms. You could get a dozen artichokes for a buck or something. Totally wiped out now.

INTERVIEWER: *True West, Buried Child, Curse of the Starving Class,* and *Lie of the Mind* are all family dramas, albeit absurdist ones. Have you drawn a lot from your own family?

SHEPARD: Yes, though less now than I used to. Most of it comes, I guess, from my dad's side of the family. They're a real bizarre bunch, going back to the original colonies. That side's got a real tough strain of alcoholism. It goes back generations and generations, so that you can't remember when there was a sober grandfather.

INTERVIEWER: Have you struggled with drinking?

SHEPARD: My history with booze goes back to high school. Back then there was a lot of Benzedrine around, and since we lived near the Mexican border I'd just run over, get a bag of bennies, and drink Ripple wine. Speed and booze together make you quite...omnipotent. You don't feel any pain. I was actually in several car wrecks that I don't understand how I survived.

At any rate, for a long time I didn't think I had a problem. Alcoholism is an insidious disease; until I confronted it I wasn't aware that it was creeping up on me. I finally did AA in the hard core down on Pico Boulevard. I said, "Don't put me in with Elton John or anything, just throw me to the lions."

INTERVIEWER: Do you feel like the drinking might have aided your writing?

SHEPARD: I didn't feel like one inspired the other, or vice versa. I certainly never saw booze or drugs as a partner to writing. That was just the way my life was tending, you know, and the writing was something I did when I was relatively straight. I never wrote on drugs, or the bourbon.

INTERVIEWER: You said the men on your dad's side of the family were hard drinkers. Is this why the mothers in your plays always seem to be caught in the middle of so much havoc?

SHEPARD: Those midwestern women from the forties suffered an incredible psychological assault, mainly by men who were disappointed in a way that they didn't understand. While growing up I saw that assault over and over again, and not only in my own family. These were men who came back from the war, had to settle down, raise a family, and send the kids to school—and they just couldn't handle it. There was something outrageous about it. I still don't know what it was—maybe living through those adventures in the war and then having to come back to suburbia. Anyway, the women took it on the nose, and it wasn't like they said, "Hey Jack, you know, down the road, I'm leaving." They sat there and took it. I think there was a kind of heroism in those women. They were tough and selfless in a way. What they sacrificed at the hands of those maniacs...

INTERVIEWER: What was your dad like?

SHEPARD: He was also a maniac, but in a very quiet way. I had a falling-out with him at a relatively young age by the standards of that era. We were always butting up against each other, never seeing eye to eye on anything, and as I got older it escalated into a really bad, violent situation. Eventually I just decided to get out.

INTERVIEWER: Is he alive?

SHEPARD: No, a couple of years ago he was killed coming out of a bar in New Mexico. I saw him the year before he died. Our last meeting slipped into this gear where I knew it was going to turn really nasty. I remember forcing myself, for some reason, not to flip out. I don't know why I made that decision, but I ended up leaving without coming back at him. He was boozed up, very violent and crazy. After that I didn't see him for a long time. I did try to track him down; a friend of his told me he got a haircut, a fishing license, and a bottle, and then took off for the Pecos River. That was the last I heard of him before he died. He turned up a year later in New Mexico, with some woman I guess he was running with. They had a big blowout in a bar, and he went out in the street and got run over.

INTERVIEWER: Did he ever see one of your plays?

SHEPARD: Yes. There's a really bizarre story about that. He found out about a production of *Buried Child* that was going on at the Greer Garson Theater in New Mexico. He went to the show smashed, just pickled, and in the middle of the play he began to identify with some character, though I'm not sure which one, since all those characters are kind of loosely structured around his family. In the second act he stood up and started to carry on with the actors, and then yelled, "What a bunch of shit this is!" The ushers tried to throw him out. He resisted, and in the end they allowed him to stay because he was the father of the playwright.

INTERVIEWER: Were you there?

SHEPARD: No, I just heard about it. I think that's the only time he ever saw a production.

You know, all that stuff about my father and my childhood is interesting up to a certain point, but I kind of capsized with the family drama a long time ago. Now I want to get away from that. Not that I won't return to it, but a certain element has been exhausted, and it feels like: why regurgitate all this stuff?

INTERVIEWER: I read somewhere that you started writing because you wanted to be a musician.

SHEPARD: Well, I got to New York when I was eighteen. I was knocking around, trying to be an actor, writer, musician, whatever happened.

INTERVIEWER: What sort of musician were you trying to be?

SHEPARD: A drummer. I was in a band called the Holy Modal Rounders.

INTERVIEWER: How did you end up in New York?

SHEPARD: After the falling-out with my father I worked on a couple of ranches— Thoroughbred layup farms, actually—out toward Chino, California. That was fine for a little while, but I wanted to get out completely, and twenty miles away wasn't far enough. So I got a job delivering papers in Pasadena, and pretty soon, by reading the ad sections, I found out about an opening with a traveling ensemble called the Bishop's Company. I decided to give it a shot, thinking that this might be a way to really get out. At the audition they gave me a little Shakespeare thing to read—I was so scared I read the stage directions —and then they hired me. I think they hired everybody.

We traveled all over the country—New England, the South, the Midwest. I think the longest we stayed in one place was two days. It was actually a great little fold-up theater. We were totally self-sufficient: we put up the lights, made the costumes, performed the play, and shut down. Anyway, one day we got to New York to do a production at a church in Brooklyn and I said, "I'm getting off the bus."

INTERVIEWER: Did you start right in?

SHEPARD: Not immediately. My first job was with the Burns Detective Agency. They sent me over to the East River to guard coal barges during these god-awful hours like three to six in the morning. It wasn't a very difficult job—all I had to do was make a round every fifteen minutes—but it turned out to be a great environment for writing. I was completely alone in a little outhouse with an electric heater and a little desk.

INTERVIEWER: Did you already think of yourself as a writer?

SHEPARD: I'd been messing around with it for a while, but nothing serious. That was the first time I felt writing could actually be useful.

INTERVIEWER: How did you hook up with the theaters?

SHEPARD: Well, I was staying on Avenue C and Tenth Street with a bunch of jazz musicians, one of whom happened to be Charlie Mingus's son. We knew each other from high school, and he got me a job as a busboy at the Village Gate. The headwaiter at the Gate was a guy named Ralph Cook. Ralph was just starting his theater at St. Mark's in the Bowery, and he said he'd heard that I'd been writing some stuff, and he wanted to see it. So, I showed him a few plays I'd written, and he said, "Well, let's do it." Things kind of took off from there. New York was like that in the sixties. You could write a one-act play and start doing it the next day. You could go to one of those theaters—Genesis, La Mama, Judson Poets—and find a way to get it done. Nothing like that exists now.

INTERVIEWER: Did off-off-Broadway plays get reviewed back then?

SHEPARD: For a while the big papers wouldn't touch them, but then they started to smell something, so they came down and wrote these snide reviews. They weren't being unfair. A lot of that stuff really was shitty and deserved to get bombed. But there was one guy who was sort of on our side. His name was Michael Smith; he worked for *The Village Voice,* and he gave a glowing review to these little one-act plays, *Cowboys* and *The Rock Garden.* I remember that distinctly, not because of the praise but because it felt like somebody finally understood what we were trying to do. He was actually hooking up with us, seeing the work for what it was.

INTERVIEWER: What were the audiences like?

SHEPARD: They were incredibly different. You really felt that the community came to see the plays. They weren't people coming from New Jersey to have a dinner party. And they weren't going to sit around if they got bored. The most hostile audience I faced was up at the American Place Theatre when we were putting on *La Turista*. They invited all these Puerto Rican kids, street kids, and they were firing at the actors with peashooters.

INTERVIEWER: Did it take a long time to find your particular voice as a writer?

SHEPARD: I was amazed, actually. I've heard writers talk about "discovering a voice," but for me that wasn't a problem. There were so many voices that I didn't know where to start. It was splendid, really; I felt kind of like a weird stenographer. I don't mean to make it sound like hallucination, but there were definitely things there, and I was just putting them down. I was fascinated by how they structured themselves, and it seemed like the natural place to do it was on a stage. A lot of the time when writers talk about their voice they're talking about a narrative voice. For some reason my attempts at narrative turned out really weird. I didn't have that kind of voice, but I had a lot of other ones, so I thought, well, I'll follow those.

INTERVIEWER: Do you feel like you're in control of those voices now?

SHEPARD: I don't feel insane, if that's what you're asking.

INTERVIEWER: What is your schedule like?

SHEPARD: I have to begin early because I take the kids to school, so usually I'm awake by six. I come back to the house afterwards and work till lunch.

INTERVIEWER: Do you have any rituals or devices to help you get started?

SHEPARD: No, not really. I mean there's the coffee and that bullshit, but as for rituals, no.

INTERVIEWER: What sort of writing situation do you have at home? Do you have an office?

SHEPARD: I've got a room out by the barn with a typewriter, a piano, some photographs and old drawings. Lots of junk and old books. I can't seem to get rid of my books.

INTERVIEWER: So, you're not a word-processor person.

SHEPARD: No, I hate green screens. The paper is important to me.

INTERVIEWER: What sort of country is it where you live?

SHEPARD: Farm country—you know, hay, horses, cattle. It's the ideal situation for me. I like the physical endeavors that go with the farm—cutting hay, cleaning out stalls, or building a barn. You go do that and then come back to the writing.

INTERVIEWER: Do you write every day?

SHEPARD: When something kicks in, I devote everything to it and write constantly until it's finished. But to sit down every day and say, "I'm going to write, come hell or high water"—no, I could never do that.

INTERVIEWER: Can you write when you're acting in a film?

SHEPARD: There are certain attitudes that shut everything down. It's very easy, for example, to get a bad attitude from a movie. I mean you're trapped in a trailer, people are pounding on the door, asking if you're ready, and at the same time you're trying to write.

INTERVIEWER: Do you actually write on the set?

SHEPARD: Film locations are a great opportunity to write. I don't work on plays while I'm shooting a movie, but I've done short stories and a couple of novels.

INTERVIEWER: What was it like the first time you saw your work being performed by actors?

SHEPARD: To a certain extent it was frustrating, because the actors were in control of the material and I wasn't used to actors. I didn't know how to talk to them and I didn't want to learn, so I hid behind the director. But slowly I started to realize that they were going through an interpretive process, just like anyone else. They don't just go in there and read the script.

INTERVIEWER: Did becoming an actor help you as a writer?

SHEPARD: It did, because it helped me to understand what kinds of dilemmas an actor faces.

INTERVIEWER: Were you impressed by any particular school, like Method acting?

SHEPARD: I am not a Strasberg fanatic. In fact, I find it incredibly self-indulgent. I've seen actors come through it because they're strong people themselves, because they're able to use it and go on, but I've also seen actors absolutely destroyed by it, which is painful to see. It has to do with this voodoo that's all about the verification of behavior, so that *I become the character.* It's not true Stanislavsky. He was on a different mission, and I think Strasberg bastardized him in a way that verges on psychosis. You forget about the material, you forget that this is a play, you forget that it's for the audience. *Hey, man, I'm in my private little world. What you talkin' about? I'm over here, I'm involved with the lemons.* On film, of course, it works because of its obsessiveness; but in theater it's a complete block and a hindrance. There's no room for self-indulgence in theater; you have to be thinking about the audience. Joe Chaikin helped me understand this. He used to have this rehearsal exercise in which the actors were supposed to play a scene for some imaginary figure in the audience. He would say, "Tonight Prince

Charles is in the audience. Play the scene for him," or, "Tonight a bag lady is in the audience."

INTERVIEWER: Is it true that you wrote *Simpatico* in a truck?

SHEPARD: Well, I started it in a truck. I don't like flying very much, so I tend to drive a lot, and I've always wanted to find a way to write while I'm on the open road. I wrote on the steering wheel.

INTERVIEWER: Really? What highway were you on?

SHEPARD: Forty West, the straightest one. I was going to Los Angeles. I think I wrote twenty-five pages by the time I got there, which was about five hundred miles of driving. There were these two characters I'd been thinking about for quite a while, and when I got to L.A. it seemed like I had a one-act play. Then another character popped up; suddenly there were two acts. And out of that second act, a third. It took me a year to finish it.

INTERVIEWER: How do you decide that a play is finished?

SHEPARD: The only way to test it is with actors, because that's who you're writing for. When I have a piece of writing that I think might be ready, I test it with actors, and then I see if it's what I imagined it to be. The best actors show you the flaws in the writing. They come to a certain place and there's nothing there, or they read a line and say, "Okay, now what?" That kind of questioning is more valuable than anything. They don't have to *say* anything. With the very best actors I can see it in the way they're proceeding. Sometimes I instinctively know that this little part at the end of scene two, act one, is not quite there, but I say to myself, "Maybe we'll get away with it." A good actor won't let me. Not that he says, "Hey, I can't do this"; I just see that he's stumbling. And then I have to face up to the problem.

INTERVIEWER: So, as you write, your thoughts are with the actors, not the audience.

SHEPARD: Well, no. I don't think you can write a play without thinking of the audience, but it's a funny deal, because I never know who the audience is. It's like a ghost. With movies you have a better notion of who's watching; there it's the whole population.

INTERVIEWER: Do you do a lot of revisions?

SHEPARD: More now than I used to. I used to be just dead set against revisions because I couldn't stand rewriting. That changed when I started working with Chaikin. Joe was so persistent about finding the essence of something. He'd say, "Does this mean what we're trying to make it mean? Can it be constructed some other way?" That fascinated me, because my tendency was to jam, like it was jazz or something. Thelonious Monk style.

INTERVIEWER: How do your plays start? Do you hear the voice of a character?

SHEPARD: It's more of an attitude than a voice. With *Simpatico*, for instance, it was these two guys in completely different predicaments who began to talk to each other, one in one attitude and the other in another.

INTERVIEWER: Do your characters always tell you where to go?

SHEPARD: The characters are definitely informing you, telling you where *they* want to go. Each time you get to a crossroads you know there are possibilities. That itself can be a dilemma, though. Several times I've written a play that seemed absolutely on the money up to a certain point, and then all of a sudden it went way left field. When that happens you really have to bring it back to the point where it diverged and try something else.

INTERVIEWER: On the subject of control, Nabokov, for one, spoke of controlling his characters with a very tight rein.

SHEPARD: Yeah, but I think the whole notion of control is very nebulous. I mean, what kind of control do you have, Vladimir? Don't get me wrong, I think he's a magnificent writer. I just question the whole notion of control.

INTERVIEWER: The monologue has become something of a Shepard trademark. You are famous for your breathtaking ones, which you've referred to as arias.

SHEPARD: Originally the monologues were mixed up with the idea of an aria. But then I realized that what I'd written was extremely difficult for actors. I mean, I was writing monologues that were three or four pages long. Now it's more about elimination, but the characters still sometimes move into other states of mind, you know, without any excuses. Something lights up and the expression expands.

INTERVIEWER: What was the genesis of *Fool for Love*? Your plays don't often have a male and a female character in conflict like that.

SHEPARD: The play came out of falling in love. It's such a dumbfounding experience. In one way you wouldn't trade it for the world. In another way it's absolute hell. More than anything, falling in love causes a certain female thing in a man to manifest, oddly enough.

INTERVIEWER: Did you know when you started *Fool for Love* that the father would play such an important role?

SHEPARD: No. I was desperately looking for an ending when he came into the story. That play baffles me. I love the opening, in the sense that I couldn't get enough of this thing between Eddie and May, I just wanted that to go on and on and on. But I knew that was impossible. One way out was to bring the father in.

I had mixed feelings about it when I finished. Part of me looks at *Fool for Love* and says, "This is great," and part of me says, "This is really corny. This is a quasi-realistic melodrama." It's still not satisfying; I don't think the play really found itself.

INTERVIEWER: Do you have any idea what the end of a play is going to be when you begin?

SHEPARD: I hate endings. Just detest them. Beginnings are definitely the most exciting, middles are perplexing, and endings are a disaster.

INTERVIEWER: Why?

SHEPARD: The temptation towards resolution, towards wrapping up the package, seems to me a terrible trap. Why not be more honest with the moment? The most authentic endings are the ones which are already revolving towards another beginning. That's genius. Somebody told me once that *fugue* means to flee, so that Bach's melody lines are like he's running away.

INTERVIEWER: Maybe that's why jazz appeals to you, because it doesn't have any endings, the music just trails away.

SHEPARD: Possibly. It's hard, you know, because of the nature of a play.

INTERVIEWER: Have you ever tried to back up from a good ending? Start with one in mind and work backwards?

SHEPARD: Evidently that's what Raymond Chandler did, but he was a mystery writer. He said he always started out knowing who did the murder. To me there's something false about an ending. I mean, because of the nature of a play, you have to end it. People have to go home.

INTERVIEWER: The endings of *True West* and *Buried Child,* for example, seem more resolved than, say, *Angel City.*

SHEPARD: Really? I can't even remember how *Angel City* ends.

INTERVIEWER: The green slime comes through the window.

SHEPARD: Ah, yes. When in doubt, bring on the goo and slime.

INTERVIEWER: What is it you have in mind when you think of the audience?

SHEPARD: You don't want to create boredom, and it becomes an easy trap for a writer to fall into. You have to keep the audience awake in very simple terms. It's easy in the theater to create boredom—easier than it is in movies. You put something in motion and it has to have momentum. If you don't do that right away, there isn't any attention.

INTERVIEWER: Do you have a secret for doing that?

SHEPARD: You begin to learn an underlying rhythmic sense in which things are shifting all the time. These shifts create the possibility for the audience to attach their attention. That sounds like a mechanical process, but in a way it's inherent in dialogue. There's a kind of dialogue that's continually shifting and moving, and each time it moves it creates something new. There's also a kind of dialogue that puts you to sleep. One is alive and the other's deadly. It could be just the shifts of attitudes, the shifts of ideas, where one line is sent out and another one comes back. Shifts are something Joe Chaikin taught me. He had a knack for marking the spot where something shifted. An actor would be going along, full of focus and concern, and then Joe would say, "No! Shift! Different! Not the same. Sun, moon—different!" And the actors would say to themselves, "Of course it's different. Why didn't I see that before?"

INTERVIEWER: Is an ear for dialogue important?

SHEPARD: I think an ear for stage dialogue is different from an ear for language that's heard in life. You can hear things in life that don't work at all when you try to reproduce them onstage. It's not the same; something changes.

INTERVIEWER: What changes?

SHEPARD: It's being listened to in a direct way, like something overheard. It's not voyeuristic, not like I'm in the other room. I'm confronted by it, and the confrontational part of theater is the dialogue. We hear all kinds of fascinating things every day, but dialogue has to create a life. It has to be self-sustaining. Conversation is definitely not dialogue.

INTERVIEWER: Do you acknowledge the influence of playwrights like Pinter and Beckett on your work?

SHEPARD: The stuff that had the biggest influence on me was European drama in the sixties. That period brought theater into completely new territory—Beckett especially, who made American theater look like it was on crutches. I don't think Beckett gets enough credit for revolutionizing theater, for turning it upside down.

INTERVIEWER: How were you affected by winning the Pulitzer Prize?

SHEPARD: You know, in a lot of ways I feel like it was given to the wrong play. *Buried Child* is a clumsy, cumbersome play. I think *A Lie of the Mind* is a much better piece of work. It's denser, more intricate, better constructed.

INTERVIEWER: Do you have a favorite among your plays?

SHEPARD: I'll tell you, I'm not attached to any of it. I don't regret them, but for me it's much more thrilling to move on to the next thing.

—MONA SIMPSON
—JEANNE MCCULLOCH
—BENJAMIN HOWE
Spring, 1997

AUGUST WILSON

Courtesy of August Wilson

Born Frederick August Kittel on April 27, 1945, August Wilson grew up in a working-class area of Pittsburgh. His father, a white German immigrant, abandoned the family when his son was only five. Wilson's mother later remarried, and the family moved to a mostly white suburb. At school there Wilson, subjected to the racism of his classmates and falsely accused of plagiarism by a teacher, dropped out of the ninth grade and began educating himself at the local library, reading the works of black authors like Langston Hughes and Richard Wright. Inspired by these, he began writing short stories and poems, supporting himself by working a number of low-paying odd jobs, among them dishwasher, mail-room clerk, and short-order cook.

In 1968, with almost no practical experience, Wilson cofounded the Black Horizons theater company, where he involved himself in, as he put it, "trying to raise consciousness through theater." He did not come into his own as a playwright, though, until 1978, when he moved to St. Paul, Minnesota.

In 1982 *Ma Rainey's Black Bottom*, which Wilson had submitted to the Eugene O'Neill Theater Center, attracted the attention of Lloyd Richards, then artistic director of the Yale Repertory Theater. Richards helped Wilson refine the play and brought it to New Haven, where in 1984 it opened to widespread acclaim. Wilson's next four plays would all premiere at the Yale Rep under Richards's direction. *Ma Rainey's Black Bottom* was produced in Philadelphia and on Broadway, and was hailed as the work of an important new playwright, receiving a Tony nomination and winning the New York Drama Critics' Circle Award.

Fences (1987), Wilson's next play, was even more successful. The story of an aging former Negro League baseball player who refuses to allow his son to accept an athletic scholarship, it won a Tony Award for best play and a Pulitzer Prize, and grossed $11 million in one year, breaking the record for a nonmusical Broadway production. Wilson earned a second Pulitzer, and another Drama Critics' Circle Award, for *The Piano Lesson* (1990).

All of Wilson's mature dramas, from *Ma Rainey's Black Bottom* through *Seven Guitars* (1996), are parts of an ambitious cycle of works devoted to the experience of African Americans during the course of the twentieth century.

———

August Wilson has been referred to (by Henry Louis Gates, Jr.) as "the most celebrated American playwright now writing, and certainly the most accomplished black playwright in this nation's history." Earlier this fall the beneficiary of Mr. Gates's praise was in Atlanta to oversee the production of one of his plays. He took time off to meet for lunch at the Sheraton Hotel's 14th Street Bar, arriving in a black turtleneck sweater under a tweed coat. The tables in the bar are set up on a balcony overlooking the yellow-gold emporium that is the hotel lobby. Wilson asked to sit in the smoking section. He gave up smoking for years but lit up a cigar upon the birth of his daughter two years ago. No cigar on hand, he had purchased a pack of cigarettes at the lobby newsstand downstairs. He said he would give up cigarettes "soon"—"ridiculous," he said, not to be around when his daughter goes to college.

Though soft-spoken, Wilson is a man of strong convictions about the role of blacks in this country. He has an astonishing memory—the envy of those aware of it—and equal abilities as a mimic. With consummate skill he can shift his voice,

[handwritten: King / he shouldn't have tried / to take his money]

STOOL PIGEON   88

I had it...seventeen...twenty seven...thirty six years now. This yours. I
think about Floyd sometimes but I know he in heaven. The angels carried
him away. He went up into heaven carried by angels. I seen them. A sky full
of angels dressed in black with black hats. The sky was all jet black. You
look and all you could see was black with fire in the middle. They snatched
him right out the ground. Time Foster lowered his body they opened the
casket and snatched him straight up into the sky. I seen them. Vera seen
them too. She dead now but she seen them too. That's when I knew that
God was a bad motherfucker after I seen that. I don't know what it was but
Hedley had his own way about him. He was quick with a knife. He cut up
them chickens whack... whack... slit... slit. He was better with a knife than
I was. Ain't too many people could say that. I used to like to watch him.
Tried to learn something. Called himself the "Conquering Lion of Judea". I
don't know what it was with him and Floyd but he didn't want the money. It
wasn't about the money. I don't know what it was. He showed me the
money. Say Buddy Bolden gave it to him. That's when I knew. I say I got to
tell. What else could you do? Ruby called me Stool Pigeon and somehow or
another it stuck. I'll tell anybody I'm a Truth Sayer. She say I killed Floyd
but she don't really believe that. She just say that to get my goat. After I
seen Floyd go up into heaven I knew God was righteous and its all
according to his will. Not man's will. God's will be done! John saw that
number spinning in the air. A hundred and forty four thousand. That's how
many people going to heaven. That's in Revelations. I say there one less
now. A hundred and forty three thousand nine hundred and ninety nine.

[handwritten margin left: B SP / It wasn't / about the / money]

[handwritten margin right: Stool / Pigeon / entry / Carvin / Wholly / wood]

(He gives him the machete)

STOOL PIGEON (cont'd)

Here. This is yours. This was your daddy's. Louise give it to me. The police
give it back to her and she wanted to get it out of the house. I say I'm gonna
keep it. I didn't know why. But now I know. This the machete that killed
Floyd Barton. That's yours. You can do with it what you want to. It took me
a long while before I could forgive Hedley for something like that. Now I
give it to you and me and Hedley come full circle. Floyd was my friend. I
give this to you and we can close the book on that chapter. I forgive. God
taught me how to do that. God can teach you a lot of things. He's a bad
motherfucker! Made the firmament. Put a circle around the sun. Called up
man out of the dust. They hung him high and stretched him wide. If he

[handwritten: B This the machete of the "Conquering Lion of Judea"]

A manuscript page from King Hedley II.

which bears hardly a trace of a regional accent, into the rich patois of the South when he mimics the railroad porters he met as a boy in Pat's Place in Pittsburgh.

In 1997 a widely publicized debate took place in New York's Town Hall between Wilson and Robert Brustein, the artistic director of the American Repertory Theater in Cambridge, Massachusetts. Wilson's position, based on W. E. B. Du Bois's principles (described in 1926 in his magazine The Crisis*), was that the plays of a true black theater must be, in brief, (1) about us, (2) by us, (3) for us, and (4) near us. Brustein criticized Wilson's views as "self-segregation" and declared that funds for "black theater" on those terms would be foundation-supported "separatism." Wilson repeated a statistic throughout the evening—that, of the sixty-five theaters belonging to the League of Regional Theaters, only one was black, the Crossroads Theater in New Brunswick, New Jersey: "The score is sixty-four to one." He pleaded for a black theater that would not have to rely on white institutions or make its appeal to white audiences. The debate was spirited if inconclusive. And reasonably polite. At its conclusion Brustein referred to Wilson as a "teddy bear." Wilson fended off the compliment: "I may be personable, but I assure you I am a lion."*

INTERVIEWER: What do you suppose Robert Brustein meant when he referred to you at the close of your Town Hall debate as a "teddy bear"?

WILSON: I think he was expecting someone with a more strident tone and antagonistic demeanor. I think he was suprised to find out I'm a pretty likable person, and that despite our different views I conducted myself with a civility and grace of manners my mother always demanded of me. For myself, I found him to be a more likable person than I had imagined. And I certainly value and respect the contributions that he has made to the theater; our differences of opinion on black theater do not dampen my respect and appreciation, nor in any way invalidate the considerable contributions that he has made.

INTERVIEWER: Can you say what first drew you to theater?

WILSON: I think it was the ability of the theater to communicate ideas and extol virtues that drew me to it. And also I was, and remain, fascinated by the idea of an audience as a community of people who gather willingly to bear witness. A novelist writes a novel and people read it. But reading is a solitary act. While it may elicit a varied and personal response, the communal nature of the audience is like having five hundred people read your novel and respond to it at the same time. I find that thrilling.

INTERVIEWER: When did you first become involved?

WILSON: In 1968, during the Black Power movement, when black Americans were, as one sociologist put it, "seeking ways to alter their relationship to the society and the shared expectations of themselves as a community of people." As a twenty-three-year-old poet concerned about the world and struggling to find a place in it, I felt it a duty and an honor to participate in that search. With my good friend Rob Penny I founded the Black Horizon Theater in Pittsburgh with the idea of using the theater to politicize the community or, as we said in those days, to raise the consciousness of the people.

INTERVIEWER: Does that mean you were looking for plays that dealt with those issues? What kind of plays did you produce?

WILSON: We did everything we could get our hands on. Scripts were rather scarce in 1968. We did a lot of Amiri Baraka's plays, the agitprop stuff he was writing. It was at a time when black student organizations were active on the campuses so we were invited to the colleges around Pittsburgh and Ohio and even as far away as Jackson, Mississippi.

INTERVIEWER: You were the director.

WILSON: And I acted when the actors didn't show up. As the director, I knew all the lines and I took over more times than I wanted to. I didn't know much about directing, but I was the only one willing to do it. Someone had looked around and said, "Who's going to be the director?" I said, "I will." I said that because I knew my way around the library. So I went to look for a book on how to direct a play. I found one called *The Fundamentals of Play Directing* and checked it out. I didn't understand anything in it. It was all about form and mass and balance. I flipped through the book and there in Appendix A I discovered what to do on the first day of rehearsal. It said, "Read the play." So I went to the first rehearsal very confidently and I said, "Okay, this is what we're going to do. We're going to read the play." We did that. Now what? I hadn't got to Appendix B. So I said, "Let's read the play again." That night I went back to the book and sort of figured out what to do from that point on.

INTERVIEWER: Did you have a theater?

WILSON: No. We worked in the elementary schools—they let us use the auditoriums there. That was our base of operations. The audiences were mostly black. We charged fifty cents admission. Eventually that got up to a dollar. We literally went into the street a half hour before the show and talked people into going in. Once they got in, they really liked it: "Hey, hey, you gonna do another play?"

"Next Thursday."

"I'm gonna be there!"

INTERVIEWER: Were you writing plays at the time?

WILSON: I was writing poetry. But I found the theater such an exciting experience that one day I went home to try. I had one character say to the other guy, "Hey, man, what's happening?" And the other guy said, "Nothing." I sat there for twenty minutes and neither of my guys would talk. So I said to myself, Well, that's all right. After all, I'm a poet. I don't have to be a playwright. To hell with writing plays. Let other people write plays.

I didn't try to write a play for a number of years after that first experience.

INTERVIEWER: What sort of luck were you having getting the poems published?

WILSON: It was early on in 1965 when I wrote some of my first poems. I sent a poem to *Harper's* magazine because they paid a dollar a line. I had an eighteen-line poem and just as I was putting it into the envelope, I stopped and decided to make it a thirty-six-line poem. It seemed like the poem came back the next day, no letter, nothing. Oh, I said to myself, I see this is serious. I'm going to have to learn how to write a poem.

INTERVIEWER: What was your first play where characters talked to each other?

WILSON: In 1977 I wrote a series of poems about a character, Black Bart, a former cattle rustler turned alchemist. A good friend, Claude Purdy, who is a stage director, suggested I turn the poems into a play. He kept after me, and not knowing any better I sat down from one Sunday to the next and wrote a 137-page, single-spaced musical satire called *Black Bart and the Sacred Hills.* Claude started taking it around to theaters, and Lou Bellamy at Penumbra Theater in St. Paul produced it in 1981. It ended up being my first professional production. I had moved to St. Paul in 1978 and got a job at the Science Museum of Minnesota writing scripts—adapting tales from the Northwest Native Americans for a group of actors attached to the anthropology department. So I began work in the script form almost without knowing it. In 1980 I sent a play, *Jitney,* to the Playwrights' Center in Minneapolis, won a Jerome Fellowship, and found myself sitting in a room with sixteen playwrights. I remember looking around and thinking that since I was sitting there, I must be a playwright too. It was then that I began to think of myself as a playwright, which is absolutely crucial to the work. It is important to claim it. I had worked so hard to earn the title "Poet" that it was hard for me to give it up. All I ever wanted was "August Wilson, Poet." So the idea of being a playwright took some adjusting to. I still write poetry and think it is the highest form of literature. But I don't call myself a Poet-Playwright. I think one of them is enough weight to carry around.

INTERVIEWER: Would an audience recognize those early works as yours?

WILSON: My early attempts writing plays, which are very poetic, did not use the language that I work in now. I didn't recognize the poetry in everyday language of black America. I thought I had to change it to create art. I had a scene in a very early play, *The Coldest Day of the Year,* between an old man and an old woman sitting on a park bench. The old man walks up and he says, "Our lives are frozen in the deepest heat and spiritual turbulence." She looks at him. He goes on, "Terror hangs over the night like a hawk." Then he says, "The wind bites at your tits." He gives her his coat. "Allow me, Madam, my coat. It is is made of the wool of a sacrificial lamb." "What's that you say?" she says. "It sounded bitter." He says, "But not as bitter as you are lovely . . . as a jay bird on a spring day." Very different from what I'm writing now.

INTERVIEWER: How do you look back on those early efforts?

WILSON: They had validity. I was exploring the same themes as I do now, but in a different language. It turns out I didn't have to do it that way.

INTERVIEWER: What have been your influences?

WILSON: My influences have been what I call my four *B*s—the primary one being the blues, then Borges, Baraka, and Bearden. From Borges, those wonderful gaucho stories from which I learned that you can be specific as to a time and place and culture and still have the work resonate with the universal themes of love, honor, duty, betrayal, et cetera. From Amiri Baraka I learned that all art is political, though I don't write political plays. That's not what I'm about. From Romare Bearden I learned that the fullness and richness of everyday ritual life can be rendered without compromise or sentimentality. To those four *B*s I could add two more. Bullins and Baldwin. Ed Bullins is a playwright with a serious body of work, much of it produced in the sixties and seventies. It was with Bullins's work that I first discovered someone writing plays about blacks with an uncompromising honesty and creating rich and memorable characters. And then James Baldwin, in particular his call for a "profound articulation of the black tradition," which he defined as "that field of manners and rituals of intercourse that can sustain a man once he's left his father's house." I thought, Let me answer the call. A profound articulation, but let's worry about the profundities later. I wanted to put that onstage, to demonstrate that the "manners and rituals" existed and that the tradition was capable of sustaining you.

INTERVIEWER: And from mainstream theater?

WILSON: Everything I could or can. While I certainly recognize that there are other forms, other approaches to theater, African ritual theater and Japanese Kabuki theater, for example, the theater that I know and embrace is essentially a European art form—the age-old dramaturgy handed down by the Greeks and rooted in Aristotle's *Poetics.* I bring an African-American cultural sensibility to that art form and try to infuse it with the principles of aesthetic statement culled from a variety of sources, but primarily—as I was saying—from the great literature of the blues.

INTERVIEWER: Can you speak about Romare Bearden and what drew you to his work?

WILSON: I first came across his work in 1977 in a book called *The Prevalence of Ritual*—representations of black life in the ritualistic terms Baldwin was speaking of... street scenes, home life, weddings, funerals. One of the things that impressed me was that it lacked the sentimentality one might have expected, but it was exciting and rich and fresh and full. When asked about his work Bearden said, "I try and explore, in terms of the life I know best, those things which are common to all cultures." The life I know best is black American life, and through Bearden I realized that you could arrive at the universal through the specific. Every artist worth his salt has a painting of a woman bathing. So Bearden's *Harlem Woman Bathing in Her Kitchen* is no different as a subject than you would find in Degas, but it is informed by African-American culture and aesthetics.

INTERVIEWER: Is it a concern to effect social change with your plays?

WILSON: I don't write particularly to effect social change. I believe writing can do that, but that's not why I write. I work as an artist. All art is political in the sense that it serves someone's politics. Here in America whites have a particular view of blacks. I think my plays offer them a different way to look at black Americans. For instance, in *Fences* they see a garbageman, a person they don't really look at, although they see a garbageman every day. By looking at Troy's life, white people find out that the content of this black garbageman's life is affected by the same things—love, honor, beauty, betrayal, duty. Recognizing that these things are as much part of his life as theirs can affect how they think about and deal with black people in their lives.

INTERVIEWER: How would that same play, *Fences*, affect a black audience?

WILSON: Blacks see the content of their lives being elevated into art. They don't always know that it is possible, and it's important for them to know that.

INTERVIEWER: Are you worried that aspects of black culture are disappearing?

WILSON: No, I find the culture robust, but I worry about a break in its traditions. I find it interesting that in the convocation ceremonies of the historically black colleges that I have attended they don't sing gospel, they sing Bach instead. It's in the areas of jazz and rap music that I find the strongest connection and celebration of black aesthetics and tradition. My older daughter called me from college, all excited, and said, "Daddy, I've joined the Black Action Society and we're studying Timbuktu." I said, "Good, but why don't you study your grandmother and work back to Timbuktu? You can't make this leap over there to those African kingdoms without understanding who you are. You don't have to go to Africa to be an African. Africa is right here in the southern part of the United States. It's our ancestral homeland. You don't need to make that leap across the ocean."

INTERVIEWER: You speak of your early plays as being poetic. What caused the change?

WILSON: When I first started writing plays I couldn't write good dialogue because I didn't respect how black people talked. I thought that in order to make art out of their dialogue I had to change it, make it into something different. Once I learned to value and respect my characters, I could really hear them. I let them start talking. The important thing is not to censor them. What they are talking about may not seem to have anything to do with what you as a writer are writing about but it does. Let them talk and it will connect, because you as a writer will make it connect. The more my characters talk, the more I find out about them. So I encourage them. I tell them, "Tell me more." I just write it down and it starts to make connections. When I was writing *The Piano Lesson*, Boy Willie suddenly announced that Sutter fell in the well. That was news to me. I had no idea who Sutter was or why he fell in the well. You have to let your characters talk for a while, trust them to do it and have the confidence that later you can shape the material.

INTERVIEWER: It's interesting that you started with poetic drama because you have such a wonderful ear for dialogue...

WILSON: The language is defined by those who speak it. There's a place in Pittsburgh called Pat's Place, a cigar store, which I read about in Claude McKay's *Home to Harlem*. It was where the railroad porters would congregate and tell stories. I thought, Hey, I know Pat's Place. I literally ran there. I was twenty-one at the time and I had no idea I was going to write about it. I wasn't keeping notes. But I loved listening to them. One of the exchanges I heard made it into *Ma Rainey's Black Bottom*. Someone said, "I came to Pittsburgh in 'forty-two on the B & O," and another guy said, "Oh no, you ain't come to Pittsburgh in 'forty-two... the B & O Railroad didn't stop in Pittsburgh in 'forty-two!" And the first guy would say, "You gonna tell *me* what railroad I came in on?" "Hell yeah I'm gonna tell you the truth." Then someone would walk in and they'd say, "Hey, Philmore! The B & O Railroad stop here in 'forty-two?" People would drift in and they'd all have various answers to that. They would argue about how far away the moon was. They'd say, "Man, the moon a million miles away." They called me Youngblood. They'd say, "Hey, Youngblood, how far the moon?" And I'd say, "150,000 miles," and they'd say, "That boy don't know nothing! The moon's a *million* miles." I just loved to hang around those old guys— you got philosophy about life, what a man is, what his duties, his responsibilities are...

Occasionally these guys would die and I would pay my respects. There'd be a message on a blackboard they kept in Pat's Place: "Funeral for Jo Boy, Saturday, one P.M." I'd look around and try to figure out which one was missing. I'd go across to the funeral home and look at him and I'd go, "Oh, it was *that* guy, the guy that wore the little brown hat all the time."

I used to hang around Pat's Place through my twenties, going there less as the time went by. That's where I learned how black people talk.

INTERVIEWER: Did they know you were interested in writing?

WILSON: No, but someone around the neighborhood must have guessed. One day there was a knock at the door of the rooming house where I was living. This guy was standing there. "They said you would buy this from me?" He had this typewriter. I knew he had stolen it and couldn't find anyone to sell it to. If he'd stolen a TV, he could have quickly sold it to anybody. So he was mad as hell walking around trying to sell this thing that in the black community had no market value. But somebody had sent him to my house, telling him, "This guy has books and papers and stuff. Maybe he'll want to buy it." So I said to him, "How much do you want for it?" He said, "Give me ten dollars." I happened to have ten dollars and I didn't have a typewriter. So I gave him ten dollars. Because it wasn't an *extra* ten dollars and I needed ten dollars to get through the week, I took the typewriter and pawned it. When I had enough money to spare, eleven dollars and twenty-five cents, I went to the pawnshop and got it back out—the $1.25 to the pawnbroker. I was eternally grateful. I kept that typewriter for ten years. We played the game many times. When I'd get into a jam I'd take it back to the pawnshop.

INTERVIEWER: You once said that you write a lot in bars and restaurants. Do you keep to this?

WILSON: I write at home now more than I've done before. I started writing poetry when I was twenty years old; you cannot sit at home as a twenty-year-old poet. You don't know anything about life. At that time many of my friends were painters and when I'd go visit them, I'd hear them complaining about needing money to buy paint. I recall visiting a painter friend of mine who was frustrated because he didn't have the three dollars to buy a tube of yellow paint. When I pointed to some yellow paint on his palette he said, "Naw, man, I'm talking about *chrome* yellow." Then I realized how lucky I was because my tools were simple: I could borrow a pencil or paper; I could write on napkins or paper bags. I'd walk around with a pen or pencil and I discovered poems everywhere. I was always prepared to write. Once when I was writing on a paper napkin, the waitress asked, "Do you write on napkins because it doesn't count?" It had never occurred to me that writing on a napkin frees me up. If I pull out a tablet, I'm saying, "Now I'm writing," and I become more conscious of being a writer. The waitress saw it; I didn't recognize it, she did. That's why I like to write on napkins. Then I go home to another kind of work—taking what I've written on napkins in bars and restaurants and typing it up, rewriting...

INTERVIEWER: Has the process changed over the years?

WILSON: My writing process is more or less the same. But I haven't found a place in Seattle where I'm comfortable writing. I went to this one place where there must have been fourteen people sitting around writing. I thought, I've found the place where writers come. I sat there and waited but nothing came. I thought, These other people are taking all the writing stuff in the air for themselves, they're taking it all away. Afterwards I made this joke about how my muse got into an argument with someone else's muse and had been thrown out of the restaurant. That was why I was sitting there waiting with nothing happening.

INTERVIEWER: If you are not writing in restaurants, where do you work?

WILSON: I work in the basement of my house. On some days it is a sanctuary. On others it's a battlefield and then at times it's a dungeon. It is a place surrounded by the familiar particulars of my life. Photographs, yellow tablets, pens, book, music. I used to have a punching bag, but as I got older I traded it in for a chair. I work at a stand-up desk which allows me to pace around. I have quotes, no more than two or three, that I use to keep me focused and inspired. For my new play, *King Hedley II,* I had a quote by Frank Gehry on his plans for the Corcoran Gallery addition: "I hope to take it to the moon." And a quote attributed to Charlie Parker: "Don't be afraid. Just play the music." And a quote from the Bhagavad-Gita: "You have the right to the work but not the reward." Other than that, I'm on my own.

INTERVIEWER: Can you say something about your work habits there?

WILSON: I write in longhand, usually on a yellow pad. I write in spurts, an explosion of writing activity that is part of a longer sustained concentration. These spurts generally last twenty minutes. When I'm working on a play, I maintain focus until the next burst of activity. It is an intense and sometimes furious activity. To find yourself there at that moment, in a way that you will never be again, is full of what I call "tremor and trust." I've discovered that I work essentially in collage. Being an admirer of Romare Bearden's collages, I try to make my plays the equal of his canvases. In creating plays I often use the image of a stewing pot in which I toss various things that I'm going to make use of: a black cat, a garden, a bicycle, a man with a scar on his face, a pregnant woman, a man with a gun. Then I assemble the pieces into a cohesive whole guided by history and anthropology and architecture and my own sense of aesthetic statement.

INTERVIEWER: How about rituals? Any to get you going?

WILSON: I always approach my work with clean hands. I will do a symbolic cleansing with my morning coffee, if nothing else is available. I do a lot of mental and spiritual preparation for what is essentially a journey on which I am going to make discoveries about myself and the nature of human life. It can sometimes be a painful process. I have a character who says, "Life without pain ain't worth living." So I'm willing to accept that. There's an awful lot of joy also. I accept that. I had dinner with Charles Johnson, the novelist, who is a Buddhist, and he was quoting his favorite passage from the Bhagavad-Gita, the quote I mentioned before which says that you have the right to the work but not the reward. I just love that. It says something I've always felt—that I'm not entitled to anything other than the work. Which is sufficient— a joy unto itself. I feel it a privilege to stand at the edge of the art having been gifted with the triumphs and failures of countless playwrights down through the ages. It's a privilege I don't want to squander.

INTERVIEWER: Can you talk about the genesis of a work? *The Piano Lesson?*

WILSON: I started with the idea from one of Romare Bearden's paintings—*The Piano Lesson*, the subtitle of which was *Homage to Mary Lou*

Williams, who was a jazz pianist in Pittsburgh. I started with a question: Can you acquire a sense of self-worth by denying your past, or is implicit in that denial a repudiation of the worth of the self? Once deciding that, I had to construct a series of events that posed that question and illustrated some possible answers. I started by having four guys carry the piano into the house. I wrote eight pages of dialogue that went like this: "Turn around the other way." "Move it up on that end." "Watch yourself!" "Come on now, lift up on that end." Once they got it in the house they began arguing about where to put it. I thought, wait a minute, where am I going? What am I doing? So I threw those pages out and started over. And then I got the idea of the brother coming into the house like a tornado, bringing in the past that his sister is trying to deny. I usually start with a line of dialogue, which contains elements of the plot, character, and the thematic idea. For instance, I started *Two Trains Running:* "When I left out of Jackson I said I was gonna buy me a V-8 Ford and drive by Mr. Henry Ford's house and honk the horn. If anybody come to the window I was gonna wave. Then I was going out and buy me a 30.06, come on back to Jackson and drive up to Mr. Stovall's house and honk the horn. Only this time I wasn't waving." That contains the attitude of the character, his approach to the world, and contributes to what became an important element about the play. So I ask myself, Who is talking? Who is he talking to? Who is Stovall? Why does he want to get a gun and go see him, et cetera. In answering the questions the play begins to emerge. Eventually I name the character, decide on a setting, and begin to construct the play in earnest.

INTERVIEWER: Is there a gestation period?

WILSON: Yes. When I finish a play, after I type "The End," I immediately begin work on the next play. I force myself to sit there until I come up with something, an idea, a title, a character, a line of dialogue, et cetera. That way I'm always working on something. So if you ask me ten minutes after I finish a play what I'm working on, I'll be able to tell you I'm working on a new play. That begins the gestation period. It can be anywhere from two months to two years. It is difficult sometimes, given the responsibility of public life, to find a block of time in which to do the work. The gestation period has become increasingly longer, which I think is ultimately good for the work.

INTERVIEWER: What areas of playwriting give you the most trouble?

WILSON: I would say the management of time. That has always been a problem. For instance, in *King Hedley II,* I have a character who plants some seeds in one scene of the play. The way the play is structured they have to be growing in the next scene. There is not enough time for this to be realistic, so you have to ask the audience to make a leap of faith, suspend disbelief and accept that the seeds are growing. Things of that sort I have not always managed well.

INTERVIEWER: What is easiest?

WILSON: The characters and their dialogue. The characters want to explain, as most people do, their entire history and philosophy, their take on the world and the vagaries of life. Sékou Touré has said that language describes the idea of the one who speaks it. I discovered that what is easiest for me, once I know who is speaking, is to translate the ideas and attitudes that I find in the blues into a language that defines and illuminates the characters, along with the elements of their philosophies and attitudes that are central to the play's thematic concerns.

INTERVIEWER: Is there a character who is a particular favorite?

WILSON: I like all my characters and I've always said that I'd like to put them all in the same play—Troy and Boy Willie and Loomis and Sterling and Floyd. I once wrote this short story called "The Best Blues Singer in the World," and it went like this: "The streets that Balboa walked were his own private ocean, and Balboa was drowning." End of story. That says it all. Nothing else to say. I've been rewriting that same story over and over again. All my plays are rewriting that same story. I'm not sure what it means, other than life is hard.

INTERVIEWER: How important is plot to you?

WILSON: Obviously if you are going to write good plays they have to be plotted. Plot is an essential tool of the dramatist. But in the way my plays are structured, plot grows out of characterization. The play doesn't flow from plot point to plot point. It emerges from the seemingly pointless banter of the characters. If you dismiss the banter as so much excessive verbiage, then you can miss the plot. In *Seven Guitars* you hear four men talking and you may think the play is not going anywhere. They are sitting in the yard reciting childhood rhymes, and it might seem that the rhymes are simply entertainment and do not contribute and advance the plot. But they do. Everything in the plays connects to something and is designed to lend resonance and support for the ideas and action of the play.

INTERVIEWER: How much does the direction of a play change as it progresses? Do you keep a tight rein on things?

WILSON: It varies. I always say if it doesn't change, you're not writing deep enough. I make discoveries as I go along. Sometimes the direction of the play can change dramatically. As far as keeping a tight rein, sometimes you just let go; sometimes your passion can carry you to places where you lose control and then something exciting happens: the characters forge their own way. Hedley in *Seven Guitars*, for example, assumed a much larger presence than I had originally imagined. He ended the first act, and I was surprised to find him onstage alone at the start of the second act. He *demanded* that I focus on him and what he had to say. He was a most unruly character. He threatened to knock down the set and remake the world to his liking. In times like that you have to reassert your authorial control.

INTERVIEWER: Is it easy to divide a work? Do you pick a dramatic closing scene and then back into it?

WILSON: I often come up with my first-act curtain early on. I look for a defining moment in the character's life that also, in large part, defines the play. In *King Hedley II*, for instance, before I knew much else about the play I knew that someone was going to step on some seeds that a character had planted and that the character was going to go berserk . . . which could be my act break.

INTERVIEWER: How much can you produce in a day's work?

WILSON: Sometimes nothing. Writing ideally is recognizing your bad writing. I mean, people ask if I write bad lines, and I say, Man, I write bad *scenes*! I put them in a drawer where nobody can see them.

INTERVIEWER: How much revision is necessary?

WILSON: It varies. But I'm a strong believer in rewrites. Rewrites are the shaping of the material you have already processed. It is an essential part of the work. The process of shaping may lead to discoveries and it may be necessary to climb back into the heat of the moment. I often make references to my notes during rewrites. They are a record of the germination of the work; sometimes contained in there is a crucial idea which you have strayed from. In architectural terms, I walk around and test the structure to make sure there is support for the ideas of the play and its validity as a work of art.

INTERVIEWER: Do you write with a particular audience in mind?

WILSON: No more than, say, Picasso painted with a particular audience in mind. The nature of the audience is built into the craft of playwriting, of course, but that's not the same as writing for a particular audience. I write to create a work of art, to contribute to the art form, and to make my aesthetic statements.

INTERVIEWER: Does it bother you that your audiences are mostly white?

WILSON: I don't think about it. Here again, to go back to Picasso, you create the work to add to the artistic storehouse of the world, to exalt and celebrate a common humanity. I don't think Picasso thought too much about whether the viewers of his paintings were French, or American or Asian or German. I think the primary concern is to do the work to the best of your ability and to fulfill its aesthetic requirements. My audience, if I thought of one, would be Ibsen, O'Neill, Miller, Williams, Baraka, and Bullins—my fellow playwrights who have wrestled with the problems of the art form and have contributed to my understanding of it. When I sit down to write, I am sitting in the same chair that Ibsen sat in, that Brecht, Tennessee Williams, and Arthur Miller sat in. I am confronted with the same problems of how to get a character onstage, how to shape the scenes to get maximum impact. I feel empowered by the chair. For years I sat in that chair and tried to best my predecessors, to write the best play that's ever been written. That was my goal until I ran across a quote by Frank Lloyd Wright, who said he didn't want to be the best architect who ever lived. He wanted to be the best architect who was ever going to live. That added fuel to the fire and raised the stakes, so to speak. Now you're not only doing battle with your predecessors but with your successors as well. It drives you to write above your talent. And I know that's possible to do because you can write beneath it.

INTERVIEWER: While white audiences can enjoy black music—jazz, blues, soul—is black theater something of a stretch for them?

WILSON: The question I can answer is whether (as a black audience member) theater based on white experience is something of a stretch for me. Can I appreciate the work of Ibsen, Chekhov, Miller, Mamet? The answer, of course, is yes, because the plays ultimately are about things I am familiar with—love, honor, duty, betrayal... the same way, for instance, I can appreciate German or Italian opera though I don't speak the language. I can appreciate good singing and dramatic incident the same way I can appreciate Wynton Marsalis, Skip James, or Bukka White. I would think the white members of the audience can appreciate my plays because the specifics and the social manners of the characters, while they may be different, can certainly be recognized as part of human conduct and endeavor.

INTERVIEWER: Do you often go to the theater?

WILSON: I don't go to the theater very much. Nor the movies. I didn't go into a movie theater for eleven years. I read the reviews and I try to keep up with what is going on. But in the evenings I play with my two-year-old daughter. I don't watch TV. I read. I listen to music. I have a large collection—classical, jazz, Eastern-Arab, Irish, all kinds of stuff... I have a large blues collection, probably the largest section of what I have, much larger than jazz because the blues have words. I've never heard a piece of music I didn't like.

INTERVIEWER: Do you try out the plays on your family?

WILSON: My first critic is my wife. But it's better to get people who are not involved in the theater, who have no preconceived ideas against which they can measure what they're seeing. My favorite critic is my brother, who has no particular interest in the theater. He'll let you know exactly what he thinks.

INTERVIEWER: What are your notions about the importance of production. Edward Albee has said that "a first-rate play exists completely on the page and is never improved by production; it is only *proved* by production." Would you agree?

WILSON: I agree with that. I don't write for a production. I write for the page, just as I would with a poem. A play exists on the page even if no one ever reads it aloud. I don't mean to underestimate a good production with actors embodying the characters, but depending on the readers' imagination they may get more by reading the play than by seeing a weak production.

INTERVIEWER: What kind of liberties do directors take with your plays?

WILSON: I like it when directors try different things, even though they don't always work. I don't want to see a production that's a near duplicate of the original. One production of *Ma Rainey* had a spiritual dancer in it. I personally didn't think it worked, but I didn't mind them trying it out. What I objected to was listing the spiritual dancer in the cast as if that dancer was part of my script. Another production had Hambone after he died coming back dressed in a white suit and looking in the window of the restaurant. The audience loved seeing this homeless person dressed in an elegant white suit. I wouldn't have done that if I were directing the play, but it worked for the audience.

INTERVIEWER: Do you go to opening nights?

WILSON: Yes. I go to opening nights and sit in the audience. But the performance that I look forward to and enjoy best is the very first time the play ever plays before an audience. There is nothing quite like that. That's the most honest collaboration between actor and audience that you're ever going to get. It's before the reviews, before the word of mouth; it's that moment of actuality when no one, actors or audience, knows what is going to happen next.

INTERVIEWER: What do you see as the essential element to be established in the drama?

WILSON: I see conflict at the center. What you do is set up a character who has certain beliefs and you establish a situation where those beliefs are challenged and the character is forced to examine those beliefs and perhaps changes. That's the kind of dramatic situation which engages an audience, forces them to go through the same inner struggle. When I teach my workshops I tell my students if a guy announces, "I'm going to kill Joe," and there's a knock on the door, the audience is going to want to know if that's Joe and why this guy wants to kill him and whether we would also want to kill him if we were in the same situation. The audience is engaged in the question.

INTERVIEWER: Are there other techniques, tricks that you suggest in your students' workshops?

WILSON: After we talk about what a play is, I ask them to invent a painting in their minds and then describe it in words.

INTERVIEWER: That frees them up?

WILSON: Absolutely. If you tell them to write a description, they get too conscious and can't do it. Let me give you an example: in his word painting a guy will describe a train station. He says, "There's a woman wearing a white dress over there and some guys sitting in another part of the station." Then I start asking questions. "Is she coming or is she going?" "Going." "Where is she going?" "To visit her grandmother." And simply by asking these questions we find out who this person is. Then we'll find out about these guys over in the other part of the station. All of a sudden the student yells, "I can write a play about this!" You've caught him by surprise. Until he began fleshing out the painting he didn't even know who the woman was.

INTERVIEWER: This word-painting technique sounds a little like your napkin writing.

WILSON: Well, it's about changing their approach. I tell them anybody can write a play, just like anybody can drive a car. All of us can learn the rules of the road, make the turns, switch on the lights. But there is Mario Andretti out there. I can't make them into Mario Andretti, obviously. But they know I've never taken a playwriting class or read any books about it. Everything I know comes from my own writing. Those students, many of whom came back for those three years I taught, really did become better playwrights; a couple of them even had productions of their plays produced. I quit teaching after the three years. But after I finish these three plays I have in mind, and the novel, I think I'd like to go back to it. But first I've got to finish those plays. That's first.

INTERVIEWER: If you hadn't found the theater, what do you think you might have done?

WILSON: I don't know. I probably would have become a novelist. The only thing I know for sure is that I would have been involved in what Borges called "the problematic practice of literature." I fell in love with words as concretized thought when I was a kid and knew somehow that I would have spent my life involved with them. I probably would have pursued my poetry with more resolve and more purpose. I remember when I was twenty years old and the world was wide open as to how I was going to live my life and make a contribution, to mark my passing, as it were, I had fallen in with a group of painters. I was intrigued and fascinated with the idea of painting. I didn't question whether I had any talent for it. In my youthful arrogance and exuberance I felt I could do anything.

INTERVIEWER: Do you see advantages in the novel form?

WILSON: The big difference in writing a novel is that the narrator can take an audience to places you can't on a stage. What I can do in a novel is to take you down this dusty road and have you taste the dust. Suddenly it gets dark and two million crows come flying across going south. They black out the sun. I can't do that onstage. But in a novel I can make you see those crows and have that mean something. I've got about sixty pages of a novel. Notes. A page here, an idea there. It really wants to be born. On occasion I have dinner with Charles Johnson, and every time I tell him I want to write a novel but that I don't know how to do it. I can't see the form of a novel—this vast ocean where I really don't know how to get from here to there. I tell him that for me writing a novel is like being on an ocean without a compass. And he says, "Well, go find a compass!" So I guess that's what I have to do. As soon as I find a compass I'll take a shot at it.

INTERVIEWER: Isn't a "compass" necessary in the writing of a play?

WILSON: For me a play is more like a river that you can navigate...a big bend there, a tree by the shore.

INTERVIEWER: If you had to construct an imaginary playwright, with what qualities would you endow him or her?

WILSON: Honesty. Something to say and the courage to say it. The will and daring to accomplish great art. Craft. Craft is what makes the will and daring work and allows playwrights to shout or whisper as they choose. A painter who has not mastered line and form, mass, perspective and proportion, who does not understand the values and properties of color, is not going to produce interesting paintings no matter the weight and measure of his heart, or the speed and power of his intellect. I don't think you can ever know too much about craft. So I would give your imaginary playwright a solid understanding of craft. All that is necessary then is ambition...which is as valid and valuable as anything else.

—GEORGE PLIMPTON
(ADDITIONAL MATERIAL BY BONNIE LYONS)
Winter, 1999

DAVID MAMET

Courtesy of David Mamet

David Mamet was born in Chicago on November 30, 1947. His father was a labor lawyer and his mother a teacher. Both sides of the family were assimilated Jews who came to Chicago in the 1920s as part of the city's last wave of central European immigrants. Mamet lived on the South Side of Chicago until age ten, when his parents divorced and he moved with his mother to a ruthlessly middle-class suburb on the edge of the prairie called Olympia Fields. He attended public school, but despite being an avid reader he never excelled academically. In 1963 he went to live with his father on Chicago's North Side and transferred to a private school with a strong theater department. The following year he went off to Goddard College in Vermont and eventually graduated, he claims, with "no skills, nor demonstrable talents."

During and after college he pursued a series of odd jobs—including driving a cab in Chicago and working in a somewhat shady real estate office—that would provide source material for later plays. Although he had been involved in theater for many years, both as an actor and as a writer, the staging of his first play in 1970 came about almost by accident. He was given a job as an instructor at Marlboro College after advertising himself as the author of a play, though in fact he had written nothing. Upon arrival at Marlboro he learned that the work was scheduled to be performed, so he hastily set about writing *Lakeboat*, a one-act drama that drew on his experiences in the merchant marine.

Following a sojourn as artist-in-residence at Goddard, Mamet returned to Chicago, where he spent four years writing, directing, and teaching (at Pontiac State Prison and the University of Chicago) while honing the rhythmic language and working-class ethos that would become his signature. But it was only when *Sexual Perversity in Chicago* won the 1974 Joseph Jefferson Award for the city's best play that he achieved his breakthrough as a playwright.

Mamet continued to write and direct, often to mixed reviews and limited box-office success. In 1976, however, *Sexual Perversity* and another Mamet play, *The Duck Variations*, opened off Broadway and ran for 293 performances; a third play, *American Buffalo*, opened in Chicago, where it won a Jefferson Award and an Obie before moving to Broadway and winning a New York Drama Critics' Circle Award. A number of setbacks followed, particularly the 1979 flop *Lone Canoe*, but then in 1983 came his most successful play, *Glengarry Glen Ross*, which won the Pulitzer Prize as well as a Drama Critics' Circle Award. His more recent plays include *Oleanna*, *The Cryptogram*, and *Death Defying Acts*.

In the eighties Mamet began to work in film, a genre that had attracted him since childhood. He has written many screenplays, including Brian De Palma's *The Untouchables* and Louis Malle's *Vanya on 42nd Street*, as well as some, like *House of Games*, that he has directed himself. He received an Academy Award nomination for his adaptation of *The Verdict*. A prolific artist, he has also published a book of poems, several novels, and numerous collections of essays and his reflections on writing and filmmaking.

INTERVIEWER: How was it that you were drawn to the theater?

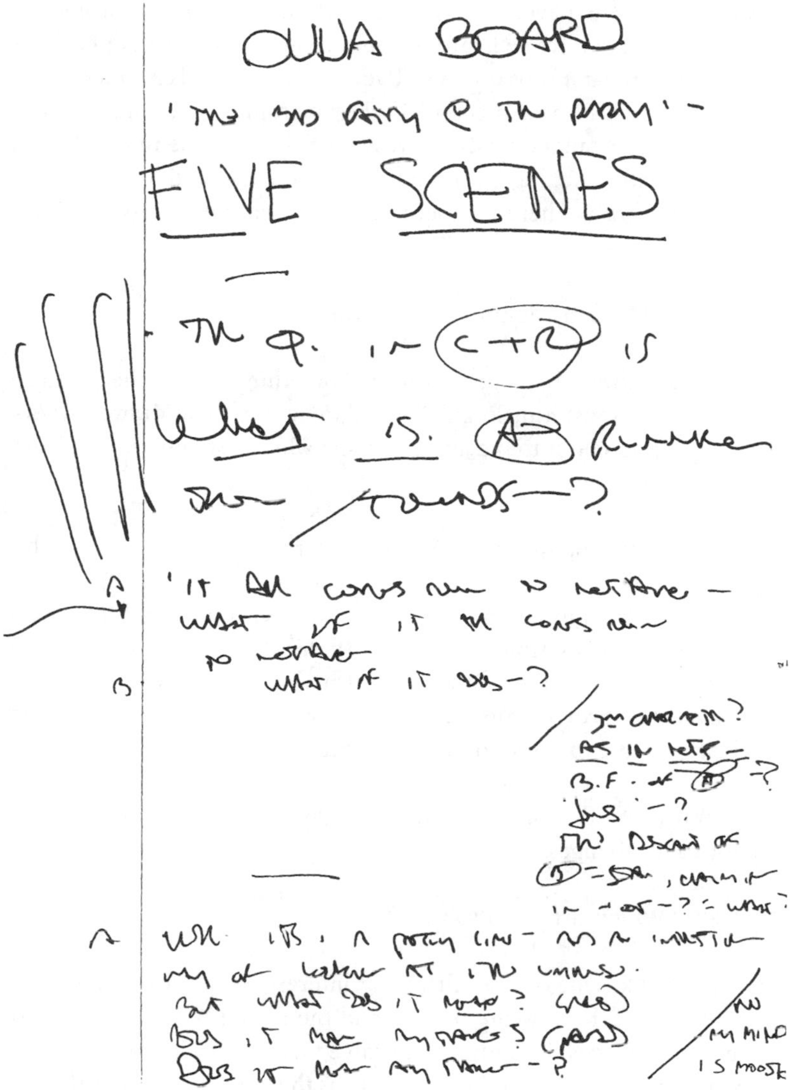

A manuscript page from the author's notebooks.

MAMET: Freud believed that our dreams sometimes recapitulate a speech, a comment we've heard or something that we've read. I always had compositions in my dreams. They would be a joke, a piece of a novel, a witticism, or a piece of dialogue from a play, and I would dream them. I would actually express them line by line in the dream. Sometimes after waking up I would remember a snatch or two and write them down. There's something in me that just wants to create dialogue.

INTERVIEWER: Can you put a date to this?

MAMET: It's always been going on. It's something my mother used to say when I was just a little kid: "David, why must you dramatize everything?" She said it to me as a criticism: why must you *dramatize* everything?

INTERVIEWER: And did you have an answer for her?

MAMET: No, but I found out (it took me forty years) that all rhetorical questions are accusations. They're very sneaky accusations because they masquerade as a request for information. If one is not aware of the anger they provoke, one can feel not only accused but inadequate for being unable to respond to the question.

INTERVIEWER: That happens in your plays a lot. There are a lot of rhetorical challenges.

MAMET: "Why must you always..."

INTERVIEWER: One of the things that interests me is how uncompromising you are, both with yourself and the audience. *The Cryptogram,* for example, forces the audience to solve this puzzle that also happens to be troubling the kid in the play. You, as the author, have put the audience and the kid in essentially the same place.

MAMET: Well, that, to me, is always the trick of dramaturgy: theoretically, perfectly, what one wants to do is put the protagonist and the audience in exactly the same position. The main question in drama, the way I was taught, is always, What does the protagonist want? That's what drama is. It comes down to that. It's not about theme, it's not about ideas, it's not about setting, but what the protagonist wants. What gives rise to the drama, what is the precipitating event, and how, at the end of the play, do we see that event culminated? Do we see the protagonist's wishes fulfilled or absolutely frustrated? That's the structure of drama. You break it down into three acts.

INTERVIEWER: Does this explain why your plays have so little exposition?

MAMET: Yes. People only speak to get something. If I say, "Let me tell you a few things about myself," already your defenses go up; you go, "Look, I wonder what he wants from me," because no one ever speaks except to obtain an objective. That's the only reason anyone ever opens their mouth, onstage or offstage. They may use a language that *seems* revealing, but if so, it's just coincidence, because what they're trying to do is accomplish an objective. "Well, well, if it isn't my younger brother just returned from Australia... have a good break?" The question is where does the *dramatist* have to lead you? Answer: the place where he or she thinks the audience needs to be led. But what does the *character* think? Does the character need to convey that information? If the answer is no, then you'd better cut it out, because you aren't putting the audience in the same position with the protagonist. You're saying, in effect, "Let's stop the play." That's what the narration is doing: stopping the play.

Now, there's a certain amount of *essential* information, without which the play does not make sense...

INTERVIEWER: And how do you fit that information in?

MAMET: As obliquely as possible. You want to give the people information before they know it's been given to them.

INTERVIEWER: So to you a character is...

MAMET: It's action, as Aristotle said. That's all that it is: exactly what the person does. It's not what they "think," because we don't know what they think. It's not what they say. It's what they do, what they're physically trying to accomplish on the stage. Which is exactly the same way we understand a person's character in life: not by what they say, but by what they do. Say someone came up to you and said, "I'm glad to be your neighbor because I'm a very honest man. That's my character. I'm honest, I like to do things, I'm forthright, I like to be clear about everything, I like to be concise." Well, you really don't know anything about that guy's character. Or the person is onstage, and the playwright has him or her make those same claims in several subtle or not-so-subtle ways, the audience will say, "Oh yes, I understand their character now; now I understand that they are a character." But in fact you don't understand anything. You just understand that they're jabbering to try to convince you of something.

INTERVIEWER: So do you end up cutting a lot of material from your earlier drafts?

MAMET: Well, you know, Hemingway said it once: "To write the best story you can, take out all the good lines."

INTERVIEWER: But do you then sometimes find that the audience has a hard time keeping up with you? It seems to me that in this climate one of the playwright's problems is that the audience expects things to be explained.

MAMET: I never try to make it hard for the audience. I may not succeed, but... Vakhtangov, who was a disciple of Stanislavsky, was asked at one point why his films were so successful, and he said, "Because I never for one moment forget about the audience." I try to adopt that as an absolute tenet. I mean, if I'm not writing for the audience, if I'm not writing to make it easier for *them*, then who the hell am I doing it for? And the way you make it easier is by following those tenets: cutting, building to a climax, leaving out exposition, and always progressing toward the single goal of the protagonist. They're very stringent rules, but they are, in my estimation and experience, what makes it easier for the audience.

INTERVIEWER: What else? Are there other rules?

MAMET: Get into the scene late, get out of the scene early.

INTERVIEWER: Why? So that something's already happened?

MAMET: Yes. That's how *Glengarry* got started. I was listening to conversations in the next booth and I thought, my God, there's nothing more fascinating than the people in the next booth. You start in the middle of the conversation and wonder, what the hell are they talking about? And you listen heavily. So I worked a bunch of these scenes with people using extremely arcane language—kind of the canting language of the real estate crowd, which I understood, having been involved with them—and I thought, well, if it fascinates me, it will probably fascinate them too. If not, they can put me in jail.

INTERVIEWER: Going back to your roots in the theater, how did you get involved initially?

MAMET: I was a kid actor. I did amateur theatricals, television, and radio in Chicago. Always loved the theater.

INTERVIEWER: You loved it, but I wonder if your plays aren't in some sort of debate with its conventions and what it should be.

MAMET: Maybe, but I always understood that as one of its conventions. Like David Ogilvy said, you don't want to create an ad that says "advertisement." That you will not look at. Concerns of content, concerns of form, it's all the same to me. It's the theatrical event. As for thinking against the sort of conventional narrative formulae of the theater.... Well, I have the great benefit of never having learned anything in school, so a lot of this stuff...

INTERVIEWER: Were you a bad student?

MAMET: I was a nonstudent. No interest, just bored to flinders. I was like the professor in *Oleanna* who all his life had been told he was an idiot, so he behaved like an idiot. Later on I realized that I enjoy accomplishing tasks. I get a big kick out of it because I never did it as a kid. Somebody said that the reason that we all have a school dream—

"I've forgotten to do my paper!" "I've forgotten to study!"—is that it's the first time that the child runs up against the expectations of the world. "The world has expectations of me, and I'm going to have to meet them or starve, meet them or die, and I'm unprepared."

INTERVIEWER: Do you ever feel unprepared?

MAMET: Much of the time. But the prescription for that is to do more, to work harder, to do more, to do it again.

INTERVIEWER: If you hadn't found the theater, what do you think you might have been?

MAMET: I think it's very likely I would have been a criminal. It seems to me to be another profession that subsumes outsiders, or perhaps more to the point, accepts people with a not-very-well-formed ego, and rewards the ability to improvise.

INTERVIEWER: Is that why con men and tricksters appear so often in your plays?

MAMET: I've always been fascinated by the picaresque. That's part of the Chicago tradition: to love our gangsters and con men, the bunko artists and so forth.

It occurred to me while I was doing *House of Games* that the difficulty of making the movie was exactly the same difficulty the confidence man has. For the confidence man it is depriving the victim of her money; for me it is misleading the audience sufficiently so they feel pleased when they find out they've been misled, tricking them so that every step is logical, and at the end they've defeated themselves. So the process of magic and the process of confidence games, and to a certain extent the process of drama, are all processes of autosuggestion. They cause the audience to autosuggest themselves in a way which seems perfectly logical, but is actually false.

You know, also being a very proud son of a bitch, I always thought that the trick was to be able to do it on a bare stage, with nothing but one or two actors. If one could do it like that, then one has done something to keep the audience's attention, make it pay off over an hour and a half, on a bare stage with nothing but two people talking.

INTERVIEWER: Did you read a lot when you were a kid?

MAMET: I always read novels. To me that was "real" writing. I liked all the midwesterners—Sinclair Lewis, Willa Cather, Sherwood Anderson.

INTERVIEWER: Was it just that the Midwest was familiar terrain, or something in the tone?

MAMET: Both. I mean, I loved Dreiser—he talked about streets that I knew and types that I knew and the kinds of people and kinds of neighborhoods that I actually knew. But I also liked the midwestern tone. It was very legato. Perhaps the rhythm of the midwestern seasons—a long, impossibly cold winter, and then a long, impossibly hot summer. It was a vast, impossibly big lake, a huge sea of wheat. It has that same rhythm, the same legato rhythm, moved on like that. Things were going to unfold in their own time, kind of like a French movie, except not quite that drawn out.

INTERVIEWER: You held a number of odd jobs while you were starting in the theater.

MAMET: Yes. After college I worked as an actor, a cabdriver, a cook, a busboy—I did all of that. At one point, after I'd been running a theater for a couple years, this guy came up to me at a party and said, "I saw the whole play. I like it very much." I said, "Thank you." He said, "You want to come be an editor at *Oui* magazine?" I said, "Why did you ask me? I have no idea what the job entails, and also, I'm sure I'm unqualified for it." And he said, "You know, I'm not sure what it entails either, but it will be a little bit of this, little bit of that, little bit of this. Make it up. And I'm sure you *are* qualified for it." And I said, "Well, I hate sitting in an office." He said, "Don't. Come in and do the work for however long it takes you, and go home." And I said *hum, hum, hummer.* And he said, "I'll pay you twenty thousand dollars a year." This was 1975. Twenty thousand was a vast amount of money—about three times more than I'd made in my life. So I said okay. I worked there for a while. Before that I was selling carpet over the telephone. Cold-calling out of the blue book, absolutely cold.

INTERVIEWER: Do you remember your spiel?

MAMET: "Mrs. Jones, this is"—you always used a fake name—"Mrs. Jones, this is Dick Richards of Walton Carpets. I don't know what you've heard about our current two-for-one special—is your husband there with you now?" "A-buh-buh." "Will he be home this evening?" "A-wah-wah-wah-wah." "Fine, which would be a better time for us to send a representative over to talk to you, seven or nine o'clock?" Because what we wanted to do, it's the same idea as the Fuller Brush men: you get your foot in the door, you offer them something, keep talking, get them in the habit of saying yes, and then you've got them in the habit of accepting what you're giving them.

INTERVIEWER: Were you a good salesman?

MAMET: No, I was terrible. I kept identifying with the people on the other end, which is something you really can't do.

INTERVIEWER: You're much more ruthless as a playwright than you would be as a salesman.

MAMET: I'm a fairly gentle guy. When Greg Mosher directed *Glengarry* we had a lot of salesmen come in to talk to the cast, guys who were making five million dollars a year selling airplanes or industrial equipment. These people were supercloser. There's a whole substratum of people who are *the* closer, like the Alec Baldwin character in the movie of *Glengarry*. But the most impressive salesman was a saleswoman, a Fuller Brush lady, who came in and showed us how to do the Fuller Brush spiel. It was great. The first thing they do is offer you a choice of two free gifts, and they make sure you take one in your hand. So it's not, "Do you want one?" It's, "Which would you rather have?" And now that you've got one of their free gifts in your hand, how could you not answer their next question, which is also going to be answered—it's going to be yes, and the next question's going to be yes, and the next…

INTERVIEWER: Does this follow a rule of drama too, for you?

MAMET: I don't know, but I was fascinated by it. And the idea was, you've absolutely got to stick to the pitch. Have to stick with it. There was a great book called *In Search of Myself* by Frederick Grove, a Canadian novelist, a great writer. Nobody's ever heard of him, but it's a great book. It's about the immigrant experience: coming here with nothing and what America does to that person. And one of the things he becomes is a book salesman who goes from door to door having to sell phony books. Heartbreaking, you know, that he has to do this. Heartbreaking.

INTERVIEWER: Going back to the odd jobs: did you see them as a means to getting your start in the theater, or were you just sort of rooting around?

MAMET: I knew I wanted to be in the theater, but I also knew I was a terrible actor. So I started, by dribs and drabs, forming a theater company that I could direct, because I figured it was something I could do.

INTERVIEWER: When did you start writing plays?

MAMET: I didn't really start writing till I was in my twenties. And I started because the company, the St. Nicholas Theatre, couldn't pay any royalties—we didn't have any money. I was very fortunate, coming from Chicago, because we had that tradition there of writing as a legitimate day-to-day skill, like bricklaying. You know, you need to build a house but you can't afford it, or you need to build a garage but you can't afford a bricklayer. Well, hell, figure out how to lay bricks. You need a script, well, hell, figure out how to write one. There was a great tradition flourishing in Chicago in the early seventies of the theater as an organic unit. The organic theater—in fact, the most important theater at the time was called the Organic Theater—but the organic (small *o*) theater consisted of a company of actors who also directed and also wrote and also designed. Everybody did everything. There was no mystery about it. One week one guy would be the director, the next week the woman would be the director and the guy would be acting, et cetera. So that was the community and the tradition that I came back to in the seventies in Chicago.

INTERVIEWER: Who were your dramatic influences?

MAMET: Well, primarily Pinter—*The Revue Sketches, A Night Out,* and *The Birthday Party.* He was my first encounter with modern drama. His work sounded real to me in a way that no drama ever had.

INTERVIEWER: What was a typical drama of the old school that struck you as dead or deadly?

MAMET: It was either a Shakespeare, which I wasn't hip enough to understand at that time in my youth, or bad translations of European plays, which were very bad translations, or American poetic realism, which just bored the bloomers off me. People talking too much—I didn't understand those people. They weren't like anybody I knew. The people I knew washed dishes or drove cabs.

INTERVIEWER: Were there advantages to starting in Chicago instead of New York?

MAMET: Being in Chicago was great. It was all happening, all the time, like jazz in New Orleans. We looked at New York as two things: one was, of course, the Big Apple, and the other was the world's biggest hick town. Because much of what we saw happening in New York was the equivalent of the Royal Nonesuch—you know, a bunch of people crawling around, barking and calling it theater. But the version in Chicago was people went to the theater just like they went to the ball game: they wanted to see a show. If it was a drama, it had to be dramatic, and if it was a comedy, it had to funny—period. And if it was those things, they'd come back. If it wasn't those things, they wouldn't come back.

INTERVIEWER: How long were you there?

MAMET: I was in Chicago from like 1973 till 1976 or 1977. And then—whore that I am—I came to New York.

INTERVIEWER: *The Cryptogram,* can we talk a little about what that was trying to figure out?

MAMET: Well, it was trying to figure out itself, for one. It was trying to figure out what the hell the mechanism of the play was. And I had all this stuff about the kid not going to sleep, and it finally occurred to me, about the billionth draft, well, it's about why can't the kid sleep? It's not *that* the kid can't sleep, but *why* can't the kid sleep? So the kid can't sleep because he knows, subconsciously, that something's unbalanced in the household. But then why is nobody paying attention to him? I thought, aha! Well, this is perhaps the question of the play.

INTERVIEWER: So you, as the writer inside *The Cryptogram,* you've sort of imagined my questions and led me gradually to revelation. You have certain designs on the audience's mind, you try to persuade them of certain psychological truths...

MAMET: No, I'm not trying to persuade them of anything; it's much more basic than that, it's much more concrete. It has to do with those black lines on the white page. Finally it comes down to—maybe this is going to sound coy—it just comes down to the writing of a play. Obviously, the point of the play is doing it for the audience—like the cook who wants to make that perfect soufflé, that perfect mousse, that perfect carbonara. Of course he isn't going to do it if he doesn't think someone's going to eat it, but the point is to cook it perfectly, not to affect the eaters in a certain way. The thing exists of itself.

INTERVIEWER: Is there a moment in one of your plays that you really didn't know was there?

MAMET: Yes. I wrote this play called *Bobby Gould in Hell.* Greg Mosher did it on a double bill with a play by Shel Silverstein over at Lincoln Center. Bobby Gould is consigned to hell, and he has to be interviewed to find out how long he's going to spend there. The Devil is called back from a fishing trip to interview Bobby Gould. And so the Devil is there, the Assistant Devil is there, and Bobby Gould. And the Devil finally says to Bobby Gould, "You're a very bad man." And Bobby Gould says, "Nothing's black and white." And the Devil says, "Nothing's black and white, nothing's black and white—what about a panda? What about a panda, you dumb fuck! What about a fucking panda!" And when Greg directed it, he had the assistant hold up a picture of a panda, kind of pan it 180 degrees to the audience at the Vivian Beaumont Theater. That was the best moment I've ever seen in any of my plays.

INTERVIEWER: What sort of writing routine do you have? How do you operate?

MAMET: I don't know. I've actually been vehemently deluding myself, thinking that I have no set habits whatever. I know that I have very good habits of thought, and I'm trying to make them better. But as for where I go, what I do, and who's around when I work—those things are never important to me.

INTERVIEWER: Those habits of thought—how do they govern your writing?

MAMET: It's really not an intellectual process. I mean, as you see, I try to apply all sorts of mechanical norms to it, and they help me order my thoughts, but finally in playwriting, you've got to be able to write dialogue. And if you write enough of it and let it flow enough, you'll probably come across something that will give you a key as to structure. I think the process of writing a play is working back and forth between the moment and the whole. The moment and the whole, the fluidity of the dialogue and the necessity of a strict construction. Letting one predominate for a while and coming back and fixing it so that eventually what you do, like a pastry chef, is frost your mistakes, if you can.

INTERVIEWER: Are you a computer man or a pad-and-pencil man?

MAMET: Pad and pencil. I want to see it, I want to see them all out in front of me, each one of the pencil adaptations, the pencil notations, and the pencil notations crossed out, and the pen on top of the pencil, and the pages...

INTERVIEWER: Do you look at all twelve drafts?

MAMET: If I have to. Theoretically, one should be able to keep the whole play in one's mind. The main thing is, I want to know that ·

they're there. The idea of taking everything and cramming it into this little electronic box designed by some nineteen-year-old in Silicon Valley... I can't imagine it.

INTERVIEWER: In looking back at your work, are there plays that you feel were more successful than others?

MAMET: The most challenging dramatic form, for me, is the tragedy. I think I'm proudest of the craft in the tragedies I've written—*The Cryptogram, Oleanna, American Buffalo,* and *The Woods.* They are classically structured tragedies.

INTERVIEWER: How do you distinguish tragedy from drama?

MAMET: Circumstance. Drama has to do with circumstance, tragedy has to do with individual choice. The precipitating element of a drama can be a person's sexuality, their wealth, their disease.... A tragedy can't be about any of those things. That's why we identify with a tragic hero more than with a dramatic hero: we understand the tragic hero to be ourselves. That's why it's easier for the audiences initially to form an affection for the drama rather than the tragedy. Although it seems that they're exercising a capacity for identification—"Oh, yes, I understand. So-and-so is in a shitload of difficulty and I identify with them, and I see where the going's bad and I see where the hero is good"—in effect they're distancing themselves, because they'll say, "Well, shit, I couldn't get into that situation because I'm not gay, or because I am gay, because I'm not crippled or because I am crippled..." They're distanced. Because I can go on with drama. That's the difference between drama and tragedy. *Glengarry,* on the other hand, falls into a very specific American genre: the gang drama or the gang comedy. The prime proponent of it, the genius proponent of it—and maybe one of its coinventors—is Sidney Kingsley. Plays like *Detective Story, Men in White, Truckline Cafe,* to some extent *Waiting for Lefty.* These are slice-of-life plays investigating a milieu of society. A good example is *Lower Depths,* where the protagonist is elaborated into many parts. In a comedy of manners like *Don Quixote,* for example, we understand that the sidekick is just another aspect of the protagonist, just like everybody in our dreams is an aspect of us. A tragedy has to be the attempt of one specific person to obtain one specific goal, and when he either gets it or doesn't get it, then we know the play is over, and we can go home and put out the baby-sitter.

INTERVIEWER: I'm interested to hear you say that you thought of *Oleanna*, which is more polemical than the other plays, as a tragedy.

MAMET: Classically it's structured as a tragedy. The professor is the main character. He undergoes absolute reversal of situation, absolute recognition at the last moment of the play. He realizes that perhaps he is the cause of the plague on Thebes.

INTERVIEWER: Did it surprise you, the way the play took off?

MAMET: It stunned them.

INTERVIEWER: You were aiming for a nerve, and you hit it.

MAMET: No, I wasn't aiming for a nerve, I was just trying to write the play. After it was finished I thought, Jesus Christ, I can't put this play on! Especially at Harvard—people were going to throw rocks through the theater windows. I was frightened. And my wife was playing the part—the part was written for her—and I was always frightened that someone was going to attack her, come over the footlights and attack her. One day we were doing some notes before the performance, and I was just looking out at the empty theater, and William Macy, who played the professor, came over and said, "Don't worry, Dave, they'll have to get through me first." I always felt they were going to put me in jail someday.

INTERVIEWER: Why?

MAMET: Well, for many reasons, not the least of which is, as a kid, I became so judgmental about the House Un-American Activities Committee. This person talked to the committee, that person talked to the committee—"How could you do that? How could you not do that? How could..." Later on I realized that everybody has their own reasons, and that unless we've walked a mile in that man or woman's moccasins it's not for us to say, "Well, okay, here's what you're going to get for criticizing others' bravery as a writer or as a creative artist."

INTERVIEWER: I suppose all your plays, in one way or another, come very close to saying something unacceptable about society, something that's very hard for people to hear.

MAMET: Well, you know, we did *American Buffalo* here on Broadway, right around the corner, and I remember some businessmen—night after night one or two of them would come storming out, muttering to themselves furiously, "What the *fuck* does this play have to do with me?" and words to that effect.

INTERVIEWER: Where did the idea for *American Buffalo* come from?

MAMET: Macy and I were in Chicago one time, and he was living in this wretched hovel—we'd both become screamingly poor—and I came over to talk to him about something, some play equipment. I opened the refrigerator, and there was this big piece of cheese. I hadn't had anything to eat in a long time, so I picked it up, cut off a big chunk, and started eating. And Macy said, "Hey, *help yourself.*" I was really hurt. I went away and fumed about that for several days. Then I just started writing, and out of that came this scene, which was the start of the play: Ruthie comes in furious because someone had just said to him, "Help yourself."

INTERVIEWER: What about when you were working on *The Village*? Did that change your routine?

MAMET: With a novel it's different. It's kind of exhilarating not to have to cut to the bone constantly. "Oh, well I can go over here for a moment." I can say what I think the guy was thinking, or what the day looked like, or what the bird was doing. If you do that as a playwright, you're dead.

INTERVIEWER: Have you considered putting stage directions in your screenplays?

MAMET: No, because if you're writing a drama, to get involved in it is kind of nonsense. It's like, you read a screenplay and it says, "BRENDA comes into the room. She's beautiful, she's sassy, she's smart, she's twenty-five, she's built like a brick shithouse: this is the kind of girl that you'll leave your wife for. When you see those deep blue eyes..." I mean, you're going to cast an actress, and she's going to look like something, right? Some idiot script reader from Yale is going to get a kick out of what you've thrown in, but it has nothing to do with making the movie, because you're going to cast an actress who will have qualities that are going to have nothing to do with what you made up. When you write stage directions: unless they're absolutely essential for the understanding of the action of the play ("He leaves." "She shoots him.") something else is going to happen when the actors and directors get them on the stage.

INTERVIEWER: What led you to the movies? It seems to me that the demands of the truth that can be told in the theater are so much deeper and more intense than on the screen. If you could tell stories, in my view, the way you tell stories, why bother with the cinema?

MAMET: I like it. I think it's a fascinating medium. It's so similar to the theater in many ways, and yet so very different. It's great: it takes place with a huge number of people, which is fine; it's very technical in ways that the theater isn't; it calls for a lot of different ways of thinking, purely mechanical ways of thinking, that I find fascinating. A lot of it, directing especially, is how many boxes are hidden in this drawing? That kind of thing. It's a fascinating medium to me.

INTERVIEWER: But I feel that if you have a gift that's so enormous in a certain area, it would be very hard not to give yourself to that entirely. Is it simply a desire to make your life interesting, or to change pace, or...?

MAMET: I think that's a large part of it.

INTERVIEWER: Where do you feel you have to work the hardest?

MAMET: That's a good question. I don't know the answer to it. I just feel like I have to work hard at all of it; it's not something that comes naturally to me. So maybe that's why I like it: I get a great sense of accomplishment from being able to complete a project with a certain level of technical efficiency. Frankly, I don't feel I have a lot of talent for it, but I love doing it and have a certain amount of hard-won technical ability.

INTERVIEWER: Do you have a lot of unfinished work?

MAMET: I've got a lot of stuff I just shelved. Some of it I come back to and some I don't.

INTERVIEWER: It tempts you.

MAMET: It challenges me, a lot of it, and it angers me.

INTERVIEWER: But are you prepared just to write and write and write, like pissing into a well or something?

MAMET: Sometimes.

INTERVIEWER: Not knowing where you're going, trying to see what the story is.

MAMET: I think it would be a lot easier to write to a formula, but it's just not fun to me. It's not challenging.

INTERVIEWER: I find it hard to understand how you can live with the tension of knowing something is unresolved, not knowing where it's going.

MAMET: But that's great. It's like Hemingway said: give yourself something to do tomorrow.

INTERVIEWER: So you let go and wait till later for a resolution. That's very hard, isn't it, to live with that?

MAMET: Well, I think that's the difference between the Christian and the Jewish ethic. Judaism is not a religion or a culture built on faith.

You don't have to have faith. You don't have to believe anything; you just have to do it.

INTERVIEWER: But what happens when you follow a character or a situation and it doesn't pan out?

MAMET: You do it again. Or, in some instances, stick it on the shelf and either do or don't come back to it sometime.

INTERVIEWER: Do you try to put in five or six hours a day writing?

MAMET: I try to do as little writing as possible, as I look back on it. I like to talk on the telephone and, you know, read magazines.

INTERVIEWER: And sit in your office and forestall writing?

MAMET: Yes, and sometimes I like to do the opposite.

INTERVIEWER: Whatever happens, you get a lot out for somebody who doesn't write a lot, or doesn't like to write.

MAMET: I never saw the point in not.

INTERVIEWER: But you just said you spend a lot of time trying not to write.

MAMET: That's true. But the actual point of being a writer, and doing something every once in a while mechanically, I just don't see the point in it, and it wouldn't be good for me. I've got to do it anyway. Like beavers, you know. They chop, they eat wood, because if they don't, their teeth grow too long and they die. And they hate the sound of running water. Drives them crazy. So, if you put those two ideas together, *they are going to build dams.*

—JOHN LAHR
Spring, 1997

WENDY WASSERSTEIN

© Jill Krementz

Wendy Wasserstein was born in Brooklyn in 1950, the youngest of four children. Her father was a textile manufacturer and her mother an amateur dancer who had grown up in Poland and moved to the United States when her father was suspected of being a spy. When Wasserstein was eleven the family moved to the Upper East Side of Manhattan, where she attended a series of young women's schools. She received her B.A. from Mount Holyoke in 1971 and an M.A. from City College, where she studied creative writing with Joseph Heller and Israel Horovitz.

In 1973, soon after she graduated from City, Wasserstein's first professional play, *Any Woman Can't*, was presented by Playwrights Horizons, a small off-Broadway theater that has played an important role in her career. But it was at the Yale School of Drama, in which she enrolled the next year, that she found her métier as a playwright. She was the lone woman among a dozen men studying playwriting, in what her friend and classmate Christopher Durang remembers as a "kind of bizarre macho class. There were an awful lot of would-be Sam Shepards, and Wendy felt a little left out."

After receiving her M.F.A. from Yale in 1976, Wasserstein returned to New York, where she has lived ever since. During the next several years, her plays, including *Uncommon Women and Others* (1977) and *Isn't It Romantic* (1983), were produced in various off-Broadway theaters. Her eighth play, *The Heidi Chronicles*, opened at Playwrights Horizons in late 1988 and quickly moved to Broadway, where it won the 1989 Pulitzer Prize and Tony Award for best play.

Since then Wasserstein has written *The Sisters Rosensweig* (1992) and *An American Daughter* (1997). In addition, she has written a collection of essays called *Bachelor Girls*, a children's book, *Pamela's First Musical*, and several screenplays, including *The Object of My Affection* (1998), all of which she considers things that happen while she is "waiting for the next play."

———

This interview is drawn from two meetings. The first took place in 1992, not long after The Sisters Rosensweig *opened on Broadway, when we met in the breakfast room of Wasserstein's apartment. It is an impressive room, with a view overlooking Central Park, and she joked, "I don't use it much; I'm not good enough." The second interview was conducted in the spring of 1997, during rehearsals for* An American Daughter.

INTERVIEWER: What do your sisters think of *The Sisters Rosensweig*?

WASSERSTEIN: I didn't show anyone in my family the play. The problem with writing plays is that everyone has an opinion. And you don't want those opinions. You want people to say, I love you no matter what. I'm a forty-two-year-old woman. What would my mother say: "Oh, it's nice, Wendy, and I notice the mother is dead"? I really didn't want any of them to see it until the opening, but my sister Sandy kept saying she wanted to come, so finally I said, "You can come but you can't call me tomorrow and make any comments, because if you call me and don't say anything, I'll know you think it's bad. So no comment, either way."

86A

                         TIMBER
She looks completely sane to me.

                         QUINCY
She's disenfranchised her femininity which will inevitably result in what
I call in Venus Raging "a good girl tragedy."

                         TIMBER
I'm just a dummy in TV News Quincy. I mostly don't understand what the
hell you print folks are talking about.

                         QUINCY
Don't worry about it. This has all been such an intense time for me. ~~I~~
~~need some advice Timber~~ *How do you do it?* ~~I need some advice~~ *I need some advice Timber*

                         TIMBER
Yes Ma'am.

                         QUINCY
I have an offer to do ~~commentary on a morning news commentary~~ *commentary on a morning show*
but I'd prefer to hold out for something ~~that can't be dismissed as soft.~~ *less soft*
TIME ZONE has expressed an interest in me but the ~~scuttlebutt~~ is before Lyssa
Hughes ~~the show~~ *that show* wasn't long for this world. *buzz*

~~Need I go on.   The point,~~ TIMBER ~~That's soft~~ *and my agent says it's*
~~perfect but~~ *and certainly that help my book.*

                         QUINCY
~~Im in a unique position to do both.~~ *Oh and certainly that help my book.* I'd really love to talk to you about it
some more. ~~I'm staying in Washington tonight.~~ We could probably both use some
time to unwind.

                         TIMBER
I never unwind. That's "paws up" to me. And I'm strictly a paws down kind
of guy.

                         QUINCY
I'm afraid now I don't understand what you're talking about,

                         TIMBER
I gotta be humble here, Quincy. You deserve someone much more evolved than
I am.
                         (HE walks away and signals for the cameras to be brought in
                         closer.)

A manuscript page from An American Daughter.

She saw it and sent me flowers the next day. They came with a note that said, "No Commitment." I realized that either the florist had made this Freudian slip or he was the florist to some Upper West Side bachelor who regularly sends out "No Commitment" flowers.

But my mother is indefatigable. I hear her talking to my nieces and saying things like, "You want to marry young. You know, you don't want to grow old like Wendy." She's fascinating. She is not a schooled person—my grandfather wrote plays and was the head of a school district in Poland, but my mother went to high school in New Jersey and then stopped. But she is deeply funny and, for someone who has not read, verbal and witty and an original thinker. She never cooked and she took great pride in having no skills at all. She had four children and then my two cousins came to live with us. And she danced. By the time I got to high school she was going to dancing lessons. That woman is over eighty and she's still dancing. Her name is Lola, and when she walks down the street, chorus boys stop her to say hello. She wears leather! She's older now and so looks more like a grandmother, but if you had hit her when I was in college—she was a number. She's from that generation of mothers who had intelligence and creativity and no place to put that except into family. If the circumstances were different, I'm sure she would have been a dancer or set designer. She thinks she's marvelous in every way. If you said, "Wendy is so talented," she'd say, "Of course, she's my daughter." My love of the theater comes from her.

My dad doesn't talk very much. He's very gentle and sweet, and my suspicion is that he's extremely bright and reflective. He invented the process that put wires into ribbons, which I guess is a little like being a furrier. They are really a yin and yang, those two.

INTERVIEWER: Did you have fun growing up?

WASSERSTEIN: I did because my mother was eccentric. In Brooklyn, a lot of mothers really did play mah-jongg and have their hair done. My mother looked like Bertolt Brecht when I was growing up. She had extremely short hair. She'd say to the hairdresser on Kings Highway, "You know how I like it, so it looks like you made a mistake." When I went to yeshiva, the rabbi's daughter would come to dinner and my mother would give us hamburgers and string beans with butter sauce. You're not supposed to have milk with meat, and she'd lie and say it was lemon juice.

Also, being so close to my brother was fun; we went exploring a lot. My sister Sandy got married when I was six. She was nineteen. My aunt Kiki fell through the floor at her wedding. She was dancing and fell through, which I thought was fabulous. Sandy eventually got divorced and went to live in England for eight years. She came back, and one day my mother had her pick me up from the June Taylor School of Dance. So there I was, a yeshiva girl, going to dance school on Saturdays; my mother had me lying to the rabbi about that. Between the lemon juice and the lying to the rabbi—I'm going straight to hell. Anyway, she told Sandy to take me to Howard Johnson's and Radio City. So Sandy took me to the House of Chen, where we had shrimp dishes—and I knew your lips fall off from the shrimp but I was too scared to tell her I can't eat this. And then, instead of going to Radio City, she took me to see *Expresso Bongo*, which was one of those English art movies. I remember a scene where the girl was wearing kilts with suspenders and no top. And then Sandy made me lie about it all to my mother.

When I was in second grade, I made up a play that I was in; I told my mother that I was in this play and the lie got larger and larger. Finally, arbitrarily, I said my play is on tomorrow, and she got me a velvet dress and made my hair in ringlets, and off I went to school. And she came to school and there was no play. She covered for me and said, "I must be confused; it must be another one of my children." Then she came home and told me I was a fibber. She must have yelled at me because to this day I have trouble with fibbing.

INTERVIEWER: Would you call *The Sisters Rosensweig* your first well-made play?

WASSERSTEIN: Yes, in terms of structure. When I see the play, I feel I'm seeing a Broadway play in 1958, or what I wish those plays had been. I remember going to them and thinking, I really like this but where are the girls? *The Sisters Rosensweig* is like those plays—the curtain goes up and there's one set, and the play is well-made, you know, beginning, middle, and end. It takes place over a weekend, the stars get applause, the stars get exit applause, they each tell their stories, it arcs in the second act, all of that. It was much harder to write than any of my other plays.

INTERVIEWER: Did your other plays prepare you for it?

WASSERSTEIN: In a way. *The Sisters Rosensweig* seems a combination of *Isn't It Romantic* and *Uncommon Women*. But those other plays are episodic, and this was a deliberate decision not to be episodic. Also, I decided not to write another play about my generation. Even though it has autobiographical materials, the focus of the play is not me. I wanted to do all those things and also evoke a fondness for plays that I love, including Chekhov. On the day I finished it I thought, this was a lot of effort just to prove to myself what a good writer Chekhov is.

INTERVIEWER: You sound as if you didn't get emotionally involved.

WASSERSTEIN: Ending *The Sisters Rosensweig* was hard, and when I finish plays I tend to get emotional and weepy. I remember the day I finished it I got weepy and then I realized it wasn't right. When we were doing the workshop in Seattle, I got weepy again and I realized it still wasn't right and I thought, how many times am I going to get weepy? Today in a taxi ride I was thinking that I would like to fix the speeches between Sara and Merv in the last scene. In the first draft, Sara sang for Merv. Then Merv sang "For Me and My Gal" in return. I was thinking, they slept together once and they're singing and running off together? What kind of play is this?

INTERVIEWER: When Sara does sing for herself—that song about Moishe Pupick, about being the only Yiddish girl in MacNamara's Band—it's an amazing moment. Jewish audiences respond to Sara's need to assimilate and her need not to. For a larger audience the moment is about identity and reconnecting with yourself after being lost for some time. When Sara first starts to sing those lyrics, the audience laughs because she's singing Yiddish words. But it's actually a deeply serious moment.

WASSERSTEIN: This play is thought of as a comedy, which is great, but to me this is a very serious play, and what you touched on in that moment is almost tonality, the heart of the play.

INTERVIEWER: One of the most moving moments in the play is when Gorgeous receives a real Chanel suit as a gift. Why is that so moving?

WASSERSTEIN: I think it comes from when I was in high school and I first realized there were people who wore real Pappagallo shoes and then there were people who wore imitation Pappagallo shoes from Chandlers. So I became very interested in this idea of what was real and what was imitation and what it felt like to wear the imitation and finally get the real.

INTERVIEWER: The Chanel suit touches on something that isn't seemly to speak of, which is that material things can give you almost a spiritual sense of happiness. It's almost like being loved in a way because it makes you feel safe and secure and beautiful or whatever, and that's something that very few people write about.

WASSERSTEIN: It was odd—we hired a rabbi as the religious adviser on the play, Rabbi Shnier, whom I kept calling Rabbi Schnorrer. We did this because Madeline didn't want to light the Sabbath candles unless she was doing it right. She didn't want to be offensive. A friend of mine was dating a rabbi, so I went to speak at his temple. We were talking about Jewish women and self-image, and I said that I never thought of myself as undesirable or unattractive, frankly, until I turned twelve and began watching these movies in which none of the men ever fell in love with anybody who looked remotely like me. No one was ever Jewish, no one was hardly ever brunette. I never thought of that before, but in retrospect it really makes me angry. Maybe that will change now. Just like when I was growing up and there were no smart girls in plays. Or if they were smart, were sort of these really mean career people.

You know what's interesting? *The Sisters Rosensweig* is a play that men like. Mort Zuckerman came up to me and said, "I love your play," and I looked at him and I said, "You do?"

INTERVIEWER: I notice that you use the word *girl* a lot.

WASSERSTEIN: I've been called on the table for years on that. I call myself a Jewish girl. Maybe it's because you can't correct semantically who in your heart you know you are. But in the last five years feminism has opened up to humor. Women who are a bit older can believe in something and also see it ironically. And younger women, who once thought that to be a feminist you had to be antimarriage, have no sense of humor, and have hairy legs, are changing. When I saw Marilyn Quayle speak at the convention in 1992, I thought, everything I do is anathema to this woman. She thinks I will rot and boil in hell. But I think of her exactly what she thinks of me: poor woman.

Feminism has affected me more in my writing than in a specifically political way. Sitting down to write a play that has three parts for women over forty, I think, is political.

INTERVIEWER: Do you feel you are doing something important by making images of older, complete women?

WASSERSTEIN: I do in a way. When Gorgeous returns the Chanel suit she is in some way heroic. For a woman to be heroic she doesn't have to save the planet. My work is often thought of as lightweight commercial comedy, and I have always thought, no, you don't understand: this is in fact a political act. *The Sisters Rosensweig* had the largest advance in Broadway history, therefore nobody is going to turn down a play on Broadway because a woman wrote it or because it's about women.

INTERVIEWER: How has the theater changed since you started out?

WASSERSTEIN: It's interesting that the two most successful straight plays the year *Sisters Rosensweig* came out were mine and Tony Kushner's *Angels in America*—a play about three women over forty and an epic about a gay fantasia. Even five years before, that wouldn't have happened.

INTERVIEWER: In conversation you sometimes are angrier and more provocative than you seem in your plays.

WASSERSTEIN: My plays are my art and not just self-revelation. Creating a well-made play means you have to round the edges so they fit into the form. Also, the plays are deliberately comedic. Humor masks a lot of anger, and it's a means of breaking up others' pretenses and of not being pretentious yourself.

INTERVIEWER: You started out in the early seventies at Playwrights Horizons with Christopher Durang, Bill Finn, and all those other people. What do you remember about the early days?

WASSERSTEIN: When I was at Yale, I sent a play called *Montpelier Pizzzazz* to Playwrights Horizons, about a week after they moved to Forty-second Street. Upstairs was still the Sex Institute of Technology. Downstairs it smelled of urine, and there were pictures of the dancers on the walls. It was not a glamour spot. That's where I met André Bishop. I sent *Uncommon Women* to Playwrights Horizons, and they did a reading of it and wanted to do it. But I eventually gave it to the Phoenix Theatre instead. I thought it would get a better production and better exposure. It was because of losing that play that André decided he would turn Playwrights into the kind of theater no playwright would turn down.

INTERVIEWER: How did Playwrights attract so much raw talent when it was new?

WASSERSTEIN: It mostly had to do with André Bishop. What André managed to do was diminish the sense of competition—we all thought this was our theater. I don't know if any other theater has been able to accomplish that, maybe the Manhattan Theatre Club with Terrence McNally and Donald Margulies, but it's not quite the same. I don't know whether it was because a lot of us had gone to school together—Christopher Durang, Alfred Uhry, and Ted Tally, who writes screenplays and won an Oscar for *Silence of the Lambs*—or because André was so gentle and sweet. It was also cockamamy because it was on Forty-second Street between Ninth and Tenth. When we did the first reading of *Uncommon Women*, my dad, when he left the theater, gave André a fifty-dollar bill and said, "Take care of yourself, son." He could not understand why this nice boy from Harvard was next to a massage parlor.

INTERVIEWER: Did you have an immediate rapport with Christopher Durang?

WASSERSTEIN: What Peter Patrone says in *The Heidi Chronicles* Christopher said to me: "You look so bored, you must be very bright." I remember in a class at Yale, E. L. Doctorow said that he was very sad because a girl at Sarah Lawrence had committed suicide. Christopher asked, "Was it for credit?" Alfred found it offensive, but I just started laughing, and I thought, this guy is great! I've never met anyone like him.

The thing about this whole group of people was that no one said, "I've got to win the Pulitzer by the time I'm thirty." That was never what it was about. It was almost like they were too eccentric, and still are, I think. They were not a slick group; they didn't go to the right parties or work a room or anything like that. But these are the people I feel aesthetically close to, as some sort of gauge of myself.

INTERVIEWER: It was André who brought you all together?

WASSERSTEIN: Well, he gave us a place where we could hear our plays read. My first play was read at Playwrights before I even went to Yale. *Any Woman Can't.*

INTERVIEWER: I've never seen it.

WASSERSTEIN: And you never will. It's an awful play. I wrote it when I took Israel Horovitz's playwriting course up at City College. My mother was walking down the street and she ran into the receptionist from the June Taylor School of Dance, where I went as a child. The receptionist asked, "How's Wendy?" My mother said, "Well, I don't know. She's not going to law school, she's not dating a lawyer; now she's writing plays. She's cuckoo." The receptionist said, "Give me Wendy's play because I work across the hall from a new theater called Playwrights Horizons." So my mother gave her *Any Woman Can't.* Bob Moss was running the theater, and they did a reading.

INTERVIEWER: You're all funny and you all tend to write rather episodically. Durang had more acts in a play than anyone had ever seen and Bill Finn wrote musical vignettes that came together as a whole in the end.

WASSERSTEIN: I think we were the next generation after Terrence McNally, Lanford Wilson, and John Guare, who were all breaking form too, from Edward Albee and Arthur Miller. I guess someone could say we were the first generation who grew up watching television and also going to the theater.

INTERVIEWER: While the previous generation only went to the theater.

WASSERSTEIN: That's right. The next generation will go to the theater even less. So the episodic writing was something that came to me. I thought writing a full-length play was something I didn't want to do and didn't know how to do. It seemed old fogyish. But I was on a committee to evaluate the Yale School of Drama, and there was this young woman, a directing student, who told me that what she wanted to do was explode text. I thought of Miss Julie exploding over the Yale School of Drama saying, "There goes *The Seagull!*" I thought, well before you explode it you should know how to do it. I thought, I would just like to try to do this. If in fact playwriting is like stained glass, if it becomes more and more this obscure craft, then it would be interesting to know how to do that craft.

INTERVIEWER: Did you learn by going?

WASSERSTEIN: Yes. When you write in an episodic mode, you know that the scene will be over. The hardest part, what's really boring, is getting people on and off the stage. You can't just bring the lights down and bring them up again. Someone has to say, "I'm leaving now."

INTERVIEWER: And there's got to be a good reason for it too. Not, "Oh, there's the phone!"

WASSERSTEIN: Exactly. That's very hard to do. I always think structurally. But for *The Sisters Rosensweig* it was very hard going. In that play there are four scenes in the first act and three in the second. I should have combined the first two scenes.

INTERVIEWER: You expressed some dissatisfaction about the end of the play. You didn't want to end with Merv and Sara singing to each other. Did that feel wrong to you?

WASSERSTEIN: I did do it originally, and it was great when Merv sang "For Me and My Gal." But suddenly this play became Mervin the Magician, this man who came into these three sisters' lives and turned the place upside down. It made the play smaller, instead of larger.

INTERVIEWER: Because it narrowed the question of whom the play was about or who got what?

WASSERSTEIN: Yes, because it was about getting a guy. For Sara, Mervin is an agent of change. But he's not the answer.

INTERVIEWER: Do you ever see actors when you write?

WASSERSTEIN: Sometimes, but they never end up doing the play. You think Julie Andrews, or people you don't even know.

INTERVIEWER: You once said that you look forward to writing because you can't wait to leave yourself.

WASSERSTEIN: Well, I was very sad when *The Sisters Rosensweig* opened the first time. People like Merv and Gorgeous are fun to write; they're nice to have in your apartment. They're really good company. So when you discover those people, *they're* talking and you're not talking anymore. I remember the day I wrote the line for Gorgeous about Benjamin Disraeli being a Jewish philanthropist: I started laughing because I thought, that's Gorgeous, there you go. The character, not my sister. If you stay with the actual people in your real life, it won't work. It's too constraining.

INTERVIEWER: What about when you are developing a character similar to yourself? Do you write what you know about yourself or do you find out things about yourself while you're writing the character?

WASSERSTEIN: It's closer to writing yourself as if you were these other people. I think the voice of the author in this play is in Geoffrey's speech to Pfeni about making the best art and the best theater. That's me, Wendy, the writer speaking, and it's interesting that I put the words into the mouth of a bisexual British man.

INTERVIEWER: Can you explain that?

WASSERSTEIN: I think because in some ways it's less inhibiting. But you're always writing different aspects of yourself into different characters. You are never writing yourself. There are aspects of me in Pfeni—the distancing aspect, the vulnerability, and the need to wander. And the ability to get involved with a bisexual. Hey—when's the mixer? There are aspects of me in Sara, too. I am a Jewish girl who's been in these Waspy institutions all my life. Ed Kliban used to say that what was interesting about me was that the family moved very quickly from being middle-class Brooklyn to upper-middle-class Upper East Side and all the pretensions of it.

INTERVIEWER: Do you tend to write about what you know?

WASSERSTEIN: I think yes. I learn things from watching and listening to people. I'm not much of a reader; I'm slightly dyslexic. Take Merv—he is someone I knew when I was eight years old. I don't run into a whole lot of Mervs right now. Nor do I run into a lot of the Gorgeouses of life. But I remember these colorful people and their language. I remember going to someone's bar mitzvah in Brooklyn with my mother and young niece. And you know when they take the Torah out? My mother said to Samantha, "Quick, kiss the Torah before the rabbi takes it out for cookies and lunch." It was such a crazy image to me.

INTERVIEWER: It sounds like a dream.

WASSERSTEIN: It was like a dream or a Philip Roth short story. But I always have this terrible memory for what people said. You always remember what someone said yesterday, so you hold them accountable—maybe that's why I tend to write about people I know.

INTERVIEWER: Where do you write?

WASSERSTEIN: I used to write in a garage out in Bridgehampton that was literally a UPS drop-off. My brother lived on fifty acres on the water, and I wrote in this place with a garage underneath, two rooms upstairs and just a little typewriter. I wrote there in the summers. I also write in this little typing room at the Society Library on Seventy-ninth Street. A friend gave me an office at Comedy Central, on Fifty-seventh and Broadway, but the problem there is that a telephone is there, and I get on the phone a lot. But when I'm alone in one of these small rooms and I'm working—if I'm in the middle of something, of a play—it's fun. That's kind of nice. I don't feel this way if I'm in the middle of something that I don't really want to be writing. That's less fun.

INTERVIEWER: You use a typewriter?

WASSERSTEIN: I've always used a typewriter or, because I go to libraries, I write longhand in a notebook. Spiral-bound, on the sides. I tend to write longhand, and then I'll start typing it on an IBM. I'll type it myself. This is why it takes me too long to write a play. Finally, I'll get it to a typist or to various young assistants, young playwrights or whomever, who type it up for me afterwards.

INTERVIEWER: Do your plays start with an image?

WASSERSTEIN: My plays start with a feeling. *The Sisters Rosensweig* started when I was living in London writing *The Heidi Chronicles*. I thought about Americans abroad, and somebody said to me, "You're terribly Jewish, just like my brother-in-law." It was that same feeling I had at Mount Holyoke, a little bit uncomfortable with myself. Like wherever I went I was always wearing a tiara with chinchilla.

INTERVIEWER: What were you doing in London?

WASSERSTEIN: I was there on a grant from the British-American Arts Association. It was for midcareer stimulation. I loved that grant. I lived in this one room at the Nell Gwyn house. I am better in one room with a hot plate. I'm not really good at working in fancy places or in places that you're supposed to write in, like your study. I don't think I'd ever write in a room that was lined with lovely curtains.

INTERVIEWER: Why is that? Does it strike you as pretentious?

WASSERSTEIN: Or maybe too perfect. Maybe writing reminds me of school. Also, I want to shut out the other things from my life.

INTERVIEWER: So you were in London writing *Heidi,* and *The Sisters Rosensweig* was germinating?

WASSERSTEIN: The play had been germinating since the night I got this message to call my brother's secretary in New York to set up dinner with him in London that night. Here I was on a four-thousand-dollar grant from these good socialist girls. Now maybe that doesn't sound too odd, but at the time it sounded nuts. So I called Bruce—he was turning forty at the time—and we had dinner in London. It was the night of Thatcher's election: he was going to Annabel's to celebrate while my friends were having a wake somewhere. So that started me thinking about Americans in London.

INTERVIEWER: What about the genesis of *An American Daughter?*

WASSERSTEIN: I always think of new plays when I'm finishing one. I was finishing *The Sisters Rosensweig,* and was prompted by Nannygate—by what happened to Zoe Baird, what happened to Lani Guinier, what is happening to Hillary Clinton. It was also a reaction to turning forty-two—to midlife decisions, to not having children. It was both personal and political. This is a darker play than *The Sisters Rosensweig.* My plays tend to skip a generation; this one is closer to *The Heidi Chronicles,* though it is also darker than that play.

INTERVIEWER: *An American Daughter* seems to be your most overtly political play. Does that come partly out of your several White House invitations in the past few years?

WASSERSTEIN: It comes from going to plays, from being on panels, from being involved with arts funding. It also comes from the assumption that artists are always liberal, and that the politics of the theater are never surprising. I thought it was time to look inward. To use the theater to do that. And yes, I've been to the White House.

INTERVIEWER: Do you think that artists are unlike other people, with different needs?

WASSERSTEIN: Well, I don't know. There is something about the happiness I feel in that garage when Merv and Gorgeous are talking to me. Sitting in the garage in a nightgown with a typewriter—it might be the only time I'm calm. It's an ageless sort of happiness. It's what made me happy when I was twenty-seven and writing *Uncommon Women,* and what made me feel happy last summer. I'm a pretty nervous gal. So there is always the anxiety of writing, which is awful, but at those moments I do feel at one.

INTERVIEWER: Can you compare the feeling of writing alone in the library to the moment when the production begins and you're suddenly surrounded by people with very intense deadlines...

WASSERSTEIN: It's exhausting. You have to get dressed and show up. And behave yourself. You can't eat all the food on the plate because there are other people there too. But it's the best part of doing plays, if the actors are asking intelligent questions, and someone like Robert Klein is telling you how good your play is. The other difference for me is Dan Sullivan, the director, who is one of those rare creatures with a wonderful analytical and theatrical mind. That's why I go to every rehearsal. I'm not gifted visually; I can only fix my plays by hearing them. Dan will turn to me and say, "This line doesn't work," and I'll rewrite it while I'm there. So I am always on my feet.

INTERVIEWER: What stage will a play be in before you show it to someone else?

WASSERSTEIN: I always finish a draft before I show it to anybody. I'll rewrite a scene thirty-seven times before I show it to anyone. Maybe it's from insecurity. I enjoy the process of polishing until finally I set a deadline and meet it. I finished both *Heidi* and *The Rosensweigs* by my birthday. On my birthday I said to myself, "I will put this in the mail to Dan Sullivan today; I'm so sick of it."

INTERVIEWER: Where were you when you heard you won the Pulitzer Prize?

WASSERSTEIN: I was home in my nightgown writing an essay about my mother that is in *Bachelor Girls*. I had heard a rumor that David Hwang was going to win it for *M. Butterfly*. I'd never been someone who won prizes. Perhaps I wasn't pretentious enough or academic enough. I never thought of myself as an intellectual or good at school. So I just assumed I wouldn't win, which would be fine. I was home, and Mark Thibodeux, the press agent for *The Heidi Chronicles*, called up and said, "You won the Pulitzer." I said, "That's not funny." He said, "No, no, I'm serious. You won the Pulitzer Prize." I kept saying, "You're the Queen of Romania, Mark, don't do this to me." He told me to call my mother, so I did, because I thought, this woman's going to hear my name on the radio and think I died or something. I called her. She asked me, "Is that as good as a Tony?" I thought, that's my mother, undermine it, don't say congratulations, just pull the rug out from under me. I wasn't in the mood, so I said, "Why don't you just call my brother and he'll explain it to you." Then the phone started ringing off the hook, it was like the phone went up and started spinning around the room. I went out that afternoon and had champagne at the Four Seasons with my brother Bruce and sister Sandra and Walter Shapiro and André Bishop. Then I went to the theater. Edward Albee was there. He told me to go onstage and take a bow. I said I was too shy. He said that I never knew when it was going to happen again. So I did it.

INTERVIEWER: Did winning the Pulitzer mean more than winning the Tony?

WASSERSTEIN: It's hard to say, because they're different. Winning the Pulitzer was never a goal of mine but it meant a great deal to me in terms of self-esteem. Getting the Tony was quite different because I knew that for the sake of the play and its commercial life that it was very important. I remember sitting in the audience with André Bishop thinking, should I go up with the scarf, without the scarf? When I went up, there were so many men standing behind me, I wanted to say, "So many men, so little time." I just couldn't do it because I was the first woman to win the Tony for best play alone, and I felt the need to dignify the occasion in some way. Because what's hard about being a playwright is, as Christopher Durang would say, it's all so random—getting your play done, how it's going to be reviewed ...

INTERVIEWER: Is it any more random than other commercial art?

WASSERSTEIN: If you want to write for television, for instance, there is a supply and demand: you can make a living. Even if you're commissioned to write a play, you are not going to get paid in the same way.

INTERVIEWER: Does that make the motives of playwrights purer?

WASSERSTEIN: In a sense. It also depends on how you think, whether you think in terms of plays. I am most interested in how people talk. If I went to a movie studio and said I wanted to do a movie about three sisters over forty with a romantic lead who is fifty-four, they'd ask me to rewrite it for Geena Davis, and then they'd probably hire Beth Henley to make them all Southern. In film the voice gets taken out of it unless you're the director.

INTERVIEWER: Are you saying that screenwriters are less writers than playwrights?

WASSERSTEIN: No, it's just a different craft; most screenwriters I know would like to be directors so that they could have some sort of control.

INTERVIEWER: Many writers detest the public life brought on by success, the awards, the speeches. I get the feeling that you enjoy it. Do you think of it as a reward for all the time you spend alone?

WASSERSTEIN: There is a part of me that thinks that playwrights deserve as much recognition as novelists or screenwriters. I also know that if you want people to come to your plays, it helps to go on David Letterman's show. One creates a persona. I'm actually a shy person. Michael Kinsley is also a shy person, and there he is on TV every night. I was talking to him about this, that fame is not about getting a restaurant reservation. It's about walking up Madison Avenue on the way to your therapist, and you're thinking, my God, I'm worthless, what am I doing with my life, I'm horrible.... Then some woman comes up to you and says, "You're Wendy Wasserstein. I can't tell you how much you mean to me." I want to say to this person, "I'm glad I mean something to you because I mean nothing to me. Thank you very much." Then I think, what is wrong with me?

I like to think that those are the people who I write for—the matinee ladies at *The Sisters Rosensweig*. I guess it is something of a release from being alone and working. It's odd for me to have chosen this profession because I'm not very good at being alone and I'm not very good at sitting still. But at the same time, I find my work very comforting.

INTERVIEWER: You are known for being nice. Can a woman afford to be too nice?

WASSERSTEIN: I have a great interest in being ladylike, but there is also something to be said for being direct. What I hate about myself and would like to change is that I get hurt very easily. I'm too vulnerable and always have been. I don't look vulnerable. I always think vulnerable girls should have Pre-Raphaelite hair, weigh two pounds, about whom everybody says, "Oh, she's so sensitive." I admire aggressiveness in women. I try to be accommodating and entertaining, and some say that's what's wrong with my plays. But I think there are very good things about being a woman that have not been taught to men—not bullshit manners but true graciousness. I think there is real anger in life to be expressed, there is great injustice, but I also think there is dignity. That is interesting, and part of the plays I want to write.

INTERVIEWER: Did you always know you were a playwright?

WASSERSTEIN: I always loved the theater, but it would have been odd to proclaim it as my vocation. I did, however, play with my Ginny doll and imagine plays for my dolls. I thought I'd be a lawyer and get married and not practice. I find it interesting how affected one is by the time in which one comes of age. I'm sure if I had gone to Mount Holyoke in 1955 I would have gotten married my sophomore year because that's what everybody did. I think of Hillary Clinton as being of that generation as well. When I went to college there was a saying: Holyoke to wed and Smith to bed. So my mother sent me to Mount Holyoke. I grew up reading the Arts and Leisure section, thinking that I would be like Celeste Holm in *All About Eve* and that it would be the husband who was the playwright and I would be the well-educated person who loved the theater. In those four years all of that changed—a transitional generation. The fact that I am the playwright has to do with that time.

INTERVIEWER: Was there any anti-Semitism at Mount Holyoke?

WASSERSTEIN: I do remember one girl at Mount Holyoke did not want me to come to her house over vacation because her father didn't particularly like Jews. They lived in Newton, Massachusetts. I came from Brooklyn, where everybody was Jewish or black or they were parochial school kids, but I didn't know them. When we moved to the Upper East Side, there were people who weren't Jewish, who went to Trinity and those fancy schools, but I didn't know them. Mount Holyoke was the first time I was ever in a house with a Christmas tree. So you did have a sense that you were Jewish and everybody else wasn't—that you were an outsider. While this could be alienating, it affected me for the better, I think; it made me feel I did not need to be anyone else. My close friends there were largely Catholic. I had one Jewish friend there from New Jersey who became a Marxist-Leninist gynecologist. How could you not love such a person? Those are the sorts of people you're supposed to meet in college.

INTERVIEWER: Who are the playwrights you most admire?

WASSERSTEIN: Chekhov, Ibsen, Wilde, Shakespeare, Chris Durang, Lanford Wilson, August Wilson, Tina Howe. I also have admiration for the women who write musicals—Betty Comden, Carolyn Leigh.

INTERVIEWER: One last question: Did you ever sit through a play of yours with your mother?

WASSERSTEIN: You mean sitting beside her? God no!

—LAURIE WINER
Spring, 1997

Notes on Contributors

Lawrence M. Bensky (Harold Pinter interview) was the Paris editor of *The Paris Review* from 1964 to 1966. He has worked mostly in broadcasting since then, first as one of the original newscasters and talk show hosts in "underground" FM radio at KSAN, and then primarily for Pacifica Radio, where he was national affairs correspondent from 1987 to 1998. Bensky teaches journalism and broadcasting at California State University, Hayward, and Stanford.

Christopher Bigsby (Arthur Miller interview) is professor of American studies and director of the Arthur Miller Center at the University of East Anglia in Norwich. He has published more than twenty-five books on aspects of British and American drama. He is the co-editor of the three-volume *Cambridge History of American Theater*.

Olga Carlisle (Arthur Miller interview), the author of a forthcoming memoir, *Far from Russia*, lives in California, where she paints and writes. She recently coauthored with her husband, Henry Carlisle, a novel, *The Idealists*.

Anne Cattaneo (John Guare interview) is the dramaturge of Lincoln Center Theater and the director of the Lincoln Center Theater Directors Lab.

William Flanagan (Edward Albee interview), was a composer of many works, including *The Death of Bessie Smith, Another August,* and *Chapters from Ecclesiastes.* He died in 1969.

Richard H. Goldstone (Thornton Wilder interview) was a professor of dramatic literature at New York University and the City College of New York, and was the author of the biography *Thornton Wilder: An Intimate Portrait.* He died in 1998.

Shusha Guppy (Tom Stoppard interview, Eugène Ionesco interview) is the London editor of *The Paris Review.* She writes on literature for a number of publications in Britain and America. Her books include *The Blindfold Horse, A Girl in Paris,* and *Looking Back.*

ANNE HOLLANDER (Lillian Hellman interview) is the author of *Seeing Through Clothes, Moving Pictures, Sex and Suits,* and *Feeding the Eye.* She is at present working on a book about the treatment of clothing in literature.

BENJAMIN HOWE (Sam Shepard interview) is a freelance journalist and an advisory editor of *The Paris Review.*

JOHN LAHR (Introduction, David Mamet interview) is the senior drama critic at *The New Yorker.* This year, three of his books—*Notes on a Cowardly Lion: The Biography of Bert Lahr; Dame Edna Everage and the Rise of Western Civilization;* and *Prick Up Your Ears: The Biography of Joe Orton*—will be reissued by the University of California Press. *Show and Tell,* a collection of his *New Yorker* profiles, will be published next year.

JAMES LIPTON (Neil Simon interview), the author of *An Exaltation of Larks,* is dean of the Actors Studio Drama School at New School University, and is executive producer, writer, and host of *Inside the Actors Studio* on the Bravo network.

BONNIE LYONS (August Wilson interview) is the author of *Passion and Craft: Conversations with Notable Writers.* The material she provided comes from her interview with Wilson, which appeared in *Contemporary Literature.*

JEANNE MCCULLOCH (Sam Shepard interview) is an editor of *The Paris Review* and an editor-at-large at *Tin House.* Her work has appeared in *The North American Review, The Paris Review, The New York Times,* and *Vogue.*

JOHN PHILLIPS (Lillian Hellman interview) was a novelist and was an advisory editor of *The Paris Review* from its founding until his death in 1998.

GEORGE PLIMPTON (August Wilson interview) is the editor of *The Paris Review.* His most recent book is the oral biography *Truman Capote: In Which Various Friends, Enemies, Acquaintances and Detractors Recall His Turbulent Career.*

DOTSON RADER (Tennessee Williams interview) is the author of many books, including *I Ain't Marching Anymore!, Blood Dues, Beau Monde,* and *Tennessee: Cry of the Heart,* a memoir.

LAWRENCE SHAINBERG (Samuel Beckett feature) is the author of two novels—*One on One* and *Memories of Amnesia*—and two works of nonfiction: *Brain Surgeon* and the recently published memoir *Ambient Zen*.

MONA SIMPSON (Sam Shepard interview) is an advisory editor of *The Paris Review*. Her novels include *The Lost Father* and *A Regular Guy*.

ROSE STYRON (Arthur Miller interview) is the author of three books of poetry, *Thieves' Afternoon, From Summer to Summer,* and *By Vineyard's Light,* as well as coauthor with Olga Carlisle of a book on Russian poets, *Poets on Street Corners*.

LAURIE WINER (Wendy Wasserstein interview) was the theater critic for the *Los Angeles Times* from 1994 to 1998. She now writes for various magazines and is at work on a screenplay.

A NOTE ON THE TYPE

The principal text of this Modern Library edition
was set in a digitized version of Janson,
a typeface that dates from about 1690 and was cut by Nicholas Kis,
a Hungarian working in Amsterdam. The original matrices have
survived and are held by the Stempel foundry in Germany.
Hermann Zapf redesigned some of the weights and sizes for Stempel,
basing his revisions on the original design.